JavaServer Faces

Introduction By Example

Josh Juneau

Apress®

JavaServer Faces: Introduction By Example

ISBN-13 (pbk): 978-1-4842-0839-7

ISBN-13 (electronic): 978-1-4842-0838-0

Managing Director: Welmoed Spahr
Lead Editor: Jonathan Gennick
Editorial Board: Steve Anglin, Gary Cornell, Louise Corrigan, Jonathan Gennick, Robert Hutchinson, Michelle Lowman, James Markham, Matthew Moodie, Jeff Olson, Jeffrey Pepper, Douglas Pundick, Ben Renow-Clarke, Gwenan Spearing, Matt Wade, Steve Weiss
Coordinating Editor: Jill Balzano
Compositor: SPi Global
Indexer: SPi Global
Artist: SPi Global
Cover Designer: Anna Ishchenko

Distributed to the book trade worldwide by Springer Science+Business Media New York, 233 Spring Street, 6th Floor, New York, NY 10013. Phone 1-800-SPRINGER, fax (201) 348-4505, e-mail orders-ny@springer-sbm.com, or visit www.springeronline.com

For information on translations, please e-mail rights@apress.com, or visit www.apress.com.

Apress and friends of ED books may be purchased in bulk for academic, corporate, or promotional use. eBook versions and licenses are also available for most titles. For more information, reference our Special Bulk Sales–eBook Licensing web page at www.apress.com/bulk-sales.

Any source code or other supplementary material referenced by the author in this text is available to readers at www.apress.com. For detailed information about how to locate your book's source code, go to www.apress.com/source-code/.

This book is dedicated to my wife, Angela, and my five children—Kaitlyn, Jacob, Matthew, Zachary, and Lucas. You are my joy and inspiration. This book is also dedicated to the many Java developers worldwide. I hope that these recipes can lead you to developing the sophisticated solutions of tomorrow.

— Josh Juneau

Contents at a Glance

Contents

About the Author

Josh Juneau has been developing software and database systems for several years. Enterprise application programming and database development has been the focus of his career since the beginning. He became an Oracle Database administrator and adopted the PL/SQL language for performing administrative tasks and developing applications for Oracle Database. In an effort to build more complex solutions, he began to incorporate Java into his PL/SQL applications and later developed stand-alone and web applications with Java. Josh wrote his early Java web applications utilizing JDBC to work with back-end databases. Later, he incorporated frameworks into his enterprise solutions, including Java EE and JBoss Seam. Today, he primarily develops enterprise web solutions utilizing Java EE and other enterprise technologies.

He extended his knowledge of the JVM by learning to develop applications with other JVM languages such as Jython and Groovy. Beginning in 2006, Josh worked as the editor and publisher for the *Jython Monthly* newsletter. In late 2008, he began a podcast dedicated to the Jython programming language. Josh was the lead author for *The Definitive Guide to Jython* (Apress, 2010), *Oracle PL/SQL Recipes* (Apress, 2010), and *Java 7 Recipes* (Apress, 2012). Most recently, Josh wrote *Java EE 7 Recipes* and *Introducting Java EE 7* (Apress, 2013). He works as an application developer and systems analyst at Fermi National Accelerator Laboratory, and and he is a member of the Chicago Java Users Group (CJUG). Josh has a wonderful wife and five children, with whom he loves to spend time and teach technology. To hear more from Josh, follow his blog, which can be found at http://jj-blogger.blogspot.com. You can also follow him on Twitter via @javajuneau.

Acknowledgments

To my wife Angela: As the years pass, I am still amazed by you and always will be. I want to thank you again for always being there for me and our children. You've helped me make it through this book, and your inspiration always keeps me moving forward. Thanks for always supporting the work I do. I love you very much.

To my children Kaitlyn, Jacob, Matthew, Zachary, and Lucas: I love you all so much and I cherish every moment we have together. You all continue to make me so proud through your schoolwork, scouting, sports, and the myriad of other things that you achieve. I hate to see you growing up so quickly...sometimes I wish that I could pause time. I hope that you will understand why I've worked so hard on the weekends when you read this book some day.

To the folks at Apress, I thank you for providing me with the chance to share my knowledge with others. I especially thank Jonathan Gennick for the continued support of my work and for providing the continued guidance to produce useful content for our readers. I also thank Jill Balzano for doing a great job coordinating this. Lastly, I'd like to thank everyone else at Apress who had a hand in this book.

To the Java community: thanks for helping to make the Java platform such an innovative and effective realm for application development. We all have the privilege of working with a mature and robust platform, and it would not be successful today if it weren't for everyone's continued contributions to the technology. I also thank all the Oracle Java experts, once again: the roadmap for the future is still looking great. I am looking forward to using Java technology for many years to come.

CHAPTER 1

Introduction to Servlets

Java servlets were the first technology for producing dynamic Java web applications. Sun Microsystems released the first Java Servlet specification in 1997. Since then it has undergone tremendous change, making it more powerful and easing development more with each release. The 3.0 version was released as part of Java EE 6 in December 2009. Although not always used directly by Java web developers, servlets are at the base of all Java EE applications. Many developers use servlet frameworks such as Java Server Pages (JSP) and Java Server Faces (JSF), both of those technologies compile pages into Java servlets behind the scenes via the servlet container. That said, a fundamental knowledge of Java servlet technology is very useful for any Java web developer.

Servlets are Java classes that conform to the Java Servlet API, which allows a Java class to respond to requests. Although servlets can respond to any type of request, they are most commonly written to respond to HTTP requests. A servlet must be deployed to a Java servlet container in order to become usable. The Servlet API provides a number of objects that are used to enable the functionality of a servlet within a web container. Such objects include the request and response objects, `pageContext`, and a great deal of others, and when these objects are used properly, they enable a Java servlet to perform just about any task a web-based application needs to perform.

As mentioned, servlets can produce not only static content but also dynamic content. Since a servlet is written in Java, any valid Java code can be used within the body of the servlet class. This empowers Java servlets and allows them to interact with other Java classes, the web container, the underlying file server, and much more.

This chapter will get you started developing and deploying servlets, and provide you with foundational knowledge to move forward with other servlet-based web frameworks In this chapter, you will learn how to install Oracle's GlassFish application server, a robust servlet container, which will enable you to deploy sophisticated Java enterprise applications. You will be taught the basics of developing servlets, how to use them with client web sessions, and how to link a servlet to another application. All the while, you will learn to use standards from the latest release of the Java Servlet API (3.2), which modernizes servlet development and makes it much easier and more productive than in years past.

Note You can run the examples within this chapter by deploying the `JSFByExample.war` file (contained in the sources) to a local Java EE application server container such as GlassFish v4.x. You can also set up the NetBeans 8.x project entitled JSFByExample that is contained in the sources, build it, and deploy to GlassFish v4.x. Otherwise, you can run the examples in Chapter 1 stand-alone using the instructions provided in the section "Packaging, Compiling, and Deploying a Servlet". If you deploy the `JSFByExample.war` file to a Java EE application server container, you can visit the following URL to load the examples for this chapter: `http://localhost:8080/JSFByExample/faces/chapter01/index.xhtml`.

Setting Up a Java Enterprise Environment

You'll need an environment in which to experiment with servlets, and then later with JavaServer Faces. Oracle's GlassFish application server is a good choice, as it is the Java EE 7 Reference Impementation. It's easy to set up, and the following example will get you started and ready to run all the subsequent examples in the book.

Example

To get started, ownload and install Oracle's GlassFish application server from the GlassFish web site. The version used for this book is the open source edition, release 4.1, and it can be downloaded from http://glassfish.java.net/ in the "Download" section. Select the .zip or .tar.gz download format, and decompress the downloaded files within a directory on your workstation. I will refer to that directory as /JAVA_DEV/GlassFish. The GlassFish distribution comes prepackaged with a domain so that developers can get up and running quickly. Once the .zip file has been unpacked, you can start the domain by opening a command prompt or terminal and starting GlassFish using the following statement:

```
/PATH_TO_GLASSFISH /GlassFish/bin/asadmin start-domain domain1
```

The domain will start, and it will be ready for use. You will see output from the server that looks similar to the following:

```
Waiting for domain1 to start ...........
Successfully started the domain : domain1
domain  Location: /PATH_TO_GLASSFISH/glassfish/domains/domain1
Log File: /PATH_TO_GLASSFISH/glassfish/domains/domain1/logs/server.log
Admin Port: 4848
Command start-domain executed successfully.
```

Explanation

The development of Java EE applications begins with a Java EE–compliant application server. A Java EE–compliant server contains all the essential components to provide a robust environment for deploying and hosting enterprise Java applications. The GlassFish application server is the industry standard for Java EE 7. As of GlassFish 4.0, there is only an open sourced distribution of the server available, meaning that it is not possible to purchase Oracle support for GlassFish. However, in a production environment, you may want to consider purchasing GlassFish 4.x support from a third-party organization so that technical support will be available if needed. An alternative is to utilize a commercially supported server that is Java EE 7 compliant, such as Oracle WebLogic 12.1.x.

Installing GlassFish is easy. It consists of downloading an archive and uncompressing it on your development machine. Once you've completed this, the application server will make use of your locally installed Java development kit (JDK) when it is started. JDK 8 is supported for use with GlassFish as of release 4.1. For GlassFish 4.0, please use JDK 7. Once the server starts, you can open a browser and go to http://localhost:4848 to gain access to the GlassFish administrative console. Most Java EE developers who deploy on GlassFish use the administrative console often. The administrative console provides developers with the tools needed to deploy web applications, register databases with Java Naming and Directory Interface (JNDI), set up security realms for a domain, and do much more. You should take some time to become familiar with the administrative console because the more you know about it, the easier it will be to maintain your Java EE environment.

Installing the GlassFish application server is the first step toward developing Java applications for the enterprise. While other applications servers such as JBoss WildFly, Apache TomEE, and WebLogic are very well adopted, GlassFish offers developers a solid environment that is suitable for production use and easy to learn. It also has the bonus of being an open source application server and the reference implementation for Java EE 7.

Developing Your First Servlet

Web applications are based upon a series of web views or pages. There is often a requirement to develop a view that has the ability to include content that may change at any given time. For instance, you may be developing a view that contains stock data, and you may wish to have that data updated often. Servlets provide the ability to produce dynamic content, allowing server-side computations and processes to update the data in the servlet at will.

Example

Develop a Java servlet class, and compile it to run within a Java servlet container. In this example, a simple servlet is created that will display some dynamic content to the web page. The The following code is the servlet code that contains the functionality for the servlet:package org.javaserverfaces.chapter01;

```java
import java.io.IOException;
import java.io.PrintWriter;
import javax.servlet.ServletException;
import javax.servlet.http.HttpServlet;
import javax.servlet.http.HttpServletRequest;
import javax.servlet.http.HttpServletResponse;

/**
 * Simple Dynamic Servlet
 * @author juneau
 */
public class SimpleServlet extends HttpServlet {

    /**
     * Processes requests for both HTTP
     * <code>GET</code> and
     * <code>POST</code> methods.
     *
     * @param request servlet request
     * @param response servlet response
     * @throws ServletException if a servlet-specific error occurs
     * @throws IOException if an I/O error occurs
     */
    protected void processRequest(HttpServletRequest request, HttpServletResponse response)
            throws ServletException, IOException {
        response.setContentType("text/html;charset=UTF-8");
        PrintWriter out = response.getWriter();
        try {
            /*
             * TODO output your page here. You may use following sample code.
             */
            out.println("<html>");
            out.println("<head>");
            out.println("<title>Servlet SimpleServlet</title>");
            out.println("</head>");
            out.println("<body>");
            out.println("<h2>Servlet SimpleServlet at " + request.getContextPath() + "</h2>");
            out.println("<br/>Welcome to JavaServer Faces: Introduction By Example!");
```

```java
            out.println("</body>");
            out.println("</html>");
        } finally {
            out.close();
        }
    }

    // <editor-fold defaultstate="collapsed" desc="HttpServlet methods. Click on the + sign on the
left to edit the code.">
    /**
     * Handles the HTTP
     * <code>GET</code> method.
     *
     * @param request servlet request
     * @param response servlet response
     * @throws ServletException if a servlet-specific error occurs
     * @throws IOException if an I/O error occurs
     */
    @Override
    protected void doGet(HttpServletRequest request, HttpServletResponse response)
            throws ServletException, IOException {
        processRequest(request, response);
    }

    /**
     * Handles the HTTP
     * <code>POST</code> method.
     *
     * @param request servlet request
     * @param response servlet response
     * @throws ServletException if a servlet-specific error occurs
     * @throws IOException if an I/O error occurs
     */
    @Override
    protected void doPost(HttpServletRequest request, HttpServletResponse response)
            throws ServletException, IOException {
        processRequest(request, response);
    }

    /**
     * Returns a short description of the servlet.
     *
     * @return a String containing servlet description
     */
    @Override
    public String getServletInfo() {
        return "Short description";
    }// </editor-fold>
}
```

The following code is the web deployment descriptor. This file is required for application deployment to a servlet container. It contains the servlet configuration and mapping that maps the servlet to a URL. Later in this chapter, will learn how to omit the servlet configuration and mapping from the web.xml file to make servlet development, deployment, and maintenance easier.

```xml
<?xml version="1.0"?>
<web-app xmlns="http://java.sun.com/xml/ns/javaee"
    xmlns:xsi="http://www.w3.org/2001/XMLSchema-instance"
    xsi:schemaLocation="http://java.sun.com/xml/ns/javaee
        http://java.sun.com/xml/ns/javaee/web-app_3_0.xsd"
    version="3.0">

    <servlet>
        <servlet-name>SimpleServlet</servlet-name>
        <servlet-class>org.javaeeexamples.chapter1.example01_02.SimpleServlet</servlet-class>
    </servlet>
    <servlet-mapping>
        <servlet-name>SimpleServlet</servlet-name>
        <url-pattern>/SimpleServlet</url-pattern>
    </servlet-mapping>
            <welcome-file-list>
        <welcome-file> /SimpleServlet </welcome-file>
    </welcome-file-list>
</web-app>
```

■ **Note** Many web applications use a page named index.html or index.xhtml as their welcome file. There is nothing wrong with doing that, and as a matter of fact, it is the correct thing to do. The use of /SimpleServlet as the welcome file in this example is to make it easier to follow for demonstration purposes.

To compile the Java servlet, use the javac command-line utility. The following line was excerpted from the command line, and it compiles the SimpleServlet.java file into a class file. First, traverse into the directory containing the SimpleServlet.java file; then, execute the following:

```
javac -cp /JAVA_DEV/GlassFish/glassfish/modules/javax.servlet-api.jar SimpleServlet.java
```

Once the servlet code has been compiled into a Java class file, it is ready to package for deployment.

■ **Note** You may want to consider installing a Java integrated development environment (IDE) to increase your development productivity. There are several very good IDEs available to developers, so be sure to choose one that contains the features you find most important and useful for development. As the author of this book on Java EE 7, I recommend installing NetBeans 8.x or newer for development. NetBeans is an open source IDE that is maintained by Oracle, and it includes support for all the cutting-edge features that the Java industry has to offer, including EJB development with Java EE 7, JavaFX 8 support, and more.

Explanation

Java servlets provide developers with the flexibility to design applications using a request-response programming model. Servlets play a key role in the development of service-oriented and web application development on the Java platform. Different types of servlets can be created, and each of them is geared toward providing different functionality. The first type is the GenericServlet, which provides services and functionality. The second type, HttpServlet, is a subclass of GenericServlet, and servlets of this type provide functionality and a response that uses HTTP. The solution to this example demonstrates the latter type of servlet because it displays a result for the user to see within a web browser.

Servlets conform to a life cycle for processing requests and posting results. First, the Java servlet container calls the servlet's constructor. The constructor of every servlet must take no arguments. Next, the container calls the servlet init method, which is responsible for initializing the servlet. Once the servlet has been initialized, it is ready for use. At that point, the servlet can begin processing. Each servlet contains a service method, which handles the requests being made and dispatches them to the appropriate methods for request handling. Implementing the service method is optional. Finally, the container calls the servlet's destroy method, which takes care of finalizing the servlet and taking it out of service.

Every servlet class must implement the javax.servlet.Servlet interface or extend another class that does. In the solution to this example, the servlet named SimpleServlet extends the HttpServlet class, which provides methods for handling HTTP processes. In this scenario, a browser client request is sent from the container to the servlet; then the servlet service method dispatches the HttpServletRequest object to the appropriate method provided by HttpServlet. Namely, the HttpServlet class provides the doGet, doPut, doPost, and doDelete methods for working with an HTTP request. The HttpServlet class is abstract, so it must be subclassed, and then an implementation can be provided for its methods. In the solution to this example, the doGet method is implemented, and the responsibility of processing is passed to the processRequest method, which writes a response to the browser using the PrintWriter. Table 1-1 describes each of the methods available to an HttpServlet.

Table 1-1. *HttpServlet Methods*

Method Name	Description
doGet	Used to process HTTP GET requests. Input sent to the servlet must be included in the URL address. For example: ?myName=Josh&myBook=JSF.
doPost	Used to process HTTP POST requests. Input can be sent to the servlet within HTML form fields.
doPut	Used to process HTTP PUT requests.
doDelete	Used to process HTTP DELETE requests.
doHead	Used to process HTTP HEAD requests.
doOptions	Called by the container to allow OPTIONS request handling.
doTrace	Called by the container to handle TRACE requests.
getLastModified	Returns the time that the HttpServletRequest object was last modified.
init	Initializes the servlet.
destroy	Finalizes the servlet.
getServletInfo	Provides information regarding the servlet.

A servlet generally performs some processing within the implementation of its methods and then returns a response to the client. The HttpServletRequest object can be used to process arguments that are sent via the request. For instance, if an HTML form contains some input fields that are sent to the server, those fields would be contained within the HttpServletRequest object. The HttpServletResponse object is used to send responses to the client browser. Both the doGet and doPost methods within a servlet accept the same arguments, namely, the HttpServletRequest and HttpServletResponse objects.

■ **Note**　The doGet method is used to intercept HTTP GET requests, and doPost is used to intercept HTTP POST requests. Generally, the doGet method is used to prepare a request before displaying for a client, and the doPost method is used to process a request and gather information from an HTML form.

In the solution to this example, both the doGet and doPost methods pass the HttpServletRequest and HttpServletResponse objects to the processRequest method for further processing. The HttpServletResponse object is used to set the content type of the response and to obtain a handle on the PrintWriter object in the processRequest method. The following lines of code show how this is done, assuming that the identifier referencing the HttpServletResponse object is response:

```
response.setContentType("text/html;charset=UTF-8");
PrintWriter out = response.getWriter();
```

A GenericServlet can be used for providing services to web applications. This type of servlet is oftentimes used for logging events because it implements the log method. A GenericServlet implements both the Servlet and ServletConfig interfaces, and to write a generic servlet, only the service method must be overridden.

How to Package, Compile, and Deploy a Servlet

Once a servlet has been developed (and compiled), it needs to be deployed to a servlet container before it can be used. After deployment to the server, the servlet needs to be mapped to a URL for invocation.

Example

Compile the sources, set up a deployable application, and copy the contents into the GlassFish deployment directory. From the command line, use the javac command to compile the sources.

```
javac -cp /PATH_TO_GLASSFISH/GlassFish/glassfish/modules/javax.servlet-api.jar SimpleServlet.java
```

After the class has been compiled, deploy it along with the web.xml deployment descriptor, conforming to the appropriate directory structure. In web.xml, declare the servlet, and map it to a URL using the following format:

```
<servlet>
    <servlet-name>SimpleServlet</servlet-name>
    <servlet-class>org.javaserverfaces.chapter01.SimpleServlet</servlet-class>
</servlet>
</servlet-mapping>
    <servlet-mapping>
    <servlet-name>SimpleServlet</servlet-name>
    <url-pattern>/SimpleServlet</url-pattern>
</servlet-mapping>
```

QUICK START FOR DEPLOYING WITHOUT AN IDE

To quickly get started with packaging, compiling, and deploying the example application for the servlet examples in this chapter on GlassFish or other servlet containers such as Apache Tomcat without an IDE, follow these steps:

1. Create a single application named SimpleServlet by making a directory named SimpleServlet.

2. Create a directory at the root of the application, and name it WEB-INF. Create an XML file in the new WEB-INF directory, and name it web.xml. In the web.xml, add the following markup:

```xml
<?xml version="1.0" encoding="UTF-8"?>
<web-app version="3.1" xmlns="http://xmlns.jcp.org/xml/ns/javaee" xmlns:xsi="
http://www.w3.org/2001/XMLSchema-instance" xsi:schemaLocation="http://xmlns.jcp.org/
xml/ns/javaee http://xmlns.jcp.org/xml/ns/javaee/web-app_3_1.xsd">
    <servlet>
        <servlet-name>SimpleServlet</servlet-name>
        <servlet-class>org.javaserverfaces.chapter01.SimpleServlet</servlet-class>
    </servlet>
    <servlet-mapping>
        <servlet-name>SimpleServlet</servlet-name>
        <url-pattern>/SimpleServlet</url-pattern>
    </servlet-mapping>
    <session-config>
        <session-timeout>
            30
        </session-timeout>
    </session-config>
</web-app>
```

3. Create "classes", and "lib" drectories inside the directory that was created in step 2. Drag the Chapter 1 sources into the WEB-INF/classes directory.

4. Set your CLASSSPATH to include any necessary JAR files. For this chapter, the JavaMail API JAR (mail.jar) is required. Place It into the WEB-INF/lib directory and set your CLASSPATH accordingly.

5. At the command prompt, change directories so that you are within the "classes" directory that was created in Step 3. Compile each class within the org.javaserverfaces. chapter01 directory with the following command:

    ```
    javac org\javaserverfaces\chapter01\*.java
    ```

6. Copy your SimpleServlet application into the /JAVA_DEV/GlassFish/glassfish/domains/ domain1/autodeploy directory for GlassFish, or the /Tomcat/webapps directory for Tomcat.

Test the application by launching a browser and going to http://localhost:8080/SimpleServlet/servlet_ name, where servlet_name corresponds to the servlet name in each example. If using Tomcat, you may need to restart the server in order for the application to deploy.

Explanation

To compile the sources, you can use your favorite Java IDE such as NetBeans or Eclipse, or you can use the command line. For the purposes of this example, I will use the command line. Note that in many of the remaining examples for this book, the NetBeans IDE is used. If you're using the command line, you must ensure you are using the `javac` command that is associated with the same Java release that you will be using to run your servlet container. In this example we will assume that GlassFish 4.1 is being used with JDK 7, and therefore assume that the location of the Java SE 7 installation is at the following path:

```
/Library/Java/JavaVirtualMachines/1.7.0.jdk/Contents/Home
```

This path may differ in your environment if you are using a different operating system and/or installation location. To ensure you are using the Java runtime that is located at this path, set the `JAVA_HOME` environment variable equal to this path. On OS X and *nix operating systems, you can set the environment variable by opening the terminal and typing the following:

```
export JAVA_HOME=/Library/Java/JavaVirtualMachines/1.7.0.jdk/Contents/Home
```

If you are using Windows, use the `SET` command within the command line to set up the `JAVA_HOME` environment variable.

```
set JAVA_HOME=C:\your-java-se-path\
```

Next, compile your Java servlet sources, and be sure to include the `javax.servlet-api.jar` file that is packaged with your servlet container (use `servlet-api.jar` for Tomcat) in your `CLASSPATH`. You can set the `CLASSPATH` by using the `-cp` flag of the `javac` command. The following command should be executed at the command line from within the same directory that contains the sources. In this case, the source file is named `SimpleServlet.java`.

```
javac -cp /path_to_jar/javax.servlet-api.jar SimpleServlet.java
```

Next, package your application by creating a directory and naming it after your application. In this case, create a directory and name it `SimpleServlet`. Within that directory, create another directory named `WEB-INF`. Traverse into the `WEB-INF` directory, and create another directory named `classes`. Lastly, create directories within the `classes` directory in order to replicate your Java servlet package structure. For this example, the `SimpleServlet.java` class resides within the Java package `org.javaserverfaces.chapter01`, so create a directory for each of those packages within the `classes` directory. Create another directory within `WEB-INF` and name it `lib`; any JAR files containing external libraries should be placed within the `lib` directory. In the end, your directory structure should resemble the following:

```
SimpleServlet
| WEB-INF
        |_classes
               |_org
                     |_javaserverfaces
                               |_chapter01

        |_lib
```

Place your `web.xml` deployment descriptor within the `WEB-INF` directory, and place the compiled `SimpleServlet.class` file within the `chapter01` directory. The entire contents of the `SimpleServlet` directory can now be copied within the deployment directory for your application server container to deploy the application. Restart the application server if using Tomcat, and visit the URL `http://localhost:8080/SimpleServlet/SimpleServlet` to see the servlet in action.

Registering Servlets Without WEB-XML

Registering servlets in the web.xml file is cumbersome. With the later releases of the Servlet specification, it is possible to deploy servlets without the requirement for a web.xml file. In this section, we will take a look at how to register servlets without the web.xml requirement.

Example

Use the @WebServlet annotation to register the servlet, and omit the web.xml registration. This will alleviate the need to modify the web.xml file each time a servlet is added to your application. The following adaptation of the SimpleServlet class that was used in the previous example includes the @WebServlet annotation and demonstrates its use:

```
package org.javaserverfaces.chapter01;

import java.io.IOException;
import java.io.PrintWriter;
import javax.servlet.ServletException;
import javax.servlet.annotation.WebServlet;
import javax.servlet.http.HttpServlet;
import javax.servlet.http.HttpServletRequest;
import javax.servlet.http.HttpServletResponse;

/**
 * Registering Servlets without WEB-XML
 * @author juneau
 */
@WebServlet(name = "SimpleServletNoDescriptor", urlPatterns = {"/SimpleServletNoDescriptor"})
public class SimpleServletNoDescriptor extends HttpServlet {

    /**
     * Processes requests for both HTTP
     * <code>GET</code> and
     * <code>POST</code> methods.
     *
     * @param request servlet request
     * @param response servlet response
     * @throws ServletException if a servlet-specific error occurs
     * @throws IOException if an I/O error occurs
     */
    protected void processRequest(HttpServletRequest request, HttpServletResponse response)
            throws ServletException, IOException {
        response.setContentType("text/html;charset=UTF-8");
        PrintWriter out = response.getWriter();
        try {
            /*
             * TODO output your page here. You may use following sample code.
             */
            out.println("<html>");
            out.println("<head>");
            out.println("<title>Servlet SimpleServlet</title>");
```

```
            out.println("</head>");
            out.println("<body>");
            out.println("<h2>Servlet SimpleServlet at " + request.getContextPath() + "</h2>");
            out.println("<br/>Look ma, no WEB-XML!");
            out.println("</body>");
            out.println("</html>");
        } finally {
            out.close();
        }
    }

    /**
     * Handles the HTTP <code>GET</code> method.
     *
     * @param request servlet request
     * @param response servlet response
     * @throws ServletException if a servlet-specific error occurs
     * @throws IOException if an I/O error occurs
     */
    @Override
    protected void doGet(HttpServletRequest request, HttpServletResponse response)
            throws ServletException, IOException {
        processRequest(request, response);
    }

    /**
     * Handles the HTTP <code>POST</code> method.
     *
     * @param request servlet request
     * @param response servlet response
     * @throws ServletException if a servlet-specific error occurs
     * @throws IOException if an I/O error occurs
     */
    @Override
    protected void doPost(HttpServletRequest request, HttpServletResponse response)
            throws ServletException, IOException {
        processRequest(request, response);
    }

}
```

In the end, the servlet will be accessible via a URL in the same way that it would if the servlet were registered within web.xml.

Explanation

There are a couple of ways to register servlets with a web container. The first way is to register them using the web.xml deployment descriptor, as demonstrated earlier in the chapter. The second way to register them is to use the @WebServlet annotation. The Servlet 3.0 API introduced the @WebServlet annotation, which provides an easier technique to use for mapping a servlet to a URL. The @WebServlet annotation is placed before the declaration of a class, and it accepts the elements listed in Table 1-2.

Table 1-2. @WebServlet Annotation Elements

Element	Description
description	Description of the servlet
displayName	The display name of the servlet
initParams	Accepts list of @WebInitParam annotations
largeIcon	The large icon of the servlet
loadOnStartup	Load on start-up order of the servlet
name	Servlet name
smallIcon	The small icon of the servlet
urlPatterns	URL patterns that invoke the servlet

In the solution to this example, the @WebServlet annotation maps the servlet class named SimpleServletNoDescriptor to the URL pattern of /SimpleServletNoDescriptor, and it also names the servlet SimpleServletNoDescriptor.

```
@WebServlet(name="SimpleServletNoDescriptor", urlPatterns={"/SimpleServletNoDescriptor"})
```

The new @WebServlet can be used rather than altering the web.xml file to register each servlet in an application. This provides ease of development and manageability. However, in some cases, it may make sense to continue using the deployment descriptor for servlet registration, such as if you do not want to recompile sources when a URL pattern changes. If you look at the web.xml file used earlier, you can see the following lines of XML, which map the servlet to a given URL and provide a name for the servlet. These lines of XML perform essentially the same function as the @WebServlet annotation in this example.

```
<servlet>
    <servlet-name>SimpleServletNoDescriptor</servlet-name>
    <servlet-class>org.javaserverfaces.chapter01.SimpleServletNoDescriptor</servlet-class>
</servlet>
<servlet-mapping>
    <servlet-name>SimpleServletNoDescriptor</servlet-name>
    <url-pattern>/SimpleServletNoDescriptor</url-pattern>
</servlet-mapping>
```

Displaying Dynamic Content with a Servlet

As mentioned previously in the chapter, it sometimes makes sense to deliver dynamic content (content that changes frequently), rather than serving static content that never changes. In this example, we will take a look at how to develop a servlet that has the ability to display dynamic content.

Example

Define a field within your servlet to contain the dynamic content that is to be displayed. Post the dynamic content on the page by appending the field containing it using the PrintWriter println method. The following example servlet declares a Date field and updates it with the current Date each time the page is loaded:

```java
package org.javaserverfaces.chapter01;

import java.io.IOException;
import java.io.PrintWriter;
import java.util.Date;
import javax.servlet.ServletException;
import javax.servlet.annotation.WebServlet;
import javax.servlet.http.HttpServlet;
import javax.servlet.http.HttpServletRequest;
import javax.servlet.http.HttpServletResponse;

/**
 * Displaying Dynamic Content with a Servlet
 *
 * @author juneau
 */
@WebServlet(name = "CurrentDateAndTime", urlPatterns = {"/CurrentDateAndTime"})
public class CurrentDateAndTime extends HttpServlet {

    /**
     * Processes requests for both HTTP <code>GET</code> and <code>POST</code>
     * methods.
     *
     * @param request servlet request
     * @param response servlet response
     * @throws ServletException if a servlet-specific error occurs
     * @throws IOException if an I/O error occurs
     */
    protected void processRequest(HttpServletRequest request, HttpServletResponse response)
            throws ServletException, IOException {
        response.setContentType("text/html;charset=UTF-8");
        PrintWriter out = response.getWriter();
        try {
            out.println("<html>");
            out.println("<head>");
            out.println("<title>Servlet CurrentDateAndTime</title>");
            out.println("</head>");
            out.println("<body>");
            out.println("<h1>Servlet CurrentDateAndTime at " + request.getContextPath() + "</h1>");
            out.println("<br/>");

            Date currDateAndTime = new Date();
            out.println("The current date and time is: " + currDateAndTime);
```

```java
            out.println("</body>");
            out.println("</html>");
        } finally {
            out.close();
        }
    }

    /**
     * Handles the HTTP <code>GET</code> method.
     *
     * @param request servlet request
     * @param response servlet response
     * @throws ServletException if a servlet-specific error occurs
     * @throws IOException if an I/O error occurs
     */
    @Override
    protected void doGet(HttpServletRequest request, HttpServletResponse response)
            throws ServletException, IOException {
        processRequest(request, response);
    }

    /**
     * Handles the HTTP <code>POST</code> method.
     *
     * @param request servlet request
     * @param response servlet response
     * @throws ServletException if a servlet-specific error occurs
     * @throws IOException if an I/O error occurs
     */
    @Override
    protected void doPost(HttpServletRequest request, HttpServletResponse response)
            throws ServletException, IOException {
        processRequest(request, response);
    }
}
```

The resulting output from this servlet will be the current date and time.

Explanation

One of the reasons why Java servlets are so useful is because they allow dynamic content to be displayed on a web page. The content can be taken from the server itself, a database, another web site, or many other web-accessible resources. Servlets are not static web pages; they are dynamic, and that is arguably their biggest strength.

In the solution to this example, a servlet is used to display the current time and date on the server. When the servlet is processed, the doGet method is called, which subsequently makes a call to the processRequest method, passing the request and response objects. Therefore, the processRequest method is where the bulk of the work occurs. The processRequest method creates a PrintWriter by calling the response.getWriter method, and the PrintWriter is used to display content on the resulting web page. Next, the current date and time are obtained from the server by creating a new Date and assigning it to the currDateAndTime field. Lastly, the processRequest method sends the web content through the out.println method, and the contents of the currDateAndTime field are concatenated to a String and sent to out.println as well. Each time the servlet is processed, it will display the current date and time at the time in which the servlet is invoked because a new Date is created with each request.

This example just scratches the surface of what is possible with a Java servlet. Although displaying the current date and time is trivial, you could alter that logic to display the contents of any field contained within the servlet. Whether it be an `int` field that displays a calculation that was performed by the servlet container or a `String` field containing some information, the possibilities are endless.

Handling Requests and Responses

Most applications allow forms that accept input, and then produce a response. This is one of the main components of an HTTP application, and servlets are ideal for handling a request-response lifecycle. It can also be useful to develop forms in HTML, and have the form submitted to a processing engine, such as a servlet.

Example

To see a request-response example in action, create a standard HTML-based web form, and when the submit button is clicked, invoke a servlet to process the end-user input and post a response. To examine this technique, you will see two different pieces of code. The following code is HTML that is used to generate the input form. Pay particular attention to the `<form>` and `<input>` tags. You will see that the form's `action` parameter lists a servlet name, `MathServlet`.

```html
<html>
    <head>
    <title>Simple Math Servlet</title>
    </head>
    <body>
        <h1>This is a simple Math Servlet</h1>
        <form method="POST" action="MathServlet">
            <label for="numa">Enter Number A: </label>
            <input type="text" id="numa" name="numa"/><br><br>
                            <label for="numb">Enter Number B: </label>
                            <input type="text" id="numb" name="numb"/><br/><br/>
            <input type="submit" value="Submit Form"/>
            <input type="reset" value="Reset Form"/>
        </form>
    </body>
</html>
```

Next, take a look at the following code for a servlet named `MathServlet`. This is the Java code that receives the input from the HTML code listed earlier, processes it accordingly, and posts a response.

```java
package org.javaserverfaces.chapter01;

import java.io.IOException;
import java.io.PrintWriter;
import java.util.Date;

import javax.servlet.*;
import javax.servlet.annotation.WebServlet;
import javax.servlet.http.*;
```

```java
/**
 * Handling Requests and Responses
 */
// Uncomment the following line to run example stand-alone
//@WebServlet(name="SessionServlet", urlPatterns={"/MathServlet"})
// The following will allow the example to run within the context of the JSFByExample example
// enterprise application (JSFByExample.war distro or Netbeans Project)
@WebServlet(name = "MathServlet", urlPatterns = {"/chapter01/MathServlet"})
public class MathServlet extends HttpServlet {

    public void doPost(HttpServletRequest req, HttpServletResponse res)
            throws IOException, ServletException {

        res.setContentType("text/html");

        // Store the input parameter values into Strings
        String numA = req.getParameter("numa");
        String numB = req.getParameter("numb");

        PrintWriter out = res.getWriter();
        out.println("<html><head>");
        out.println("<title>Test Math Servlet</title>");
        out.println("\t<style>body { font-family: 'Lucida Grande', "
                + "'Lucida Sans Unicode';font-size: 13px; }</style>");
        out.println("</head>");
        out.println("<body>");

        try {
            int solution = Integer.valueOf(numA) + Integer.valueOf(numB);

            /*
             * Display some response to the user
             */
            out.println("<p>Solution: "
                    + numA + " + " + numB + " = " + solution + "</p>");

        } catch (java.lang.NumberFormatException ex) {
            // Display error if an exception is raised
            out.println("<p>Please use numbers only...try again.</p>");
        }

        out.println("</body></html>");

        out.close();
    }
}
```

> ■ **Note**   To run the example, deploy the JSFByExample application to your application server container, and then enter the following address into your browser: `http://localhost:8080/JSFByExample/chapter01/math.html`. This assumes you are using default port numbers for your application server installation. If using the NetBeans project that was packaged with the sources, you do not need to worry about copying the code as everything is pre-configured.

Explanation

Servlets make it easy to create web applications that adhere to a request and response life cycle. They have the ability to provide HTTP responses and also process business logic within the same body of code. The ability to process business logic makes servlets much more powerful than standard HTML code. The solution to this example demonstrates a standard servlet structure for processing requests and sending responses. An HTML web form contains parameters that are sent to a servlet. The servlet then processes those parameters in some fashion and publishes a response that can be seen by the client. In the case of an `HttpServlet` object, the client is a web browser, and the response is a web page.

Values can be obtained from an HTML form by using HTML `<input>` tags embedded within an HTML `<form>`. In the solution to this example, two values are accepted as input, and they are referenced by their `id` attributes as `numa` and `numb`. There are two more `<input>` tags within the form; one of them is used to submit the values to the form `action`, and the other is used to reset the form fields to blank. The form action is the name of the servlet that the form values will be passed to as parameters. In this case, the action is set to `MathServlet`. The `<form>` tag also accepts a form-processing method, either `GET` or `POST`. In the example, the `POST` method is used because form data is being sent to the action; in this case, data is being sent to `MathServlet`. You could, of course, create an HTML form as detailed as you would like and then have that data sent to any servlet in the same manner. This example is relatively basic; it serves to give you an understanding of how the processing is performed.

The `<form>` action attribute states that the `MathServlet` should be used to process the values that are contained within the form. The `MathServlet` name is mapped back to the `MathServlet` class via the `web.xml` deployment descriptor or the `@WebServlet` annotation. Looking at the `MathServlet` code, you can see that a `doPost` method is implemented to handle the processing of the `POST` form values. The `doPost` method accepts `HttpServletRequest` and `HttpServletResponse` objects as arguments. The values contained with the HTML form are embodied within the `HttpServletRequest` object. To obtain those values, call the request object's `getParameter` method, passing the `id` of the input parameter you want to obtain. In this example, those values are obtained and stored within local `String` fields.

```
String numA = req.getParameter("numa");
String numB = req.getParameter("numb");
```

Once the values are obtained, they can be processed as needed. In this case, those `String` values are converted into `int` values, and then they are added together to generate a sum and stored into an `int` field. That field is then presented as a response on a resulting web page.

```
int solution = Integer.valueOf(numA) + Integer.valueOf(numB);
```

As mentioned, the HTML form could be much more complex, containing any number of `<input>` fields. Likewise, the servlet could perform more complex processing of those field values. This example is merely the tip of the iceberg, and the possibilities are without bounds. Servlet-based web frameworks such as Java Server Pages and Java Server Faces hide many of the complexities of passing form values to a servlet and processing a response. However, the same basic framework is used behind the scenes.

Listening for Servlet Container Events

There are cases when it may be useful for an application to perform some tasks when it is being started up or shut down. In such cases, servlet context event listeners can become useful.

Example

Create a servlet context event listener to alert when the application has started up or when it has been shut down. The following solution demonstrates the code for a context listener, which will log application start-up and shutdown events and send e-mail alerting of such events:

```java
package org.javaserverfaces.chapter01;

import java.util.Properties;
import javax.mail.Message;
import javax.mail.Session;
import javax.mail.Transport;
import javax.mail.internet.InternetAddress;
import javax.mail.internet.MimeMessage;
import javax.servlet.ServletContextListener;
import javax.servlet.ServletContextEvent;
import javax.servlet.annotation.WebListener;

@WebListener
public class StartupShutdownListener implements ServletContextListener {

    @Override
    public void contextInitialized(ServletContextEvent event) {
        System.out.println("Servlet startup...");
        System.out.println(event.getServletContext().getServerInfo());
        System.out.println(System.currentTimeMillis());
        sendEmail("Servlet context has initialized");
    }

    @Override
    public void contextDestroyed(ServletContextEvent event) {
        System.out.println("Servlet shutdown...");
        System.out.println(event.getServletContext().getServerInfo());
        System.out.println(System.currentTimeMillis());
        // See error in server.log file if mail is unsuccessful
        sendEmail("Servlet context has been destroyed...");
    }

    /**
     * This implementation uses the GMail smtp server
     * @param message
     * @return
     */
```

```java
    private boolean sendEmail(String message) {
        boolean result = false;
        String smtpHost = "smtp.gmail.com";
        String smtpUsername = "username";
        String smtpPassword = "password";
        String from = "fromaddress";
        String to = "toaddress";
        int smtpPort = 587;
        System.out.println("sending email...");
        try {
            // Send email here

            //Set the host smtp address
            Properties props = new Properties();
            props.put("mail.smtp.host", smtpHost);
            props.put("mail.smtp.auth", "true");
            props.put("mail.smtp.starttls.enable", "true");

            // create some properties and get the default Session
            Session session = Session.getInstance(props);

            // create a message
            Message msg = new MimeMessage(session);

            // set the from and to address
            InternetAddress addressFrom = new InternetAddress(from);
            msg.setFrom(addressFrom);
            InternetAddress[] address = new InternetAddress[1];
            address[0] = new InternetAddress(to);
            msg.setRecipients(Message.RecipientType.TO, address);
            msg.setSubject("Servlet container shutting down");
            // Append Footer
            msg.setContent(message, "text/plain");
            Transport transport = session.getTransport("smtp");
            transport.connect(smtpHost, smtpPort, smtpUsername, smtpPassword);

            Transport.send(msg);

            result = true;
        } catch (javax.mail.MessagingException ex) {
            ex.printStackTrace();
            result = false;
        }
        return result;
    }
}
```

■ **Note**   To run this example, you may need additional external JARs in your CLASSPATH. Specifically, make sure you have mail.jar and javaee.jar.

Explanation

Sometimes it is useful to know when certain events occur within the application server container. This concept can be useful under many different circumstances, but most often it would likely be used for initializing an application upon start-up or cleaning up after an application upon shutdown. A servlet listener can be registered with an application to indicate when it has been started up or shut down. Therefore, by listening for such events, the servlet has the opportunity to perform some actions when they occur.

To create a listener that performs actions based upon a container event, you must develop a class that implements the ServletContextListener interface. The methods that need to be implemented are contextInitialized and contextDestroyed. Both of the methods accept a ServletContextEvent as an argument, and they are automatically called each time the servlet container is initialized or shut down, respectively. To register the listener with the container, you can use one of the following techniques:

- Utilize the @WebListener annotation, as demonstrated by the solution to this example.

- Register the listener within the web.xml application deployment descriptor.

- Use the addListener methods defined on ServletContext.

For example, to register this listener within web.xml, you would need to add the following lines of XML:

```
<listener>
    <listener-class> org.javaserverfaces.chapter01.StartupShutdownListener</listener-class>
</listener>
```

Neither way is better than the other. The only time that listener registration within the application deployment descriptor (web.xml) would be more helpful is if you had the need to disable the listener in some cases. On the other hand, to disable a listener when it is registered using @WebListener, you must remove the annotation and recompile the code. Altering the web deployment descriptor does not require any code to be recompiled.

There are many different listener types, and the interface that the class implements is what determines the listener type. For instance, in this example, the class implements the ServletContextListener interface. Doing so creates a listener for servlet context events. If, however, the class implements HttpSessionListener, it would be a listener for HTTP session events. The following is a complete listing of listener interfaces:

```
javax.servlet.ServletRequestListener
javax.servlet.ServletRequestAttrbiteListener
javax.servlet.ServletContextListener
javax.servlet.ServletContextAttributeListener
javax.servlet.HttpSessionListener
javax.servlet.HttpSessionAttributeListener
```

It is also possible to create a listener that implements multiple listener interfaces. To learn more about listening for different situations such as attribute changes, please see the section entitled Listening for Attribute Changes.

Setting Initialization Parameters

It is possible to set initialization parameters for servlets as well. Doing so can be handy in cases where you would like to implement a task with default values if none were given.

Example #1

Set the servlet initialization parameters using the @WebInitParam annotation. The following code sets an initialization parameter that is equal to a String value:

```java
package org.javaserverfaces.chapter01;

import java.io.IOException;
import java.io.PrintWriter;

import javax.servlet.*;
import javax.servlet.annotation.WebInitParam;
import javax.servlet.annotation.WebServlet;
import javax.servlet.http.*;

@WebServlet(name="SimpleServletCtx1", urlPatterns={"/SimpleServletCtx1"},
initParams={ @WebInitParam(name="name", value="Duke") })
public class SimpleServletCtx1 extends HttpServlet {

        @Override
    public void doGet(HttpServletRequest req, HttpServletResponse res)
        throws IOException, ServletException {

        res.setContentType("text/html");

        PrintWriter out = res.getWriter();

        /* Display some response to the user */

        out.println("<html><head>");
        out.println("<title>Simple Servlet Context Example</title>");
        out.println("\t<style>body { font-family: 'Lucida Grande', " +
            "'Lucida Sans Unicode';font-size: 13px; }</style>");
        out.println("</head>");
        out.println("<body>");

        out.println("<p>This is a simple servlet to demonstrate context!  Hello "
                              + getServletConfig().getInitParameter("name") + "</p>");

        out.println("</body></html>");
        out.close();
    }
}
```

To execute the example using the sources for this book, load the following URL into your web browser: http://localhost:8080/JSFByExample/SimpleServletCtx1. The resulting web page will display the following text:

```
This is a simple servlet to demonstrate context! Hello Duke
```

Example #2

Place the `init` parameters inside the `web.xml` deployment descriptor file. The following lines are excerpted from the `web.xml` deployment descriptor for the `SimpleServlet` application. They include the initialization parameter names and values.

```
<web-app>
    <servlet>
        <servlet-name>SimpleServletCtx1</servlet-name>
        <servlet-class> org.javaserverfaces.chapter01.SimpleServletCtx1</servlet-class>

        <init-param>
            <param-name>name</param-name>
            <param-value>Duke</param-value>
        </init-param>
    ...
    </servlet>
    ...
</web-app>
```

Explanation

Oftentimes there is a requirement to set initialization parameters for a servlet in order to initialize certain values. Servlets can accept any number of initialization parameters, and there are a couple of ways in which they can be set. The first example is to annotate the servlet class with the @WebInitParam annotation, and the second way to set an initialization parameter is to declare the parameter within the web.xml deployment descriptor, as demonstrated in the second example. Either way will work; however, the solution using @WebInitParam is based upon the newer Java Servlet 3.0 API. Therefore, Example #1 is the more contemporary approach, but Example #2 remains valid for following an older model or using an older Java servlet release.

To use the @WebInitParam annotation, it must be embedded within the @WebServlet annotation. Therefore, the servlet must be registered with the web application via the @WebServlet annotation rather than within the web.xml file. For more information on registering a servlet via the @WebServlet annotation, see the section entitled Registering Servlets Without web.xml.

The @WebInitParam annotation accepts a name-value pair as an initialization parameter. In the solution to this example, the parameter name is name, and the value is Duke.

```
@WebInitParam(name="name", value="Duke")
```

Once set, the parameter can be used within code by calling getServletConfig().getInitializationParameter() and passing the name of the parameter, as shown in the following line of code:

```
out.println("<p>This is a simple servlet to demonstrate context!  Hello "
                        + getServletConfig().getInitParameter("name") + "</p>");
```

The annotations have the benefit of providing ease of development, and they also make it easier to maintain servlets as a single package rather than jumping back and forth between the servlet and the deployment descriptor. However, those benefits come at the cost of compilation because in order to change the value of an initialization parameter using the @WebInitParam annotation, you must recompile the code. Such is not the case when using the web.xml deployment descriptor. It is best to evaluate your application circumstances before committing to a standard for naming initialization parameters.

Filtering Web Requests

Another useful technique can be to apply a filter against a specified URL for a servlet. A filter can then invoke custom processing each time the URL is visited, and the filter will be executed prior to the servlet.

Example

Create a servlet filter that will be processed when the specified URL format is used to access the application. In this example, the filter will be executed when a URL conforming to the format of /* is used. This format pertains to any URL in the application. Therefore, any page will cause the servlet to be invoked.

```java
package org.javaserverfaces.chapter01;

import java.io.IOException;
import java.io.PrintWriter;
import java.util.Date;
import javax.servlet.*;
import javax.servlet.annotation.WebFilter;
import javax.servlet.http.*;

/**
 * This filter obtains the IP address of the remote host and logs
 * it.
 *
 * @author juneau
 */
@WebFilter("/*")
public class LoggingFilter implements Filter {

    private FilterConfig filterConf = null;

    public void init(FilterConfig filterConf) {
        this.filterConf = filterConf;
    }

    public void doFilter(ServletRequest request,
            ServletResponse response,
            FilterChain chain)
            throws IOException, ServletException {
        String userAddy = request.getRemoteHost();
        filterConf.getServletContext().log("Vistor User IP: " + userAddy);
        chain.doFilter(request, response);
    }

    @Override
    public void destroy() {
        throw new UnsupportedOperationException("Not supported yet.");
    }
}
```

The filter could contain any processing; the important thing to note is that this servlet is processed when a specified URL is used to access the application.

■ **Note**   To invoke the filter, load a URL for the application with which the filter is associated. For the purposes of this example, load the following URL (for the previous example) to see the filter add text to the server log:

`http://localhost:8080/JSFByExample/SimpleServletCtx1.`

How It Works

Web filters are useful for preprocessing requests and invoking certain functionality when a given URL is visited. Rather than invoking a servlet that exists at a given URL directly, any filter that contains the same URL pattern will be invoked prior to the servlet. This can be helpful in many situations, perhaps the most useful for performing logging, authentication, or other services that occur in the background without user interaction.

Filters must implement the `javax.servlet.Filter` interface. Methods contained within this interface include `init`, `destroy`, and `doFilter`. The `init` and `destroy` methods are invoked by the container. The `doFilter` method is used to implement tasks for the filter class. As you can see from this example, the filter class has access to the `ServletRequest` and `ServletResponse` objects. This means the request can be captured, and information can be obtained from it. This also means the request can be modified if need be. For example, including the user name in the request after an authentication filter has been used.

If you want to chain filters or if more than one filter exists for a given URL pattern, they will be invoked in the order in which they are configured in the `web.xml` deployment descriptor. It is best to manually configure the filters if you are using more than one per URL pattern rather than using the `@WebFilter` annotation. To manually configure the `web.xml` file to include a filter, use the `<filter>` and `<filter-mapping>` XML elements along with their associated child element tags. The following excerpt from a `web.xml` configuration file shows how the filter that has been created for this example may be manually configured within the `web.xml` file:

```
<filter>
    <filter-name>LoggingFilter</filter-name>
    <filter-class>LoggingFilter</filter-class>
</filter>
<filter-mapping>
    <filter-name>LogingFilter</filter-name>
    <url-pattern>/*</url-pattern>
</filter-mapping>
```

Of course, the `@WebFilter` annotation takes care of the configuration for you, so in this case the manual configuration is not required.

■ **Note**   As of Servlet 3.1 API, if a filter invokes the next entity in the chain, each of the filter `service` methods must run in the same thread as all filters that apply to the servlet.

Listening for Attribute Changes

Servlets can perform listening event tasks when HTTP session attributes are changed by implementing the HttpSessionAttributeListener interface.

Example

This example demonstrates how to generate an attribute listener servlet to listen for such events as attributes being added, removed, or modified. The following class demonstrates this technique by implementing HttpSessionAttributeListener and listening for attributes that are added, removed, or replaced within the HTTP session:

```
package org.javaserverfaces.chapter01;

import javax.servlet.ServletContext;
import javax.servlet.ServletContextEvent;
import javax.servlet.ServletContextListener;
import javax.servlet.annotation.WebListener;
import javax.servlet.http.HttpSession;
import javax.servlet.http.HttpSessionAttributeListener;
import javax.servlet.http.HttpSessionBindingEvent;

/**
 * Attribute Listener
 */
@WebListener
public final class AttributeListener implements ServletContextListener,
        HttpSessionAttributeListener {

    private ServletContext context = null;

    @Override
    public void attributeAdded(HttpSessionBindingEvent se) {
        HttpSession session = se.getSession();
        String id = session.getId();
        String name = se.getName();
        String value = (String) se.getValue();
        String message = new StringBuffer("New attribute has been added to session: \n").
        append("Attribute Name: ").append(name).append("\n").append("Attribute Value:").
        append(value).toString();
        log(message);
    }

    /**
     *
     * @param se
     */
    @Override
    public void attributeRemoved(HttpSessionBindingEvent se) {
        HttpSession session = se.getSession();
        String id = session.getId();
```

```
        String name = se.getName();
        if (name == null) {
            name = "Unknown";
        }
        String value = (String) se.getValue();
        String message = new StringBuffer("Attribute has been removed: \n")
        .append("Attribute Name: ").append(name).append("\n").append("Attribute Value:")
        .append(value).toString();
        log(message);
    }

    @Override
    public void attributeReplaced(HttpSessionBindingEvent se) {
        String name = se.getName();
        if (name == null) {
            name = "Unknown";
        }
        String value = (String) se.getValue();
        String message = new StringBuffer("Attribute has been replaced: \n ").append(name).
        toString();
        log(message);
    }

    private void log(String message) {
        if (context != null) {
            context.log("SessionListener: " + message);
        } else {
            System.out.println("SessionListener: " + message);
        }
    }

    @Override
    public void contextInitialized(ServletContextEvent event) {
        this.context = event.getServletContext();
        log("contextInitialized()");
    }

    @Override
    public void contextDestroyed(ServletContextEvent event) {
// Do something
    }
}
```

Messages will be displayed within the server log file indicating when attributes have been added, removed, or replaced.

Explanation

In some situations, it can be useful to know when an attribute has been set or what an attribute value has been set to. This example demonstrates how to create an attribute listener in order to determine this information. To create a servlet listener, you must implement one or more of the servlet listener interfaces. To listen for HTTP session attribute changes, implement HttpSessionAttributeListener. In doing so, the listener will implement the attributeAdded, attributeRemoved, and attributeReplaced methods. Each of these methods accepts HttpSessionBindingEvent as an argument, and their implementation defines what will occur when an HTTP session attribute is added, removed, or changed, respectively.

In this example, you can see that each of the three methods listed in the previous paragraph contains a similar implementation. Within each method, the HttpSessionBindingEvent is interrogated and broken down into String values, which represent the ID, name, and value of the attribute that caused the listener to react. For instance, in the attributeAdded method, the session is obtained from HttpSessionBindingEvent, and then the session ID is retrieved from that via the use of getSession. The attribute information can be obtained directly from the HttpSessionBindingEvent using the getId and getName methods, as shown in the following lines of code:

```
HttpSession session = se.getSession();
String id = session.getId();
String name = se.getName();
String value = (String) se.getValue();
```

After these values are obtained, the application can do whatever it needs to do with them. In this example, the attribute ID, name, and session ID are simply logged and printed.

```
String message = new StringBuffer("New attribute has been added to session: \n")
.append("Attribute Name: ").append(name).append("\n")
.append("Attribute Value:").append(value).toString();
log(message);
```

The body of the attributeReplaced and attributeRemoved methods contain similar functionality. In the end, the same routine is used within each to obtain the attribute name and value, and then something is done with those values.

A few different options can be used to register the listener with the container. The @WebListener annotation is the easiest way to do so, and the only downfall to using it is that you will need to recompile code in order to remove the listener annotation if you ever need to do so. The listener can be registered within the web deployment descriptor, or it can be registered using one of the addListener methods contained in ServletContext.

Although the example does not perform any life-changing events, it does demonstrate how to create and use an attribute listener. In the real world, such a listener could become handy if an application needed to capture the user name of everyone who logs in or needed to send an e-mail whenever a specified attribute is set.

Applying a Listener to a Session

In the same way that a listener can be applied to an HTTP session to listen for attribute changes, a listener can be applied for performing tasks when sessions are created and destroyedAssume in the following example that you wish to listen for sessions to be created so that you can count how many active sessions your application currently contains, as well as perform some initialization for each session.

Example

Create a session listener, and implement the sessionCreated and sessionDestroyed methods accordingly. In the following example, a servlet is used to keep track of active sessions. Each time someone works with the application, a counter has one added to it. Likewise, each time a person leaves the application, then the counter goes down by one.

```java
package org.javaserverfaces.chapter01;

import javax.servlet.annotation.WebListener;
import javax.servlet.http.HttpSession;
import javax.servlet.http.HttpSessionEvent;
import javax.servlet.http.HttpSessionListener;

/**
 * Applying a Session Listener
 *
 * @author juneau
 */
@WebListener
public class SessionListener implements HttpSessionListener {

    private int numberOfSessions;

    public SessionListener() {
        numberOfSessions = 0;
    }

    public int getNumberOfSessions() {
        return numberOfSessions;
    }

    @Override
    public void sessionCreated(HttpSessionEvent arg) {
        HttpSession session = arg.getSession();
        session.setMaxInactiveInterval(60);
        session.setAttribute("testAttr", "testVal");
        synchronized (this) {
            numberOfSessions++;
        }
        System.out.println("Session created, current count: " + numberOfSessions);
    }

    @Override
    public void sessionDestroyed(HttpSessionEvent arg) {
        HttpSession session = arg.getSession();
        synchronized (this) {
            numberOfSessions--;
        }
        System.out.println("Session destroyed, current count: " + numberOfSessions);
        System.out.println("The attribute value: " + session.getAttribute(("testAttr")));
    }
}
```

Each time a new visitor visits the application, a new session is started, and testAttr is set. When the session times out, then it will be destroyed, and any attributes that have been set for the session will be removed.

Explanation

A meaningful way to track web application users is to place values in their HttpSession object. Using a Java servlet, session attributes can be set, which will exist for the life of the HttpSession. Once the session is invalidated, the attributes will be removed. To set up a session listener, create a Java servlet, annotate it with the @WebListener annotation, and implement javax.servlet.http.HttpSessionListener. Doing so will force the implementation of both the sessionCreated and sessionDestroyed methods, which is where the session magic occurs.

In this example, the sessionCreated method first obtains a handle on the current HttpSession object by calling the HttpSessionEvent object's getSession method. The handle is assigned to an HttpSession variable named session. Now that you have that variable initialized with the session object, it can be used to set the time of life and place attributes that will live and die with the session's life. The first session configuration performed in the example is to set the maximum inactive life to 60 (seconds), after which time the servlet container will invalidate the session. Next an attribute named testAttr is set in the session and given a value of testVal.

```
HttpSession session = arg.getSession();
session.setMaxInactiveInterval(60);
session.setAttribute("testAttr", "testVal");
```

A field within the servlet named numberOfSessions is declared, and it is incremented each time a new session is started. Following the session.setAttribute() call, the counter is incremented within a synchronized statement. Finally, a message is printed to the server log indicating that a new session was created and providing the total active session count.

■ **Note** Placing the increment within the synchronized statement helps avoid concurrency issues with the field. For more information on Java synchronization and concurrency, please see the online documentation at http://docs.oracle.com/javase/tutorial/essential/concurrency/locksync.html.

The sessionDestroyed method is called on a session once the maximum number of inactive seconds has passed. In this example, the method will be called after 60 seconds of inactivity. Within the sessionDestroyed method, another synchronization statement decrements the numberOfSessions field value by one, and then a couple of lines are printed to the server log indicating that a session has been destroyed and providing the new total number of active sessions.

Session listeners can be used to set cookies and perform other useful tactics to help manage a user's experience. They are easy to use and very powerful.

Managing Session Attributes

It is possible to maintain information throughout the life of an individual session. Servlets can make use of session attributes to retain information on a per-session basis. That information can then be used at any time, so long as the session remains available.

Example

Make use of session attributes to retain session-based information. To do so, use the `HttpServletRequest` object to obtain access to the session, and then use the `getAttribute()` and `setAttribute()` methods accordingly to set information into the session. In the following scenario, an HTML page is used to capture a user's e-mail address, and then the e-mail address is placed into a session attribute. The attribute is then used by Java servlets across different pages of the application in order to maintain state.

The following code demonstrates what the HTML form (chapter01/sessionAttributeDemo.html) may look like in this scenario:

```html
<html>
    <head>
        <title></title>
        <meta http-equiv="Content-Type" content="text/html; charset=UTF-8">
    </head>
    <body>
        <h1>Provide an email address to use with this transaction</h1>
        <br/>
        <form method="POST" action="SessionServlet">
            <input type="text" id="email" name="email"/>
            <br/>
            <input type="submit" value="Submit"/>
        </form>
    </body>
</html>
```

Next, the Java servlet named `SessionServlet` using a URL pattern of `/SessionServlet` is initiated when the form is submitted. Any form input values are passed to `SessionServlet` and processed accordingly.

```java
package org.javaserverfaces.chapter01;

import java.io.*;
import javax.servlet.*;
import javax.servlet.annotation.WebServlet;
import javax.servlet.http.*;

// Uncomment the following line to run example stand-alone
//@WebServlet(name="SessionServlet", urlPatterns={"/SessionServlet"})

// The following will allow the example to run within the context of the JSFByExample example
// enterprise application (JSFByExample.war distro or Netbeans Project)
@WebServlet(name="SessionServlet", urlPatterns={"/chapter01/SessionServlet"}) public class
SessionServlet extends HttpServlet {
  public void doPost (HttpServletRequest req, HttpServletResponse res)
        throws ServletException, IOException {

    // Obtain he Session object

        HttpSession session = req.getSession(true);
```

```
// Set up a session attribute

    String email = (String)
    session.getAttribute ("session.email");
    if (email == null) {
        email = req.getParameter("email");
        session.setAttribute ("session.email", email);
    }
    String sessionId = session.getId();

    res.setContentType("text/html");
    PrintWriter out = res.getWriter();
    out.println("<html>");
    out.println("<head><title>Working with sessions</title></head>");
    out.println("<body>");
    out.println("<h1>Session Test</h1>");
    out.println ("Your email address is: " + email + "<br/><br/>");
    out.println ("Your session id: " + sessionId);
    out.println("</body></html>");
  }
}
```

In the end, the e-mail address that was entered within the original HTML form was captured and used throughout the different pages in the application.

How It Works

Since the beginning of web development, session attributes have been used to retain important information regarding a user's session. This concept holds true when developing using Java servlets as well, and servlets make it easy to maintain attribute values. All HttpServlet classes must implement doGet or doPost methods in order to process web application events. In doing so, these methods have access to the HttpServletRequest object as it is passed to them as an argument. An HttpSession object can be gleaned from the HttpServletRequest, and therefore, it can be used to retrieve and set attributes as needed.

In this example, an HTTP session attribute is used to store an e-mail address. That address is then used throughout the application within different servlet classes by obtaining the session object and then retrieving the attribute value.

```
// Obtain the Session object
   HttpSession session = req.getSession(true);
// Set up a session attribute
   String email = (String)
   session.getAttribute ("session.email");
   if (email == null) {
       email = req.getParameter("email");
       session.setAttribute ("session.email", email);
   }
```

Any attributes will remain in the HttpSession object as long as the session remains valid. The session ID will remain consistent when traversing between pages. You can see that the solution to this example obtains and prints the current session ID for reference. Using attributes in the HttpSession is a good way to pass data around to maintain a session's state.

Downloading a File Using a Servlet

Servlet applications have the ability to download a given file using a series of InputStreams and OutputStreams.

Example

Write a servlet that will accept the name and path of a chosen file and then read the file and stream it to the file requestor. The following web page can be used to select a file for the servlet to download. Although the following HTML (chapter01/download.html) contains a statically typed file name, it could very well contain a dynamic list of files from a database or other source:

```
<!DOCTYPE html>
<html>
    <head>
        <title></title>
        <meta http-equiv="Content-Type" content="text/html; charset=UTF-8">
    </head>
    <body>
        <h1>Click on the link below to download the file.</h1>
        <br/>
        <a href="DownloadServlet?filename=downloadTest.txt">Download test file</a>
        <br/>

    </body>
</html>
```

■ **Note** For the example, you can create and edit a file in your root directory next to the WEB-INF folder, and name the file downloadTest.txt to see the servlet transfer the data to your browser client.

When a user clicks the link presented on the web page from the previous HTML, the following servlet will be used to download the given file by passing the HttpServletRequest and HttpServletResponse objects to it along with the file that should be downloaded:

```
package org.javaserverfaces.chapter01;

import java.io.DataInputStream;
import java.io.File;
import java.io.FileInputStream;
import java.io.IOException;
import java.io.InputStream;
import java.io.PrintWriter;
import javax.servlet.ServletContext;
import javax.servlet.ServletException;
import javax.servlet.ServletOutputStream;
import javax.servlet.annotation.WebServlet;
import javax.servlet.http.HttpServlet;
import javax.servlet.http.HttpServletRequest;
import javax.servlet.http.HttpServletResponse;
```

```java
/**
 *
 * @author juneau
 */
// Uncomment the following line to run example stand-alone
//@WebServlet(name = "DownloadServlet", urlPatterns = {"/DownloadServlet"})

// The following will allow the example to run within the context of the JSFByExample
// enterprise application (JSFByExample.war distro or Netbeans Project)
@WebServlet(name = "DownloadServlet", urlPatterns = {"/chapter01/DownloadServlet"})
public class DownloadServlet extends HttpServlet {

    /**
     * Handles the HTTP
     * <code>GET</code> method.
     *
     * @param request servlet request
     * @param response servlet response
     * @throws ServletException if a servlet-specific error occurs
     * @throws IOException if an I/O error occurs
     */
    @Override
    protected void doGet(HttpServletRequest request, HttpServletResponse response)
            throws ServletException, IOException {
        // Read parameter from form that contains the filename to download
        String fileToDownload = request.getParameter("filename");
        // Call the download method with the given file
        System.err.println("Downloading file now...");
        doDownload(request, response, fileToDownload);
    }


    /**
     * Sends a file to the output stream.
     *
     * @param req The request
     * @param resp The response
     * @param original_filename The name the browser should receive.
     */
    private void doDownload( HttpServletRequest request, HttpServletResponse response,
                             String originalFile) throws IOException {
        final int BYTES = 1024;
        int               length  = 0;
        ServletOutputStream outStream = response.getOutputStream();
        ServletContext      context  = getServletConfig().getServletContext();


        response.setContentType( (context.getMimeType( originalFile ) != null) ?
                context.getMimeType( originalFile ) : "text/plain" );
        response.setHeader( "Content-Disposition", "attachment; filename=\"" + originalFile + "\"" );
```

```
        InputStream in = context.getResourceAsStream("/" + originalFile);
        byte[] bbuf = new byte[BYTES];

        while ((in != null) && ((length = in.read(bbuf)) != -1))
        {
            outStream.write(bbuf,0,length);
        }

        outStream.flush();
        outStream.close();
    }

    /**
     * Returns a short description of the servlet.
     *
     * @return a String containing servlet description
     */
    @Override
    public String getServletInfo() {
        return "Short description";
    }
}
```

The servlet will not produce a response; it will simply download the given file to the end user when the user clicks the link to download the file.

Explanation

Downloading files is an essential task for almost any web application. Performing the steps that are provided by this example will make it easy to achieve this task. This example demonstrates an easy case in which users can visit a web page, click a file to download, and have the file retrieved from the server and copied to their machine. The HTML is very simplistic in this example, and it lists a URL link that invokes the servlet and passes the name of the file that is to be downloaded. When the user clicks the link, the name of the file is passed to /DownloadServlet as a parameter with the name filename. When the link is clicked, the servlet doGet method is invoked. The first task that is performed in the doGet method is to read the filename parameter from the invoking web page. That information is then passed to the doDownload method along with the HttpServletRequest and HttpServletResponse objects.

In the doDownload method, the ServletOutputStream is obtained from the HttpServletResponse object, and the ServletContext is obtained for later use. To download a file, the servlet must provide a response of the same type that matches that of the file to be downloaded. It must also indicate in the response header that an attachment is to be included. Therefore, the first tasks to be performed by the doDownload method involve setting up the HttpServletResponse appropriately.

```
response.setContentType( (context.getMimeType( originalFile ) != null) ?
            context.getMimeType( originalFile ) : "text/plain" );
response.setHeader( "Content-Disposition", "attachment; filename=\"" + originalFile + "\"" );
```

The file name, in this case originalFile, is used to obtain the MIME type of the file. If the MIME type of the file is null, then text/plain will be returned. The attachment is set up in the response header as well, by appending the file name as an attachment to the Content-Disposition. Next, the doDownload method obtains a reference to the file that is to be downloaded by calling the ServletContext getResourceAsStream method and passing the name of the file. This will return an InputStream object that can be used to read the contents of the indicated file. A byte buffer is then created, which will be used to obtain chunks of data from the file when it is being read. The final real task is to read the file contents and copy them to the output stream. This is done using a `while` loop, which will continue to read from the `InputStream` until everything has been processed. Chunks of data are read in and written to the output stream using the loop.

```
while ((in != null) && ((length = in.read(bbuf)) != -1))
{
    outStream.write(bbuf,0,length);
}
```

Lastly, the `ServletOutputStream` object's `flush` method is called to clear the contents, and it is then closed to release resources. The magic of downloading files using a Java servlet may be a bit obfuscated by this example, however, because a static file is being used as the download source in this example. In real life, the HTML page would probably contain a list of files that are contained within a database or on a file system, and then when the user selects a file to download, the servlet will process that file accordingly, even extracting the file from the database if necessary.

Dispatching Requests

The concept of handing off tasks to other workers to perform action can be mirrored with real-world scenarios. If your car stops functioning properly, you take it to a mechanic. Servlet processing can follow a similar technique by handing off tasks to the appropriate worker servlets. This process is also known as dispatching. Furthermore, servlets have the ability to hand off tasks without redirecting the client to another site, and therefore, the URL in the browser does not change.

Example

To begin, create a request dispatcher servlet, which will decide which task needs to be completed and then send the request to an appropriate servlet to achieve that task. The following example demonstrates this concept via an HTML form that accepts two numbers from the user and allows the user to decide what type of mathematical evaluation should be performed by the server. The servlet processes the request by first determining which type of mathematical evaluation should be performed and then dispatching the request to the appropriate servlet to perform the task.

The following HTML form accepts two numbers from the user and allows them to choose which type of math to perform against the numbers:

```html
<html>
    <head>
        <title></title>
        <meta http-equiv="Content-Type" content="text/html; charset=UTF-8">
    </head>
    <body>
        <h1>Request Dispatch Example</h1>
        <p>Perform a mathematical evaluation.  Insert two numbers to be evaluated and then
            choose the type of evaluation to perform.</p>
        <form method="POST" action="MathDispatcher">
            <label for="numa">Enter Number A: </label>
            <input type="text" id="numa" name="numa"/><br><br>
            <label for="numb">Enter Number B: </label>
            <input type="text" id="numb" name="numb"/><br/><br/>
            <select id="matheval" name="matheval">
                <option value="add">Add the numbers</option>
                <option value="subtract">Subtract the numbers</option>
```

```
            <option value="multiply">Multiply the numbers</option>
            <option value="divide">Divide the numbers</option>
        </select>
        <input type="submit" value="Submit Form"/>
        <input type="reset" value="Reset Form"/>
    </form>
  </body>
</html>
```

The next piece of code is the servlet that will dispatch requests accordingly depending upon the value of the mathEval field:

```java
package org.javaserverfaces.chapter01;

import java.io.IOException;
import javax.servlet.RequestDispatcher;
import javax.servlet.ServletContext;
import javax.servlet.ServletException;
import javax.servlet.ServletRequest;
import javax.servlet.annotation.WebServlet;
import javax.servlet.http.HttpServlet;
import javax.servlet.http.HttpServletRequest;
import javax.servlet.http.HttpServletResponse;

/**
 *
 * @author juneau
 */
// Uncomment the following line to run example stand-alone
//@WebServlet(name = "MathDispatcher", urlPatterns = {"/MathDispatcher"})

// The following will allow the example to run within the context of the JSFByExample
// enterprise application (JSFByExample.war distro or Netbeans Project)
@WebServlet(name = "MathDispatcher", urlPatterns = {"/chapter01/MathDispatcher"})
public class MathDispatcher extends HttpServlet {

    /**
     * Handles the HTTP
     * <code>POST</code> method.
     *
     * @param request servlet request
     * @param response servlet response
     * @throws ServletException if a servlet-specific error occurs
     * @throws IOException if an I/O error occurs
     */
    @Override
    protected void doPost(HttpServletRequest request, HttpServletResponse response)
            throws ServletException, IOException {
        System.out.println("In the servlet...");
```

```java
        // Store the input parameter values into Strings
            String eval = request.getParameter("matheval");
            ServletContext sc = getServletConfig().getServletContext();
            RequestDispatcher rd = null;
            int evaluate = 0;
            int add = 0;
            int subtract = 1;
            int multiply = 2;
            int divide = 3;
            if(eval.equals("add"))
                evaluate = add;
            if (eval.equals("subtract"))
                evaluate = subtract;
            if (eval.equals("multiply"))
                evaluate = multiply;
            if(eval.equals("divide")){
                evaluate = divide;
            }
            switch(evaluate){
                case(0): rd =  sc.getRequestDispatcher("/AddServlet");
                                rd.forward(request, response);
                                break;
                case(1): rd =  sc.getRequestDispatcher("/SubtractServlet");
                                rd.forward(request, response);
                                break;
                case(2): rd =  sc.getRequestDispatcher("/MultiplyServlet");
                                rd.forward(request, response);
                                break;
                case(3): rd =  sc.getRequestDispatcher("/DivideServlet");
                                 rd.forward(request, response);
                                 break;
            }

    }


    /**
     * Returns a short description of the servlet.
     *
     * @return a String containing servlet description
     */
    @Override
    public String getServletInfo() {
        return "Short description";
    }
}
```

Next is an example of one of the servlets that the request will be dispatched to. The following is the code for the AddServlet, which will add the two numbers and return the sum to the user:

```java
package org.javaserverfaces.chapter01;

import java.io.IOException;
import java.io.PrintWriter;
import javax.servlet.ServletException;
import javax.servlet.annotation.WebServlet;
import javax.servlet.http.HttpServlet;
import javax.servlet.http.HttpServletRequest;
import javax.servlet.http.HttpServletResponse;

/**
 *
 * @author juneau
 */
// Uncomment the following line to run example stand-alone
//@WebServlet(name = "AddServlet", urlPatterns = {"/AddServlet"})

// The following will allow the example to run within the context of the JSFByExample
// enterprise application (JSFByExample.war distro or Netbeans Project
@WebServlet(name = "AddServlet", urlPatterns = {"/chapter01/AddServlet"})
public class AddServlet extends HttpServlet {

    /**
     * Processes requests for both HTTP
     * <code>GET</code> and
     * <code>POST</code> methods.
     *
     * @param request servlet request
     * @param response servlet response
     * @throws ServletException if a servlet-specific error occurs
     * @throws IOException if an I/O error occurs
     */
    protected void processRequest(HttpServletRequest request, HttpServletResponse response)
            throws ServletException, IOException {
        response.setContentType("text/html;charset=UTF-8");
        PrintWriter out = response.getWriter();
        // Store the input parameter values into Strings
                String numA = request.getParameter("numa");
                String numB = request.getParameter("numb");
                int sum = Integer.valueOf(numA) + Integer.valueOf(numB);
        try {
            out.println("<html>");
            out.println("<head>");
            out.println("<title>The Sum of the Numbers</title>");
            out.println("</head>");
            out.println("<body>");
            out.println("<h1>Sum: " + sum + "</h1>");
            out.println("<br/>");
            out.println("<a href=example01_14.html>Try Again</a>");
```

```java
            out.println("</body>");
            out.println("</html>");
        } finally {
            out.close();
        }
    }

    /**
     * Handles the HTTP
     * <code>GET</code> method.
     *
     * @param request servlet request
     * @param response servlet response
     * @throws ServletException if a servlet-specific error occurs
     * @throws IOException if an I/O error occurs
     */
    @Override
    protected void doGet(HttpServletRequest request, HttpServletResponse response)
            throws ServletException, IOException {
        processRequest(request, response);
    }

    /**
     * Handles the HTTP
     * <code>POST</code> method.
     *
     * @param request servlet request
     * @param response servlet response
     * @throws ServletException if a servlet-specific error occurs
     * @throws IOException if an I/O error occurs
     */
    @Override
    protected void doPost(HttpServletRequest request, HttpServletResponse response)
            throws ServletException, IOException {
        processRequest(request, response);
    }

    /**
     * Returns a short description of the servlet.
     *
     * @return a String containing servlet description
     */
    @Override
    public String getServletInfo() {
        return "Short description";
    }
}
```

Each of the other servlets is very similar to AddServlet, except the mathematical evaluation is different. To see a full listing of the code, please take a look at the sources for this book.

Explanation

Sometimes it is a good idea to hide the forwarding of requests from the end user. Other times it just makes sense to hand off a request from one servlet to another so that another type of processing can take place. These are just two examples of when it is handy to perform a request dispatch within a servlet. Forwarding a request versus dispatching a request is different because a forwarded request hands off the request on the client side, whereas a dispatched request hands off the request on the server side. The difference can be quite large since the end user has no idea of server-side dispatches, whereas the browser is redirected to a different URL when the request is forwarded on the client side.

Dispatching requests is an easy task. The facilities for doing so are built right into the ServletContext, so once you obtain a reference to ServletContext, then you simply call the getRequestDispatcher method to obtain a RequestDispatcher object that can be used to dispatch the request. When calling the getRequestDispatcher method, pass a String containing the name of the servlet that you want to hand off the request to. You can actually obtain a RequestDisptacher object for any valid HTTP resource within the application by passing the appropriate URL for the resource in String format to the getRequestDispatcher method. Therefore, if you'd rather dispatch to a JSP or HTML page, you can do that as well. After a RequestDispatcher object has been obtained, invoke its forward method by passing the HttpServletRequest and HttpServletResponse objects to it. The forward method performs the task of handing off the request.

```
rd = sc.getRequestDispatcher("/AddServlet");
rd.forward(request, response);
```

In the case of this example, you can dispatch requests to different servlets in order to perform a specific task. Once handed off, the servlet that has obtained the request is responsible for providing the response to the client. In this case, the servlet returns the result of the specified mathematical evaluation.

Redirecting to Another Application or Site

In certain situations, it can be useful to redirect from a servlet to a different application on the same server or a different site altogether.

Example

Use the HttpServletResponse object's sendRedirect() method to redirect from the servlet to another URL. In the following example, when a URL that matches the /redirect pattern is used, then the servlet will redirect the browser to another site:

```
import java.io.IOException;
import javax.servlet.*;
import javax.servlet.annotation.WebServlet;
import javax.servlet.http.*;

@WebServlet(name="RedirectServlet", urlPatterns={"/redirect"})
public class RedirectServlet extends HttpServlet {

        @Override
    public void doGet(HttpServletRequest req, HttpServletResponse res)
```

```
        throws IOException, ServletException {
            String site = "http://www.apress.com";

        res.sendRedirect(site);
    }
}
```

In this example, the servlet will redirect to the `www.apress.com` web site.

Explanation

There are some cases in which a web application needs to redirect traffic to another site or URL within the same or another application. For such cases, the `HttpServletResponse` `sendRedirect` method can be of use. The `sendRedirect` method accepts a URL in `String` format and then redirects the web browser to the given URL. Given that `sendRedirect` accepts a `String`-based URL makes it easy to build dynamic URLs as well. For instance, some applications may redirect to a different URL based upon certain parameters that are passed from a user. Dynamic generation of a URL in such cases may look something like the following:

```
String redirectUrl = null;
If(parameter.equals("SOME STRING")
    redirectUrl = "/" + urlPathA;
else
    redirectUrl = "/" + urlPathB;
res.sendRedirect(redirectUrl);
```

The `sendRedirect()` method can also come in handy for creating the control for web menus and other page items that can send web traffic to different locations.

■ **Note** This simple redirect, as opposed to servlet chaining, does not pass the `HttpRequest` object along to the target address.

Utilizing Cookies Within the Browser Securely

If an application must maintain state, it should be maintained in a secure manner. Cookies are oftentimes used to pass data around as a means of maintaining state. Servlets can safeguard cookies by marking them as HTTP only.

Example

Use "HTTP only" browser cookies to save the state. In the following example, one servlet is used to place some session information into a cookie in the browser. Another servlet is then called, which reads the cookie information and displays it to the user. The following servlet demonstrates how to store a cookie in the browser using a Java servlet:

```java
package org.javaserverfaces.chapter01;

import java.io.IOException;
import java.io.PrintWriter;
import javax.servlet.ServletException;
import javax.servlet.annotation.WebServlet;
import javax.servlet.http.Cookie;
import javax.servlet.http.HttpServlet;
import javax.servlet.http.HttpServletRequest;
import javax.servlet.http.HttpServletResponse;

/**
 * Securing State within the Browser
 * @author juneau
 */
@WebServlet(name = "SetCookieServlet", urlPatterns = {"/SetCookieServlet"})
public class SetCookieServlet extends HttpServlet {


    protected void processRequest(HttpServletRequest request, HttpServletResponse response)
            throws ServletException, IOException {
        response.setContentType("text/html;charset=UTF-8");
        PrintWriter out = response.getWriter();
        Cookie cookie = new Cookie("sessionId","12345");
        cookie.setHttpOnly(true);
        cookie.setMaxAge(-30);
        response.addCookie(cookie);
        try {
            out.println("<html>");
            out.println("<head>");
            out.println("<title>SetCookieServlet</title>");
            out.println("</head>");
            out.println("<body>");
            out.println("<h1>Servlet SetCookieServlet is setting a cookie into the browser</h1>");
            out.println("<br/><br/>");
            out.println("<a href='DisplayCookieServlet'>Display the cookie contents.</a>");
            out.println("</body>");
            out.println("</html>");
        } finally {
            out.close();
        }
    }
```

```java
    @Override
    protected void doGet(HttpServletRequest request, HttpServletResponse response)
            throws ServletException, IOException {
        processRequest(request, response);
    }

    @Override
    protected void doPost(HttpServletRequest request, HttpServletResponse response)
            throws ServletException, IOException {
        processRequest(request, response);
    }

}
```

The next code listing demonstrates a servlet that reads the cookies in the browser and prints out the contents:

```java
package org.javaserverfaces.chapter01;

import java.io.IOException;
import java.io.PrintWriter;
import javax.servlet.ServletException;
import javax.servlet.annotation.WebServlet;
import javax.servlet.http.Cookie;
import javax.servlet.http.HttpServlet;
import javax.servlet.http.HttpServletRequest;
import javax.servlet.http.HttpServletResponse;

/**
 * Securely Maintaining State within the Browser
 * @author juneau
 */
@WebServlet(name = "DisplayCookieServlet", urlPatterns = {"/DisplayCookieServlet"})
public class DisplayCookieServlet extends HttpServlet {

    protected void processRequest(HttpServletRequest request, HttpServletResponse response)
            throws ServletException, IOException {
        response.setContentType("text/html;charset=UTF-8");
        PrintWriter out = response.getWriter();
        Cookie[] cookies = request.getCookies();

        try {
            out.println("<html>");
            out.println("<head>");
            out.println("<title>Display Cookies</title>");
            out.println("</head>");
            out.println("<body>");
            for(Cookie cookie:cookies){
                out.println("<p>");
                out.println("Cookie Name: " + cookie.getName());
                out.println("<br/>");
                out.println("Value: " + cookie.getValue());
                out.println("</p>");
            }
```

```
                out.println("</body>");
                out.println("</html>");
        } finally {
            out.close();
        }
    }

    @Override
    protected void doGet(HttpServletRequest request, HttpServletResponse response)
            throws ServletException, IOException {
        processRequest(request, response);
    }

    @Override
    protected void doPost(HttpServletRequest request, HttpServletResponse response)
            throws ServletException, IOException {
        processRequest(request, response);
    }

}
```

Explanation

Using cookies to store data within the browser is a technique that has been in practice for years. Since Servlet 3.0 API, the ability to mark a cookie as HTTP only has become available. This allows the cookie to be safeguarded against client-side scripting attacks, making the cookie more secure. Any standard servlet can create a cookie and place it into the current session. Similarly, any servlet that is contained within the same session can read or update a session's cookies values. In this example, two servlets are used to demonstrate how cookies work. The first servlet that is listed is responsible for creating a new cookie and setting it into the browser session. The second servlet is responsible for displaying the contents of the cookie to the user.

To create a cookie, simply instantiate a new javax.servlet.http.Cookie object and assign a name and value to it. Passing both the name and value into the Cookie constructor at the time of instantiation can assign a name and value, or it can be done by passing values to the cookie's setName and setValue methods. Once the cookie has been instantiated, properties can be set that will help to configure the cookie. In this example, the cookie's setMaxAge and setHttpOnly methods are called, setting the time of life for the cookie and ensuring that it will be guarded against client-side scripting. For a complete listing of cookie properties, please refer to Table 1-3. Finally, the cookie is placed into the response by passing it to the response object's addCookie method.

```
Cookie cookie = new Cookie("sessionId","12345");
cookie.setHttpOnly(true);
cookie.setMaxAge(-30);
response.addCookie(cookie);
```

Table 1-3. *Cookie Property Methods*

Property	Description
setComment	Sets a comment to describe the cookie.
setDomain	Specifies the domain in which the cookie belongs.
setHttpOnly	Marks the cookie as HTTP only.
setMaxAge	Sets the maximum lifetime of the cookie. A negative value indicates that the cookie will expire when the session ends.
setPath	Specifies a path for the cookie to which the client should return it.
setSecure	Indicates that the cookie should be sent only using a secure protocol.
setValue	Assigns a value to the cookie.
setVersion	Specifies the version of the cookie protocol that the cookie will comply with.

The second servlet, `DisplayCookieServlet`, is responsible for reading and displaying the session's cookies values. When `DisplayCookieServlet` is invoked, its `processRequest` method is called, which obtains the cookies within the `response` object by calling `response.getCookies()` and setting the result to an array of `Cookie` objects.

```
Cookie[] cookies = request.getCookies();
```

The `cookie` object array can now be iterated over in order to obtain each cookie and print out its contents. The servlet does so by using a `for` loop and printing out each cookie's name and value.

```
for(Cookie cookie:cookies){
        out.println("<p>");
        out.println("Cookie Name: " + cookie.getName());
        out.println("<br/>");
        out.println("Value: " + cookie.getValue());
        out.println("</p>");
}
```

Finalizing Servlet Tasks

It is easy to perform cleanup tasks within the context of a servlet.

Example

To cleanup or perform finalization within a servlet, first provide code for performing any cleanup within the servlet `destroy` method. Second, in the case that there are potentially long-running methods, code them so that you will become aware of a shutdown and, if necessary, halt and return so that the servlet can shut down cleanly. The following code excerpt is a small example of a `destroy` method. In this code, it is being used to initialize local variables and is setting the `beingDestroyed` boolean value to indicate that the servlet is shutting down.

```
...
/**
     * Used to finalize the servlet
     */
    public void destroy() {
        // Tell the servlet it is shutting down
        setBeingDestroyed(true);
        // Perform any cleanup
        thisString = null;

    }
...
```

The code within the destroy method may successfully achieve a full cleanup of the servlet, but in the case where there may be a long-running task, then it must be notified of a shutdown. The following excerpt is a block of code that signifies a long-running task. The task should stop processing once the shutdown is indicated by the beingDestroyed value becoming true.

```
for (int x = 0; (x <= 100000 && !isBeingDestroyed()); x++) {
    doSomething();
}
```

Explanation

The finalization of a servlet can be very important, especially if the servlet is using some resources that may lead to a memory leak, making use of a reusable resource such as a database connection or in order to persist some values for another session. In such cases, it is a good idea to perform cleanup within the servlet destroy method. Every servlet contains a destroy method (which may be implemented to overload default behavior) that is initiated once the servlet container determines that a servlet should be taken out of service.

The destroy method is called once all of a servlet's service methods have stopped running. However, if there is a long-running service method, then a server grace period can be set that would cause any running service to be shut down when the grace period is reached. As mentioned earlier, the destroy method is the perfect place to clean up resources. However, the destroy method is also a good place to help clean up after long-running services. Cleanup can be done by setting a servlet-specific local variable to indicate that the servlet is being destroyed and by having the long-running service check the state of that variable periodically. If the variable indicates that the destroy method has been called, then it should stop executing.

Reading and Writing with Nonblocking I/O

First generation web applications oftentimes were plagued with the user clicking a button to submit a request to perform a read or write operation, and then waiting for a period of time so that the task could complete. Sometimes this was a momentary wait, and other timesit was a longer wait. Modern implementations of the Servlet API make it possible to perform asynchronous I/O, helping to alleviate this issue.

Example

Use the Non-Blocking I/O API that is part of the Servlet 3.1 release to create an asynchronous solution. To use the new technology, implement the new ReadListener interface when performing nonblocking reads, and implement the WriteListener interface for performing nonblocking writes. The implementation class can then be registered to a ServletInputStream or ServletOutputStream so that reads or writes can be performed when the listener finds that servlet content can be read or written without blocking.

The following sources are those of a ReadListener implementation that reside in the source file org.javaserverfaces.chapter01.AcmeReadListenerImpl.java, and they demonstrate how to implement the ReadListener:

```java
package org.javaserverfaces.chapter01;

import java.io.IOException;
import java.util.logging.Level;
import java.util.logging.Logger;
import javax.servlet.AsyncContext;
import javax.servlet.ReadListener;
import javax.servlet.ServletInputStream;

public class AcmeReadListenerImpl implements ReadListener {

    private ServletInputStream is = null;
    private AsyncContext async = null;

    public AcmeReadListenerImpl(ServletInputStream in, AsyncContext ac) {
        this.is = in;
        this.async = ac;
        System.out.println("read listener initialized");
    }

    @Override
    public void onDataAvailable() {
        System.out.println("onDataAvailable");
        try {
            StringBuilder sb = new StringBuilder();
            int len = -1;
            byte b[] = new byte[1024];
            while (is.isReady()
                    && (len = is.read(b)) != -1) {
                String data = new String(b, 0, len);
                System.out.println(data);
            }
        } catch (IOException ex) {
            Logger.getLogger(AcmeReadListenerImpl.class.getName()).log(Level.SEVERE, null, ex);
        }
    }

    @Override
        public void onAllDataRead() {
        System.out.println("onAllDataRead");
        async.complete();

    }
```

```
    @Override
        public void onError(Throwable thrwbl) {
        System.out.println("Error: " + thrwbl);
        async.complete();
    }

}
```

Next, use the listener by registering it to a ServletInputStream (in the case of the ReadListener) or a ServletOutputStream (in the case of a WriteListener). For this example, I'll show a servlet that utilizes the AcmeReadListenerImpl class. The sources for the following class reside within the file org.javaserverfaces. chapter01.AcmeReaderExample.java:

```
package org.javaserverfaces.chapter01;

import java.io.IOException;
import java.io.InputStream;
import java.io.PrintWriter;
import java.util.concurrent.CountDownLatch;
import javax.servlet.AsyncContext;
import javax.servlet.ServletContext;
import javax.servlet.ServletException;
import javax.servlet.ServletInputStream;
import javax.servlet.ServletOutputStream;
import javax.servlet.annotation.WebServlet;
import javax.servlet.http.HttpServlet;
import javax.servlet.http.HttpServletRequest;
import javax.servlet.http.HttpServletResponse;

@WebServlet(urlPatterns = {"/AcmeReaderServlet"}, asyncSupported=true)
public class AcmeReaderServlet extends HttpServlet {

    protected void processRequest(HttpServletRequest request, HttpServletResponse response)
            throws ServletException, IOException {
        response.setContentType("text/html;charset=UTF-8");
        try (PrintWriter output = response.getWriter()) {
            String filename = "test.txt";
            ServletContext context = getServletContext();

            InputStream in = context.getResourceAsStream(filename);
            output.println("<html>");
            output.println("<head>");
            output.println("<title>Acme Reader</title>");
            output.println("</head>");
            output.println("<body>");
            output.println("<h1>Welcome to the Acme Reader Servlet</h1>");
            output.println("<br/><br/>");
            output.println("<p>Look at the server log to see data that was read asynchronously from
            a file<p>");
            AsyncContext asyncCtx = request.startAsync();
```

```
            ServletInputStream input = request.getInputStream();
            input.setReadListener(new AcmeReadListenerImpl(input, asyncCtx));

            output.println("</body>");
            output.println("</html>");
        } catch (Exception ex){
            System.out.println("Exception Occurred: " + ex);
        }
    }
}


  // Http Servlet Methods ...
...
}
```

The last piece of code that we need is the servlet that invokes the AcmeReaderServlet, passing the message that needs to be processed. In this example, a file from the server is passed to the AcmeReaderServlet as input, which then is asynchronously processed via the AcmeReadListenerImpl class. The following code is taken from org.javaserverfaces.chapter01.ReaderExample.java.

```
package org.javaserverfaces.chapter01;

import java.io.BufferedReader;
import java.io.BufferedWriter;
import java.io.IOException;
import java.io.InputStream;
import java.io.InputStreamReader;
import java.io.OutputStreamWriter;
import java.io.PrintWriter;
import java.net.HttpURLConnection;
import java.net.URL;
import java.util.logging.Level;
import java.util.logging.Logger;
import javax.servlet.ServletContext;
import javax.servlet.ServletException;
import javax.servlet.annotation.WebServlet;
import javax.servlet.http.HttpServlet;
import javax.servlet.http.HttpServletRequest;
import javax.servlet.http.HttpServletResponse;

@WebServlet(name = "ReaderExample", urlPatterns = {"/ReaderExample"})
public class ReaderExample extends HttpServlet {

    protected void processRequest(HttpServletRequest request, HttpServletResponse response)
            throws ServletException, IOException {
        response.setContentType("text/html;charset=UTF-8");
        String filename = "/WEB-INF/test.txt";
        ServletContext context = getServletContext();
```

```java
        InputStream in = context.getResourceAsStream(filename);
        try (PrintWriter out = response.getWriter()) {
            String path = "http://"
                        + request.getServerName()
                        + ":"
                        + request.getServerPort()
                        + request.getContextPath()
                        + "/AcmeReaderServlet";
            out.println("<html>");
            out.println("<head>");
            out.println("<title>Intro to Java EE 7 - Servlet Reader Example</title>");
            out.println("</head>");
            out.println("<body>");
            out.println("<h1>Servlet ReaderExample at " + request.getContextPath() + "</h1>");
            out.println("Invoking the endpoint: " + path + "<br>");
            out.flush();
            URL url = new URL(path);
            HttpURLConnection conn = (HttpURLConnection) url.openConnection();
            conn.setChunkedStreamingMode(2);
            conn.setDoOutput(true);
            conn.connect();
            if (in != null) {
                InputStreamReader inreader = new InputStreamReader(in);
                BufferedReader reader = new BufferedReader(inreader);
                String text = "";
                out.println("Beginning Read");
                try (BufferedWriter output = new BufferedWriter(new OutputStreamWriter(conn.
                getOutputStream()))) {
                    out.println("got the output...beginning loop");
                    while ((text = reader.readLine()) != null) {
                        out.println("reading text: " + text);
                        out.flush();
                        output.write(text);

                        Thread.sleep(1000);
                        output.write("Ending example now..");
                        out.flush();
                    }
                output.flush();
                    output.close();
                }
            }
            out.println("Review the GlassFish server log for messages...");
            out.println("</body>");
            out.println("</html>");
        } catch (InterruptedException | IOException ex) {
            Logger.getLogger(ReaderExample.class.getName()).log(Level.SEVERE, null, ex);
        }
    }
```

```java
@Override
    protected void doGet(HttpServletRequest request, HttpServletResponse response)
            throws ServletException, IOException {
        processRequest(request, response);
    }

@Override
    protected void doPost(HttpServletRequest request, HttpServletResponse response)
            throws ServletException, IOException {
        processRequest(request, response);
    }

@Override
    public String getServletInfo() {
        return "Short description";
    }
}
```

When the servlet is visited, the asynchronous, nonblocking read of the test.txt file will occur, and its text will be displayed in the server log.

Explanation

Servlet technology has allowed only traditional (blocking) input/output during request processing since its inception. In the Servlet 3.1 release, the new Non-Blocking I/O API makes it possible for servlets to read or write without any blocking. This means other tasks can be performed at the same time that a read or write is occurring, without any wait. Such a solution opens up a new realm of possibilities for servlets, making them much more flexible for use along with modern technologies such as the WebSockets protocol.

To implement a nonblocking I/O solution, new programming interfaces have been added to ServletInputStream and ServletOutputStream, as well as two event listeners: ReadListener and WriteListener. ReadListener and WriteListener interfaces make the servlet I/O processing occur in a nonblocking manner via callback methods that are invoked when servlet content can be read or written without blocking. Use the ServletInputStream.setReadListener(ServletInputStream, AsyncContext) method to register a ReadListener with a ServletInputStream, and use the I/O read ServletInputStream.setWriteListener(ServletOutputStream, AsyncContext) method for registering a WriteListener. The following lines of code demonstrate how to register a ReadListener implementation with a ServletInputStream:

```java
AsyncContext context = request.startAsync();
ServletInputStream input = request.getInputStream();
input.setReadListener(new ReadListenerImpl(input, context));
```

■ **Note**   In Servlet 3.0, AsyncContext was introduced to represent an execution context for an asynchronous operation that is initiated on a servlet request. To use the asynchronous context, a servlet should be annotated as a @WebServlet, and the asyncSupported attribute of the annotation must be set to true. The @WebFilter annotation also contains the asyncSupported attribute.

After a listener has been registered with a ServletInputStream, the status on a nonblocking read can be checked by calling the methods ServletInputStream.isReady and ServletInputStream.isFinished. For instance, a read can begin once the ServletInputStream.isReady method returns a true, as shown here:

```
while (is.isReady() && (b = input.read()) != -1)) {
len = is.read(b);
String data = new String(b, 0, len);
}
```

To create a ReadListener or WriteListener, three methods must be overridden: onDataAvailable, onAllDataRead, and onError. The onDataAvailable method is invoked when data is available to be read or written, onAllDataRead is invoked once all the data has been read or written, and onError is invoked if an error is encountered. The code for AcmeReadListenerImpl in the solution to this example demonstrates how to override these methods.

The AsyncContext.complete method is called in the onAllDataRead method to indicate that the read has been completed and to commit the response. This method is also called in the onError implementation so that the read will complete, so it is important to perform any cleanup within the body of the onError method to ensure that no resources are leaked, and so on.

To implement a WriteListener, make use of the new ServletOutputStream.canWrite method, which determines whether data can be written in a nonblocking fashion. A WriteListener implementation class must override a couple of methods: onWritePossible and onError. The onWritePossible method is invoked when a nonblocking write can occur. The write implementation should take place within the body of this method. The onError method is much the same as its ReadListener implementation counterpart, because it is invoked when an error occurs.

The following lines of code demonstrate how to register a WriteListener with a ServletOutputStream:

```
AsyncContext context = request.startAsync();
ServletOutputStream os = response.getOutputStream();
os.setWriteListener(new WriteListenerImpl(os, context));
```

The WriteListener implementation class must include overriding methods for onWritePossible and onError. The following is an example for a WriteListener implementation class:

```
import javax.servlet.AsyncContext;
import javax.servlet.ServletOutputStream;
import javax.servlet.WriteListener;

public class WriteListenerImpl implements WriteListener {

    ServletOutputStream os;
    AsyncContext context;

    public WriteListenerImpl(ServletOutputStream out, AsyncContext ctx){
        this.os = out;
        this.context = ctx;
        System.out.println("Write Listener Initialized");
    }

    @Override
    public void onWritePossible() {
        System.out.println("Now possible to write...");
```

```
        // Write implementation goes here...
    }

    @Override
    public void onError(Throwable thrwbl) {
        System.out.println("Error occurred");
        context.complete();
    }

}
```

■ **Note**   In most cases, the ReadListener and WriteListener implementation classes can be embedded within the calling servlet. They have been broken out into separate classes for the examples in this book for demonstration purposes.

The new Non-Blocking I/O API helps bring the Servlet API into compliance with new web standards. The new API makes it possible to create web-based applications that perform well in an asynchronous fashion.

CHAPTER 2

JavaServer Pages

The JavaServer Pages (JSP) web framework introduced a great productivity boost for Java web developers over the Java Servlet API. When the JSP technology was introduced in 1999, it was Sun's answer to PHP and ASP, which provided web developers with a quick way to create dynamic web content. JSPs contain a mix of XML and HTML but can also contain embedded Java code within scripting elements known as *scriptlets*. Indeed, JSPs are easy to learn and allow developers to quickly create dynamic content and use their favorite HTML editor to lay out nice-looking pages. JSP was introduced several years ago and still remains one of the most important Java web technologies available. Although JSP technology has changed over the years, there are still many applications using older JSP variations in the world today.

Over the years, the creation of dynamic web content has solidified, and the techniques used to develop web applications have become easier to maintain down the road. Whereas early JSP applications included a mix of Java and XML markup within the pages, today the separation of markup from business logic is increasingly important. Newer releases of the JSP technology have accounted for these changes in the web space, and the most recent releases allow developers the flexibility to develop highly dynamic content without utilizing any embedded Java code but, instead, making use of markup and custom tags within pages.

This chapter will show you the ins and outs of JSP development. Starting with creating a simple JSP application, you will learn how to develop applications using JSP technology from the ground up and harness the productivity and power that the technology has to offer. The chapter also brushes upon advanced techniques such as the development of custom JSP tags and the invocation of Java functions utilizing conditional tags. Although entire books have been written on JSP, the examples within this chapter will lay a solid foundation on which you can begin to develop applications utilizing JSP.

Note Utilizing a Java integrated development environment (IDE) can significantly reduce development time, especially when working with Java web technologies such as JSP.

Development of a Simple JSP Page

JSPs are a perfect match for developing web pages that contain dynamic content. JSPs allow developers to mix HTML markup with dynamic content via the use of JSP Scriptlets.

Example

JavaServer Pages can be used to create web pages that combine standard markup with blocks of Java code that are embedded within the markup. The following JSP markup demonstrates how to include dynamic code into a page:

```
<%--
    Document    : simplejsp
    Author      : juneau
--%>

<%@page contentType="text/html" pageEncoding="UTF-8"%>
<!DOCTYPE html>
<html>
    <head>
        <meta http-equiv="Content-Type" content="text/html; charset=UTF-8">
        <title>JSP Page Example</title>
    </head>
    <body>
        <jsp:useBean id="dateBean" scope="application" class="org.javaserverfaces.chapter02.
DateBean"/>
        <h1>Hello World!</h1>
        <br/>
        <p>
            The current date is: ${dateBean.currentDate}!
        </p>
    </body>
</html>
```

The previous JSP code uses a JavaBean to pull the current date into the page. The following Java code is the JavaBean that is used by the JSP code:

```java
package org.javaserverfaces.chapter02;

import java.time.LocalDateTime;

/**
 * Creating a Simple JSP
 * @author juneau
 */
public class DateBean {

    private LocalDateTime currentDate = LocalDateTime.now();

    /**
     * @return the currentDate
     */
    public LocalDateTime getCurrentDate() {
        return currentDate;
    }
```

```
/**
 * @param currentDate the currentDate to set
 */
public void setCurrentDate(LocalDateTime currentDate) {
    this.currentDate = currentDate;
}
}
```

The following output would result. Of course, the page will display the current date when you run the code.

```
Hello World!

The current date is: 2014-10-16T12:30:04.714!
```

Explanation

The JavaServer Pages technology makes it easy to develop web pages that can utilize both static and dynamic web content by providing a set of tags and value expressions to expose dynamic Java fields to a web page. Using the JSP technology, a page developer can access the underlying JavaBeans classes to pass content between the client and the server. In the example within this example, a JSP page is used to display the current date and time, which is obtained from a JavaBean class on the server. Therefore, when a user visits the JSP page in a browser, the current time and date on the server will be displayed.

A JSP page should use a document extension of `.jsp` if it is a standard HTML-based JSP page. Other types of JSP pages contain different extensions; one of those is the JSP document type. A JSP document is an XML-based well-formed JSP page. JSP pages can contain HTML markup, special JSP tags, page directives, JavaScript, embedded Java code, and more. This example contains the `<jsp:useBean>` tag, as well as a value expression to display the content of a field that is contained within the JavaBean. The `<jsp:useBean>` tag is used to include a reference to a Java class that will be referenced in the JSP page. In this case, the class that is referenced is named `org.javaserverfaces.chapter02.DateBean`, and it will be referenced as `dateBean` within the page. For a full description of the `<jsp:useBean>` tag, please reference the section entitled "Separating Business Logic from View Code".

```
<jsp:useBean id="dateBean" scope="application" class="org.javaserverfaces.chapter02.DateBean"/>
```

Since the `<jsp:useBean>` tag contains a reference to the DateBean Java class, the JSP page that includes the tag can make use of any public fields or methods that are contained within the class or private fields through public "getter" methods. This is demonstrated by the use of the Expression Language (EL) value expression, which is enclosed within the ${} characters. To learn more about JSP EL expressions, please see the section entitled "Yielding and Setting Values". In the example, the value of the JavaBean field named `currentDate` is displayed on the page. The value of the private field is retrieved automatically via the pubic "getter" method, getCurrentDate.

```
The current date is: ${dateBean.currentDate}!
```

LIFE CYCLE OF A JSP PAGE

The life cycle of a JSP page is very much the same as that of a Java servlet. This is because a JSP page is translated to a servlet (the `HttpJspBase` JSP servlet class) behind the scenes by a special servlet. When a request is sent to a JSP page, the special servlet checks to ensure that the JSP page's servlet is not older than the page itself. If it is, the JSP is retranslated into a servlet class and compiled. The JSP-to-servlet translation is automatic, which is one of the most productive reasons to use JSP.

When a JSP page is translated, a servlet with a name such as `0002fjspname_jsp.java` is created, where `jspname` is the name of the JSP page. If errors result during the translation, they will be displayed when the JSP page response is displayed.

Different portions of the JSP page are treated differently during the translation to a Java servlet.

- Template data is translated into code.

- JSP scripting elements are inserted into the JSP page's servlet class.

- `<jsp:XXX .../>` elements are converted into method calls.

After translation, the life cycle works similarly to the servlet life cycle:

- If the JSP page's servlet does not already exist, then the container does the following:

  1. Loads the servlet class

  2. Instantiates the servlet class

  3. Initializes the servlet instance with a call to the `jspInit` method

This example contains only beginning knowledge of what is possible with the JSP technology. To learn more regarding the technology and best practices when using JSP, please continue reading the examples in this chapter.

Embedding Java into a JSP Page

JSPs allow one to embed Java code into a page. As such, it is very easy to create dynamic content and forms for processing data with JSPs.

Example

To embed Java code into the page, use JSP scripting elements. The following JSP code demonstrates how to import the Java `Date` class and then use it to obtain the current date without using a server-side JavaBean class:

```
<%--
    Document    : embeddingJava.jsp
    Author      : juneau
--%>

<%@page import="java.time.LocalDateTime"%>
<%@page contentType="text/html" pageEncoding="UTF-8"%>
<!DOCTYPE html>
<%! LocalDateTime currDate = LocalDateTime.now(); %>
```

```html
<html>
    <head>
        <meta http-equiv="Content-Type" content="text/html; charset=UTF-8">
        <title>Embedding Java in a JSP</title>
    </head>
    <body>
        <h1>Hello World!</h1>
        <br/>
        <br/>
        The current date and time is: <%= currDate %>

    </body>
</html>
```

This page will display the current system date from the server that hosts the JSP application.

Explanation

Using scripting elements within a JSP page allows you to embed Java code directly in a web page. However, it should be noted that this is not the best approach to web development. Scripting element programming used to be one of the best ways to code web applications using JSP technology. However, when it came time to perform maintenance activities on a JSP page or to introduce new developers to a code base that used scripting elements in JSP, nightmares ensued because in order to debug a problem, the developer had to search through scripts embedded within HTML, as well as Java classes themselves. Sometimes it is still nice to have the ability to embed Java code directly into a page, even if for nothing more than testing, so that is why I show how it is done in this example. A better approach would be to separate the business logic from the view code, which you will see in the next example.

In this example, the current date is pulled into the JSP page via the use of the Java LocalDateTime class. A new LocalDateTime instance is assigned to a field that is named currDate. An import page directive is used to import the java.time.LocalDateTime class into the JSP page using the following line:

```
<%@page import="java.time.LocalDateTime"%>
```

The declaration of currDate is done within a declaration scripting element. Declaration scripting elements begin with the character sequence <%! and end with the character sequence %>. Excerpted from the example, the currDate field is declared and initialized in the following line of code:

```
<%! LocalDateTime currDate = LocalDateTime.now(); %>
```

Anything that is contained inside declarations goes directly to the jspService() method of the generated JSP servlet class, creating a global declaration for the entire servlet to make use of. Any variable or method can be declared within declarations' character sequences.

■ **Note**   Declarations are executed only once for the JSP page, when it is initially converted into a servlet. If any code on the JSP page changes, it will be translated to a servlet again, and the declaration will be evaluated again at that time. If you want for code to be executed each time the JSP page is loaded by the browser, do not place it in a declaration.

In the example, you can see that there are no JSP tags used to reference a server-side JavaBean class to create a new instance of the LocalDateTime class, and that is because the instantiation is done right within the JSP code in between character sequences known as *scriptlets*, <% %>. Scriptlets basically have the same syntax as declarations, except that they do not include the exclamation point in the first character sequence. Scriptlets are used to embed any Java code that you want to have run each time the JSP is loaded, at request-processing time. At translation time, anything contained within a scriptlet is placed into a method named _jspService within the translated JSP servlet, and that method is executed with each request on the JSP page. Scriptlets are the most common place to use embedded Java in a JSP page. Since in this example you want the current date to be displayed each time the page is loaded, the new LocalDateTime class could instead be invoked, assigning the results of the now() method to the currDate variable within a scriptlet.

```
<% currDate = LocalDateTime.now(); %>
```

Later in the JSP page, the currDate field is displayed using an expression, which is enclosed using the <%= and %> character sequences. Expressions are used to display content, and anything that is contained within an expression is automatically converted to a String when a request is processed. After the String conversion, it is displayed as output on the page.

```
The current date and time is: <%= currDate %>
```

■ **Note**   If the code within an expression is unable to be converted into a String, an exception will occur.

While embedding Java code in a JSP page is possible to do, it is frowned upon within the Java community since the Model-View-Controller (MVC) paradigm makes coding much cleaner. To learn more about coding JSP applications without using scripting elements, please see the next example.

Separating Business Logic from View Code

It is considered good practice to separate the business logic from the code that is used to create a view within your web application. This can be done easily within JSP applications by separating the JSP from the Java code, and by using scriptlets to display the results.

Example

Separate the business logic into a JavaBean class, and use JSP tags to incorporate the logic into the view. In the following example, a JavaBean is referenced from within a JSP page, and one of the JavaBean fields is displayed on the page. Each time the page is refreshed, the field value is updated because the page calls the underlying JavaBean field's getter method, where the field is initialized.

The following JSP markup contains a reference to a JavaBean named RandomBean and displays a field from the bean on the page:

```
<%--
    Document    : separatingLogic
    Author      : juneau
--%>
```

```
<%@page contentType="text/html" pageEncoding="UTF-8"%>
<!DOCTYPE html>
<html>
    <head>
        <meta http-equiv="Content-Type" content="text/html; charset=UTF-8">
        <title>Separating Business Logic from View Code</title>
    </head>
    <body>
        <jsp:useBean id="randomBean" scope="application" class="org.javaserverfaces.chapter02.
RandomBean"/>
        <h1>Display a Random Number</h1>
        <br/>
        <br/>
        <p>
            Your random number is ${randomBean.randomNumber}.  Refresh page to see another!
        </p>
    </body>
</html>
```

The next code is that of the JavaBean class referenced in the JSP code, known as RandomBean:

```
package org.javaserverfaces.chapter02;

import java.util.Random;

/**
 * @author juneau
 */
public class RandomBean {
    Random randomGenerator = new Random();
    private int randomNumber = 0;

    /**
     * @return the randomNumber
     */
    public int getRandomNumber() {
        randomNumber = randomGenerator.nextInt();
        return randomNumber;
    }

}
```

The resulting output for the page resembles the following, although the random number will be different every time the page is loaded:

```
Your random number is -1200578984. Refresh page to see another!
```

Explanation

Sometimes embedding Java code directly into a JSP page can be helpful, and it can satisfy the requirement. However, in most cases, it is a good idea to separate any Java code from markup code that is used to create the web view. Doing so makes maintenance easier, and it allows a page developer to focus on creating nice-looking web pages rather than wading through Java code. In some organizations, a Java developer can then write the server-side business logic code, and a web developer can focus on the view. In many organizations today, the same person is performing both tasks, and using the MVC methodology can help separate the logic and increase productivity.

In the early days of JSP, embedding Java directly into a JSP page was the only way to go, but as time went on, the MVC paradigm caught on, and JSP has been updated to follow suit. As a best practice, it is good to use JSP tags to separate Java code from page markup. In the example, the `<jsp:useBean>` element is used to reference a server-side JavaBean class so that the public fields and methods from that class, as well as private fields via public "getter" methods, can be incorporated into the JSP page. The `jsp:useBean` element requires that you provide an ID and a scope, along with a class name or a beanName. In the example, the `id` attribute is set to `randomBean`, and this `id` is used to reference the bean within the JSP page. The `scope` attribute is set to `application`, which means that the bean can be used from any JSP page within the application. Table 2-1 displays all the possible scopes and what they mean. The `class` attribute is set to the fully qualified name of the Java class that will be referenced via the name that is set with the `id` attribute, in this case, `randomBean`.

Table 2-1. *`jsp:useBean` Element Scopes*

Scope	Description
page (default)	The bean can be used within the same JSP page that contains the `jsp:useBean` element.
request	The bean can be used from any JSP page processing the same request.
session	The bean can be used from any JSP page within the same session as the JSP page that contains the `jsp:useBean` element that created the bean. The page that creates the bean must have a page directive with `session="true"`.
application	The bean can be used from any JSP within the same application as the JSP page that created it.

After the `jsp:useBean` element has been added to a page, JavaBean properties can be used in the JSP page, and public methods can be called from the page. The example demonstrates how to display the value of a JavaBean property using the `${ }` notation. Any variable that contains a "getter" and a "setter" method in the JavaBean can be accessed from a JSP page by referencing the class member field in between the `${` and `}` character sequences, better known as an Expression Language expression. To learn more about EL expressions, please see the next example. The following excerpt from the example demonstrates how to display the `randomNumber` field from the JavaBean:

```
Your random number is ${randomBean.randomNumber}.  Refresh page to see another!
```

The key to separating business logic from view logic in the JSP technology is the `jsp:useBean` element. This will allow you to use JavaBean classes from within the JSP page, without embedding the code directly in the page. Separating business logic from view code can help make it easier to maintain code in the future and make the code easier to follow.

Yielding or Setting Values

As mentioned previously, JSPs are a good medium for development of application forms. An application form must have the capability to set and retrieve field values.

Example

It is possible to expose the values from a JavaBean in a JSP page using EL expressions with the ${ bean.value } syntax. In the following JSP code, a Java class by the name of EasyBean will be used to hold the value that is entered into a text field by a user. The value will then be read from the bean and displayed on the page using EL expressions.

The following code shows a JSP page that contains an input form and displays the value that is entered into the text box:

```
<%--
    Document    : settingAndYieldingValues
    Author      : juneau
--%>

<%@page contentType="text/html" pageEncoding="UTF-8"%>
<!DOCTYPE html>
<html>
    <head>
        <meta http-equiv="Content-Type" content="text/html; charset=UTF-8">
        <title>Yielding and Setting Values</title>
    </head>
    <body>
        <jsp:useBean id="easyBean" scope="page" class="org.javaserverfaces.chapter02.EasyBean"/>
        <jsp:setProperty name="easyBean" property="*"/>
        <form method="post">
        Use the input text box below to set the value, and then hit submit.
        <br/><br/>
        Set the field value:
        <input id="fieldValue" name="fieldValue" type="text" size="30"/>
        <br/>
        The value contained within the field is currently:
        <jsp:getProperty name="easyBean" property="fieldValue"/>

        <input type="submit">
        </form>
    </body>
</html>
```

Next, the JavaBean class, which is used to hold the value that is used by the page, looks like the following:

```
package org.javaserverfaces.chapter02;

/**
 * Yielding and Setting Values
 * @author juneau
 */
```

```
public class EasyBean implements java.io.Serializable {
    private String fieldValue;

    public EasyBean(){
        fieldValue = null;
    }

    /**
     * @return the fieldValue
     */
    public String getFieldValue() {
        return fieldValue;
    }

    /**
     * @param fieldValue the fieldValue to set
     */
    public void setFieldValue(String fieldValue) {
        this.fieldValue = fieldValue;
    }

}
```

This simple example demonstrates how to enter a value, "set" it into the JavaBean variable, and then display it on the page.

Explanation

Perhaps one of the most useful web constructs is the input form, which allows a user to enter information into text boxes on the page and submit them to a server for processing. JSP makes it easy to submit values from an HTML form, and it is equally easy to display them back on a page. To do so, a field is declared in a Java class and accessor methods (aka getters and setters) are provided so that other classes can save values to the field and obtain values that are currently stored in it. Sometimes Java classes that contain fields with accessor methods are referred to as JavaBean *classes*. The classes can also contain other methods that can be used to perform tasks, but it is a best practice to keep JavaBeans as simple as possible. JavaBean classes should also implement java.io.Serializable so that they can be easily stored and resurrected.

In this example, a Java class named EasyBean contains a private field named fieldValue. The accessor methods getFieldValue and setFieldValue can be used to obtain and store the value in fieldValue, respectively. Those accessor methods are declared as public, and thus they can be used from another Java class or JSP page. The JSP page uses the jsp:useBean element to obtain a reference to the EasyBean class. The scope is set to page so that the class can be used only within the JSP page that contains the jsp:useBean element. Table 2-1, which can be found in the previous example, lists the different scopes available for use with the jsp:useBean element.

```
<jsp:useBean id="easyBean" scope="page" class="org.javaserverfaces.chapter02.EasyBean"/>
```

Next, an HTML form is defined in the JSP page with the POST method, and it contains an input field named fieldValue, which allows a user to enter a String of text that will be submitted as a request parameter when the form is submitted. Note that the form in the example does not have an action specified; this means that the same URL will be used for form submission, and the same JSP will be used for form submission and will be displayed again once the form is submitted. Since the JSP has a jsp:useBean element specified on the page, all request parameters will be sent to that bean when the page is submitted. The key to ensuring that the value entered into the fieldValue input text field is stored into the fieldValue variable within the Java class is using the jsp:setProperty element within the form. The jsp:setProperty element allows one or more properties to be set in a JavaBean class using the corresponding setter methods. In the example, <jsp:useBean> is used to instantiate the EasyBean Java class, and <jsp:setProperty> is used to set the value that is entered within the fieldValue input text box to the fieldValue variable within the EasyBean class. The jsp:setProperty name attribute must equal the value of the jsp:useBean id attribute. The jsp:setProperty property attribute can equal the name of the field within the Java class that you want to set in the bean, or it can be a wildcard * character to submit all input fields to the bean. The value attribute of jsp:setProperty can be used to specify a static value for the property. The following excerpt from the example shows how the jsp:setProperty tag is used:

```
<jsp:setProperty name="easyBean" property="*"/>
```

■ **Note**   The ordering of the JSP elements is very important. <jsp:useBean> must come before <jsp:setProperty> because the jsp:useBean element is responsible for instantiating its corresponding Java class. Since the JSP page is executed from the top of the page downward, the bean would be unavailable for use to any elements prior to when jsp:useBean is specified.

When the user enters a value into the input field and submits the request, it is submitted as a request parameter to the Java class that corresponds to the jsp:useBean element for that page. There are a couple of different ways to display the data that has been populated in the JavaBean field. The example demonstrates how to use the jsp:getProperty element to display the value of the fieldValue variable. The <jsp:getProperty> element must specify a name attribute, which corresponds to the id of the Java class that was specified within the jsp:useBean element. It must also specify a property attribute, which corresponds to the name of the JavaBean property that you want to display. The following excerpt from the example demonstrates the use of the jsp:getProperty tag:

```
<jsp:getProperty name="easyBean" property="fieldValue"/>
```

It is also possible to display the value of a JavaBean property using EL expressions, using the id of specified in the jsp:useBean element, along with the property name. To try this, you can replace the jsp:getProperty element with the following EL expression:

```
${easyBean.fieldValue}
```

The JSP framework makes the development of web applications using Java technology much easier than using servlets. Input forms such as the one demonstrated in this example show how much more productive JSP is compared to standard servlet coding. As with anything, both servlets and JSP technology have their place in your toolbox. For creating simple data entry forms, JSP definitely takes the cake.

Invoking a Function in a Conditional Expression

Utilizing some of the concepts that have been demonstrated in the previous examples, it is possible to invoke Java functions within the context of a JSP.

Example

To invoke a Java method from a JSP, code the function in a JavaBean class and then register the bean with the JSP via the <jsp:useBean> tag. You will then need to register the function within a tag library descriptor (TLD) so that it can be made usable on the JSP page via a tag. Finally, set up a page directive for the TLD in which the function is registered, and use the function tag within the page. In the example that follows, a JSP page will use a function to tell the user whether a given Java type is a primitive type. The user will enter a String value into a text box, and that value will be submitted to a JavaBean field. The contents of the field will then be compared against a list of Java primitive types to determine whether it is a match. If the value entered into the field is a primitive, a message will be displayed to the user.

The following code is the Java class that contains the implementation of the function, which is going to be used from within the JSP. The bean also contains a field that will be used from the JSP page for setting and getting the value that is entered by the user.

```java
package org.javaserverfaces.chapter02;

/**
 * @author juneau
 */
public class ConditionalClass implements java.io.Serializable {
    private String typename = null;
    public static String[] javaTypes = new String[8];

    public ConditionalClass(){
        javaTypes[0] = "byte";
        javaTypes[1] = "short";
        javaTypes[2] = "int";
        javaTypes[3] = "long";
        javaTypes[4] = "float";
        javaTypes[5] = "double";
        javaTypes[6] = "boolean";
        javaTypes[7] = "char";
    }

    public static boolean isPrimitive(String value){
        boolean returnValue = false;
        for(int x=0; x<=javaTypes.length-1; x++){
            if(javaTypes[x].equalsIgnoreCase(value)){
                returnValue = true;
            }
        }
        return returnValue;
    }

    /**
     * @return the typename
     */
    public String getTypename() {
        return typename;
    }
```

```java
    /**
     * @param typename the typename to set
     */
    public void setTypename(String typename) {
        this.typename = typename;
    }
}
```

The field typename will be used from the JSP page to set the value that is entered by the user and to retrieve it for passing to the function named isPrimitive(), which is used to compare the given value to a list of Java primitives. Next is a listing of the TLD that is used to register the function so that it can be used as a tag within the JSP. For simplicity, the TLD file is named functions.tld. The file should be places within the WEB-INF folder of the web application.

```xml
<?xml version="1.0" encoding="UTF-8"?>
<taglib version="2.1" xmlns="http://java.sun.com/xml/ns/javaee"
xmlns:xsi="http://www.w3.org/2001/XMLSchema-instance" xsi:schemaLocation="http://java.sun.com/xml/
ns/javaee http://java.sun.com/xml/ns/javaee/web-jsptaglibrary_2_1.xsd">
    <tlib-version>1.0</tlib-version>
    <short-name>fct</short-name>
    <uri>functions</uri>
    <function>
        <name>isPrimitive</name>
        <function-class>org.javaserverfaces.chapter02.ConditionalClass</function-class>
        <function-signature>boolean isPrimitive(java.lang.String)</function-signature>
    </function>
</taglib>
```

Last is the JSP code that contains the page directive for using the TLD and the conditional call to the function isPrimitive() via a tag:

```jsp
<%--
    Document    : invokingAFunction
    Author      : juneau
--%>

<%@page contentType="text/html" pageEncoding="UTF-8"%>
<!DOCTYPE html>
<%@ taglib uri="http://java.sun.com/jsp/jstl/core"
     prefix="c" %>
<%@ taglib uri="/WEB-INF/tlds/functions.tld" prefix="fct" %>
<html>
    <head>
        <meta http-equiv="Content-Type" content="text/html; charset=UTF-8">
        <title>Invoking a Function in an Expression</title>
    </head>
    <body>
```

```
<form method="get">
    <p>Name one of the primitive Java types:
        <input type="text" id="typename" name="typename" size="40"/>
    </p>
    <br/>
    <input type="submit">
</form>
<jsp:useBean id="conditionalBean" scope="page" class="org.javaserverfaces.chapter02.
ConditionalClass"/>
<jsp:setProperty name="conditionalBean" property="typename"/>
<c:if test="${fct:isPrimitive(conditionalBean.typename)}" >
    ${ conditionalBean.typename } is a primitive type.
</c:if>

<c:if test="${conditionalBean.typename ne null and !fct:isPrimitive(conditionalBean.
typename)}" >
    ${ conditionalBean.typename } is not a primitive type.
</c:if>
    </body>
</html>
```

Following the strategy used in this solution, it is possible to create a conditional test that is usable via a JSP tag .

Explanation

A few different steps need to be taken before a Java function can become accessible from a JSP page. One of the most commonly overlooked conditions is that the function must be declared with a static modifier in the Java class. In the example, the function isPrimitive is declared as static, and it returns a boolean value indicating whether the web page user types the name of a Java primitive type.

The next step toward making a function accessible via a JSP page is to register it with a TLD. In the example, a TLD named functions.tld is created, although if there is already a custom TLD in your application, then you could register the function with it rather than creating an additional one if you want. The TLD in this example has a short-name attribute of fct, which will be used from within JSP tags. To actually register the function, a function element must be created within the TLD, providing a function name, indicating the class that the function resides within, and, finally, specifing the function signature.

```
<function>
    <name>isPrimitive</name>
    <function-class>org.javaserverfaces.chapter02.ConditionalClass</function-class>
    <function-signature>boolean isPrimitive(java.lang.String)</function-signature>
</function>
```

The function is now ready for use within the JSP. To make the function accessible via the JSP, register the TLD that contains the function element by including a taglib directive specifying the uri and prefix for the TLD. The uri is the path to the TLD, and the prefix should match the name given in the short-name element of the TLD. The following excerpt from the JSP in this example shows the taglib directive:

```
<%@ taglib uri="/WEB-INF/tlds/functions.tld" prefix="fct" %>
```

The function will now be accessible via an EL expression within the JSP by specifying the `taglib` prefix along with the name of the function as it is registered in the TLD. The EL expression in the example calls the function, passing the `typename` parameter. The `isPrimitive` function is used to determine whether the text contained within the `typename` bean field is equal to one of the Java primitive types.

```
<c:if test="${fct:isPrimitive(conditionalBean.typename)}" >
```

The solution also uses the Java Standard Tag Library (JSTL) core. Depending upon the server environment being used, this may be a separate download. The JSTL provides an extension to the standard set of tags provided with the JSP API. For more information regarding JSTL, please refer to the online documentation, which can be found at www.oracle.com/technetwork/java/index-jsp-135995.html.

The JSTL `<c:if>` tag can be used to test conditions, executing the markup between its opening and closing tags if the condition test returns a `true` value. Not surprisingly, the `<c:if>` tag includes a `test` attribute that specifies an EL expression that indicates the test that needs to be performed. In the example, the `isPrimitive` function is called within the EL expression, passing the bean value. If the test returns a `true`, then a message is printed indicating that the given value is equal to a Java primitive type. Another `<c:if>` test follows the first in the example, and this time it tests to ensure that the property value is not equal to `null` and also that it is not a Java primitive type. Expression Language is used to determine whether the property value is equal to `null` via the `ne` expression. The `and` expression ties both the first and second conditional expressions together within the EL expression, meaning that both of the expressions must evaluate to a `true` value in order for the condition to be met. If both conditions are met, then the value specified by the user is not a Java primitive type, and a corresponding message is printed.

```
<c:if test="${conditionalBean.typename ne null and !fct:isPrimitive(conditionalBean.typename)}" >
          ${ conditionalBean.typename } is not a primitive type.
</c:if>
```

It takes only a few easy steps to create a conditional function for use within JSPs. First, in the JavaBean class, you must create a public static function, which returns a `boolean` value. Second, create a TLD, which will make the function available via a JSP tag. Lastly, use the custom tag from within the JSP page along with JSTL conditional test tags to display the content conditionally.

Creating a JSP Document

In some situations, it is better for a JSP to adhere to the XML standard and contain only valid HTML and JSP tags. JSP Documents can be used in such cases rather than standard JSP files.

Example

JSP document is an XML-based representation of a standard JSP document that conforms to the XML standard. The following JSP document contains the same code that is used in the JSP code for the previous example, but it uses the JSP document format instead. As you can see, not much is different because well-formed tags were already used to create the standard JSP document. The page is also saved with an extension of `jspx` rather than `jsp`.

```
<!--
    Document    : jspDocument
    Author      : juneau
-->
<html xmlns:jsp="http://java.sun.com/JSP/Page" version="2.0"
     xmlns:c="http://java.sun.com/jsp/jstl/core"
     xmlns:fct="/WEB-INF/tlds/functions.tld">

    <jsp:directive.page contentType="text/html" pageEncoding="UTF-8"/>
```

```
        <body>
            <form method="get">
                <p>Name one of the primitive Java types:
                    <input type="text" id="typename" name="typename" size="40"/>
                </p>
                <br/>
                <input type="submit"/>
            </form>
            <jsp:useBean id="conditionalBean" scope="request" class="org.javaserverfaces.chapter02.
ConditionalClass"/>
            <jsp:setProperty name="conditionalBean" property="typename"
                            value="${param.typename}" />
            <c:if test="${fct:isPrimitive(conditionalBean.typename)}" >
                ${ conditionalBean.typename } is a primitive type.
            </c:if>

            <c:if test="${fn.length(conditionalBean.typename) > 0 and !fct:isPrimitive(conditionalBean.
typename)}" >
                ${ conditionalBean.typename } is not a primitive type.
            </c:if>

        </body>
</html>
```

This JSP document will yield the same output as the one in the previous example. However, a well-formed document will be enforced, and this will exclude the use of scripting elements within the page.

Explanation

Separating business logic from markup code can be important for many reasons. Standard JSP pages can adhere to the MVC paradigm, but they are not forced into doing so. Sometimes it makes sense to enforce the separation of business logic, by strictly adhering to a well-formed XML document using only JSP tags to work with server-side Java classes. Well-formed means that there should be only one root element, and each starting tag must have a corresponding ending tag. Creating a JSP document is one answer because such documents enforce well-formed XML and do not allow scripting elements to be used within the JSP page.

Several JSP tags can be used to communicate with Java classes, perform JSP-specific functionality, and make markup easy to follow. As such, modern JSP-based applications should make use of well-formed JSP documents utilizing such JSP tags, rather than embedding scripting elements throughout markup. Table 2-2 describes what the different JSP tags do.

Table 2-2. *JSP Tags*

Tag	Description
`<jsp:attribute>`	Defines attributes for a JSP page.
`<jsp:body>`	Defines an element body.
`<jsp:declaration>`	Defines page declarations.
`<jsp:directive>`	Defines page includes and page directives.
`<jsp:doBody>`	Executes the body of the JSP tag that is used by the calling JSP page to invoke the tag.
`<jsp:element>`	Generates an XML element dynamically.
`<jsp:expression>`	Inserts the value of a scripting language expression, converted into a string.
`<jsp:forward>`	Forwards a request to another page. The new page can be HTML, JSP, or servlet.
`<jsp:getProperty>`	Obtains the value of a bean property and places it in the page.
`<jsp:include>`	Includes another JSP or web resource in the page.
`<jsp:invoke>`	Invokes a specified JSP fragment.
`<jsp:output>`	Specifies the document type declaration.
`<jsp:plugin>`	Executes an applet or bean with the specified plug-in.
`<jsp:root>`	Defines standard elements and tag library namespaces.
`<jsp:scriptlet>`	Embeds code fragment into a page if necessary.
`<jsp:setProperty>`	Sets specified value(s) into a bean property.
`<jsp:text>`	Encloses template data.
`<jsp:useBean>`	References and instantiates (if needed) a JavaBean class using a name and providing a scope.

Creating a well-formed JSP can lead to easier development, ease of maintenance, and better overall design. Since it is so important, the remaining examples in this chapter will use the JSP document format.

Embedding Expressions in EL

The use of JSP tags makes it possible to introduce conditional expressions and/or arithmetic within your JSP without embedding Java code using scripting elements.

Example

This example will look at two examples of EL expressions. The first example demonstrates how to perform conditional logic using EL expressions. Note that the JSTL tag library is also used in this case, to conditionally display a message on the page if the expression results to true.

```
<!--
    Document    : conditionalLogic
    Author      : juneau
-->
<html xmlns:jsp="http://java.sun.com/JSP/Page"
      xmlns:c="http://java.sun.com/jsp/jstl/core"
      version="2.0">

    <jsp:directive.page contentType="text/html" pageEncoding="UTF-8"/>
    <head>
        <title>Embedding Expressions in EL</title>
    </head>
    <body>
        <h1>Conditional Expressions</h1>
        <p>
            The following portion of the page will only display conditional expressions
            which result in a true value.
        </p>
        <c:if test="${1 + 1 == 2}">
            The conditional expression (1 + 1 == 2) results in TRUE.
            <br/>
        </c:if>

        <c:if test="${'x' == 'y'}">
            The conditional expression (x == y) results in TRUE.
            <br/>
        </c:if>

        <c:if test="${(100/10) gt 5}">
            The conditional expression ((100/10) > 5) results in TRUE.
            <br/>
        </c:if>

        <c:if test="${20 mod 3 eq 2}">
            The conditional expression (20 mod 3 eq 2) results in TRUE.
            <br/>
        </c:if>
    </body>
</html>
```

This JSP page will result in the following output being displayed:

```
...
The conditional expression (1 + 1 == 2) results in TRUE.
The conditional expression ((100/10) > 5) results in TRUE.
The conditional expression (20 mod 3 eq 2) results in TRUE.
...
```

Arithmetic expressions can also be evaluated using EL. The following JSP code demonstrates some examples of using arithmetic within EL:

```
<!--
    Author      : juneau
-->
<html xmlns:jsp="http://java.sun.com/JSP/Page"
      xmlns:c="http://java.sun.com/jsp/jstl/core"
      version="2.0">

    <jsp:directive.page contentType="text/html" pageEncoding="UTF-8"/>
    <head>
        <title>Embedding Expressions in EL</title>
    </head>
    <body>
        <jsp:useBean id="expBean" class="org.javaserverfaces.chapter02.Expressions"/>
        <h1>Arithmetic Expressions</h1>
        <p>
            The following expressions demonstrate how to perform arithmetic using EL.
        </p>
        10 - 4 = ${10 - 4}
        <br/>
        85 / 15 = ${85 / 15}
        <br/>
        847 divided by 6 = ${847 div 6}
        <br/>
        ${expBean.num1} * ${expBean.num2} = ${expBean.num1 * expBean.num2}

    </body>

</html>
```

The preceding JSP will result in the following output being displayed:

```
...
10 - 4 = 6
85 / 15 = 5.666666666666667
847 divided by 6 = 141.16666666666666
5 * 634.324 = 3171.62
...
```

Explanation

The JSP technology makes it easy to work with expressions. Conditional page rendering can be performed using a combination of EL value expressions, which are enclosed within the ${ } character sequences, and JSTL tags. Arithmetic expressions can also be performed using EL expressions. To make things easier, the Expression Language contains keywords or characters that can be used to help form expressions. The example contains various expressions and conditional page rendering using the JSTL <c:if> tag.

In the first JSP page displayed in the example, there are some examples of conditional page rendering. To use the `<c:if>` tag to perform the conditional tests, you must be sure to import the JSTL tag library with the JSP page. To do so, add an import for the JSTL tag library and assign it to a character or string of characters. In the following excerpt from the example, the JSTL library is assigned to the character c:

```
<html xmlns:jsp="http://java.sun.com/JSP/Page"
      xmlns:c="http://java.sun.com/jsp/jstl/core"
      version="2.0">
```

An EL value expression is contained within the ${ and } character sequences. Anything within these characters will be treated as EL, and as such, the syntax must be correct, or the JSP page will not be able to compile into a servlet, and it will throw an error. All expressions using the ${ } syntax are evaluated immediately, and they are read-only expressions. That is, no expressions using this syntax can be used to set values into a JavaBean property. The JSP engine first evaluates the expression, and then it converts into a `String` and lastly returns the value to the tag handler. Four types of objects can be referenced within a value expression. Those are JavaBean components, collections, enumerated types, and implicit objects. If using a JavaBean component, the JavaBean must be registered with the JSP page using the `jsp:useBean` element. Collections or enumerated types can also be referenced from a JavaBean that has been registered with the page. Implicit objects are those that allow access to page context, scoped variables, and other such objects. Table 2-3 lists different implicit objects that can be referenced from within EL expressions.

Table 2-3. *Implicit JSP Objects*

Object	Type	Description
pageContext	Context	Provides access to the context of the page and various subobjects
servletContext	Page context	Context for JSP page servlet and web components
session	Page context	Session object for the client
request	Page context	Request that invoked the execution of the page
response	Page context	Response that is returned by the JSP
param	N/A	Responsible for mapping parameter names to values
paramValues	N/A	Maps request parameter to an array of values
header	N/A	Responsible for mapping a header name to a value
headerValues	N/A	Maps header name to an array of values
cookie	N/A	Maps a cookie name to a single cookie
initParam	N/A	Maps a context initialization parameter to a value
pageScope	Scope	Maps page scope variables
requestScope	Scope	Maps request scope variables
sessionScope	Scope	Maps session scope variables
applicationScope	Scope	Maps application scope variables

The following are some examples of expressions that make use of JavaBean components, collections, enumerated types, and implicit objects:

```
// Displays the value of a variable named myVar within a JavaBean referenced as elTester
${ elTester.myVar }
// Does the same thing as the line above
${ elTester["myVar"] }

// Evaluates an Enumerated Type in which myEnum is an instance of MyEnum
${ myEnum == "myValue" }
// Reference a getter method of the Enum named getTestVal()
${ myEnum.testVal}

// References a collection named myCollection within the JavaBean referenced as elTester
${ elTester.myCollection }

// Obtain the parameter named "testParam"
${ param.testParam }  // Same as: request.getParameter("testParam")
// Obtain session attribute named "testAttr"
${ sessionScope.testAttr } // Same as: session.getAttribute("testAttr")
```

In the example, the `<c:if>` tag is used to test a series of value expressions and conditionally display page content. The test attribute of `<c:if>` is used to register a test condition, and if the test condition returns a `true` result, then the content contained between the `<c:if>` starting and ending tags is displayed. The following excerpt from the example demonstrates how a test is performed:

```
<c:if test="${'x' == 'y'}">
        The conditional expression (x == y) results in TRUE.
        <br/>
    </c:if>
```

EL expressions can contain a series of reserved words that can be used to help evaluate the expression. For instance, the following expression utilizes the gt reserved word to return a value indicating whether the value returned from the calculation of 100/10 is greater than 5:

```
<c:if test="${(100/10) gt 5}">
        The conditional expression ((100/10) > 5) results in TRUE.
        <br/>
</c:if>
```

Table 2-4 lists all the JSP EL expression reserved words and their meanings.

Table 2-4. *EL Expression Reserved Words*

Reserved Word	Description
and	Combines expressions and returns true if all of them evaluate to true
or	Combines expressions and returns true if one of them evaluates to true
not	Negates an expression
eq	Equal
ne	Not equal
lt	Less than
gt	Greater than
le	Less than or equal
ge	Greater than or equal
true	True value
false	False value
null	Null value
instanceof	Used to test whether an object is an instance of another object
empty	Determines whether a list or collection is empty
div	Divided by
mod	Modulus

Arithmetic expressions are demonstrated by the second example. The following arithmetic operators can be utilized within expressions:

- + (addition), - (binary and unary), * (multiplication), / and div (division), %, and mod (modulus)

- and, &&, or, ||, not, !

- ==, !=, <, >, <=, >=

- X ? Y : Z (ternary conditional)

Entire chapters of books have been written on the use of EL expressions within JSPs. This example only touches upon the possibilities of using value expressions. The best way to get used to expressions is to create a test JSP page and experiment with the different options that are available.

Accessing Parameters in Multiple Pages

There are times in which a parameter is required to be maintained across multiple pages. JSPs can make use of the request object to store parameters and pass them to the next page.

Example

In the following example, an input form is used to submit parameters to the request object, and then the request object is utilized to retrieve the values in another page. The JSP page that contains an input form is used to pass values to another JSP page by setting the HTML form action attribute to the value of the JSP page that will utilize the parameters. In the case of this example, the receiving JSP page merely displays the parameter values, but other work could be performed as well.

The following JSP code demonstrates the use of an input form to save parameters into the request object and pass them to a page named accessingParametersb.jspx:

```
<!--
    Document    : accessingParametersa
    Author      : juneau
-->
<html xmlns:jsp="http://java.sun.com/JSP/Page"
      xmlns:c="http://java.sun.com/jsp/jstl/core"
      version="2.0">

    <jsp:directive.page contentType="text/html" pageEncoding="UTF-8"/>
    <head>
        <title>Passing Parameters</title>
    </head>
    <body>

        <h1>Passing Parameters</h1>
        <p>
            The following parameters will be passed to the next JSP.
        </p>
        <form method="get" action="accessingParametersb.jspx">
        Param 1: <input id="param1" name="param1" type="text" value="1"/>
        <br/>
        Param 2: <input id="param2" name="param2" type="text" value="2 + 0"/>
        <br/>
        Param 3: <input id="param3" name="param3" type="text" value="three"/>
        <br/>
        <input type="submit" value="Go to next page"/>
        </form>
    </body>

</html>
```

The next JSP code receives the parameters and displays their values:

```
<!--
    Document    : accessingParametersb
    Author      : juneau
-->
<html xmlns:jsp="http://java.sun.com/JSP/Page"
      xmlns:c="http://java.sun.com/jsp/jstl/core"
      version="2.0">
```

```
<jsp:directive.page contentType="text/html" pageEncoding="UTF-8"/>
<head>
    <title>Passing Parameters</title>
</head>
<body>

    <h1>Passing Parameters</h1>
    <p>
        The following parameters will were passed from the original JSP.
    </p>
    <form method="post" action=" accessingParametersa.jspx">
    Param 1: <jsp:expression>request.getParameter("param1") </jsp:expression>
    <br/>
    Param 2: <jsp:expression> request.getParameter("param2") </jsp:expression>
    <br/>
    Param 3: <jsp:expression> request.getParameter("param3") </jsp:expression>
    <br/>
    OR using value expressions
    <br/>
    Param 1: ${ param.param1 }
    <br/>
    Param 2: ${ param.param2 }
    <br/>
    Param 3: ${ param.param3 }
    <br/>

    <input type="submit" value="Back to Page 1"/>
    </form>
</body>

</html>
```

As you can see, a couple of variations can be used to display the parameter values. Both of the variations will display the same result.

Explanation

Request parameters are one of the most useful features of web applications. When a user enters some data into a web form and submits the form, the request contains the parameters that were entered into the form. Parameters can also be statically embedded within a web page or concatenated onto a URL and sent to a receiving servlet or JSP page. The data contained in request parameters can then be inserted into a database, redisplayed on another JSP page, used to perform a calculation, or a myriad of other possibilities. The JSP technology provides an easy mechanism for using request parameters within other JSP pages, and the example demonstrates how to do just that.

■ **Note**   Request parameters are always translated into String values.

Note that in the example, the first JSP page uses a simple HTML form to obtain values from a user and submit them to the request. Another JSP page named accessingParametersb.jspx is set as the form action attribute, so when the form is submitted, it will send the request to accessingParametersb.jspx. The input fields on the first JSP page specify both an id attribute and a name attribute, although only the name attribute is required. The name that is given to the input fields is the name that will be used to reference the value entered into it as a request parameter.

▪ **Note**   It is a good programming practice to always include an id attribute. The ID is useful for performing work with the DOM and for referencing elements via a scripting language such as JavaScript.

The receiving action, accessingParametersb.jspx in this example, can make a call to response.getParameter(), passing the name of a parameter (input field name) to obtain the value that was entered into its corresponding text field. To adhere to JSP document standards, the scriptlet containing the call to response.getParameter() must be enclosed within <jsp:expression> tags. The following excerpt demonstrates how this is done:

```
Param 1: <jsp:expression>request.getParameter("param1") </jsp:expression>
```

Optionally, an EL expression can contain a reference to the implicit param object and obtain the request parameter in the same way. When the expression ${param.param1} is called, it is evaluated by the JSP engine, and it is translated into response.getParameter("param1"). The following excerpt demonstrates this use of EL expressions:

```
Param 1: ${ param.param1 }
```

Either technique will perform the same task; the named request parameter will be obtained and displayed on the page.

Creating a Custom JSP Tag

JSP tags provide an encapsulation of functionality for a developer. There are a number of predefined JSP tags, but sometimes there are circumstances that require functionality that is not offered by one of the standard JSP tags. In such cases, the JSP 2.0 simple tag support can be utilized to create a custom tag.

Example

Suppose you want to create a custom tag that will insert a signature into the JSP where the tag is placed. The custom tag will print out a default signature, but it will also accept an authorName attribute, which will include a given author's name to the signature if provided. To get started, you'll first need to define a Java class that extends the SimpleTagSupport class. This class will provide the implementation for your tag. The following code is the implementation for a class named Signature, which provides the implementation for the custom tag.

▪ **Note**   To compile the following code, you will need to add javax.servlet.jsp to classpath: cd customTagExample
javac -cp ...\glassfish4\glassfish\modules\javax.servlet.jsp-api.jar *.java

---

```java
package org.javaserverfaces.chapter02;

import javax.servlet.jsp.JspException;
import javax.servlet.jsp.JspWriter;
import javax.servlet.jsp.PageContext;
import javax.servlet.jsp.tagext.SimpleTagSupport;

/**
 * Creating a Custom JSP Tag
 * @author juneau
 */
public class Signature extends SimpleTagSupport {

    private String authorName = null;

    /**
     * @param authorName the authorName to set
     */
    public void setAuthorName(String authorName) {
        this.authorName = authorName;
    }

    @Override
    public void doTag() throws JspException {
        PageContext pageContext = (PageContext) getJspContext();
        JspWriter out = pageContext.getOut();

        try {
            if(authorName != null){
                out.println("Written by " + authorName);
                out.println("<br/>");
            }
            out.println("Published by Apress");

        } catch (Exception e) {
            System.out.println(e);
        }

    }
}
```

Next, a TLD to be created to map the Signature class tag implementation to a tag. The TLD that includes the custom tag mapping is listed here:

```xml
<?xml version="1.0" encoding="UTF-8"?>
<taglib version="2.1" xmlns="http://java.sun.com/xml/ns/javaee" xmlns:xsi="http://www.w3.org/2001/
XMLSchema-instance" xsi:schemaLocation="http://java.sun.com/xml/ns/javaee http://java.sun.com/xml/
ns/javaee/web-jsptaglibrary_2_1.xsd">
  <tlib-version>1.0</tlib-version>
  <short-name>cust</short-name>
  <uri>custom</uri>
  <tag>
```

```
    <name>signature</name>
    <tag-class>org.javaserverfaces.chapter02.Signature</tag-class>
    <body-content>empty</body-content>
    <attribute>
        <name>authorName</name>
        <rtexprvalue>true</rtexprvalue>
        <required>false</required>
    </attribute>
 </tag>
</taglib>
```

Once the class implementation and the TLD are in place, the tag can be used from within a JSP page. The following JSP code is an example of using the custom tag on a page:

```
<!--
    Document    : customTagExample
    Author      : juneau
-->
<html xmlns:jsp="http://java.sun.com/JSP/Page"
      xmlns:c="http://java.sun.com/jsp/jstl/core"
      xmlns:cust="custom"
      version="2.0">

    <jsp:directive.page contentType="text/html" pageEncoding="UTF-8"/>
    <head>
        <title>Creating a Custom JSP Tag</title>
    </head>
    <body>

        <h1>Custom JSP Tag</h1>
        <p>
            The custom JSP tag is used as the footer for this page.
            <br/>
        </p>
        <cust:signature authorName="Josh Juneau"/>

    </body>

</html>
```

The custom tag output will now be displayed in place of the cust:signature element within the JSP page.

Explanation

One of the most useful new features of JSP 2.0 was the inclusion of the SimpleTagSupport class, which provides an easier way for developers to create custom tags. Prior to the 2.0 release, custom tag creation took a good deal of more work, because the developer had to provide much more code to implement the tag within the tag's implementation class. The SimpleTagSupport class takes care of much implementation for the developer so that the only thing left to do is implement the doTag method in order to provide an implementation for the custom tag.

In the example, a custom tag is created that will print out a signature on the JSP page in the position where the tag is located. To create a custom tag implementation, create a Java class that will extend the `SimpleTagSupport` class, and provide an implementation for the `doTag` method. The example class also contains a field named `authorName`, which will be mapped within the TLD as an attribute for the custom tag. In the `doTag` method, a handle on the JSP page context is obtained by calling the `getJspContext` method. `getJspContext` is a custom method that is implemented for you within `SimpleTagSupport` and makes it easy to get ahold of the JSP page context. Next, to provide the ability to write to the JSP output, a handle is obtained on the `JspWriter` by calling `PageContext`'s `getOut` method.

```
PageContext pageContext = (PageContext) getJspContext();
JspWriter out = pageContext.getOut();
```

The next lines within `doTag` provide the implementation for writing to the JSP output via a series of calls to `out.println`. Any content that is passed to `out.println` will be displayed on the page. Note that in the example, the `authorName` field is checked to see whether it contains a `null` value. If it does not contain a `null` value, then it is displayed on the page; otherwise, it is omitted. Therefore, if the tag within the JSP page contains a value for the `authorName` attribute, then it will be printed on the page. The `out.println` code is contained within a `try-catch` block in case any exceptions occur.

■ **Note** To allow your tag to accept scriptlets, you will need to use the Classic Tag Handlers. The classic tag handlers existed before the JSP 2.0 era and can still be used today alongside the Simple Tag Handlers. The Simple Tag Handlers revolve around the `doTag()` method, whereas the Classic Tag Handlers deal with a `doStartTag()` method and a `doEndTag()` method, as well as others. Since the Simple Tag Handlers can be used alongside the Classic Tag Handlers, it is possible to use some of the more complex Classic Tag methods, while utilizing Simple Tag methods in the same application. This eases the transition from the Classic Tag Handlers to the Simple Tag Handlers. For more information regarding the differences between the two APIs, please see some online documentation by searching for the keywords *Simple vs. Classic Tag Handlers*.

That's it; the implementation for the tag is complete. To map the implementation class to the Document Object Model (DOM) via a tag name, a TLD must contain a mapping to the class. In the example, a TLD is created named `custom.tld`, and it contains the mapping for the class. The `short-name` element specifies the name that must be used within the JSP page to reference the tag. The `uri` element specifies the name of the TLD, and it is used from within the JSP page to reference the TLD file itself. The meat of the TLD is contained within the `tag` element. The name element is used to specify the name for the tag, and it will be used within a JSP page in combination with the `short-name` element to provide the complete tag name. The `tag-class` element provides the name of the class that implements the tag, and `body-content` specifies a value to indicate whether the body content for the JSP page will be made available for the tag implementation class. It is set to `empty` for this example. To specify an attribute for the tag, the `attribute` element must be added to the TLD, including the name, `rtexprvalue`, and `required` elements. The name element of attribute specifies the name of the attribute, `rtexprvalue` indicates whether the attribute can contain an EL expression, and `required` indicates whether the attribute is required.

To use the tag within a JSP page, the `custom.tld` TLD must be mapped to the page within the `<html>` element in a JSP document or a taglib directive within a standard JSP. The following lines show the difference between these two:

```
<!—JSP Document syntax -->
xmlns:cust="custom"

<!—JSP syntax -->
<%@taglib prefix="cust" uri="custom" %>
```

To use the tag within the page, simply specify the TLD short-name along with the mapping name for the tag implementation and any attributes you want to provide.

```
<cust:signature authorName="Josh Juneau"/>
```

Creating custom tags within JSP is easier than it was in the past. Custom tags provide developers with the ability to define custom actions and/or content that can be made accessible from within a JSP page via a tag rather than scriptlets. Custom tags help developers follow the MVC architecture, separating code from business logic.

Including Other JSPs into a Page

JSPs can be utilized to perform a modular style of programming. Utilization of the <jsp:include> tag enables multiple JSPs to be combined to form a single JSP. This makes it easy to divide a web page into different segments, such as a header, footer, and content section.

Example

The <jsp:include> tag can be used to embed either static or dynamic pages in your JSP page. The following example demonstrates the inclusion of two JSP pages within another. One of the JSP pages is used to formulate the header of the page, and another is used for the footer. The following page demonstrates the main JSP page, which includes two others using the <jsp:include> tag. The JSPX files named header.jspx and footer.jspx are included within the body of the main JSP page in order to provide the header and footer sections of the page.

```
<html xmlns:jsp="http://java.sun.com/JSP/Page"
      xmlns:c="http://java.sun.com/jsp/jstl/core"
      version="2.0">

    <jsp:directive.page contentType="text/html" pageEncoding="UTF-8"/>
    <head>
        <title>Including Other JSPs into a Page</title>
    </head>
    <body>
        <jsp:include page="header.jspx" />
        <h1>This is the body of the main JSP.</h1>
        <p>
            Both the header and footer for this page were created as separate JSPs.
        </p>
        <jsp:include page="footer.jspx"/>

    </body>

</html>
```

Next is the JSP code that comprises the page header. It's nothing fancy but is a separate JSP page nonetheless.

```
<html xmlns:jsp="http://java.sun.com/JSP/Page" version="2.0">

    <jsp:directive.page contentType="text/html" pageEncoding="UTF-8"/>

    <p>This is the page header</p>
</html>
```

The next JSP code makes up the page footer:

```
<html xmlns:jsp="http://java.sun.com/JSP/Page" version="2.0">

    <jsp:directive.page contentType="text/html" pageEncoding="UTF-8"/>

    <p>This is the page footer</p>

</html>
```

In the end, these three pages create a single page that contains a header, a body, and a footer.

Explanation

Including other JSP pages helps increase developer productivity and reduces maintenance time. Using this technique, a developer can extract any JSP features that appear in multiple pages and place them into a separate JSP page. Doing so will allow a single point of maintenance when one of these features needs to be updated.

To include another page within a JSP page, use the `<jsp:include>` tag. The `<jsp:include>` tag allows embedding a static file or another web component. The tag includes a page attribute, which is used to specify the relative URL or an expression that results in another file or web component to include in the page.

■ **Note**   The tag also has an optional flush attribute, which can be set to either true or false to indicate whether the output buffer should be flushed prior to the page inclusion. The default value for the flush attribute is false.

Optionally, `<jsp:param>` clauses can be placed between the opening and closing `<jsp:include>` tags to pass one or more name-value pairs to the included resource if the resource is dynamic. An example of performing this technique would resemble something like the following lines of code. In the following lines, a parameter with a name of bookAuthor and a value of Juneau is passed to the header JSP page.

```
<jsp:include page="header.jspx">
    <jsp:param name="bookAuthor" value="Juneau"/>
</jsp:include>
```

The ability to include other content within a JSP page provides a means to encapsulate resources and static content. This allows developers to create content once and include it in many pages.

Creating an Input Form for a Database Record

One of the most important constructs for a web based application is the input form. Providing users with the ability to enter information into a form and then submit to a data store is a foundational concept for any application. JSPs provide the ability to create an input form via the use of a Java servlet action method.

Example

This example requires a JSP document and a Java servlet in order to complete the database input form. An input form is created within a JSP document to populate records within a database table named EXAMPLES. When the user enters the information into the text fields on the form and clicked the submit button, a servlet is called that performs the database insert transaction.

The following code is the JSP document that is used to create the input form for the database application:

```
<!--
    Document    : inputForms
    Author      : juneau
-->
<html xmlns:jsp="http://java.sun.com/JSP/Page"
      xmlns:c="http://java.sun.com/jsp/jstl/core"
      version="2.0">

    <jsp:directive.page contentType="text/html" pageEncoding="UTF-8"/>
    <head>
        <title>Creating an Input Form</title>
    </head>
    <body>
        <h1>Example Input Form</h1>
        <p>
            Please insert example details using the text fields below.
        </p>
        ${ exampleBean.message }
        <form method="POST" action="/JSFByExample/ExampleServlet">
            Example Number: <input id="exampleNumber" name="exampleNumber" size="30"/>
            <br/>
            Example Name: <input id="name" name="name" size="30"/>
            <br/>
            Example Description: <input id="description" name="description" size="30"/>
            <br/>
            Example Text: <input id="text" name="text" size="30"/>
            <br/>
            <br/>
            <input type="submit"/>
        </form>
    </body>
</html>
```

Next is the code for a servlet named ExampleServlet. It is responsible for reading the request parameters from the JSP document input form and inserting the fields into the database.

```
package org.javaserverfaces.chapter02;

import java.io.IOException;
import java.io.PrintWriter;
import java.sql.Connection;
import java.sql.PreparedStatement;
import java.sql.SQLException;
import javax.servlet.ServletException;
import javax.servlet.annotation.WebServlet;
import javax.servlet.http.HttpServlet;
import javax.servlet.http.HttpServletRequest;
import javax.servlet.http.HttpServletResponse;
```

```java
/**
 * Creating an Input Form
 * @author juneau
 */
@WebServlet(name = "ExampleServlet", urlPatterns = {"/ExampleServlet"})
public class ExampleServlet extends HttpServlet {


    /**
     * Processes requests for both HTTP
     * <code>GET</code> and
     * <code>POST</code> methods.
     *
     * @param request servlet request
     * @param response servlet response
     * @throws ServletException if a servlet-specific error occurs
     * @throws IOException if an I/O error occurs
     */
    protected void processRequest(HttpServletRequest request, HttpServletResponse response)
            throws ServletException, IOException {
        response.setContentType("text/html;charset=UTF-8");
        PrintWriter out = response.getWriter();
        int result = -1;
        try {
            /*
             * TODO Perform validation on the request parameters here
             */
            result = insertRow (request.getParameter("exampleNumber"),
                        request.getParameter("name"),
                        request.getParameter("description"),
                        request.getParameter("text"));
            out.println("<html>");
            out.println("<head>");
            out.println("<title>Example Servlet</title>");
            out.println("</head>");
            out.println("<body>");
            out.println("<h1>Example Servlet at " + request.getContextPath() + "</h1>");
            out.println("<br/><br/>");

            if(result > 0){
                out.println("<font color='green'>Record successfully inserted!</font>");
                out.println("<br/><br/><a href='/JSFByExample/chapter02/inputForms.jspx'>Insert
another record</a>");
            } else {
                out.println("<font color='red'>Record NOT inserted!</font>");
                out.println("<br/><br/><a href='/JSFByExample/chapter02/inputForms.jspx'>
                Try Again</a>");
            }

            out.println("</body>");
            out.println("</html>");
        } finally {
```

```java
            out.close();
        }
    }

    public int insertRow(String exampleNumber,
                         String name,
                         String description,
                         String text) {

        String sql = "INSERT INTO EXAMPLES VALUES(" +
                     "EXAMPLES_SEQ.NEXTVAL,?,?,?,?)";
        PreparedStatement stmt = null;
        int result = -1;
        try {
            CreateConnection createConn = new CreateConnection();
            Connection conn = createConn.getConnection();
            stmt = (PreparedStatement) conn.prepareStatement(sql);
            stmt.setString(1, exampleNumber);
            stmt.setString(2, name);
            stmt.setString(3, description);
            stmt.setString(4, text);
            // Returns row-count or 0 if not successful
            result = stmt.executeUpdate();
            if (result > 0){
                System.out.println("-- Record created --");
            } else {
                System.out.println("!! Record NOT Created !!");
            }
        } catch (SQLException e) {
            e.printStackTrace();
        } finally {
            if (stmt != null) {
                try {
                    stmt.close();
                } catch (SQLException ex) {
                    ex.printStackTrace();
                }
            }

        }
        return result;
    }


    @Override
    protected void doGet(HttpServletRequest request, HttpServletResponse response)
            throws ServletException, IOException {
        processRequest(request, response);
    }
```

```
    @Override
    protected void doPost(HttpServletRequest request, HttpServletResponse response)
            throws ServletException, IOException {
        processRequest(request, response);
    }
}
```

If the request is successful, the record will be inserted into the database, and the user will be able to click a link to add another record. Of course, in a real-life application, you would want to code some validation using JavaScript either within the input form or within the server-side Java code to help ensure database integrity.

Explanation

A fundamental task to almost every enterprise application is the use of a database input form. Database input forms make it easy for end users to populate database tables with data. When using JSP technology along with servlets, this operation can become fairly simple. As you have seen in the example, writing a JSP input form is straightforward and can be coded using basic HTML. The key is to set up a Java servlet to receive a submitted request and process the records using the servlet. This provides an easy mechanism for separating web content from the application logic.

In the example, a JSP document named inputForms.jspx contains a standard HTML form with a method of POST and an action of /JSFByExample/ExampleServlet. The input form contains four fields, which map to database columns into which the data will eventually be inserted. The input tags contain the name of four corresponding fields (exampleNumber, name, description, and text), which will be passed to the form action when submitted. As you can see, the only reference to the Java code is the name of the servlet that is contained within the form action attribute.

The Java servlet named ExampleServlet is responsible for obtaining the request parameters that were submitted via the JSP document, validating them accordingly (not shown in the example), and inserting them into the database. When the page is submitted, ExampleServlet is invoked, and the request is sent to the doPost method since the HTML action method is POST. Both the doGet and doPost methods are really just wrapper methods for a processing method named processRequest, which is responsible for most of the work. The processRequest method is responsible for obtaining the request parameters, inserting them into the database, and sending a response to the client. A PrintWriter object is declared and created by making a call to response.getWriter() first because this object will be used later to help form the response that is sent to the client. Next, an int value named result is set up and initialized to -1. This variable will be used for determining whether the SQL insert worked or failed. After those declarations, a try-catch block is opened, and the first line of the try block is a call to the insertRow method, passing the request parameters as values. The result variable is going to accept the int value that is returned from the execution of the insertRows method, indicating whether the insert was successful.

```
result = insertRow (request.getParameter("exampleNumber"),
                    request.getParameter("name"),
                    request.getParameter("description"),
                    request.getParameter("text"));
```

As such, an SQL insert statement is assigned to a String named sql, and it is set up using the PreparedStatement format. Each question mark in the SQL string corresponds to a parameter that will be substituted in the string when the SQL is executed.

```
String sql = "INSERT INTO EXAMPLES VALUES(" +
                " EXAMPLES_SEQ.NEXTVAL,?,?,?,?)";
```

Next, a `PreparedStatement` and `int` values are initialized, and then a `try-catch-finally` block is opened, which will contain the SQL insert code. Within the block, a `Connection` object is created by calling a helper class named `CreateConnection`. `CreateConnection` will return a database connection that can then be used to work with the database. If for some reason the connection fails, the `catch` block will be executed, followed by the `finally` block. A `PreparedStatement` object is created from the successful connection, and the SQL string that contains the database insert is assigned to it. Each of the request parameter values, in turn, is then set as a parameter to the `PreparedStatement`. Lastly, the `PreparedStatement`'s `executeUpdate` method is called, which performs an insert to the database. The return value of `executeUpdate` is assigned to the result variable and then returned to the `processRequest` method. Once the control is returned to `processRequest`, the servlet response is created using a series of `PrintWriter` statements. If the insert was successful, then a message indicating success is displayed. Likewise, if unsuccessful, then a message indicating failure is displayed.

Developing database input forms with JSP is fairly easy to do. To preserve the MVC structure, using a Java servlet for handing the request and database logic is the best choice.

Looping Through Database Records Within a Page

In many solutions, it can be beneficial to encapsulate the database logic in a Java class and access it from the JSP page. This allows one to list all of the records within a database table, for example.

Example

Use the JSTL `c:forEach` element to iterate through the database rows and display them on the page. Two Java classes would be used for working with the data in this situation. One of the classes would represent the table, which you are querying from the database, and it would contain fields for each column in that table. Another JavaBean class would be used to contain the database business logic for querying the database.

The example will display the first and last names of each author contained within the AUTHORS database table. The following code is used to create the JSP document that will display the data from the table using a standard HTML-based table along with the JSTL `<c:forEach>` tag to loop through the rows:

```
<!--
    Document    : loopingThroughRecords
    Author      : juneau
-->
<html xmlns:jsp="http://java.sun.com/JSP/Page"
      xmlns:c="http://java.sun.com/jsp/jstl/core"
      version="2.0">

    <jsp:directive.page contentType="text/html" pageEncoding="UTF-8"/>
    <jsp:useBean id="authorBean" scope="session" class="org.javaserverfaces.chapter02.AuthorBean"/>
    <head>
        <title>Looping Through Database Records within a Page </title>
    </head>
    <body>
        <h1>Authors</h1>
        <p>
            The authors from the books which Josh Juneau has worked on are printed below.
        </p>
        <table border="1">

        <c:forEach items="${authorBean.authorList }" var="author">
            <tr>
```

89

```
                <td> ${ author.first } ${ author.last }</td>
            </tr>
        </c:forEach>
        </table>
    </body>
</html>
```

As you can see, `<c:forEach>` is used to loop through the items contained within `${authorBean.authorList}`. Each item within the list is an object of type `Author`. The following Java code is that of the `Author` class, which is used for holding the data contained within each table row:

```java
package org.javaserverfaces.chapter02;

/**
 *
 * @author juneau
 */
public class Author implements java.io.Serializable {
    private int id;
    private String first;
    private String last;

    public Author(){
        id = -1;
        first = null;
        last = null;
    }

    /**
     * @return the id
     */
    public int getId() {
        return id;
    }

    /**
     * @param id the id to set
     */
    public void setId(int id) {
        this.id = id;
    }

    /**
     * @return the first
     */
    public String getFirst() {
        return first;
    }
```

```java
    /**
     * @param first the first to set
     */
    public void setFirst(String first) {
        this.first = first;
    }

    /**
     * @return the last
     */
    public String getLast() {
        return last;
    }

    /**
     * @param last the last to set
     */
    public void setLast(String last) {
        this.last = last;
    }
}
```

Lastly, the JSP document makes reference to a JavaBean named AuthorBean, which contains the business logic to query the data and return it as a list to the JSP page. The following code is what is contained within the AuthorBean class:

```java
package org.javaserverfaces.chapter02;

import java.sql.Connection;
import java.sql.PreparedStatement;
import java.sql.ResultSet;
import java.sql.SQLException;
import java.util.ArrayList;
import java.util.List;
import org.javaserverfaces.common.CreateConnection;

/**
 *
 * @author juneau
 */
public class AuthorBean implements java.io.Serializable {

    public static Connection conn = null;
    private List authorList = null;


    public AuthorBean(){

    }
```

```java
public List queryAuthors(){
    String sql = "SELECT ID, FIRST, LAST FROM BOOK_AUTHOR";
    List 272103_1_En authorList = new ArrayList272103_1_En();
    PreparedStatement stmt = null;
    ResultSet rs = null;
    int result = -1;
    try {
        CreateConnection createConn = new CreateConnection();
        conn = createConn.getConnection();
        stmt = (PreparedStatement) conn.prepareStatement(sql);

        // Returns row-count or 0 if not successful
        rs = stmt.executeQuery();
        while (rs.next()){
            Author author = new Author();
            author.setId(rs.getInt("ID"));
            author.setFirst((rs.getString("FIRST")));
            author.setLast(rs.getString("LAST"));
            authorList.add(author);
        }
    } catch (SQLException e) {
        e.printStackTrace();
    } finally {
        if (stmt != null) {
            try {
                stmt.close();
            } catch (SQLException ex) {
                ex.printStackTrace();
            }
        }

    }
    return authorList;
}

public List getAuthorList(){
    authorList = queryAuthors();
    return authorList;
}
}
```

The names of the authors contained within the records in the table will be displayed on the page.

Explanation

Almost any enterprise application performs some sort of database querying. Oftentimes results from a database query are displayed in a table format. The example demonstrates how to query a database and return the results to a JSP page for display in a standard HTML table. The JSP page in this example makes use of the JSTL c:forEach element to iterate through the results of the database query. Note that there is more than one way to develop this type of database query using JSP; however, the format demonstrated in this example is most recommended for use in a production enterprise environment.

As mentioned previously, the JSP page in this example uses a combination of the `jsp:useBean` element and the `c:forEach` element to iterate over the results of a database query. The logic for querying the database resides within a server-side JavaBean class that is referenced within the `jsp:useBean` element on the page. In the example, the JavaBean is named `AuthorBean`, and it is responsible for querying a database table named AUTHORS and populating a list of `Author` objects with the results of the query. When the `c:forEach` element is evaluated with the `items` attribute set to `${authorBean.authorList }`, it calls upon the JavaBean method named `getAuthorList` because JSP expressions always append "get" to a method call behind the scenes and also capitalizes the first letter of the method name within the call. When the `getAuthorList` method is called, the `authorList` field is populated via a call to `queryAuthors`. The `queryAuthors` method utilizes a Java Database Connectivity (JDBC) database call to obtain the authors from the AUTHORS table. A new `Author` object is created for each row returned by the database query, and each new `Author` object is, in turn, added to the `authorList`. In the end, the populated `authorList` contains a number of `Author` objects, and it is returned to the JSP page and iterated over utilizing the `c:forEach` element.

The `c:forEach` element contains an attribute named `var`, and this should be set equal to a string that will represent each element in the list that is being iterated over. The `var` is then used between the opening and closing `c:forEach` element tags to reference each element in the list, printing out each author's first and last names.

This example provides some insight on how to combine the power of JSTL tags with other technologies such as JDBC to produce very useful results. To learn more about the different JSTL tags that are part of JSP, please visit the online documentation at `www.oracle.com/technetwork/java/jstl-137486.html`.

Handling JSP Errors

It is important to create a user-friendly error page that will be displayed if an error occurs in a JSP.

Example

The following JSP document, in JSP format (not JSPX), demonstrates a standard error page to display if an error occurs within a JSP application. If an exception occurs within any JSP page in the application, the following error page will be displayed.

■ **Note** The uses the JSTL fmt library, which provides convenient access to formatting capabilities that allow for localization of text as well as date and number formatting. Text localization capabilities allow locales to be set so that text can be formatted into different languages, depending upon the user locale. Tags used for date manipulation make it easy for developers to format dates and times easily within a JSP page and also provide a way to parse dates and times for data input. Lastly, number-formatting tags provide a way to format and parse numeric data within pages. To learn more about the JSTL fmt tag library, please refer to the online documentation at `http://jstl.java.net/`.

```
<%--
    Document    : errorPage
    Author      : juneau
--%>

<%@page contentType="text/html" pageEncoding="UTF-8"%>
<%@ page isErrorPage="true" %>
<%@ taglib uri="http://java.sun.com/jsp/jstl/core"
    prefix="c" %>
<%@ taglib uri="http://java.sun.com/jsp/jstl/fmt"
```

```
        prefix="fmt" %>
<!DOCTYPE html>
<html>
    <head>
        <meta http-equiv="Content-Type" content="text/html; charset=UTF-8">
        <title>JSP Error Page</title>
    </head>
    <body>
        <h1>Error Encountered</h1>
        <br/>
        <br/>
        <p>
            The application has encountered the following error:
            <br/>
            <fmt:message key="ServerError"/>: ${pageContext.errorData.statusCode}

        </p>
    </body>
</html>
```

For example, the following JSP would create an error (NullPointerException) if the parameter designated as param is null. If this occurs, the indicated error page would be displayed.

```
<!--
    Document    : errorPage2
    Author      : juneau
-->
<html xmlns:jsp="http://java.sun.com/JSP/Page"
      xmlns:c="http://java.sun.com/jsp/jstl/core"
      version="2.0">

    <jsp:directive.page contentType="text/html" pageEncoding="UTF-8"/>
    <jsp:directive.page errorPage="errorPage.jsp"/>

    <head>
        <title> </title>
    </head>
    <body>
        <h1>There is an error on this page</h1>
        <p>
            This will produce an error:
            <jsp:scriptlet>
             if (request.getParameter("param").equals("value")) {
                System.out.println("test");
             }
            </jsp:scriptlet>
        </p>
    </body>

</html>
```

Explanation

One of the most annoying issues for users while working with applications is when an error is thrown. A nasty, long stack trace is often produced, and the user is left with no idea how to resolve the error. It is better to display a nice and user-friendly error page when such an error occurs. The JSP technology allows an error page to be designated by adding a page directive to each JSP page that may produce an error. The directive should designate an error page that will be displayed if the page containing the directive produces an error.

The second JSP document in the solution demonstrates a JSP page that will throw an error if the parameter being requested within the page is null. If this were to occur and there were no error page specified, then a NullPointerException error message would be displayed. However, this JSP indicates an error page by designating it within a page directive using the following syntax:

```
<jsp:directive.page errorPage="errorPage.jsp"/>
```

When an error occurs on the example page, errorPage.jsp is displayed. The first JSP document listed in the solution contains the sources for the errorPage.jsp page. It is flagged as an error page because it includes a page directive indicating as such:

```
<%@ page isErrorPage="true" %>
```

An error page is able to determine the error code, status, exception, and an array of other information by using the pageContext implicit object. In the example, the ${pageContext.errorData.statusCode} expression is used to display the status code of the exception. Table 2-5 displays the other possible pieces of information that can be gleaned from the pageContext object.

Table 2-5. *pageContext Implicit Object Exception Information*

Expression	Value
pageContext.errorData	Provides access to the error information
pageContext.exception	Returns the current value of the exception object
pageContext.errorData.requestURI	Returns the request URI
pageContext.errorData.servletName	Returns the name of the servlet invoked
pageContext.errorData.statusCode	Returns the error status code
pageContext.errorData.throwable	Returns the throwable that caused the error

Providing user-friendly error pages in any application can help create a more usable and overall more functional experience for the end user. JSP and Java technology provide robust exception handling and mechanisms that can be used to help users and administrators alike when exceptions occur.

Disabling Scriptlets in Pages

Since it is a bad idea to mix Java code inside of JSPs, scriptlets should only be used in rare circumstances. In fact, recent releases of JSP have provided the ability to disable scriptlets.

Example

Set the `scripting-invalid` element within the web deployment descriptor to `true`. The following excerpt from a `web.xml` deployment descriptor demonstrates how to do so:

```
<jsp-config>
    <jsp-property-group>
        <scripting-invalid>true</scripting-invalid>
    </jsp-property-group>
</jsp-config>
```

Explanation

When working in an environment that encourages the use of the Model-View-Controller architecture, it can be useful to prohibit the use of scriptlets within JSP pages and documents. When JSP 2.1 was released, it provided solutions to help developers move Java code out of JSP pages and into server-side Java classes where it belonged. In the early years of JSP, pages were cluttered with scriptlets and markup. This made it difficult for developers to separate business logic from content, and it was hard to find good tools to help develop such pages effectively. JSP 2.1 introduced tags, which make it possible to eliminate the use of scriptlets within JSP pages, and this helps maintain the use of the MVC architecture.

To prohibit the use of scriptlets within JSP pages in an application, add the `jsp-config` element within the `web.xml` file of the application of which you want to enforce the rule. Add a subelement of `jsp-property-group` along with the `scripting-invalid` element. The value of the `scripting-invalid` element should be set to `true`.

Ignoring EL in Pages

In some situations, EL should be allowed to pass expressions through without processing them. In other words, applications will be able to pass through expressions verbatim. For instance, if an expression property contains HTML that needs to be rendered, we do not want EL to process the content.

Example #1

Escape the EL expressions within the page by using the \ character before any expressions. For instance, the following expressions will be ignored because the \ character appears before them:

```
\${elBean.myProperty}
\${2 + 4}
```

Example #2

Configure a JSP property group within the `web.xml` file for the application. Within the `web.xml` file, a `<jsp-property-group>` element can contain child elements that characterize how the JSP page evaluates specified items. By including an `<el-ignored>true</el-ignored>` element, all EL within the application's JSP documents will be ignored and treated as literals. The following excerpt from `web.xml` demonstrates this feature:

```
<jsp-property-group>
    <el-ignored>true</el-ignored>
 </jsp-property-group>
```

Example #3

Include a page directive including the isELIgnored attribute, and set it to true. The following page directive can be placed at the top of a given JSP document to allow each EL expression to be treated as a literal:

```
<jsp:directive.page isELIgnored="true"/>
```

or in a standard JSP:

```
<%@ page isELIgnored="true" %>
```

Explanation

There may be a situation in which the evaluation of JSP EL expressions should be turned off. This occurs most often in cases of legacy applications using older versions of JSP technology; EL expressions were not yet available. There are a few different ways to turn off the evaluation of EL expressions, and this example demonstrates each of them.

In the first example, the escape technique is demonstrated. An EL expression can be escaped by placing the \ character directly before the expression, as shown in the example. Doing so will cause the JSP interpreter to treat the expression as a string literal, and the output on the page will be the expression itself, rather than its evaluation. The second example demonstrates adding a jsp-property-group to the web.xml deployment descriptor in order to ignore EL. All EL within an application will be ignored by including the isELIgnored element and providing a true value for it. Lastly, the final example demonstrates how to ignore EL on a page-by-page basis by including a page directive with the isELIgnored attribute set to true.

Each of the different solutions for ignoring EL allows coverage to different parts of the application. The solution you choose should depend upon how broadly you want to ignore EL throughout an application.

CHAPTER 3

■ ■ ■

The Basics of JavaServer Faces

In 2004 Sun Microsystems introduced a Java web framework called JavaServer Faces (JSF) in an effort to help simplify web application development. It is an evolution of the JavaServer Pages (JSP) framework, adding a more organized development life cycle and the ability to more easily utilize modern web technologies. JSF uses XML files for view construction and uses Java classes for application logic, making it adhere to the MVC architecture. JSF is request-driven, and each request is processed by a special servlet named the `FacesServlet`. The `FacesServlet` is responsible for building the component trees, processing events, determining which view to process next, and rendering the response. JSF 1.*x* used a special resource file named the `faces-config.xml` file for specifying application details such as navigation rules, registering listeners, and so on. While the `faces-config.xml` file can still be used in JSF 2.*x*, the more modern releases of JSF have focused on being easy to use, minimizing the amount of XML configuration, and utilizing annotations in place of XML where possible. Such will be the trend with the future releases of JSF as well, since it has now become a mature web framework.

The framework is very powerful, including easy integration with technologies such as Ajax and making it effortless to develop dynamic content. JSF works well with databases, using JDBC, EJB, or RESTful technology to work with the back end. JavaBeans, known as JSF *managed beans*, are used for application logic and support the dynamic content within each view. They can adhere to different life spans depending upon the scope that is used. Views can invoke methods within the beans to perform actions such as data manipulation and form processing. Properties can also be declared within the beans and exposed within the views, providing a convenient way to pass request values. JSF allows developers to customize their applications with preexisting validation and conversion tags that can be used on components with the view. It is also easy to build custom validators, as well as custom components, that can be applied to components in a view.

This chapter includes examples that will be useful for those who are getting started with JSF and also those who are looking to beef up their basic knowledge of the framework. You will learn how to create managed beans, work with standard components, and handle page navigation. There are also examples that cover useful techniques such as building custom validators and creating bookmarkable URLs. The examples are refined to include the most current techniques and provide the most useful methodologies for using them. After studying the examples in this chapter, you will be ready to build standard JSF applications, sprinkling in some custom features as well.

Writing a Simple JSF Application

One of the best ways to learn quickly is to jump right in with an example. In this section, a simple JSF application will be built, explaining some basic concepts throughout the process.

Example #1

This JSF web application is comprised of a single XHTML page and a single JSF managed bean, along with other required JSF configuration files. The application in this example simply displays a message that is initialized within a JSF managed bean.

> ■ **Note** It is recommended that you utilize a Java IDE to make life easier. If you have not yet created a JSF
> application and are interested in learning how to create one from scratch with an IDE, then please see Example #2. This
> book features the NetBeans IDE, a cutting-edge Java development environment that is usually the first to support new
> Java features. However, there are many excellent IDE choices. You can choose the IDE you want and follow along with its
> instructions for working with JSF.

Displaying a JSF Managed Bean Field Value

The following code makes up the XHTML view that will be used to display the JSF managed bean field value:

```
<?xml version="1.0" encoding="UTF-8"?>
<!--
Book: JavaServerFaces
Example: Simple JSF Application
Author: J. Juneau
Filename: chapter03/simpleJSF1.xhtml
-->
<!DOCTYPE html PUBLIC "-//W3C//DTD XHTML 1.0 Strict//EN" "http://www.w3.org/TR/xhtml1/DTD/
xhtml1-strict.dtd">
<html xmlns="http://www.w3.org/1999/xhtml"
      xmlns:f="http://xmlns.jcp.org/jsf/core"
      xmlns:h="http://xmlns.jcp.org/jsf/html">
    <h:head>
        <meta http-equiv="Content-Type" content="text/html; charset=UTF-8"/>
        <title>A Simple JSF Application</title>
    </h:head>
    <h:body>
        <p>
            This simple application utilizes a request-scoped JSF managed bean
            to display the message below. If you change the message within the
            managed bean's constructor and then recompile the application, the
            new message appears.
            <br/>
            <br/>
            #{helloWorldController.hello}
            <br/>
            or
            <br/>
            <h:outputText id="helloMessage" value="#{helloWorldController.hello}"/>
        </p>
    </h:body>
</html>
```

As you can see, the JSF page utilizes a JSF expression, #{helloWorldController.hello}. Much like JSP
technology, a backing JavaBean, otherwise known as a *JSF managed bean*, is referenced in the expression along with
the field to expose.

Examining the JSF Managed Bean

The following code is that of HelloWorldController, the JSF managed bean example:

```java
package org.javaserverfaces.chapter03;

import java.io.Serializable;
import javax.enterprise.context.SessionScoped;
import javax.inject.Named;

/**
 * A Simple JSF Application
 * @author juneau
 */
@Named(value = "helloWorldController")
@SessionScoped
public class HelloWorldController implements Serializable {
    private String hello;

    /**
     * Creates a new instance of HelloWorldController
     */
    public HelloWorldController() {
        hello = "Hello World";
    }

    /**
     * @return the hello
     */
    public String getHello() {
        return hello;
    }

    /**
     * @param hello the hello to set
     */
    public void setHello(String hello) {
        this.hello = hello;
    }
}
```

■ **Note** Prior to JSF 2.0, in order to enable the JSF servlet to translate the XHTML page, you needed to ensure that the web.xml file contained a servlet element indicating the javax.faces.webapp.FacesServlet class and its associated servlet-mapping URL. Since the release of JSF 2.0, if using a Servlet 3.x container, the FacesServlet is automatically mapped for you, so there is no requirement to adjust the web.xml configuration.

Ensuring the JSF Application Functions Properly in a Pre-JSF 2.0 Environment

The listing that follows is an excerpt taken from the web.xml file for the sources to this book, and it demonstrates the features that must be added to the web.xml file in order to make the JSF application function properly.

```
...
<servlet>
    <servlet-name>Faces Servlet</servlet-name>
    <servlet-class>javax.faces.webapp.FacesServlet</servlet-class>
    <load-on-startup>1</load-on-startup>
  </servlet>
  ...
  <servlet-mapping>
    <servlet-name>Faces Servlet</servlet-name>
    <url-pattern>/faces/*</url-pattern>
  </servlet-mapping>
...
  <welcome-file-list>
    <welcome-file>faces/index.xhtml</welcome-file>
  </welcome-file-list>
```

Let's take a deeper look at the web.xml configuration for a JSF application. It is not very complex, but a few elements could use some explanation. The javax.faces.webapp.FacesServlet servlet must be declared within the web.xml file. The declaration must contain a servlet-name; the servlet-class element, which lists the fully qualified class name; and a load-on-startup value of 1 to ensure that the servlet is loaded when the application is started up by the container. The web.xml file must then map that servlet to a given URL within a servlet-mapping element. The servlet-mapping element must include the servlet-name, which is the same value as the servlet-name element that is contained in the servlet declaration, and a url-pattern element, which specifies the URL that will be used to map JSF pages with the servlet. When a URL is specified that contains the /faces/ mapping, the FacesServlet will be used to translate the view.

To load the application in your browser, visit http://localhost:8080/JSFByExample/faces/chapter03/simpleJSF1.xhtml, and you will see the following text:

This simple application utilizes a request-scoped JSF managed bean to display the message below. If you change the "hello" variable within the managed bean's constructor and then recompile and run the application, the new message appears.

```
Hello World
or
Hello World
```

Example #2

Use an IDE, such as NetBeans, to create a JSF application. To get started with NetBeans, first download the most recent release of NetBeans from the Netbeans.org web site. The examples in this example make use of NetBeans 8.x. Once installed, create a new project by clicking the File ➤ New Project menu option.

Creare a NetBeans Web Project. Net, modify the index.xhtml file by making the page the same as the JSF view that is listed in Example #1's "Displaying JSF Managed Bean Field Value" section. Once done, add the managed bean to your application that will be used to supply the business logic for the index.xhtml page. To create the managed bean, right-click the Source Packages navigation menu for your project, and choose New ➤ JSF Managed Bean from the context menu. This will open the New JSF Managed Bean dialog (Figure 3-1), which will allow you to specify several options for your managed bean, including the name, location, and scope.

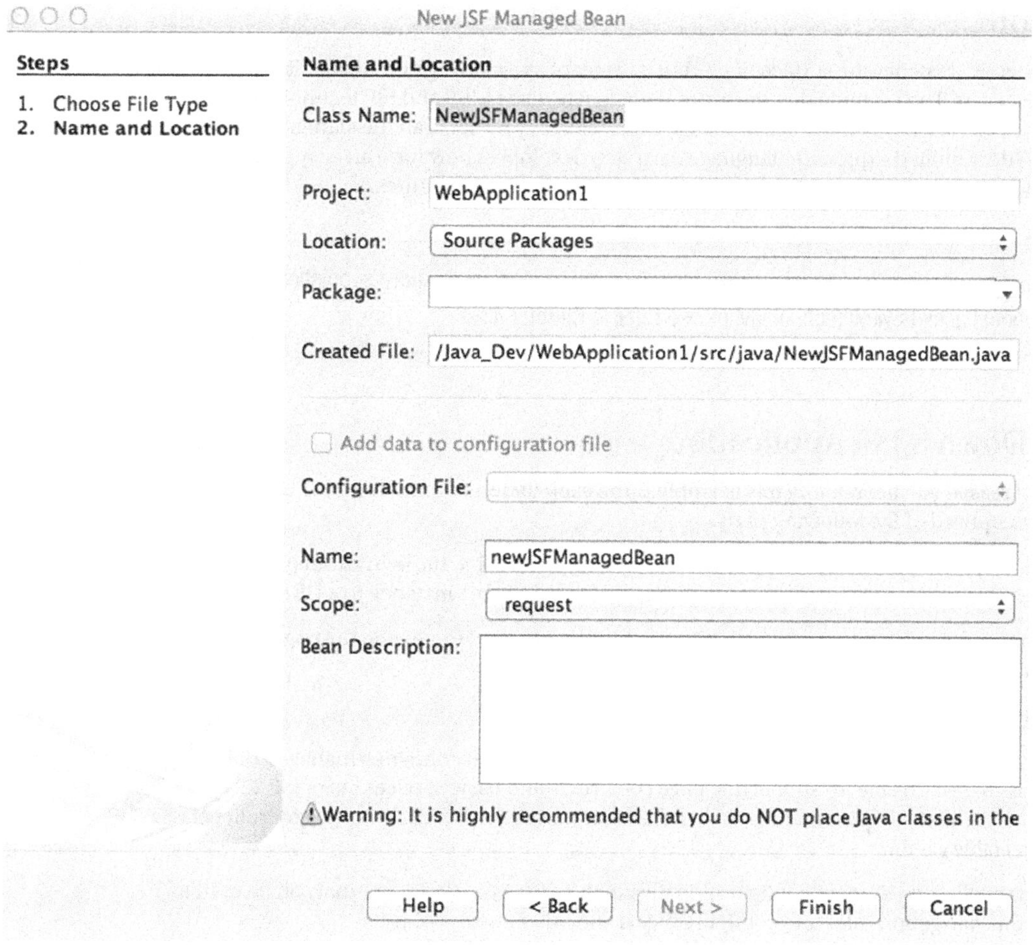

Figure 3-1. *New JSF managed bean*

For the purposes of this example, change the name of the bean to `HelloWorldController`, and leave the rest of the options at their defaults; then click Finish. Copy and paste the code from Example #1's "Examining the JSF Managed Bean" section into the newly created managed bean class. Once finished, right-click the application project from the Project navigation menu and choose Deploy to deploy your application.

To load the application in your browser, visit `http://localhost:8080/JSFByExample/faces/chapter03/index.xhtml`, and you will see the following text:

This simple application utilizes a request-scoped JSF managed bean to display the message below. If you change the "hello" variable within the managed bean's constructor and then recompile and run the application, the new message appears.

```
Hello World
or
Hello World
```

Explanation

This example merely scratches the surface of JSF, but it is meant as a starting point to guide you along the path of becoming a JSF expert. The example demonstrates how closely related JSF and JSP technologies are. In fact, the only difference in the two view pages is the use of the JSF expression #{} rather than the standard JSP value expression ${}. Thanks to the JSP 2.0 unified expression language, Java web developers now have an easy transition between the two technologies, and they now share many of the same expression language features.

■ **Note**   JSF 2.x can make use of Facelets view technology to produce even more sophisticated and organized designs. To learn more about Facelets view technology, please refer to Chapter 4.

Breaking Down a JSF Application

Now for the real reason you are reading this example. . .the explanation for building a JSF application! A JSF application is comprised of the following parts:

- If using or maintaining JSF applications written using JSF 1.x, the web.xml deployment descriptor that is responsible for mapping the FacesServlet instance to a URL path

- One or more web pages on which JSF components are used to provide the page layout (may or may not utilize Facelets view technology)

- JSF component tags

- One or more managed beans, which are simple, lightweight container-managed objects that are responsible for supporting page constructs and basic services. As of JSF 2.2+, we should utilize CDI annotations, rather than @ManagedBean to make these controller classes injectable via EL.

- Optionally, one or more configuration files such as faces-config.xml that can be used to define navigation rules and configure beans and other custom objects

- Optionally, supporting objects such as listeners, converters, or custom component

- Optionally, custom tags for use on a JSF view

```
LIFE CYCLE OF A JSF APPLICATION
```

The JSF view processing life cycle contains six stages. These stages are as follows:

1. Restore View

2. Apply Request Values

3. Process Validations

4. Update Model Values

5. Invoke Application

6. Render Response

Restore View is the first phase in the JSF life cycle, and it is responsible for constructing the view. The component tree then applies the request parameters to each of the corresponding component values using the component tree's decode method. This occurs during the Apply Request Values phase. During this phase, any value conversion errors will be added to FacesContext for display as error messages during the Render Response phase. Next, all of the validations are processed. During the Process Validations phase, each component that has a registered validator is examined, and local values are compared to the validation rules. If any validation errors arise, the Render Response phase is entered, rendering the page with the corresponding validation errors.

If the Process Validations phase exits without errors, the Update Model Values phase begins. During this phase, managed bean properties are set for each of the corresponding input components within the tree that contain local values. Once again, if any errors occur, then the Render Response phase is entered, rendering the page with the corresponding errors displayed. After the successful completion of the Update Model Values phase, the application-level events are handled during the Invoke Applications phase. Such events include page submits or redirects to other pages. Finally, the Render Response phase occurs, and the page is rendered to the user. If the application is using JSP pages, then the JSF implementation allows the JSP container to render the page.

The example uses the minimum number of these parts. To run the example, you will need to ensure that the web.xml file contains the proper JSF configuration if running in a pre-JSF 2.x environment. You will need to have a managed bean declaring the field that is exposed on the JSF view along with the necessary accessor methods to make it work properly. And lastly, you will need to have the XHTML JSF view page containing the JSF expression that exposes the field that is declared within the managed bean.

A JSF managed bean is a lightweight, container-managed object that is associated with a JSF page. The managed bean is much like a JSP JavaBean in that it provides the application logic for a particular page so that Java code does not need to be embedded into the view code. Components (a.k.a. JSF tags) that are used within a JSF view are mapped to server-side fields and methods contained within the JSF managed bean. Oftentimes, JSF managed beans contain *Controller* within their name because they are indeed the controllers for the page logic. In the example, the JSF managed bean is named HelloWorldController, and a field named hello is declared, exposing itself to the public via the getHello and setHello methods. The JSF managed bean is instantiated and initialized when a page that contains a reference to the bean is requested, and the managed bean scope determines the life span of the bean. In the case of this example, the managed bean contains a request scope, via the @RequestScoped (javax.enterprise.context. RequestScoped) annotation. Therefore, its life span is that of a single request, and it is re-instantiated each time the page in the example is reloaded. To learn more about the scope and annotations that are available for a managed bean, please see the next example.

JSF technology utilizes a web view declaration framework known as Facelets. Facelets uses a special set of XML tags, similar in style to the standard JSF tags, to help build componentized web views. To learn more about Facelets, please see Chapter 4. While this example does not use Facelets, it is a vital part of JSF view technology. Facelets pages typically use XHTML, which is an HTML page that is comprised of well-formed XML components. The example JSF view is well-structured, and it contains two JSF EL expressions that are responsible for instantiating the managed bean and displaying the content for the hello field. When the EL expression #{helloWorldBean.hello} is translated by the FacesServlet, it makes the call to the HelloBeanController's getHello() method.

Lots of information was thrown at you within this introductory example. The simple example provides a good starting point for working with JSF technology. Continue with the examples in this chapter to gain a broader knowledge of each component that is used for developing JavaServer Faces web applications.

Writing a Managed Bean

JSF views have the ability to access fields and methods that are contained within JSF Managed Bean controller classes. This example will cover how to develop a managed bean, and how to access it within a JSF view using Expression Language.

Example

The JSF managed bean is a lightweight container-managed component, which provides the application logic for use within your JSF application web pages. Typically each view within a JSF application is paired with a managed bean controller class. As such, this example is comprised of a JSF view and a JSF managed bean. The application calculates two numbers that are entered by the user and then adds, subtracts, multiplies, or divides them depending upon the user's selection. The following code is the managed bean that is responsible for declaring fields for each of the numbers that will be entered by the user, as well as a field for the result of the calculation. The managed bean is also responsible for creating a list of Strings that will be displayed within an h:selectOneMenu element within the JSF view and retaining the value that is chosen by the user.

Although it may seem as though this managed bean is doing a lot of work, it actually is very simple! The managed bean is really a beefed-up Plain Old Java Object (POJO) that includes some methods that can be called from JSF view components.

Managed Bean

The following code is for the managed bean that is used for the calculation example. The bean is named CalculationController, and it is referenced as calculationController from within the JSF view. JSF uses convention over configuration for its naming conventions. By default, JSF views can contain EL that references a managed bean by specifying the class name with the first character in lowercase.

```java
package org.javaserverfaces.chapter03;

import java.io.Serializable;
import java.util.ArrayList;
import java.util.List;
import javax.enterprise.context.SessionScoped;
import javax.faces.application.FacesMessage;

import javax.faces.context.FacesContext;
import javax.faces.model.SelectItem;
import javax.inject.Named;

/**
 * Writing a JSF Managed Bean
 * @author juneau
 */
```

```java
@SessionScoped
@Named(value="calculationController")
public class CalculationController implements Serializable {

    private int num1;
    private int num2;
    private int result;
    private String calculationType;
    private static String ADDITION = "Addition";
    private static String SUBTRACTION = "Subtraction";
    private static String MULTIPLICATION = "Multiplication";
    private static String DIVISION = "Division";
    List<SelectItem> calculationList;

    /**
     * Creates a new instance of CalculationController
     */
    public CalculationController() {
        // Initialize variables
        num1 = 0;
        num2 = 0;
        result = 0;
        calculationType = null;
        // Initialize the list of values for the SelectOneMenu
        populateCalculationList();
    }

    /**
     * @return the num1
     */
    public int getNum1() {
        return num1;
    }

    /**
     * @param num1 the num1 to set
     */
    public void setNum1(int num1) {
        this.num1 = num1;
    }

    /**
     * @return the num2
     */
    public int getNum2() {
        return num2;
    }

    /**
     * @param num2 the num2 to set
     */
```

```java
public void setNum2(int num2) {
    this.num2 = num2;
}

    /**
 * @return the result
 */
public int getResult() {
    return result;
}

/**
 * @param result the result to set
 */
public void setResult(int result) {
    this.result = result;
}

/**
 * @return the calculationType
 */
public String getCalculationType() {
    return calculationType;
}

/**
 * @param calculationType the calculationType to set
 */
public void setCalculationType(String calculationType) {
    this.calculationType = calculationType;
}

public List<SelectItem> getCalculationList(){
    return calculationList;
}

private void populateCalculationList(){
    calculationList = new ArrayList<SelectItem>();
    calculationList.add(new SelectItem(ADDITION));
    calculationList.add(new SelectItem(SUBTRACTION));
    calculationList.add(new SelectItem(MULTIPLICATION));
    calculationList.add(new SelectItem(DIVISION));
}

public void performCalculation() {
    if (getCalculationType().equals(ADDITION)){
        setResult(num1 + num2);
    } else if (getCalculationType().equals(SUBTRACTION)){
        setResult(num1 - num2);
    } else if (getCalculationType().equals(MULTIPLICATION)){
        setResult(num1 * num2);
    } else if (getCalculationType().equals(DIVISION)){
```

```
        try{
            setResult(num1 / num2);
        } catch (Exception ex){
            FacesMessage facesMsg = new FacesMessage(FacesMessage.SEVERITY_ERROR,
"Invalid Calculation", "Invalid Calculation");
            FacesContext.getCurrentInstance().addMessage(null, facesMsg);
        }
    }
}
}
```

Next is the view that composes the web page, which is displayed to the user. The view is composed within an XHTML document and is well-formed XML.

JSF View

The view contains JSF components that are displayed as text boxes into which the user can enter information, a pick-list of different calculation types for the user to choose from, a component responsible for displaying the result of the calculation, and an h:commandButton component for submitting the form values.

```
<?xml version="1.0" encoding="UTF-8"?>
<!--
Example: Writing a JSF Managed Bean
Author: J. Juneau
-->
<!DOCTYPE html PUBLIC "-//W3C//DTD XHTML 1.0 Strict//EN" "http://www.w3.org/TR/xhtml1/DTD/
xhtml1-strict.dtd">
<html xmlns="http://www.w3.org/1999/xhtml"
      xmlns:f="http://xmlns.jcp.org/jsf/core"
      xmlns:h="http://xmlns.jcp.org/jsf/html">
    <h:head>
        <meta http-equiv="Content-Type" content="text/html; charset=UTF-8"/>
        <title>Writing a JSF Managed Bean</title>
    </h:head>
    <h:body>
        <f:view>

            <h2>Perform a Calculation</h2>
            <p>
                Use the following form to perform a calculation on two numbers.
                <br/>
                Enter the numbers in the two text fields below, and select a calculation to
                <br/>
                perform, then hit the "Calculate" button.
                <br/>
                <br/>
                <h:messages errorStyle="color: red" infoStyle="color: green" globalOnly="true"/>
                <br/>
```

```
<h:form id="calulationForm">
    Number1:
    <h:inputText id="num1" value="#{calculationController.num1}"/>
    <br/>
    Number2:
    <h:inputText id="num2" value="#{calculationController.num2}"/>
    <br/>
    <br/>
    Calculation Type:
    <h:selectOneMenu id="calculationType" value="#{calculationController.
    calculationType}">
        <f:selectItems value="#{calculationController.calculationList}"/>
    </h:selectOneMenu>
    <br/>
    <br/>
    Result:
    <h:outputText id="result" value="#{calculationController.result}"/>
    <br/>
    <br/>
    <h:commandButton action="#{calculationController.performCalculation()}"
    value="Calculate"/>
</h:form>
            </p>
        </f:view>
    </h:body>
</html>
```

The resulting JSF view looks like Figure 3-2 when displayed to the user.

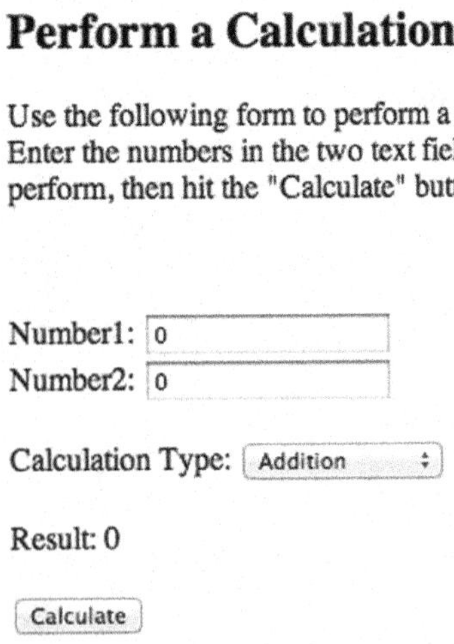

Perform a Calculation

Use the following form to perform a calculation on two numbers.
Enter the numbers in the two text fields below, and select a calculation to
perform, then hit the "Calculate" button.

Number1: 0
Number2: 0

Calculation Type: Addition

Result: 0

Calculate

Figure 3-2. Resulting JSF view page

Explanation

The JSF managed bean is responsible for providing the application logic for a JSF-based web application. Much like the JavaBean is to a JSP, the managed bean is the backbone for a JSF view. They are also referred to as *backing beans*, because there is typically one JSF managed bean per each JSF view. Managed beans have changed a bit since the JSF technology was first introduced. There used to be configuration required for each managed bean within a faces-config.xml configuration file and also within the web.xml file for use with some application servers. Starting with the release of JSF 2.0, managed beans became easier to use, and coding powerful JSF applications became easier. This example focuses on newer managed bean technology.

The example demonstrates many of the most important features of a JSF managed bean. The view components refer to the managed bean as calculationController. By default, a JSF managed bean can be referred to within a JSF view using the name of the bean class with a lowercase first letter. However, using the @Named annotation, the string that is used to reference the bean from within a view can be changed. In the example, calculationController is also used as the value passed to the @Named annotation, but it could have easily been some other string. The @Named annotation should be placed before the class declaration.

```
@Named(value = "calculationController")
```

Scopes

The bean in the example will be initialized when it is first accessed by a session and destroyed when the session is destroyed. It is a managed bean that "lives" with the session. The scope of the bean is configured by an annotation on the class, just before the class declaration. There are different annotations that can be used for each available scope. In this case, the annotation is @SessionScoped, denoting that the managed bean is session-scoped. All of the possible managed bean scopes are listed within Table 3-1.

Table 3-1. *Managed Bean Scopes*

Scope Annotation	Description
@ApplicationScoped	Specifies that a bean is application scoped. Initialized when the application is started up. Destroyed when the application is shut down. Managed beans with this scope are available to all application constructs in the same application throughout the life of a session.
@ConversationScoped	Specifies that a bean is conversation scoped. Initialized when a conversation is started and destroyed when the conversation ends. Managed beans with this scope are available throughout the life cycle of a conversation, and belong to a single HTTP session. If the HTTP session ends, all conversation contexts that were created during the session are destroyed.
@Dependent	Specifies that a bean belongs to a dependent pseudo-scope. Beans that use this scope behave differently than managed beans containing any of the other scopes.
@NormalScope	Specifies that every client executing within a certain thread sees the same contextual instance of the bean.
@RequestScoped	Specifies that a bean is request scoped. Initialized when a request to the bean is made and destroyed when the request is complete.
@SessionScoped	Specifies that a bean is session scoped. Initialized when first accessed within a session. Destroyed when the session ends. Available to all servlet requests that are made within the same session.

Prior to JSF 2.0, a managed bean had to be declared within the `faces-config.xml` file. The addition of annotations has made JSF managed beans XML configuration-free. It is important to note that the managed bean implements `java.io.Serializable`; all managed beans should be specified as `Serializable` so that they can be persisted to disk by the container if necessary.

Fields declared within a managed bean should be specified as private in order to adhere to object-oriented methodology. To make a field accessible to the public and usable from JSF views, accessor methods should be declared for it. Any field that has a corresponding "getter" and "setter" is known as a JSF managed bean *property*. Properties are available for use within JSF views by utilizing lvalue JSF EL expressions, meaning that the expression is contained within the #{ and } character sequences and that it is readable and writable. For instance, to access the field num1 that is declared within the managed bean, the JSF view can use the #{calculationController.num1} expression, as you can see in the JSF view code for the example.

Any pubic method contained within a JSF managed bean is accessible from within a JSF view using the same EL expression syntax, that is, by specifying #{beanName.methodName} as the expression. In the example, the `performCalculation` method of the managed bean is invoked from within the JSF view using an `h:commandButton` JSF component. The component action is equal to the EL expression that will invoke the JSF managed bean method. To learn more about JSF components and how to use them in view, Chapter 5.

```
<h:commandButton action="#{calculationController.performCalculation}" value="Calculate"/>
```

■ **Note**   The input form for this example contains no `action` attribute. JSF forms do not contain action attributes since JSF components within the view are responsible for specifying the action method, rather than the form itself.

JSF managed beans are a fundamental part of the JSF web framework. They provide the means for developing dynamic, robust, and sophisticated web applications with the Java platform.

Building Sophisticated JSF Views with Components

The JSF framework is bundled with a number of components. The components encapsulate all JavaScript and CSS that should be required to render elements on screen. A JSF view can contain any number of components, and they be used together to build sophisticated user interfaces.

Example

Make use of bundled JSF components to construct JSF views. JSF components contain bundled application logic and view constructs that can be used within applications by merely adding tags to a view. In the following example, several JSF components are used to create a view that displays the authors for an Apress book and allows for a new author to be added to the list. The following code is the XHTML for the JSF view:

```
<?xml version="1.0" encoding="UTF-8"?>
<!--
Example: Organizing the Presentation for a JSF View
Author: J. Juneau
-->
<!DOCTYPE html PUBLIC "-//W3C//DTD XHTML 1.0 Strict//EN" "http://www.w3.org/TR/xhtml1/DTD/
xhtml1-strict.dtd">
<html xmlns="http://www.w3.org/1999/xhtml"
      xmlns:f="http://xmlns.jcp.org/jsf/core"
      xmlns:h="http://xmlns.jcp.org/jsf/html">
```

```
<h:head>
    <meta http-equiv="Content-Type" content="text/html; charset=UTF-8"/>
    <title>ReciBuilding Sophisticated JSF Views with Components</title>
</h:head>
<h:body>
    <h:form id="componentForm">
        <h1>JSF Components, Creating a Sophisticated Page</h1>
        <p>
            The view for this page is made up entirely of JSF standard components.
            <br/>As you can see, there are many useful components bundled with JSF out of the box.
            <br/>
        </p>
        <p>Book Recommendation: Java 7 Recipes
            <br/>
            <h:graphicImage id="java7recipes" library="image" name="java7recipes.png"/>
            <br/>

            <p>
                Use the following form to add an author to the list.
            </p>
            <h:outputLabel for="newAuthorFirst" value="New Author First Name: "/>
            <h:inputText id="newAuthorFirst" value="#{authorController.newAuthorFirst}"/>
            <br/>
            <h:outputLabel for="newAuthorLast" value="New Author Last Name: "/>
            <h:inputText id="newAuthorLast" value="#{authorController.newAuthorLast}"/>
            <br/>
            <h:outputLabel for="bio" value="Bio:"/>
            <br/>
            <h:inputTextarea id="bio" cols="20" rows="5"
                             value="#{authorController.bio}"/>
            <br/>
            <br/>
            <h:commandButton id="addAuthor" action="#{authorController.addAuthor}"
                             value="Add Author"/>
            <br/>
            <br/>
            <h:dataTable id="authorTable" value="#{authorController.authorList}"
                         var="author">
                <f:facet name="header">
                    Java 7 Recipes Authors
                </f:facet>
        <h:column>
                <h:outputText id="authorName" value="#{author.first} #{author.last}"/>
        </h:column>
            </h:dataTable>
            <br/>
            <br/>
        </p>
    </h:form>
</h:body>
</html>
```

This example utilizes a JSF managed bean named AuthorController. The managed bean declares a handful of properties that are exposed in the view, and it also declares and populates a list of authors that is displayed on the page within a JSF h:dataTable component.

```
package org.javaserverfaces.chapter03;

import java.io.Serializable;
import java.util.ArrayList;
import java.util.List;
import javax.enterprise.context.SessionScoped;
import javax.inject.Named;

/**
 * @author juneau
 */
@Named(value = "authorController")
@SessionScoped
public class AuthorController implements Serializable {

    private String newAuthorFirst;
    private String newAuthorLast;
    private String bio;
    private List<Author> authorList;

    /**
     * Creates a new instance of AuthorController
     */
    public AuthorController() {
        populateAuthorList();
    }

    private void populateAuthorList(){
        System.out.println("initializng authors");
        authorList = new ArrayList<>();
        authorList.add(new Author("Josh", "Juneau", null));
        authorList.add(new Author("Carl", "Dea", null));
        authorList.add(new Author("Mark", "Beaty", null));
        authorList.add(new Author("John", "O'Conner", null));
        authorList.add(new Author("Freddy", "Guime", null));

    }

    public void addAuthor() {
        getAuthorList().add(
                new Author(this.getNewAuthorFirst(),
                        this.getNewAuthorLast(),
                        this.getBio()));
    }
```

```
/**
 * @return the authorList
 */
public List<Author> getAuthorList() {
    return authorList;
}

/**
 * @param authorList the authorList to set
 */
public void setAuthorList(List<Author> authorList) {
    this.authorList = authorList;
}

/**
 * @return the newAuthorFirst
 */
public String getNewAuthorFirst() {
    return newAuthorFirst;
}

/**
 * @param newAuthorFirst the newAuthorFirst to set
 */
public void setNewAuthorFirst(String newAuthorFirst) {
    this.newAuthorFirst = newAuthorFirst;
}

/**
 * @return the newAuthorLast
 */
public String getNewAuthorLast() {
    return newAuthorLast;
}

/**
 * @param newAuthorLast the newAuthorLast to set
 */
public void setNewAuthorLast(String newAuthorLast) {
    this.newAuthorLast = newAuthorLast;
}

/**
 * @return the bio
 */
public String getBio() {
    return bio;
}
```

```
    /**
     * @param bio the bio to set
     */
    public void setBio(String bio) {
        this.bio = bio;
    }
}
```

Finally, the Author class is used to hold instances of Author objects that are loaded into the authorList. The following code is for the Author class:

```
package org.javaserverfaces.chapter03;

/**
 * @author juneau
 */
public class Author implements java.io.Serializable {
    private String first;
    private String last;
    private String bio;

    public Author(){
        this.first = null;
        this.last = null;
        this.bio = null;
    }

    public Author(String first, String last, String bio){
        this.first = first;
        this.last = last;
        this.bio = bio;
    }
    /**
     * @return the first
     */
    public String getFirst() {
        return first;
    }

    /**
     * @param first the first to set
     */
    public void setFirst(String first) {
        this.first = first;
    }
```

```java
/**
 * @return the last
 */
public String getLast() {
    return last;
}

/**
 * @param last the last to set
 */
public void setLast(String last) {
    this.last = last;
}

/**
 * @return the bio
 */
public String getBio() {
    return bio;
}

/**
 * @param bio the bio to set
 */
public void setBio(String bio) {
    this.bio = bio;
}
}
```

The resulting web page would resemble the page shown in Figure 3-3.

JSF Components, Creating a Sophisticated Page

The view for this page is made up entirely of JSF standard components.
As you can see, there are many useful components bundled with JSF out of the box.

Book Recommendation: Java 7 Recipes

Java 7 Recipes Authors

Josh Juneau

Carl Dea

Mark Beaty

John O'Conner

Freddy Guime

Use the following form to add an author to the list.

New Author First Name:

New Author Last Name:

Figure 3-3. *Sophisticated JSF view example*

Explanation

JSF views are comprised of well-formed XML, being a mixture of HTML and JSF component tags. Any well-formed HTML can be used within a JSF view, but the components are the means by which JSF communicates with managed bean instances. There are components shipped with JSF that can be used for adding images to views, text areas, buttons, checkboxes, and much more. Moreover, there are several very good component libraries that include additional JSF components, which can be used within your applications. This example is meant to give you an overall understanding of JSF components and how they work. You can learn more details regarding JSF components and the use of external component libraries by reading the examples in Chapter 5.

The first step toward using a component within a JSF view is to declare the tag library on the page. This is done within the HTML element at the top of the page. The example declares both the JSF core component library and the JSF HTML component library within the HTML element near the top of the page. These two libraries are standard JSF component libraries that should be declared in every JSF view.

```
...
<html xmlns="http://www.w3.org/1999/xhtml"
      xmlns:f="http://xmlns.jcp.org/jsf/core"
      xmlns:h="http://xmlns.jcp.org/jsf/html">
...
```

Once a library is declared, a component from within that library can be used in the view by specifying the library namespace, along with the component you want to use. For instance, to specify an HTML element for displaying text, use the JSF h:outputText component tag, along with the various component attributes.

Prior to JSF 2.0, it was important to enclose a JSF view along with all of the components within the f:view tag. As of JSF 2.0, the tag is no longer required because the underlying Facelets view technology is part of every JSF view by default, so it takes care of specifying the view automatically. However, the f:view element can still be useful for specifying locale, content type, or encoding. Please see the online documentation for more information regarding the use of those features: http://docs.oracle.com/cd/E17802_01/j2ee/javaee/javaserverfaces/2.0/docs/pdldocs/facelets/index.html.

The <h:head> and <h:body> tags can be used to specify the header and body for a JSF web view. However, using the standard HTML <head> and <body> tags is fine also. Some Java IDEs will automatically use <h:head> and <h:body> in place of the standard HTML tags when writing JSF views. An important note is that you must enclose any content that will be treated as an HTML input form with the <h:form> JSF tag. This tag encloses a JSF form and renders an HTML form using a POST method if none is specified. No action attribute is required for a JSF form tag because the JSF managed bean action is invoked using one of the JSF action components such as h:commandButton or h:commandLink.

■ **Tip** Always specify an id for the h:form tag because the form id is added as a prefix to all JSF component tag ids when the page is rendered. For instance, if a form id of myform contained a component tag with an id of mytag, the component id will be rendered as myform:mytag. If you do not specify an id, then one will be generated for you automatically. If you want to use JavaScript to work with any of the page components, you will need to have an id specified for h:form, or you will never be able to access them.

■ **Note** This example provides a quick overview of a handful of the standard JSF components. For an in-depth explanation of JSF components and their usage, please see Chapter 5.

The standard JSF component library contains a variety of components, and a few of them are utilized in the example. The h:graphicImage tag can be used to place an image on the page and utilize a JSF managed bean if needed. The h:graphicImage tag is rendered into an HTML component, and as with all of the other JSF components, it accepts JSF EL expressions within its attributes, which allows for the rendering of dynamic images. In this example, a static image is specified with the url attribute, but an expression could also be used, making use of a JSF managed bean field. The library attribute is used to specify the directory in which the resource, in this case an image, resides.

```
<h:graphicImage id="java7recipes" library="image" name="java7recipes.png"/>
```

The h:outputLabel tag is useful for reading managed bean properties and displaying their values when the view is rendered. They are rendered as a label for a corresponding field within the view. The example utilizes static values for the h:outputLabel component, but they could include JSF expressions if needed. The h:outputText component is also useful for reading managed bean properties and displaying their values. This component renders basic text on the page. The difference between h:outputLabel and h:outputText is that they are rendered into different HTML tags. Both components can accept JSF managed bean expressions for their value attributes.

In the example, a couple of text fields are displayed on the page using the h:inputText component, which renders an input field. The value attribute for h:inputText can be set to a JSF managed bean field, which binds the text field to the corresponding managed bean property. For instance, the example includes an h:inputText component with a value of #{authorController.newAuthorFirst}, which binds the component to the newAuthorFirst property within the AuthorController class. If the field contains a value, then a value will be present within a text field when the page is rendered. If a value is entered into the corresponding text field and the form is submitted, the value will be set into the newAuthorFirst field using its setter method. The h:inputText tag allows for both reading and writing of managed bean properties because it uses lvalue JSF EL expressions. The h:inputTextarea tag is very similar to h:inputText in that it works the same way, but it renders a text area rather than a text field.

The h:commandButton component is used to render a submit button on a page. Its action attribute can be set to a JSF managed bean method. When the button is pressed, the corresponding managed bean method will be executed, and the form will be submitted. The request will be sent to the FacesServlet controller, and any properties on the page will be set. The h:commandButton used in the example has an action attribute of #{authorController.addAuthor}, which will invoke the addAuthor method within the AuthorController managed bean. As you can see from the method, when invoked it will add a new Author object to the authorList, utilizing the values that were populated within the corresponding h:inputText components for the newAuthorFirst, newAuthorLast, and bio fields. The following excerpt from the example's JSF view lists the h:commandButton component:

```
<h:commandButton id="addAuthor" action="#{authorController.addAuthor}"
                         value="Add Author"/>
```

The last component in the example that bears some explanation is the h:dataTable. This JSF component is rendered into an HTML table, and it enables developers to dynamically populate tables with collections of data from a managed bean. In the example, the h:dataTable value attribute is set to the managed bean property of #{authorController.authorList}, which maps to an instance of ArrayList that is populated with Author objects. The dataTable var attribute contains a String that will be used to reference the different objects contained within each row of the table. In the example, the var attribute is set to author, so referencing #{author.first} within the dataTable will return the value for the current Author object's first property. The dataTable in the example effectively prints out the first and last names of each Author object within the authorList. This is just a quick overview of how the JSF dataTable component works. For more details, please refer to the example focused on dataTable later in this chapter.

As you work more with constructing JSF views, you will become very familiar with the component library. The tags will become second nature, and you will be able to construct highly sophisticated views for your application. Adding external JSF component libraries into the mix along with using Ajax for updating components is the real icing on the cake! You will learn more about spreading the icing on the cake and creating beautiful and user-friendly views in Chapter 5!

Displaying Messages in JSF Pages

JSF contains a component that is devoted to the display of messages within a view. Oftentimes it is useful to display a message after a form is submitted, or after an on-screen action occurs.

Example

Add the h:messages component to your JSF view and create messages as needed within the view's managed bean using FacesMessage objects. The following JSF view contains an h:messages component tag that will render any messages that were registered with FacesContext within the corresponding page's managed bean. It also includes an h:message component that is bound to an h:inputText field. The h:message component can display messages that are specific to the corresponding text field.

```
<?xml version="1.0" encoding="UTF-8"?>
<!--
Displaying Messages in JSF Pages
Author: J. Juneau
-->
<!DOCTYPE html PUBLIC "-//W3C//DTD XHTML 1.0 Strict//EN" "http://www.w3.org/TR/xhtml1/DTD/
xhtml1-strict.dtd">
<html xmlns="http://www.w3.org/1999/xhtml"
      xmlns:f="http://xmlns.jcp.org/jsf/core"
      xmlns:h="http://xmlns.jcp.org/jsf/html">
    <h:head>
        <meta http-equiv="Content-Type" content="text/html; charset=UTF-8"/>
        <title>Displaying Messages in JSF Pages</title>
    </h:head>
    <h:body>
        <h:form id="componentForm">
            <h1>JSF Messages</h1>
            <p>
                This page contains a JSF message component below. It will display
                messages from a JSF managed bean once the bean has been initialized.
            </p>
            <h:messages errorStyle="color: red" infoStyle="color: green" globalOnly="true"/>
            <br/>
            <br/>
            Enter the word Java here:
            <h:inputText id="javaText" value="#{messageController.javaText}"/>
            <h:message for="javaText" errorStyle="color: red" infoStyle="color: green"/>
            <br/><br/>
            <h:commandButton id="addMessage" action="#{messageController.newMessage}"
                             value="New Message"/>

        </h:form>
    </h:body>
</html>
```

The managed bean in this example is named MessageController. It will create a JSF message upon initialization, and then each time the newMessage method is invoked, another message will be displayed. Also, if the text *java* is entered into the text field that corresponds to the h:inputText tag, then a success message will be displayed for that component. Otherwise, if a different value is entered into that field or if the field is left blank, then an error message will be displayed. The following listing is that of MessageController:

```java
package org.javaserverfaces.chapter03;

import java.util.Date;
import javax.enterprise.context.SessionScoped;

import javax.faces.application.FacesMessage;
import javax.faces.context.FacesContext;
import javax.inject.Named;
/**
 * @author juneau
 */
@SessionScoped
@Named
public class MessageController implements java.io.Serializable {
    int hitCounter = 0;
    private String javaText;

    /**
     * Creates a new instance of MessageController
     */
    public MessageController() {
        javaText = null;
        FacesMessage facesMsg = new FacesMessage(FacesMessage.SEVERITY_INFO, "Managed Bean
                          Initialized", null);

        FacesContext.getCurrentInstance().addMessage(null, facesMsg);
    }

    public void newMessage(){
        String hitMessage = null;
        hitCounter++;
        if(hitCounter > 1){
            hitMessage = hitCounter + " times";
        } else {
            hitMessage = hitCounter + " time";
        }

        Date currDate = new Date();
        FacesMessage facesMsg = new FacesMessage(FacesMessage.SEVERITY_ERROR,
                "You've pressed that button " + hitMessage + "! The current date and time: "
                + currDate, null);
        FacesContext.getCurrentInstance().addMessage(null, facesMsg);
```

```
        if (getJavaText().equalsIgnoreCase("java")){
            FacesMessage javaTextMsg = new FacesMessage(FacesMessage.SEVERITY_INFO,
                "Good Job, that is the correct text!", null);
            FacesContext.getCurrentInstance().addMessage("componentForm:javaText", javaTextMsg);
        } else {
            FacesMessage javaTextMsg = new FacesMessage(FacesMessage.SEVERITY_ERROR,
                "Sorry, that is NOT the correct text!", null);
            FacesContext.getCurrentInstance().addMessage("componentForm:javaText", javaTextMsg);
        }
    }

    /**
     * @return the javaText
     */
    public String getJavaText() {
        return javaText;
    }

    /**
     * @param javaText the javaText to set
     */
    public void setJavaText(String javaText) {
        this.javaText = javaText;
    }
}
```

The message will be displayed on the page in red text if it is an error message and in green text if it is an informational message. In this example, the initialization message is printed green, and the update message is printed in red.

Explanation

It is always a good idea to relay messages to application users, especially in the event that some action needs to be taken by the user. The JSF framework provides an easy façade that allows messages to be added to a view from the JSF managed bean. To use the façade, add the h:message component to a view for displaying messages that are bound to specific components, and add the h:messages component to a view for displaying messages that are not bound to specific components. The h:message component contains a number of attributes that can be used to customize message output and other things. It can be bound to a component within the same view by specifying that component's id in the for attribute of h:message. The most important attributes for the h:message component are as follows:

- id: Specifies a unique identifier for the component

- rendered: Specifies whether the message is rendered

- errorStyle: Specifies the CSS styles to be applied to error messages

- errorClass: Indicates the CSS class to apply to error messages

- infoStyle: Specifies the CSS styles to be applied to informational messages

- infoClass: Indicates the CSS class to apply to informational messages

- for: Specifies the component for which the message belongs

For a list of all attributes available for the h:message component, please refer to the online documentation. In the example, the h:message component is bound to the h:inputText component with an id of javaText. When the page is submitted, the newMessage method within the MessageController class is invoked. That method is used in this example for generating messages to display on the page. If the text entered within the javaText property matches Java, then a successful message will be printed on the page. To create a message, an instance of the javax.faces.application.FacesMessage class is generated, passing three parameters that correspond to message severity, message summary, and message detail. A FacesMessage object can be created without passing any parameters, but usually it is more productive to pass the message into the constructor at the time of instantiation. The general format for creating a FacesMessage object is as follows:

```
new FacesMessage(FacesMessage.severity severity, String summary, String detail)
```

Passing a static field from the FacesMessage class specifies the message severity. Table 3-2 shows the possible message severity values along with their descriptions.

Table 3-2. *FacesMessage Severity Values*

Severity	Description
SEVERITY_ERROR	Indicates that an error has occurred
SEVERITY_FATAL	Indicates that a serious error has occurred
SEVERITY_INFO	Indicates an informational message rather than an error
SEVERITY_WARN	Indicates that an error may have occurred

In the example, if the value entered for the javaText property equals Java, then an informational message is created. Otherwise, an error message is created. In either case, once the message is created, then it needs to be passed into the current context using FacesContext.getCurrentInstance().addMessage(String componentId, FacesMessage message). In the example, the method is called, passing a component ID of componentForm:javaText. This refers to the component within the JSF view that has an ID of javaText (h:inputText component). The componentForm identifier belongs to the form (h:form component) that contains the h:inputText component, so in reality the h:inputText component is nested within the h:form component. To reference a nested component, combine component IDs using a colon as a delimiter. The following is an excerpt from the example, demonstrating how to create a message and send it to the h:message component:

```
FacesMessage javaTextMsg = new FacesMessage(FacesMessage.SEVERITY_ERROR,
              "Sorry, that is NOT the correct text!", null);
FacesContext.getCurrentInstance().addMessage("componentForm:javaText", javaTextMsg);
```

The h:messages component can be used for displaying all messages that pertain to a view, or it can be used for displaying only non-component-related messages by using the globalOnly attribute. All other attributes for h:messages are very similar to the h:message component. By indicating a true value for the globalOnly attribute, you are telling the component to ignore any component-specific messages. Therefore, any FacesMessage that is sent to a specific component will not be displayed by h:messages. In the example, the message that is displayed by h:messages is generated in the same manner as the component-specific message, with the exception of specifying a specific component to which the message belongs. The following excerpt demonstrates sending an error message to the h:messages component. Note that the last argument that is sent to the FacesMessage call is a null value. This argument should be the clientId specification, and by setting it to null, you are indicating that there is no specified client identifier. Therefore, the message should be a global message rather than tied to a specific component.

```
FacesMessage facesMsg = new FacesMessage(FacesMessage.SEVERITY_ERROR,
            "You've pressed that button " + hitMessage + "! The current date and time: "
            + currDate, null);
FacesContext.getCurrentInstance().addMessage(null, facesMsg);
```

Displaying the appropriate message at the right time within an application is very important. By utilizing FacesMessages objects and displaying them using either the h:message or h:messages component, you can ensure that your application users will be well informed of the application state.

Navigation Based Upon Conditions

JSF allows you to construct a series of navigational cases based upon a condition. Moreover, the framework provides more than one technique for doing so.

Example

JSF provides the following techniques for performing navigation within JSF applications:

- Utilize explicit navigation through the use of a JSF managed bean method along with a corresponding faces-config.xml configuration file to control the navigation for your application.

- Use implicit navigation for specifying the next view to render from within the managed bean.

- Use implicit navigation by specifying the name of the view to render as the action attribute of a component tag, bypassing the managed bean altogether.

This example consists of four JSF views, and each one contains h:commandButton components that invoke navigation to another view. The h:commandButton components are linked to managed bean methods that are present within the view's corresponding managed bean named NavigationController. The first view listed here contains two h:commandButton components, each of which invokes a method within the managed bean named NavigationController. The first button utilizes explicit JSF navigation, and the second uses implicit navigation.

```
<?xml version="1.0" encoding="UTF-8"?>
<!--
Author: J. Juneau
-->
<!DOCTYPE html PUBLIC "-//W3C//DTD XHTML 1.0 Strict//EN" "http://www.w3.org/TR/xhtml1/DTD/
xhtml1-strict.dtd">
<html xmlns="http://www.w3.org/1999/xhtml"
    xmlns:f="http://xmlns.jcp.org/jsf/core"
    xmlns:h="http://xmlns.jcp.org/jsf/html">
    <h:head>
        <meta http-equiv="Content-Type" content="text/html; charset=UTF-8"/>
        <title>Navigation Example</title>
    </h:head>
```

```
    <h:body>
        <h:form id="componentForm">
            <h1>JSF Navigation - Page 1</h1>
            <p>
                Clicking the submit button below will take you to Page #2.
            </p>

            <br/>
            <h:commandButton id="navButton" action="#{navigationController.pageTwo}"
                             value="Go To Page 2"/>
            <br/>
            <br/>
            <h:commandButton id="navButton2" action="#{navigationController.nextPage}"
                             value="Implicitly Navigate to Page 3"/>

        </h:form>
    </h:body>
</html>
```

The source for the second JSF view is very similar, except that a different managed bean method is specified within the action attribute of the view's h:commandButton component.

```
<?xml version="1.0" encoding="UTF-8"?>
<!--
Author: J. Juneau
-->
<!DOCTYPE html PUBLIC "-//W3C//DTD XHTML 1.0 Strict//EN" "http://www.w3.org/TR/xhtml1/DTD/
xhtml1-strict.dtd">
<html xmlns="http://www.w3.org/1999/xhtml"
    xmlns:f="http://xmlns.jcp.org/jsf/core"
    xmlns:h="http://xmlns.jcp.org/jsf/html">
    <h:head>
        <meta http-equiv="Content-Type" content="text/html; charset=UTF-8"/>
        <title>JSF Navigation</title>
    </h:head>
    <h:body>
        <h:form id="componentForm">
            <h1>JSF Navigation - Page 2</h1>
            <p>
                Clicking the submit button below will take you to Page #1.
            </p>

            <br/>
            <h:commandButton id="navButton" action="#{navigationController.pageOne}"
                             value="Go To Page 1"/>
        </h:form>
    </h:body>
</html>
```

The third JSF view contains an h:commandButton component that invokes a managed bean action and utilizes conditional navigation, rendering pages depending upon a conditional outcome within the faces-config.xml.

```
<?xml version="1.0" encoding="UTF-8"?>
<!--
Author: J. Juneau
-->
<!DOCTYPE html PUBLIC "-//W3C//DTD XHTML 1.0 Strict//EN" "http://www.w3.org/TR/xhtml1/DTD/
xhtml1-strict.dtd">
<html xmlns="http://www.w3.org/1999/xhtml"
      xmlns:f="http://xmlns.jcp.org/jsf/core"
      xmlns:h="http://xmlns.jcp.org/jsf/html">
    <h:head>
        <meta http-equiv="Content-Type" content="text/html; charset=UTF-8"/>
        <title>JSF Navigation</title>
    </h:head>
    <h:body>
        <h:form id="componentForm">
            <h1>JSF Navigation - Page 3</h1>
            <p>
                The button below will utilize conditional navigation to take a user
                to the next page.
            </p>

            <br/>
            <h:commandButton id="loginButton" action="#{navigationController.login}"
                             value="Login Action"/>
        </h:form>
    </h:body>
</html>
```

Lastly, the fourth JSF view in the navigational example application contains an h:commandButton that invokes a method and uses implicit navigation to return to the third JSF view, specifying the view name within the action attribute directly and bypassing the managed bean altogether.

```
<?xml version="1.0" encoding="UTF-8"?>
<!--
Author: J. Juneau
-->
<!DOCTYPE html PUBLIC "-//W3C//DTD XHTML 1.0 Strict//EN" "http://www.w3.org/TR/xhtml1/DTD/
xhtml1-strict.dtd">
<html xmlns="http://www.w3.org/1999/xhtml"
      xmlns:f="http://xmlns.jcp.org/jsf/core"
      xmlns:h="http://xmlns.jcp.org/jsf/html">
    <h:head>
        <meta http-equiv="Content-Type" content="text/html; charset=UTF-8"/>
        <title>JSF Navigation</title>
    </h:head>
```

```
    <h:body>
        <h:form id="componentForm">
            <h1>JSF Navigation - Page 4</h1>
            <p>
                Clicking the submit button below will take you to Page #1 using conditional
                navigation rules.
            </p>

            <br/>
            <h:commandButton id="navButton2" action="navigation3"
                             value="Implicitly Navigate to Page 3"/>
        </h:form>
    </h:body>
</html>
```

Now let's take a look at the source listing for `NavigationController`. It contains the methods that are specified within each page's `h:commandButton` `action` attribute. Some of the methods return a `String` value, and others do not. However, after the methods are invoked, then the `FacesServlet` processes the request, and the `faces-config.xml` configuration file is traversed, if needed, to determine the next view to render.

```java
package org.javaserverfaces.chapter03;

import javax.enterprise.context.RequestScoped;
import javax.inject.Named;

/**
 * @author juneau
 */
@Named(value = "navigationController")
@RequestScoped
public class NavigationController implements java.io.Serializable{

    private boolean authenticated = false;

    /**
     * Creates a new instance of NavigationController
     */
    public NavigationController() {
    }

    public String pageOne(){
        return "PAGE_1";
    }

    public String pageTwo(){
        return "PAGE_2";
    }
```

```java
    /**
     * Utilizing implicit navigation, a page name can be returned from an
     * action method rather than listing a navigation-rule within faces-config.xml
     * @return
     */
    public String nextPage(){
        // Perform some task, then implicitly list a page to render

        return "navigation3";
    }

    /**
     * Demonstrates the use of conditional navigation
     */
    public void login(){
        // Perform some task and then return boolean
        setAuthenticated(true);
        System.out.println("Here");
    }

    /**
     * @return the authenticated
     */
    public boolean isAuthenticated() {
        return authenticated;
    }

    /**
     * @param authenticated the authenticated to set
     */
    public void setAuthenticated(boolean authenticated) {
        this.authenticated = authenticated;
    }
}
```

At the heart of the navigation is the faces-config.xml file. It specifies which view should be displayed after a corresponding outcome. Two of the navigation-rules use standard JSF navigation, and the last navigation-rule makes use of conditional navigation.

```xml
<?xml version='1.0' encoding='UTF-8'?>

<!-- =========== FULL CONFIGURATION FILE =================================== -->

<faces-config version="2.2"
              xmlns="http://xmlns.jcp.org/xml/ns/javaee"
              xmlns:xsi="http://www.w3.org/2001/XMLSchema-instance"
              xsi:schemaLocation="http://xmlns.jcp.org/xml/ns/javaee
http://xmlns.jcp.org/xml/ns/javaee/web-facesconfig_2_2.xsd">
```

```
<navigation-rule>
    <from-view-id>/chapter03/navigation1.xhtml</from-view-id>
    <navigation-case>
        <from-outcome>PAGE_2/from-outcome>
        <to-view-id>/chapter03/navigation2.xhtml</to-view-id>
    </navigation-case>
</navigation-rule>

<navigation-rule>
    <from-view-id>/chapter03/navigation2.xhtml</from-view-id>
    <navigation-case>
        <from-outcome>PAGE_1</from-outcome>
        <to-view-id>/chapter03/navigation1.xhtml</to-view-id>
    </navigation-case>
</navigation-rule>

<navigation-rule>
    <navigation-case>
        <from-action>#{navigationController.login}</from-action>
        <if>#{navigationController.authenticated}</if>
        <to-view-id>/chapter03/navigation4.xhtml</to-view-id>
        <redirect/>
    </navigation-case>
</navigation-rule>
</faces-config>
```

Explanation

One of the most daunting tasks when building a web application is to determine the overall page navigation. Many web frameworks have instituted XML configuration files for organizing page navigation. This holds true for the JavaServer Faces web framework, and the navigational XML is placed within a JSF application's faces-config.xml configuration file. When using standard navigation, JSF utilizes navigation rules to determine which view to render based upon the outcome of page actions. If using standard JSF navigation, when a page action occurs, the managed bean method that is associated with the action can return a String value. That value is then evaluated using the navigational rules that are defined within the faces-config.xml file and used to determine which page to render next.

The standard navigation infrastructure works well in most cases, but in some instances it makes more sense to directly list the next page to be rendered within the managed bean, rather than making a navigation rule in the configuration file. When a managed bean action is invoked, it can return the name of a view, without the .xhtml suffix. Such navigation was introduced with the release of JSF 2.0, and it is known as *implicit navigation*. As shown in the fourth example, you can also perform implicit navigation by specifying the name of a view without the suffix for an action attribute of the component tag.

Yet another type of navigation was introduced with JSF 2.0, taking navigation to the next level by allowing the use of JSF EL expressions within the faces-config.xml navigation rules. Conditional navigation allows for an <if> element to be specified within the navigational rule, which corresponds to a JSF EL condition. If the condition evaluates to true, then the specified view is rendered.

Navigation rules are constructed in XML residing within the faces-config.xml descriptor, and each rule has a root element of navigation-rule. Within each rule construct, the from-view-id element should contain the name of the view from which the action method was invoked. A series of navigation-cases should follow the from-view-id element. Each navigation-case contains a from-outcome element, which should be set to a String value corresponding to the String value that is returned from a subsequent action method. For instance, when the pageOne method is invoked in the example, the String "PAGE_1" is returned, and it should be specified within the from-outcome element within a navigation-case in the faces-config.xml file. Lastly, the to-view-id element should follow the from-outcome element within the navigation-case, and it should specify which view to render if the String in from-outcome is returned from the action method. The following excerpt shows the standard navigation rule that allows for navigation from page 1 to page 2 of the application:

```
<navigation-rule>
        <from-view-id>/chapter03/navigation1.xhtml</from-view-id>
        <navigation-case>
            <from-outcome>PAGE_1</from-outcome>
            <to-view-id>/chapter03/navigation2.xhtml</to-view-id>
        </navigation-case>
</navigation-rule>
```

Implicit navigation does not require any XML navigation rules to be declared. The action method that is invoked via an h:commandButton returns a String that is equal to the name of the view that should be rendered next. In the example, the second h:commandButton on view 1 invokes the nextPage managed bean method, which returns the name of the next view that should be rendered.

```
public String nextPage(){
        // Perform some task, then implicitly list a page to render

        return "navigation3";
}
```

If you want to use implicit navigation, you can bypass the managed bean altogether and specify the name of the view that you want to render directly within the action attribute of h:commandButton or h:commandLink. The fourth JSF view in the example demonstrates this technique.

The third view in the example, named navigation3.xhtml, demonstrates conditional navigation. Its h:commandButton action invokes the login method within the NavigationController managed bean. That method does not contain much business logic in this example, but it does set the bean's authenticated field equal to true. Imagine that someone entered an incorrect password and failed to authenticate; in such a case, then the authenticated field would be set to false. After the login method is executed, the faces-config.xml file is parsed for the next view to render, and the conditional navigation rule utilizes JSF EL to specify the navigation condition. The from-action element is set equal to the JSF EL that is used to invoke the login method, and an <if> element is specified, referencing the navigationController.authenticated field via JSF EL. If that field is equal to true, then the view specified within the to-view-id element will be rendered. Note that the <redirect/> is required to tell JSF to redirect to the view listed in the <to-view-id> element since JSF uses a redirect rather than a forward.

```
<navigation-rule>
        <navigation-case>
            <from-action>#{navigationController.login}</from-action>
            <if>#{navigationController.authenticated}</if>
            <to-view-id>/chapter03/navigation4.xhtml</to-view-id>
            <redirect/>
        </navigation-case>
    </navigation-rule>
</faces-config>
```

Standard JSF navigation allows enough flexibility for most cases, and its architecture is much more sophisticated than other web frameworks. However, in JSF 2.0, two new navigational techniques known as *implicit* and *conditional navigation* were introduced. With the addition of the new techniques, JSF navigation is more robust and easier to manage.

Updating Messages Without Recompiling

JSF makes it possible to specify the messages within a property file so that they can be edited on the fly. If a message is hard coded as a String, then the code must be recompiled if the message requires a change.

Example

A resource bundle can be used to specify your application messages. Then retrieve the messages from the bundle and add them to the FacesMessages objects rather than hard-coding a String value. In the example that follows, a resource bundle is used to specify a message that is to be displayed on a page. If you need to change the message at any time, simply modify the resource bundle and reload the page in the browser.

The following code is for a JSF view that contains the h:messages component for displaying the message from a corresponding managed bean:

```xml
<?xml version="1.0" encoding="UTF-8"?>
<!--
Author: J. Juneau
-->
<!DOCTYPE html PUBLIC "-//W3C//DTD XHTML 1.0 Strict//EN"
"http://www.w3.org/TR/xhtml1/DTD/xhtml1-strict.dtd">
<html xmlns="http://www.w3.org/1999/xhtml"
      xmlns:f="http://xmlns.jcp.org/jsf/core"
      xmlns:h="http://xmlns.jcp.org/jsf/html">
    <h:head>
        <meta http-equiv="Content-Type" content="text/html; charset=UTF-8"/>
        <title>Specifying Updatable Messages</title>
    </h:head>
    <h:body>
        <h:form id="componentForm">
            <h1>Utilizing a resource bundle</h1>
            <p>
                The message below is displayed from a resource bundle. The h:outputText
                component has been added to the page only to instantiate the bean for this
                example. To change the message, simply modify the corresponding message within the
                bundle and then refresh the page.
            </p>
            <h:outputText id="exampleProperty" value="#{exampleController.exampleProperty}"/>
            <br/>
            <h:messages errorStyle="color: red" infoStyle="color: green" globalOnly="true"/>
        </h:form>
    </h:body>
</html>
```

Next, the managed bean class is responsible for creating the message and sending it to the h:messages component via the FacesContext. The following source is for ExampleController, which is the managed bean for the JSF view in this example:

```java
package org.javaserverfaces.chapter03;

import java.util.ResourceBundle;
import javax.enterprise.context.RequestScoped;

import javax.faces.application.FacesMessage;
import javax.faces.context.FacesContext;
import javax.inject.Named;

@Named(value = "exampleController")
@RequestScoped
public class ExampleController {
    private String exampleProperty;

    /**
     * Creates a new instance of ExampleController
     */
    public ExampleController() {
        exampleProperty = "Used to instantiate the bean.";
        FacesMessage facesMsg = new FacesMessage(FacesMessage.SEVERITY_INFO,
                ResourceBundle.getBundle("/org/javaserverfaces/chapter03/Bundle").
                getString("ExampleMessage"), null);
        FacesContext.getCurrentInstance().addMessage(null, facesMsg);
    }

    /**
     * @return the exampleProperty
     */
    public String getExampleProperty() {
        return exampleProperty;
    }

    /**
     * @param exampleProperty the exampleProperty to set
     */
    public void setExampleProperty(String exampleProperty) {
        this.exampleProperty = exampleProperty;
    }
}
```

The resource bundle, which contains the message, is read by the managed bean to obtain the message. If you want to update the message, you can do so without recompiling any code.

```
# This file is an example resource bundle
ExampleMessage=This message can be changed by updating the message bundle!
```

When the page is loaded, the h:outputText component instantiates ExampleController, which in turn creates the FacesMessage objects that are used to display the message on the screen.

Explanation

Oftentimes it is useful to have the ability to update custom system or user messages rather than hard-coding them. This could be useful in the case that some custom information that is contained within a particular message may have the possibility of changing in the future. It'd be nice to simply update the message in text format rather than editing the code, recompiling, and redeploying your application. It is possible to create updateable messages using a resource bundle. A resource bundle is simply a properties file, which contains name-value pairs. When adding custom messages to a bundle, name the message appropriately and then add the custom message as the value portion of the property. An application can then look up the property by name and utilize its value. In this case, the value is a `String` that will be used to create a `FacesMessage` instance.

In the example, the bundle contains a property named `ExampleMessage`, along with a corresponding value. When the JSF view is loaded into the browser, the `ExampleController` managed bean is instantiated, causing its constructor to be executed. A `FacesMessage` instance is created, generating a message of type `FacesMessage.SEVERITY_INFO`, and it reads the resource bundle and obtains the value for the `ExampleMessage` property. The following excerpt demonstrates how to obtain a specified message value from the resource bundle:

```
ResourceBundle.getBundle("/org/javaserverfaces/chapter03/Bundle").getString("ExampleMessage"), null);
```

After the message is created, it is added to the current instance of `FacesContext` and, subsequently, displayed on the page when it is rendered. Using a resource bundle to specify your messages can make life much easier because you'll no longer be required to recompile code in order to update such messages.

Validating User Input

It is imperative to validate any data that is entered into a JSF form before it. JSF provides a powerful mechanism for validating input via the validator API.

Example

To utilize a JSF validator, register a validator on any text field components or other input components that need to be validated. Use predefined JSF validators where applicable, and create custom validator classes when needed. The example utilizes predefined validators for two `h:inputText` components in order to ensure that the values entered into them are of proper length. A custom validator is added to a third text field, and it is responsible for ensuring that the text contains a specified `String`. The three fields make up an employee input form, and when an employee is entered and the data validates successfully, a new `Employee` object is created and added to a list of employees. An `h:dataTable` element in the view is used to display the list of employees if there are any. This is perhaps not the most true-to-life example, but you can apply the basic philosophy to validate real-world needs within your own applications.

The following listing is for the JSF view that constructs the employee input form, including the validation tags for each input text field:

```
<?xml version="1.0" encoding="UTF-8"?>
<!--
Author: J. Juneau
-->
<!DOCTYPE html PUBLIC "-//W3C//DTD XHTML 1.0 Strict//EN" "http://www.w3.org/TR/xhtml1/DTD/
xhtml1-strict.dtd">
<html xmlns="http://www.w3.org/1999/xhtml"
      xmlns:f="http://xmlns.jcp.org/jsf/core"
      xmlns:h="http://xmlns.jcp.org/jsf/html">
    <h:head>
        <meta http-equiv="Content-Type" content="text/html; charset=UTF-8"/>
        <title>Validating Data</title>
    </h:head>
    <h:body>
        <h:form id="employeeForm">
            <h1>Java Developer Employee Information</h1>
            <br/>
            <h:messages globalOnly="true" errorStyle="color: red" infoStyle="color: green"/>
            <br/>
            <h:dataTable id="empTable" var="emp"
                        border="1" value="#{employeeController.employeeList}"
                        rendered="#{employeeController.employeeList.size() > 0}">
                <f:facet name="header">
                    Current Employees
                </f:facet>
                <h:column id="empNameCol">
                    <f:facet name="header">Employee</f:facet>
                    <h:outputText id="empName" value="#{emp.employeeFirst} #{emp.employeeLast}"/>
                </h:column>
                <h:column id="titleCol">
                    <f:facet name="header">Title</f:facet>
                    <h:outputText id="title" value="#{emp.employeeTitle}"/>
                </h:column>

            </h:dataTable>
            <p>
                Please use the form below to insert employee information.
            </p>
            <h:panelGrid columns="3">
                <h:outputLabel for="employeeFirst" value="First: />
                <h:inputText id="employeeFirst" value="#{employeeController.employeeFirst}">
                    <f:validateLength minimum="3" maximum="30"/>
                </h:inputText>
                <h:message for="employeeFirst" errorStyle="color:red"/>
```

```
                    <h:outputLabel for="employeeLast" value="Last: " />
                    <h:inputText id="employeeLast" value="#{employeeController.employeeLast}">
                        <f:validateLength minimum="3" maximum="30"/>
                    </h:inputText>
                    <h:message for="employeeLast" errorStyle="color:red"/>

                    <h:outputLabel for="employeeTitle" value="Title (Must be a Java Position): " />
                    <h:inputText id="employeeTitle" value="#{employeeController.employeeTitle}">
                        <f:validator validatorId="employeeTitleValidate" />
                    </h:inputText>
                    <h:message for="employeeTitle" errorStyle="color:red"/>

            </h:panelGrid>
            <h:commandButton id="employeeInsert" action="#{employeeController.insertEmployee}"
                            value="Insert Employee"/>
        </h:form>
    </h:body>
</html>
```

The third h:inputText component in the view utilizes a custom validator. The f:validator tag is used to specify a custom validator, and its validatorId attribute is used to specify a corresponding validator class. The following listing is the Java code for a class named EmployeeTitleValidate, the custom validation class for the text field:

```java
package org.javaserverfaces.chapter03;

import java. util.Date;
import java.util.Locale;
import java.util.ResourceBundle;
import javax.faces.application.FacesMessage;
import javax.faces.component.UIComponent;
import javax.faces.context.FacesContext;
import javax.faces.validator.FacesValidator;
import javax.faces.validator.Validator;
import javax.faces.validator.ValidatorException;

/**
 *
 * @author juneau
 */
@FacesValidator("employeeTitleValidate")
public class EmployeeTitleValidate implements Validator {

    @Override
    public void validate(FacesContext facesContext, UIComponent uiComponent, Object value)
            throws ValidatorException {

        checkTitle(value);

    }
```

```
        private void checkTitle(Object value) {
            String title = value.toString();
            if (!title.contains("Java")) {
                String messageText = "Title does not include the word Java";
                throw new ValidatorException(new FacesMessage(FacesMessage.SEVERITY_ERROR,
                        messageText, messageText));
            }
        }
    }
}
```

Now let's take a look at the JSF managed bean for the JSF view that contains the validation tags. The managed bean class is named EmployeeController, and the action method, insertEmployee, is used to add new Employee objects containing valid data to an ArrayList.

```
package org.javaserverfaces.chapter03;

import java.io.Serializable;
import java.util.ArrayList;
import java.util.List;
import java.util.ResourceBundle;
import javax.faces.bean.SessionScoped;
import javax.faces.application.FacesMessage;
import javax.faces.context.FacesContext;
import javax.faces.bean.ManagedBean;


/**
 * @author juneau
 */
@ManagedBean(name = "employeeController")
@SessionScoped
public class EmployeeController implements Serializable {

    private String employeeFirst;
    private String employeeLast;
    private String employeeTitle;

    private List <Employee> employeeList;

    public EmployeeController(){
        employeeFirst = null;
        employeeLast = null;
        employeeTitle = null;
        employeeList = new ArrayList();
    }
```

```java
public void insertEmployee(){
    Employee emp = new Employee(employeeFirst,
                                employeeLast,
                                employeeTitle);
    employeeList.add(emp);
    FacesMessage facesMsg = new FacesMessage(FacesMessage.SEVERITY_INFO, "Employee Successfully
                                             Added", null);
    FacesContext.getCurrentInstance().addMessage(null, facesMsg);
}

/**
 * @return the employeeFirst
 */
public String getEmployeeFirst() {
    return employeeFirst;
}

/**
 * @param employeeFirst the employeeFirst to set
 */
public void setEmployeeFirst(String employeeFirst) {
    this.employeeFirst = employeeFirst;
}

/**
 * @return the employeeLast
 */
public String getEmployeeLast() {
    return employeeLast;
}

/**
 * @param employeeLast the employeeLast to set
 */
public void setEmployeeLast(String employeeLast) {
    this.employeeLast = employeeLast;
}

/**
 * @return the employeeTitle
 */
public String getEmployeeTitle() {
    return employeeTitle;
}

/**
 * @param employeeTitle the employeeTitle to set
 */
public void setEmployeeTitle(String employeeTitle) {
    this.employeeTitle = employeeTitle;
}
```

```
    /**
     * @return the employeeList
     */
    public List <Employee> getEmployeeList() {
        return employeeList;
    }

    /**
     * @param employeeList the employeeList to set
     */
    public void setEmployeeList(List <Employee> employeeList) {
        this.employeeList = employeeList;
    }
}
```

Finally, the Employee class is a POJO that declares three fields: employeeFirst, employeeLast, and employeeTitle. Each of these three fields is declared as private, and there are accessor methods that are used by the JSF view for accessing the fields.

```
package org.javaserverfaces.chapter03;

import java.io.Serializable;

/**
 * @author juneau
 */
public class Employee implements Serializable {
    private String employeeFirst;
    private String employeeLast;
    private String employeeTitle;

    /**
     * Creates a new instance of EmployeeController
     */
    public Employee() {
        employeeFirst = null;
        employeeLast = null;
        employeeTitle = null;
    }

    public Employee(String first, String last, String title){
        employeeFirst = first;
        employeeLast = last;
        employeeTitle = title;
    }
    /**
     * @return the employeeFirst
     */
    public String getEmployeeFirst() {
        return employeeFirst;
    }
```

```java
/**
 * @param employeeFirst the employeeFirst to set
 */
public void setEmployeeFirst(String employeeFirst) {
    this.employeeFirst = employeeFirst;
}
/**
 * @return the employeeLast
 */
public String getEmployeeLast() {
    return employeeLast;
}

/**
 * @param employeeLast the employeeLast to set
 */
public void setEmployeeLast(String employeeLast) {
    this.employeeLast = employeeLast;
}

/**
 * @return the employeeTitle
 */
public String getEmployeeTitle() {
    return employeeTitle;
}

/**
 * @param employeeTitle the employeeTitle to set
 */
public void setEmployeeTitle(String employeeTitle) {
    this.employeeTitle = employeeTitle;
}
}
```

In the end, the validators will raise exceptions if a user attempts to enter an employee first or last name using an invalid length or a title that does not contain the word *Java*. When user input validation fails, error messages are displayed next to the components containing the invalid entries.

Explanation

The JSF framework contains many features that make it more convenient for developers to customize their applications. Validators are one of those features, because they can be used to solidify application data and ensure data is correct before storing in a database or other data store. The JSF framework ships with a good deal of validators that are already implemented. To use these predefined validators, simply embed the appropriate validator tag within a component tag in a view to validate that component's data values. Sometimes there are cases where the standard validators will not do the trick. In such cases, JSF provides a means for developing custom validator classes that can be used from within a view in the same manner as the predefined validators.

In the example, two of the h:inputText components contain standard JSF validators used to validate the length of the values entered. The f:validateLength tag can be embedded into a component for String length validation, and the tag's minimum and maximum attributes can be populated with the minimum and maximum String length, respectively. As mentioned previously, JSF ships with a good number of these predefined validators. All that the developer is required to do is embed the validator tags within the components that they want to validate. Table 3-3 lists all standard validator tags and what they do. For a detailed look at each of the validator attributes, please see the online documentation.

Table 3-3. *Standard Validators*

Validator Tag	Description
validateLength	Checks the length of a String
validateLongRange	Checks the range of a numeric value
validateDoubleRange	Checks the range of a floating-point value
validateRequired	Ensures the input field is not empty (also an alternative to using the required attribute on an input field component tag)
validateRegex	Validates the component against a given regular expression pattern

Oftentimes, there is a need for some other type of validation to take place for a specified component. In such cases, developing a custom validator class may be the best choice. Many developers shy away from writing their own validators, because it seems to be a daunting task at first glance. However, JSF 2.0 took great strides toward making custom validator classes easier to write and understand.

To create a custom validator class, implement the javax.faces.validator.Validator class. Annotate the validator class with the @FacesValidator annotation, specifying the string you want to use for registering your validator within the f:validator tag. In the example, the name used to reference the validator class is employeeTitleValidate. The only requirement is that the validator class overrides the validate method, which is where the custom validation takes place. The validate method contains the following signature:

```
public void validate(FacesContext facesContext, UIComponent uiComponent, Object value)
            throws ValidatorException
```

Utilizing the parameters that are passed into the method, you can obtain the current FacesContext, a handle on the component being validated, as well as the component's value. In the example, a helper method is called from within the validate method, and it is used to check the component's value and ensure that the word *Java* is contained somewhere within it. If it does not validate successfully, a ValidatorException is created and thrown. The message that is placed within the ValidatorException is what will appear next to the component being validated if the validation fails. The following excerpt from the validation class demonstrates creating and throwing a ValidatorException:

```
throw new ValidatorException(new FacesMessage(FacesMessage.SEVERITY_ERROR,
                messageText, messageText));
```

So, when does the validation occur? That is the key to the validator, isn't it? The answer is immediately, before the request is sent to the managed bean action method. Any validation occurs during the *process validation* phase, and if one or more components being validated within a view throws a ValidatorException, then the processing stops, and the request is not sent to the action method. When the user clicks the submit button, the validation takes place first, and if everything is OK, then the request is passed to the action method.

■ **Note** A means of validating that an input component simply contains a value is to use the `required` attribute. The `required` attribute of input component tags can be set to `true` in order to force a value to be entered for that component.

The validation of components within a JSF view using standard validators can really save a developer some time and increase the usability and accountability of an application. The ability to create custom validators allows validation to be performed for any scenario. Be constructive, use validation on all of your application's input forms, and create custom validators to perform validation using unique techniques. Your application users will appreciate it!

Evaluation of Page Expressions Immediately

By convention, component validation occurs after a form has been submitted. However, there are circumstances in which it makes sense to perform validation prior to form submission. JSF makes it possible to do so, and you can enable that behavior by specifying the `immediate` and `onchange` component attributes.

Example

To perform immediate validation, specify `true` for the component tag's `immediate` attribute, and also specify the component's `onchange` attribute and set it equal to `submit()`. This will cause the input form to be submitted immediately when the value for the component is changed, and JSF will skip the render response phase when doing so and will execute all components that specify an `immediate` attribute set to `true` during the Apply Request Values phase. The example uses the same employee form that was demonstrated in a previous example. However, instead of waiting until the form is submitted, the first and last `h:inputText` components will be evaluated and validated during the Apply Request Values phase immediately when their values change. The following source is for the JSF view named `immediateValidation.xhtml`:

```
<?xml version="1.0" encoding="UTF-8"?>
<!--
Author: J. Juneau
-->
<!DOCTYPE html PUBLIC "-//W3C//DTD XHTML 1.0 Strict//EN" "http://www.w3.org/TR/xhtml1/DTD/
xhtml1-strict.dtd">
<html xmlns="http://www.w3.org/1999/xhtml"
      xmlns:f="http://xmlns.jcp.org/jsf/core"
      xmlns:h="http://xmlns.jcp.org/jsf/html">
    <h:head>
        <meta http-equiv="Content-Type" content="text/html; charset=UTF-8"/>
        <title>Immediate View Evaluation</title>
    </h:head>
    <h:body>
        <h:form id="employeeForm">
            <h1>Java Developer Employee Information</h1>
            <br/>
            <h:messages globalOnly="true" errorStyle="color: red" infoStyle="color: green"/>
            <br/>
```

```
<h:dataTable id="empTable" var="emp"
             border="1" value="#{employeeController.employeeList}"
             rendered="#{employeeController.employeeList.size() > 0}">
    <f:facet name="header">
        Current Employees
    </f:facet>
    <h:column id="empNameCol">
        <f:facet name="header">Employee</f:facet>
        <h:outputText id="empName" value="#{emp.employeeFirst} #{emp.employeeLast}"/>
    </h:column>
    <h:column id="titleCol">
        <f:facet name="header">Title</f:facet>
        <h:outputText id="title" value="#{emp.employeeTitle}"/>
    </h:column>

</h:dataTable>
<p style="width: 40%;">
    Please use the form below to insert employee information. The first and
    last text fields will result in immediate evaluation during the apply request
    values phase, whereas the text field in the middle will result in standard
    evaluation and be validated during
    the invoke application phase.
    <br/><br/>
    To test, try inserting just one character in the first text field
    and then tab to the next field.  You should see an immediate result.
</p>
<h:panelGrid columns="3">
    <h:outputLabel for="employeeFirst" value="First: " />
    <h:inputText id="employeeFirst" immediate="true" onchange="submit()"
    value="#{employeeController.employeeFirst}">
        <f:validateLength minimum="3" maximum="30"/>
    </h:inputText>
    <h:message for="employeeFirst" errorStyle="color:red"/>
    <h:outputLabel for="employeeLast" value="Last: "  />
    <h:inputText id="employeeLast" value="#{employeeController.employeeLast}">
        <f:validateLength minimum="3" maximum="30"/>
    </h:inputText>
    <h:message for="employeeLast" errorStyle="color:red"/>

    <h:outputLabel for="employeeTitle" value="Title (Must be a Java Position): " >
    <h:inputText id="employeeTitle" immediate="true" value="#{employeeController.
    employeeTitle}">
        <f:validator validatorId="employeeTitleValidate" />
    </h:inputText>
    <h:message for="employeeTitle" errorStyle="color:red"/>

</h:panelGrid>
<h:commandButton id="employeeInsert" action="#{employeeController.insertEmployee}"
                 value="Insert Employee"/>
    </h:form>
  </h:body>
</html>
```

As you can see, the h:inputText components with ids of employeeFirst and employeeTitle specify both the immediate="true" and the onchange="submit()" attributes. These two attributes cause the components to be validated immediately rather than when the h:commandButton action is invoked.

Explanation

Event handling that occurs immediately can be useful in cases where you do not want to validate the entire form in order to process input but, rather, when you want chosen components to be validated immediately. As mentioned previously, when a JSF view is processed, a number of phases are executed. As such, when a form is submitted, the Invoke Application phase initiates the event handlers for view components, and validation occurs. When the immediate attribute for a component is set to true, the event handlers for that component execute during the Apply Request Values phase, which occurs before the Process Validation phase, where component validation normally occurs. This allows for an immediate validation response for the specified components, resulting in immediate error messages if needed.

As mentioned previously, specify the immediate attribute for a component and set it to true if you want to have that component evaluated immediately. This will cause the component to be evaluated and validated during the Apply Request Values phase. The real fun comes into play when you also specify the onclick attribute and set it equal to submit(), causing the form to be submitted when the value for the component changes. Specifying attributes as such will cause any component within the view that has an immediate attribute set to true to be validated when the component value changes.

■ **Note** The immediate attribute can also be useful when used on a commandButton component in such instances where you do not want any form processing to take place, such as if you want to set up a Cancel button or another button that bypasses form processing.

Passing Page Parameters to Methods

JSF EL provides an easy medium for invoking action methods that reside within managed bean controllers. More times than not, the actions being invoked do not require a passed argument. However, in some cases it can be beneficial to pass an argument to an action method via EL.

Example

Use a standard JSF EL expression to invoke a managed bean method, and enclose the parameters that you want to pass to the method within parentheses. In the example, an h:dataTable component is used to display a list of Author objects in a view. Each row within the h:dataTable contains an h:commandLink component, which invokes a JSF managed bean method when selected. The h:commandLink displays the current row's author name and invokes the AuthorController class displayAuthor method when clicked, passing the last name for the author being displayed in the current row. In the displayAuthor method, the list of authors is traversed, finding the element that contains the same last name as the parameter, which is passed into the method. The current author is then displayed in a subsequent page, which is rendered using implicit navigation.

The following source is for the JSF view entitled passingParameters.xhtml, which displays the list of authors using an h:dataTable component:

```
<?xml version="1.0" encoding="UTF-8"?>
<!--
Passing Page Parameters to Methods
Author: J. Juneau
-->
<!DOCTYPE html PUBLIC "-//W3C//DTD XHTML 1.0 Strict//EN"
"http://www.w3.org/TR/xhtml1/DTD/xhtml1-strict.dtd">
<html xmlns="http://www.w3.org/1999/xhtml"
      xmlns:f="http://xmlns.jcp.org/jsf/core"
      xmlns:h="http://xmlns.jcp.org/jsf/html">
    <h:head>
        <meta http-equiv="Content-Type" content="text/html; charset=UTF-8"/>
        <title>Passing Page Parameters to Methods</title>
    </h:head>
    <h:body>
        <h:form id="componentForm">
            <h1>Author List</h1>
            <p>
                Below is the list of authors. Click on the author's last name
                for more information regarding the author.
            </p>

            <h:graphicImage id="java7recipes" style="width: 10%; height: 20%"  library="image"
                            name="java7recipes.png"/>
            <br/>
            <h:dataTable id="authorTable" border="1" value="#{authorTableController.authorList}"
                    var="author">
                <f:facet name="header">
                    Java 7 Recipes Authors
                </f:facet>
                <h:column>
                <h:commandLink id="authorName" action="#{authorTableController.displayAuthor(author.
                                          last)}"
                            value="#{author.first} #{author.last}"/>
                </h:column>
            </h:dataTable>
            <br/>
            <br/>

        </h:form>
    </h:body>
</html>
```

The next listing is that of the managed bean controller for the preceding JSF view. The managed bean populates an ArrayList with Author objects upon instantiation.

```java
package org.javaserverfaces.chapter03;

import java.io.Serializable;
import java.util.ArrayList;
import java.util.List;
import javax.enterprise.context.SessionScoped;
import javax.inject.Named;
/**
 *
 * @author juneau
 */
@Named(name = "authorTableController")
@SessionScoped
public class AuthorController implements Serializable {

    private List<Author> authorList = null;
    private String juneauBio =
            "Josh Juneau has been developing software"
            + " since the mid-1990s. PL/SQL development and database programming"
            + " was the focus of his career in the beginning, but as his skills developed,"
            + " he began to use Java and later shifted to it as a primary base for his"
            + " application development. Josh has worked with Java in the form of graphical"
            + " user interface, web, and command-line programming for several years. "
            + "During his tenure as a Java developer, he has worked with many frameworks"
            + " such as JSF, EJB, and JBoss Seam. At the same time, Josh has extended his"
            + " knowledge of the Java Virtual Machine (JVM) by learning and developing applications"
            + " with other JVM languages such as Jython and Groovy. His interest in learning"
            + " new languages that run on the JVM led to his interest in Jython. Since 2006,"
            + " Josh has been the editor and publisher for the Jython Monthly newsletter. "
            + "In late 2008, he began a podcast dedicated to the Jython programming language.";

    private String deaBio = "This is Carl Dea's Bio";
    private String beatyBio = "This is Mark Beaty's Bio";
    private String oConnerBio = "This is John O'Connor's Bio";
    private String guimeBio = "This is Freddy Guime's Bio";
    private Author current;
    /**
     * Creates a new instance of AuthorController
     */
    public AuthorController() {
        populateAuthorList();
    }
```

```java
    private void populateAuthorList() {

        if(authorList == null){
            System.out.println("initializng authors list");
            authorList = new ArrayList<Author>();
            authorList.add(new Author("Josh", "Juneau", juneauBio));
            authorList.add(new Author("Carl", "Dea", deaBio));
            authorList.add(new Author("Mark", "Beaty", beatyBio));
            authorList.add(new Author("John", "O'Conner", oConnerBio));
            authorList.add(new Author("Freddy", "Guime", guimeBio));
        }
    }

    public String displayAuthor(String last){
        for(Author author:authorList){
            if(author.getLast().equals(last)){
                current = author;
                break;
            }
        }
        return "passingParameters2";
    }

    /**
     * @return the authorList
     */
    public List getAuthorList() {
        System.out.println("Getting the authorlist =>" + authorList.size());
        return authorList;
    }

    /**
     * @return the current
     */
    public Author getCurrent() {
        return current;
    }

    /**
     * @param current the current to set
     */
    public void setCurrent(Author current) {
        this.current = current;
    }
}
```

The Author class is the same Author POJO that was utilized previously. For the source of the Author class, please refer to that example. Lastly, the following code is for a JSF view entitled passingParameters2.xhtml, the detail view for each author. When an author name is clicked from the h:dataTable component in the first view, the component's corresponding managed bean method is invoked, and then this view is rendered to display the selected author's information.

```
<?xml version="1.0" encoding="UTF-8"?>
<!--
Author: J. Juneau
-->
<!DOCTYPE html PUBLIC "-//W3C//DTD XHTML 1.0 Strict//EN" "http://www.w3.org/TR/xhtml1/DTD/
xhtml1-strict.dtd">
<html xmlns="http://www.w3.org/1999/xhtml"
      xmlns:f="http://xmlns.jcp.org/jsf/core"
      xmlns:h="http://xmlns.jcp.org/jsf/html">
    <h:head>
        <meta http-equiv="Content-Type" content="text/html; charset=UTF-8"/>
        <title>Passing Page Parameters to Methods</title>
    </h:head>
    <h:body>
        <h:form id="componentForm">
            <h1>#{authorTableController.current.first} #{authorTableController.current.last}</h1>
            <p>
                <h:graphicImage id="java7recipes" style="width: 10%; height: 20%" url="../images/
                                java7recipes.png"/>
                <br/>
                #{authorTableController.current.bio}
            </p>

            <h:link value="Go Back to List" outcome="passingParameters"/>

        </h:form>
    </h:body>
</html>
```

Explanation

The release of JSF 2.0 contained many enhancements that made the life of JSF developers much easier than before. The ability to pass parameters to managed bean methods from within JSF views is one such enhancement. As you can see from the example, it is possible to pass parameters to a method within a JSF EL construct in the same manner that you would call any method with parameters in Java: by enclosing the argument(s) within parentheses after the method name. It cannot get much simpler than that!

Let's take a look at the lines of code that make this example hum. The first JSF view displays a table of author names, and each name is displayed using an h:commandLink component. The value attribute for the h:commandLink component is set to the author name, and the action attribute is set to the JSF EL, which invokes a managed bean action method named displayAuthor. Notice that within the call to the managed bean method, the EL for the author's last name is passed as a String parameter.

```
<h:dataTable id="authorTable" border="1" value="#{authorTableController.authorList}"
                           var="author">
       <f:facet name="header">
                 Java 7 Recipes Authors
       </f:facet>
       <h:column>
               <h:commandLink id="authorName" action="#{authorTableController.displayAuthor(author.
last)}"
                               value="#{author.first} #{author.last}"/>
       </h:column>
 </h:dataTable>
```

The displayAuthor method within the managed bean accepts a String parameter value, which is the author's last name, and then finds an Author object within the list of authors that contains the same last name. When found, a class field named current is set equal to the Author object for the matching List element. The subsequent JSF view then displays content utilizing the current Author information.

Prior to JSF 2.0, developers were unable to pass parameters to managed bean methods from within a view. This made it a bit more difficult to perform such techniques and usually involved a bit more code.

Arithmetic and Reserved Words in Expressions

JSF Expression Language (EL) not only enables access to managed bean properties and methods, but it also allows you to perform arithmetic and use reserved words.

Example

JSF EL expressions can contain arithmetic using standard arithmetic operators. It is also possible to combine two or more expressions utilizing some of JSF ELs reserved words. In the following example, some JSF EL expressions are used to display mathematical results on a page. Both the usage of arithmetic and reserved words are used within the expressions.

```
<?xml version="1.0" encoding="UTF-8"?>
<!--
Author: J. Juneau
-->
<!DOCTYPE html PUBLIC "-//W3C//DTD XHTML 1.0 Strict//EN" "http://www.w3.org/TR/xhtml1/DTD/
xhtml1-strict.dtd">
<html xmlns="http://www.w3.org/1999/xhtml"
      xmlns:f="http://xmlns.jcp.org/jsf/core"
      xmlns:h="http://xmlns.jcp.org/jsf/html"
      xmlns:c="http://xmlns.jcp.org/jsp/jstl/core">
   <h:head>
       <meta http-equiv="Content-Type" content="text/html; charset=UTF-8"/>
       <title>Arithmetic and Reserved Words</title>
   </h:head>
```

```
    <h:body>
        <h:form id="componentForm">
            <h1>JSF Arithmetic and Reserved Words in EL</h1>
            <p>
                The following examples use JSF EL to perform some arithmetic.
            </p>
            1 + 1 = #{1 + 1}
            <br/>
            <h:outputText value="20 / 5 = #{20 / 5}"/>
            <br/>

            <h:outputText rendered="#{1 + 1 eq 2}" value="1 + 1 DOES equal 2"/>
            <br/>
            <h:outputText rendered="#{5 * 4 ne 20}" value="Is 5 * 4 equal to 20?"/>
            <br/>
            <h:outputText rendered="#{5 * 5 eq 25 and 1 + 1 eq 2}" value="Combining some
                                    expressions"/>
            <br/>
            <c:if test=)"#{evaluationController.expr1()}">
                This will be displayed if expr1() evaluates to true.
            </c:if>
            <br/>
            <c:if test="#{evaluationController.expr2() or evaluationController.field1}">
                This will be displayed if expr2() or field1 evaluates to true.
            </c:if>
        </h:form>
    </h:body>
</html>
```

Some of the expressions contain managed bean references for a bean named EvaluationController. The listing for this managed bean is as follows:

```
package org.javaserverfaces.chapter03;

import javax.enterprise.context.RequestScoped;
import javax.inject.Named;
/**

 * @author juneau
 */
@Named(value = "evaluationController")
@RequestScoped
public class EvaluationController {

    private boolean field1 = true;

    /**
     * Creates a new instance of EvaluationController
     */
    public EvaluationController() {
    }
```

```java
    public boolean expr1(){
        return t)rue;
    }

    public boolean expr2(){
        return false;
    }

    /**
     * @return the field1
     */
    public boolean isField1() {
        return field1;
    }

    /**
     * @param field1 the field1 to set
     */
    public void setField1(boolean field1) {
        this.field1 = field1;
    }
}
```

The resulting page will look as follows:

```
The following examples use JSF EL to perform some arithmetic.
1 + 1 = 2
20 / 5 = 4.0
1 + 1 DOES equal 2

Combining some expressions
This will be displayed if expr1() evaluates to true.
This will be displayed if expr1() or field1 evaluates to true.
```

Explanation

It is possible to use standard arithmetic and combine expressions using reserved words within JSF EL expressions. All standard arithmetic operators are valid within EL, but a couple of things are different. For instance, instead of writing an expression such as #{1 + 1 = 2}, you could use the eq reserved characters so that the expression reads #{1 + 1 eq 2}. Similarly, the != symbol could be used to specify that some value is not equal to another value, but rather, in this example, the ne reserved word is used. Table 3-4 describes all such reserved words.

Table 3-4. *JSF EL Reserved Words*

Reserved Word	Description
and	Combines two or more expressions
div	Used to divide
empty	Used to refer to an empty list
eq	Equal to
false	Boolean false
ge	Greater than or equal to
gt	Greater than
instanceof	Used to evaluate whether an object is an instance of another
le	Less than or equal
lt	Less than
mod	Modulus
ne	Not equal
not	Used for negation
null	Evaluates a null value
or	Combines two or more expressions
true	Boolean true

Table 3-5 lists the available ope)rators that can be used within JSF EL expressions, in order of precedence.

Table 3-5. *Operators for Use in Expressions*

Operator
[]
()
- (unary), not, !, empty
*, /, div, %, mod
+, -   (binary)
<, >, <=, >=, lt, gt, le, ge
==, !, eq, ne
&&, and
||, or
?, :

Creating Bookmarkable URLs

JSF *view parameters* can be used to create link-able or "bookmarkable" URLs. For example, a bookmarkable URL can be used to load data at page load time. Views can be made bookmarkable by accepting and setting parameter values into the appropriate resource to retrieve the data.

Example

Add view parameters to a JSF view for which you want to create a bookmarkable URL by defining the parameter in an f:viewParam tag, which is a subtag of the f:metadata tag. Doing so will allow a page to become accessible via a URL that contains request parameters that can be used for record identification. In this example, the view contains a view parameter, via the f:viewParam tag, that allows for the specification of an author's last name when the view is requested. For the example, the managed bean that was created in earlier in the chapter has been modified to include a new property named authorLast in order to accommodate the new view parameter.

The sources for the view named bookmarkable.xhtml are listed next. They are very similar to the view named passingparameters2.xhtml, except that they include an f:viewParam element, which is enclosed between opening and closing f:metadata elements.

```
<?xml version="1.0" encoding="UTF-8"?>
<!--
Author: J. Juneau
-->
<!DOCTYPE html PUBLIC "-//W3C//DTD XHTML 1.0 Strict//EN" "http://www.w3.org/TR/xhtml1/DTD/
xhtml1-strict.dtd">
<html xmlns="http://www.w3.org/1999/xhtml"
      xmlns:f="http://xmlns.jcp.org/jsf/core"
      xmlns:h="http://xmlns.jcp.org/jsf/html">
    <h:head>
        <meta http-equiv="Content-Type" content="text/html; charset=UTF-8"/>
        <title>Creating Bookmarkable URLs</title>

    </h:head>
    <h:body>

        <f:metadata>
            <f:viewParam name="authorLast" value="#{authorTableController.authorLast}"/>
        </f:metadata>
        <h:form id="componentForm">
            <h1>#{authorTableController.current.first} #{authorTableController.current.last}</h1>
            <p>
                <h:graphicImage id="java7recipes" style="width: 10%; height: 20%" url="../images/
                                java7recipes.png"/>
                <br/>
                #{authorTableController.current.bio}
            </p>

            <h:link value="Go Back to List" outcome="passingParameters"/>

        </h:form>

    </h:body>
</html>
```

The updated code for the org.javaserverfaces.chapter03.AuthorController managed bean class is listed next:

```java
package org.javaserverfaces.chapter03;

import java.io.Serializable;
import java.util.ArrayList;
import java.util.List;
import javax.enterprise.context.SessionScoped;
import javax.inject.Named;

@Named(value = "authorTableController")
@SessionScoped
public class AuthorController implements Serializable {

    ...
    private String authorLast;
    ...

    /**
     * @return the authorLast
     */
    public String getAuthorLast() {
        return authorLast;
    }

    /**
     * @param authorLast the authorLast to set
     */
    public void setAuthorLast(String authorLast) {
        displayAuthor(authorLast);
    }
}
```

As mentioned previously, a property has been added to the bean named authorList. This property makes it possible for the JSF view listed in the example to accept a request parameter named authorList via a GET URL and pass it to the bean when the page is requested. In the end, the URL for accessing the view and requesting the details for the author Josh Juneau would be as follows:

```
http://my-server.com/JSFByExample/chapter03/bookmarkable.xhtml?authorLast=Juneau
```

Explanation

In the past, JSF applications had a weakness in that they used to require a launch view, which created an entry point for accessing the application. This gave the application a view that would set up an initial state for the application session. While this concept is nice because each user session would begin their session with an initialized application state, it prohibited the ability for records to be linked directly via a URL. Sometimes it is very useful to have the ability to link a view to a URL that contains request parameters so that record(s) matching the given parameters can be returned to the view without further user interaction; for instance, say a web site included information regarding a book and wanted to include a URL to find out more about the book's author. It's much nicer to directly link to a view containing that author's information rather than redirecting the user to a web site that requires them to perform a manual search for the author. Such URLs are also known as *bookmarkable* URLs because the URL contains all of the state that is required to make the request. Therefore, they allow the user of a web application to bookmark the URL for direct access to a specific point within an application.

JSF 2.0 introduced the ability to include view parameters, adding the ability for views to accept request parameters. Utilizing a GET-based URL, a request parameter can be appended to the end along with its value, and a view containing the new view parameter can then pass the parameter to a managed bean before the response is rendered. The bean can then accept the parameter value and query a database or search through some other collection of data to find a record that matches the given value before rendering the response.

To include one or more view parameters within a view, you must add an opening and closing f:metadata element to the view and embed the number of f:viewParam elements between them. The f:viewParam element includes two attributes that must have values, those being the name and value attributes. The name attribute specifies the name of the request parameter as you would like it to appear within the bookmarkable URL, and the value attribute specifies the managed bean field that should be mapped to that request parameter. In the example, the JSF view contains a view parameter named authorLast, and the associated authorLast field within the managed bean contains a setter method, which is invoked when the page is requested. The following excerpt from the view demonstrates the lines for adding the metadata and view parameter:

```
<f:metadata>
    <f:viewParam name="authorLast" value="#{authorTableController.authorLast}"/>
</f:metadata>
```

With the addition of the view parameter, the page can be requested with a URL containing the authorLast request parameter as follows:

```
http://my-server.com/JSFByExample/chapter03/bookmarkable.xhtml?authorLast=Juneau
```

When the page is requested, the view parameter's value invokes the setAuthorLast method within the managed bean, which then searches for an author record that contains a last name equal to the given request parameter value.

```
...
public void setAuthorLast(String authorLast) {
        displayAuthor(authorLast);
    }
...
```

The addition of view parameters to JSF 2.0 has made it easy to create bookmarkable URLs. This allows applications to be more flexible and produce results immediately without requiring a user to navigate through several pages before producing a result.

Displaying Lists of Objects

The JSF h:dataTable component can be used to display list objects, iterating over each object in a list and displaying the specified values. They can also be handy for performing searches, and in some cases editing, of records in a list.

Example

The h:dataTable component is very customizable and can be configured to display content in a variety of layouts. The following JSF view contains two h:dataTable components that are used to display the authors for the *Java 7 Recipes* book using managed beans developed in previous examples. The first table in the view is straightforward and displays the names of each author. It has been formatted to display alternating row colors. The second table contains two rows for each corresponding list element, displaying the author names on the first row and their bios on the second.

```
<?xml version="1.0" encoding="UTF-8"?>
<!--
Author: J. Juneau
-->
<!DOCTYPE html PUBLIC "-//W3C//DTD XHTML 1.0 Strict//EN" "http://www.w3.org/TR/xhtml1/DTD/
xhtml1-strict.dtd">
<html xmlns="http://www.w3.org/1999/xhtml"
      xmlns:f="http://xmlns.jcp.org/jsf/core"
      xmlns:h="http://xmlns.jcp.org/jsf/html">
    <h:head>
        <meta http-equiv="Content-Type" content="text/html; charset=UTF-8"/>
        <title>Displaying Lists of Objects</title>

        <link href="#{facesContext.externalContext.requestContextPath}/css/styles.css"
              rel="stylesheet" type="text/css" />

    </h:head>
    <h:body>

        <h:form id="componentForm">
            <p>

                <h:graphicImage id="java7recipes" style="width: 10%; height: 20%" url="../images/
                                java7recipes.png"/>
                <br/>
                #{authorTableController.current.bio}
            </p>

            <h:dataTable id="authorTable" border="1"
                        value="#{authorTableController.authorList}"
                        styleClass="authorTable"
                        rowClasses="authorTableOdd, authorTableEven"
                        var="author">
                <f:facet name="header">
                    Java 7 Recipes Authors
                </f:facet>
```

```
                <h:column>
                <h:outputText id="authorName" value="#{author.first} #{author.last}"/>
                </h:column>
            </h:dataTable>
            <br/><br/>
            <h:dataTable id="authorTable2" border="1" value="#{authorTableController.authorList}"
                        var="author" width="500px;">
                <f:facet name="header">
                    Java 7 Recipes Authors
                </f:facet>
                <h:column>
                    <h:panelGrid columns="2" border="1" width="100%">
                        <h:outputText id="authorFirst" value="#{author.first}" style="width: 50%"/>
                        <h:outputText id="authorLast" value="#{author.last}" style="width:50%"/>

                    </h:panelGrid>
                    <h:outputText id="authorBio" value="#{author.bio}"/>
                </h:column>
            </h:dataTable>

        </h:form>

    </h:body>
</html>
```

The example utilizes a cascading style sheet to help format the colors on the table. The source for the style sheet is as follows:

```
.authorTable{
        border-collapse:collapse;
}
.authorTableOdd{
        text-align:center;
        background:none repeat scroll 0 0 #CCFFFF;
        border-top:1px solid #BBBBBB;
}

.authorTableEven{
        text-align:center;
        background:none repeat scroll 0 0 #99CCFF;
        border-top:1px solid #BBBBBB;
}
```

The resulting page should look similar to Figure 3-4.

Java 7 Recipes Authors
Josh Juneau
Carl Dea
Mark Beaty
John O'Conner
Freddy Guime

Java 7 Recipes Authors	
Josh	Juneau

Josh Juneau has been developing software since the mid-1990s. PL/SQL development and database programming was the focus of his career in the beginning, but as his skills developed, he began to use Java and later shifted to it as a primary base for his application development. Josh has worked with Java in the form of graphical user interface, web, and command-line programming for several years. During his tenure as a Java developer, he has worked with many frameworks such as JSF, EJB, and JBoss Seam. At the same time, Josh has extended his knowledge of the Java Virtual Machine (JVM) by learning and developing applications with other JVM languages such as Jython and Groovy. His interest in learning new languages that run on the JVM led to his interest in Jython. Since 2006, Josh has been the editor and publisher for the Jython Monthly newsletter. In late 2008, he began a podcast dedicated to the Jython programming language.

Carl	Dea

This is Carl Dea's Bio

Mark	Beaty

This is Mark Beaty's Bio

Figure 3-4. JSF DataTable component examples

Explanation

A JSF h:dataTable component can be used to display lists of objects within a page. When rendered, an HTML table is constructed, populating the cells of the table with the data for each list element or record of data. The h:dataTable can iterate over a collection of data, laying it out in a columnar format including column headers and the ability to customize the look using Cascading Style Sheets (CSS). The component contains a number of important attributes, as listed in Table 3-6. Perhaps the most important of them are the value and var attributes. The value attribute specifies the collection of data to iterate, and the var attribute lists a String that will be used to reference each individual row of the table. The collection usually comes from the managed bean, such as in the example. The legal data types for the value attribute are Array, DataModel, List, and Result. The var attribute is used within each column to reference a specific field within an object for the corresponding row.

Table 3-6. DataTable Attributes

Attribute	Description
id	ID for the component
border	An integer indicating border thickness; 0 is default
bgcolor	Background color of table
cellpadding	Padding between the cell wall and its contents
cellspacing	Spacing within the cells
width	Overall width of the table, specified in pixels or percentages
first	The first entry in the collection to display
rows	Total number of rows to display
styleClass, captionClass, headerClass, footerClass, rowClasses, columnClasses	CSS attributes
rendered	Boolean value indicating whether the component will be rendered

The h:dataTable can contain any number of columns, and each is specified within the h:dataTable component in the JSF view. The h:column nested element encloses the output for each column. A column can contain just about any valid component or HTML, even embedded dataTables. An h:column normally does not have any attributes specified, but it always contains an expression or hard-coded value for display.

```
<h:column>my column value</h:column>
```

or

```
<h:column>#{myTable.myColValue}</h:column>
```

Normally, columns within an HTML table contain headers. You can add headers to the h:dataTable or individual columns by embedding an f:facet element within the h:dataTable and outside of the column specifications or within each h:column by specifying the name attribute as header. The f:facet element can also specify caption for the name attribute in order to add a caption to the table. The following excerpt from the example demonstrates an h:dataTable that includes each of these features:

```
<h:dataTable id="authorTable" border="1"
                        value="#{authorTableController.authorList}"
                        styleClass="authorTable"
                        rowClasses="authorTableOdd, authorTableEven"
                        var="author">
    <f:facet name="header">
        Java 7 Recipes Authors
    </f:facet>
    <h:column>
        <h:outputText id="authorName" value="#{author.first} #{author.last}"/>
    </h:column>
</h:dataTable>
```

In the example, you can see that the h:dataTable value attribute is listed as #{authorTableController.authorList}, a List of Author objects declared within the managed bean. The var attribute establishes a variable named author that refers to the current author who is being processed from the author list. The author variable can then be accessed from within each h:column, displaying the data associated with the current list element.

An important piece of the puzzle to help make tables easier to read and follow is the CSS that can be used to style the table. The h:dataTable supports various attributes that allow you to apply externally defined CSS classes to your table, specifically, the styleClass, captionClass, headerClass, footerClass, rowClasses, and columnClasses attributes. Each of them can contain a CSS class specification for formatting. The example demonstrates this feature.

Invoking Managed Bean Actions on Life-Cycle Phase Events

A ViewAction component can be used to invoke action methods when a specified life cycle phase occurs. For instance, when a view is loading, it is possible to invoke a managed bean action that performs a conditional verification based upon the user who is visiting the page.

Example

Utilize a JSF view action by adding the f:viewAction facet to the JSF view. Use the facet to specify the managed bean action to invoke, as well as when to invoke the action. In the following excerpt from the view chapter03/invokingActions.xhtml, a managed bean method action named validateUser is invoked:

```
<f:metadata>
        <f:viewAction action="#{viewActionManagedBean.validateUser()}"/>
</f:metadata>
```

Explanation

In JSF 2.1 and prior, it was difficult to invoke action methods within a managed bean unless they were bound to a command component. Sometimes it makes sense to invoke a method when the page is loading, after the page has been fully loaded, and so on. In the past, this was done by using a preRenderView event listener, which invokes a method contained within a managed before the view is rendered. Utilization of the preRenderView event listener works, but it does not provide the level of control that is required to invoke a method during different phases of the view life cycle. The preRenderView also requires developers to programmatically check the request type and work with the navigation handler.

In the JSF 2.2 release, a new technique can be used to invoke action methods within a managed bean during specified life-cycle events that occur within the view. A new tag, f:viewAction, can be bound to a view, and it can be incorporated into the JSF life cycle in both non-JSF (initial) and JSF (postback) requests. To use the tag, it must be a child of the metadata facet. View parameters can be specified within the metadata facet as well, and they will become available from within the managed bean when the action method is invoked.

In the example, the action method named validateUser is invoked using the viewAction. In the example method, a String is returned, which enables implicit navigation based upon the action method results. If null is returned, the navigation handler is invoked, but the same view will be rendered again so long as there are no navigation condition expressions that change the navigation. If a String-based view name is returned, then the navigation handler will render that view once the method has completed. This can come in handy for situations such as authentication handling, where an action method is used to check the user's role and then the appropriate view is rendered based upon the authenticated user role.

```
public String validateUser() {
        String viewName;
        System.out.println("Look in the server log to see this message");
        // Here we would perform validation based upon the user visiting the
        // site to ensure that they had the appropriate permissions to view
        // the selected view. For the purposes of this example, this
        // conditional logic is just a prototype.
        if (visitor.isAdmin()){
            // visit the current page
            viewName = null;
            System.out.println("Current User is an Admin");
        } else {
            viewName = "notAdmin";
            System.out.println("Current User is NOT an Admin");
        }
        return viewName;
}
```

As mentioned previously, f:viewAction facet can be customized to allow the action method to be invoked at different stages within the view life cycle. By default, the viewAction will be initiated before postback because the specified action method is expected to execute whether the request was Faces or non-Faces. However, this can be changed by setting the onPostback attribute of the f:viewAction tag to true.

```
<f:viewAction action="#{viewActionManagedBean.validateUser()}" onPostback="true"/>
```

If you need to get even more granular and invoke a view action during specified life-cycle phase, it is possible by setting the phase attribute to the phase required. Table 3-7 specifies the different phases along with their phase value.

Table 3-7. *JSF Life-Cycle Phases*

Phase	Tag Value
Restore View	RESTORE_VIEW
Apply Request Values	APPLY_REQUEST_VALUES
Process Validations	PROCESS_VALIDATIONS
Update Model Values	UPDATE_MODEL_VALUES
Invoke Application	INVOKE_APPLICATION
Render Response	RENDER_RESPONSE

The following example demonstrates the f:viewAction facet that will cause the action to be invoked during the Process Validations phase:

```
<f:viewAction action="#{viewActionManagedBean.validateUser()}"
                    phase="PROCESS_VALIDATIONS"/>
```

CHAPTER 4

Facelets

In the early days of web development, web pages consisted of many HTML tables for structuring layout and lots of redundancy across application pages. This made development of web pages cumbersome and difficult to maintain at best. Over the years, other technologies such as Cascading Style Sheets (CSS) have come along to help web developers organize and style their pages. Such technologies encouraged organization by allowing developers to encapsulate styles into separate files, leaving the markup within pages easier to follow. Other technologies such as Tiles came along to help reduce the amount of redundancy that was incurred by providing a similar layout to all pages of an application. Tiles allowed developers to construct a single layout and apply it to several different web pages. Facelets is a view definition language that was introduced to help organize JSF views. Facelets follows in the footsteps of Tiles, in that it allows developers to encapsulate layouts into separate files and apply them to different JSF views...and that functionality only scratches the surface! While Facelets can be used to create layouts and build templates for JSF applications, it also brings with it many other significant advantages.

Facelets became the default view definition language of JSF with the release of JSF 2.0. Prior to that, Facelets had to be applied to an application separately. Developers of JSF 2.0+ applications can begin to use Facelets out of the box, without any additional application configuration. In addition to helping build application templates, Facelets provides built-in components to facilitate iteration over collections of data, debugging, inserting view fragments into other views, and so forth.

This chapter will cover an array of examples to help developers gain an understanding of some beginning, intermediate, and advanced Facelets techniques.

Creating a Page Template

Facelets' view definition language can be applied to JSF views within an application apply a similar layout to each view.

Example

The first step to applying a cohesive structure throughout an application is to create a page template using the Facelets view definition language. Facelets ships as part of JavaServer Faces, and you can use it to create highly sophisticated layouts for your views in a proficient manner. The template demonstrated in this example will be used to define the standard layout for all pages within an application. The demo application for this chapter is for a bookstore web site. The site will display a number of book titles on the left side of the screen, a header at the top, a footer at the bottom, and a main view in the middle. When a book title is clicked in the left menu, the middle view changes, displaying the list of authors for the selected book.

To create a template, you must first develop a new XHTML view file and then add the appropriate HTML/JSF/XML markup to it. Content from other views will displace the ui:insert elements in the template once the template has been applied to one or more JSF views. The following source is that of a template named custom_template.xhtml; this is the template that will be used for all views within the application:

```
<?xml version='1.0' encoding='UTF-8' ?>
<!--
Author: J. Juneau
-->
<!DOCTYPE html PUBLIC "-//W3C//DTD XHTML 1.0 Transitional//EN" "http://www.w3.org/TR/xhtml1/DTD/
xhtml1-transitional.dtd">
<html xmlns="http://www.w3.org/1999/xhtml"
      xmlns:ui="http://xmlns.jcp.org/jsf/facelets"
      xmlns:h="http://xmlns.jcp.org/jsf/html">

    <h:head>
        <meta http-equiv="Content-Type" content="text/html; charset=UTF-8" />
        <h:outputStylesheet library="css" name="default.css"/>
        <h:outputStylesheet library="css" name="cssLayout.css"/>
        <h:outputStylesheet library="css" name="styles.css"/>
        <title>#{faceletsAuthorController.storeName}</title>
    </h:head>

    <h:body>

        <div id="top">
            <h2>#{faceletsAuthorController.storeName}</h2>
        </div>
        <div>
            <div id="left">
                <h:form id="navForm">
                    <h:commandLink action="#{faceletsAuthorController.
                    populateJavaRecipesAuthorList}" >Java 7 Recipes</h:commandLink>
                    <br/>
                    <br/>
                    <h:commandLink action="#{faceletsAuthorController.populateJavaEERecipesAuthorList}"
                    >Java EE 7 Recipes </h:commandLink>
                </h:form>
            </div>
            <div id="content" class="left_content">
                <ui:insert name="content">Content</ui:insert>
            </div>
        </div>
        <div id="bottom">
            Written by Josh Juneau, Apress Author
        </div>

    </h:body>

</html>
```

The template defines the overall structure for the application views. However, it uses a CSS style sheet to declare the formatting for each of the `<div>` elements within the template. The style sheet, entitled `default.css`, should be contained within a `resources` directory in the application so that it will be accessible to the views.

■ **Note**   The CSS style sheets are automatically generated for you if using the NetBeans IDE.

There are also a couple of JSF EL expressions utilized within the template. The EL references a JSF managed bean by the name of `AuthorController`, which is referenced by `faceletsAuthorController`. While the source for this class is very important for the overall application, you'll wait to look at that code until the next example since it does not play a role in the application template layout.

Explanation

To create a unified application experience, the views should be coherent in that they look similar and function in a uniform fashion. The idea of developing web page templates has been around for a number of years, but unfortunately many template implementations contain duplicate markup on every application page. While duplicating the same layout for every separate web page works, it creates a maintenance nightmare. What happens when there is a need to update a single link within the page header? Such a conundrum would cause a developer to visit and manually update every web page for an application if the template was duplicated on every page. The Facelets view definition language provides a robust solution for the development of view templates, and it is one of the major bonuses of working with the JSF technology.

Facelets provides the ability for a single template to be applied to one or more views within an application. This means a developer can create one view that constructs the header, footer, and other portions of the template, and then this view can be applied to any number of other views that are responsible for containing the main view content. This technique mitigates issues such as changing a single link within the page header, because now the template can be updated with the new link, and every other view within the application will automatically reflect the change.

To create a template using Facelets, create an XHTML view, declare the required namespaces, and then add HTML, JSF, and Facelets tags accordingly to design the layout you desire. The template can be thought of as an "outer shell" for a web view, in that it can contain any number of other views within it. Likewise, any number of JSF views can have the same template applied, so the overall look and feel of the application will remain constant. Figure 4-1 provides a visual demonstrating the concept of an application template.

Figure 4-1. *Visual representation of a Facelets template and client*

You may have noticed from the view listing in the solution to this example that there are some tags toting the `ui:` prefix. Those are the Facelets tags that are responsible for controlling the view layout. To utilize these Facelets tags, you'll need to declare the XML namespace for the Facelets tag library in the `<html>` element within the template. Note that the XML namespace for the standard JSF tag libraries is also specified here.

```
<html xmlns="http://www.w3.org/1999/xhtml"
      xmlns:ui="http://xmlns.jcp.org/jsf/facelets"
      xmlns:h="http://xmlns.jcp.org/jsf/html">
...
```

■ **Note**   The Facelets template must include the `<html>`, `<head>`, or `<h:head>`, and `<body>` or `<h:body>`, elements because they are what define the overall layout for each view that uses it. The `<h:head>` and `<h:body>` elements will be covered in detail in Chapter 5. Each view that makes use of a Facelets template is known as a *composition*. One template can be used by multiple compositions or views. In actuality, everything outside of the `<ui:composition>` opening and closing tags within a composition is ignored. You'll learn more about that in the next example!

Facelets contains a number of special tags that can be used to help control page flow and layout. Table 4-1 in the next example lists the Facelets tags that are useful for controlling page flow and layout. The only Facelets tag that is used within the template for this example is `ui:insert`. The `ui:insert` tag contains a name attribute, which is set to the name of the corresponding `ui:define` element that will be included in the view. Taking a look at the source for this example, you can see the following `ui:insert` tag:

```
<ui:insert name="content">Content</ui:insert>
```

Table 4-1. *Facelets Page Control and Template Tags*

Tag	Description
ui:component	Defines a template component and specifies a file name for the component
ui:composition	Defines a page composition and encapsulates all other JSF markup
ui:debug	Creates a debug component, which captures debugging information, namely, the state of the component tree and the scoped variables in the application, when the component is rendered
ui:define	Defines content that is inserted into a page by a template
ui:decorate	Decorates pieces of a page
ui:fragment	Defines a template fragment, much like ui:component, except that all content outside of tag is not disregarded
ui:include	Allows another XHTML page to be encapsulated and reused within a view
ui:insert	Inserts content into a template
ui:param	Passes parameters to an included file or template
ui:repeat	Iterates over a collection of data
ui:remove	Removes content from a page

If a view that uses the template, a.k.a. template client, specifies a ui:define tag with the same name as the ui:insert name, then any content that is placed between the opening and closing ui:define tags will be inserted into the view in that location. However, if the template client does not contain a ui:define tag with the same name as the ui:insert tag, then the content between the opening and closing ui:insert tags within the template will be displayed.

Templates can be created via an IDE, such as NetBeans, to provide a more visual representation of the layout you are trying to achieve. To create a Facelets template from within NetBeans, right-click the project folder into which you want to place the template, and select New ➤ Other from the contextual menu to open the New File window. Once that's open, select JavaServer Faces from the Category menu and then Facelets Template from within the file types, as shown in Figure 4-2.

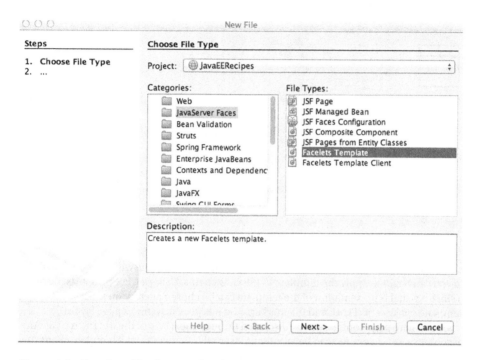

Figure 4-2. *Creating a Facelets template from within NetBeans*

After you've selected the Facelets Template file type, click the Next button to open the New Facelets Template window (Figure 4-3). This window will allow you to select the overall layout that you would like to compose for your application views, as well as choose the location and name for the template.

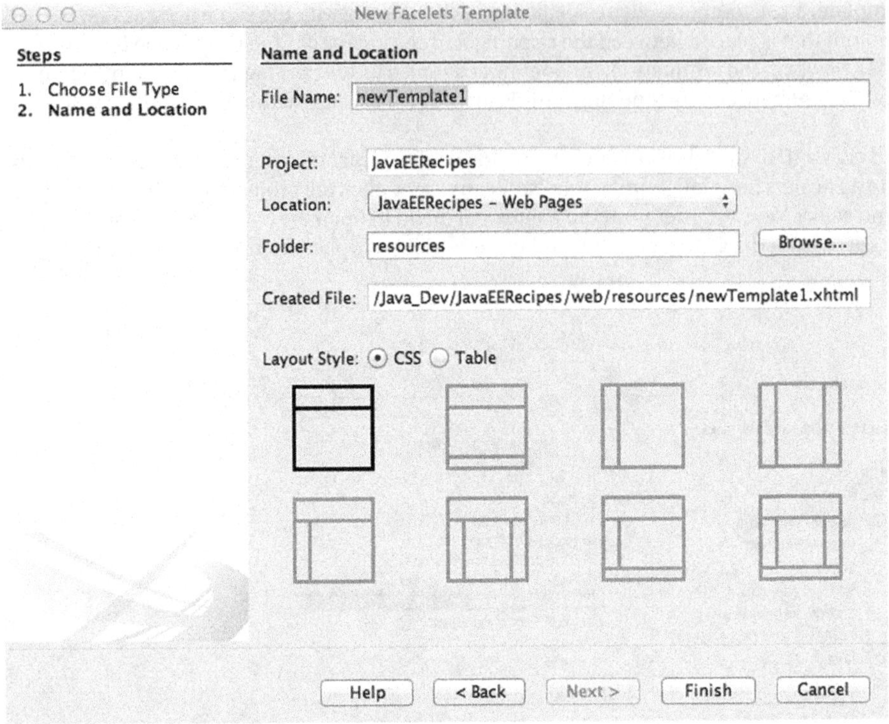

Figure 4-3. New Facelets Template window in NetBeans

After you've selected the layout of your choice and filled in the other options, the template will be opened within the NetBeans code editor, and you can begin to apply the template to JSF view clients. Using a wizard such as the one offered by NetBeans can help since a visual representation of the template can be chosen at creation time.

In summary, a Facelets template consists of HTML and JSF markup, and it is used to define a page layout. Sections of the template can specify where page content will be displayed through the usage of the ui:insert tag. Any areas within the template that contain a ui:insert tag can have content inserted into them from a template client. To learn more about applying a template to your views, please see the next example.

Applying a Template to Your Views

Once a Facelets template has been generated, it needs to be applied to one or more Facelets template clients. Use the ui:composition tag within each view that will utilize the template.

Example

The ui:composition tag should be used to invoke the template, and ui:define tags should be placed where content should be inserted. The following listings demonstrate how Facelets templates are applied to various views.

View #1: example04_01a.xhtml

The file exapmle04_01a.xhtml holds the markup for a view within the bookstore application that is used to display the authors for the *Java 7 Recipes* book. The template that was created in the first example in this chapter is applied to the view, and individual ui:define tags are used within the view to specify the content that should be inserted into the page/view.

```
<?xml version='1.0' encoding='UTF-8' ?>
<!--
Author: J. Juneau
-->
<!DOCTYPE html PUBLIC "-//W3C//DTD XHTML 1.0 Transitional//EN" "http://www.w3.org/TR/xhtml1/DTD/
xhtml1-transitional.dtd">
<html xmlns="http://www.w3.org/1999/xhtml"
      xmlns:ui="http://xmlns.jcp.org/jsf/facelets"
      xmlns:f="http://xmlns.jcp.org/jsf/core"
      xmlns:h="http://xmlns.jcp.org/jsf/html">

    <body>

        <ui:composition template="./layout/custom_template.xhtml">
            <ui:define name="top">
            </ui:define>
            <ui:define name="left">
            </ui:define>

            <ui:define name="content">
                <h:form id="componentForm">
                    <h1>Author List for Java 7 Recipes</h1>
                    <p>
                        Below is the list of authors.  Click on the author's last name
                        for more information regarding the author.
                    </p>

                    <h:graphicImage id="javarecipes" style="width: 100px; height: 120px"
                    library="image" name="java7recipes.png"/>
                    <br/>
                    <h:dataTable id="authorTable" border="1" value="#{faceletsAuthorController.
                    authorList}"
                                    var="author">
                        <f:facet name="header">
                            Java 7 Recipes Authors
                        </f:facet>
                        <h:column>
                            <h:commandLink id="authorName" action="#{faceletsAuthorController.
                            displayAuthor(author.last)}"
                                            value="#{author.first} #{author.last}"/>
                        </h:column>
                    </h:dataTable>
                    <br/>
                    <br/>
```

```
                </h:form>
            </ui:define>

            <ui:define name="bottom">
                bottom
            </ui:define>

        </ui:composition>
    </body>
</html>
```

View #2: example04_01b.xhtml

The file example04_01b.xhtml contains the sources for the second view within the bookstore application. It is used to list the authors for the *Java EE 7 Recipes* book. Again, note that the template has been applied to the view by specifying the template attribute within the ui:composition tag.

```
<?xml version='1.0' encoding='UTF-8' ?>
<!--
Author: J. Juneau
-->
<!DOCTYPE html PUBLIC "-//W3C//DTD XHTML 1.0 Transitional//EN" "http://www.w3.org/TR/xhtml1/DTD/
xhtml1-transitional.dtd">
<html xmlns="http://www.w3.org/1999/xhtml"
      xmlns:ui="http://xmlns.jcp.org/jsf/facelets"
      xmlns:f="http://xmlns.jcp.org/jsf/core"
      xmlns:h="http://xmlns.jcp.org/jsf/html">

    <body>

        <ui:composition template="./layout/custom_template.xhtml">

            <ui:define name="top">
            </ui:define>

            <ui:define name="left">
            </ui:define>

            <ui:define name="content">
                <h:form id="componentForm">
                    <h1>Author List for Java EE 7 Recipes</h1>
                    <p>
                        Below is the list of authors.  Click on the author's last name
                        for more information regarding the author.
                    </p>

                    <h:graphicImage id="javarecipes" style="width: 100px; height: 120px"
                    library="image" name="java7recipes.png"/>
                    <br/>
```

```
                <h:dataTable id="authorTable" border="1" value="#{faceletsAuthorController.
                authorList}"
                                var="author">
                    <f:facet name="header">
                        Java 7 Recipes Authors
                    </f:facet>
                    <h:column>
                        <h:commandLink id="authorName" action="#{faceletsAuthorController.
                        displayAuthor(author.last)}"
                                    value="#{author.first} #{author.last}"/>
                    </h:column>
                </h:dataTable>
                <br/>
                <br/>

            </h:form>
        </ui:define>

        <ui:define name="bottom">
            bottom
        </ui:define>

    </ui:composition>
  </body>
</html>
```

View #3: example04_01c.xhtml

In example04_01c.xhtml, you'll find the sources for another view listing that is part of the bookstore application. This view is responsible for displaying the individual author detail. Again, the template is applied to this page.

```
<?xml version="1.0" encoding="UTF-8"?>
<!--
Author: J. Juneau
-->
<!DOCTYPE html PUBLIC "-//W3C//DTD XHTML 1.0 Strict//EN" "http://www.w3.org/TR/xhtml1/DTD/xhtml1-
strict.dtd">
<html xmlns="http://www.w3.org/1999/xhtml"
    xmlns:f="http://xmlns.jcp.org/jsf/core"
    xmlns:ui="http://xmlns.jcp.org/jsf/facelets"
    xmlns:h="http://xmlns.jcp.org/jsf/html">
    <h:head>
        <meta http-equiv="Content-Type" content="text/html; charset=UTF-8"/>
        <title>Facelets Page Template</title>
    </h:head>
    <h:body>
        <ui:composition template="./layout/custom_template.xhtml">

            <ui:define name="top">
            </ui:define>
```

```
            <ui:define name="left">
            </ui:define>

            <ui:define name="content">
                <h:form id="componentForm">
                    <h1>#{faceletsAuthorController.current.first} #{faceletsAuthorController.
                    current.last}</h1>
                    <p>
                        <h:graphicImage id="java7recipes" style="width: 10%; height: 20%" url="../
                        images/java7recipes.png"/>
                        <br/>
                        #{faceletsAuthorController.current.bio}
                    </p>
                </h:form>
            </ui:define>

            <ui:define name="bottom">
                bottom
            </ui:define>

        </ui:composition>
    </h:body>
</html>
```

Managed Bean Controller: AuthorController

Of course, all the business logic and navigation is occurring from within a JSF managed bean. AuthorController is the bean that handles all the logic for the bookstore application. Note that the @Named annotation specifies a String value of faceletsAuthorController, which is used to reference the bean from within the views.

```
package org.javaserverfaces.chapter04;

import java.io.Serializable;
import java.util.ArrayList;
import java.util.List;
import javax.enterprise.context.SessionScoped;
import javax.inject.Named;


/**
 * @author juneau
 */
@Named(value = "faceletsAuthorController")
@SessionScoped
public class AuthorController implements Serializable {

    private List<Author> authorList;
    private String storeName = "Acme Bookstore";
```

```java
private String juneauBio =
        "Josh Juneau has been developing software"
        + " since the mid-1990s. PL/SQL development and database programming"
        + " was the focus of his career in the beginning, but as his skills developed,"
        + " he began to use Java and later shifted to it as a primary base for his"
        + " application development. Josh has worked with Java in the form of graphical"
        + " user interface, web, and command-line programming for several years. "
        + "During his tenure as a Java developer, he has worked with many frameworks"
        + " such as JSF, EJB, and JBoss Seam. At the same time, Josh has extended his"
        + " knowledge of the Java Virtual Machine (JVM) by learning and developing applications"
        + " with other JVM languages such as Jython and Groovy. His interest in learning"
        + " new languages that run on the JVM led to his interest in Jython. Since 2006,"
        + " Josh has been the editor and publisher for the Jython Monthly newsletter. "
        + "In late 2008, he began a podcast dedicated to the Jython programming language.";
private String deaBio = "This is Carl Dea's Bio";
private String beatyBio = "This is Mark Beaty's Bio";
private String oConnerBio = "This is John O'Connor's Bio";
private String guimeBio = "This is Freddy Guime's Bio";
private Author current;
private String authorLast;

/**
 * Creates a new instance of RecipeController
 */
public AuthorController() {
    populateJavaRecipesAuthorList();
}

public String populateJavaRecipesAuthorList() {

    authorList = new ArrayList<>();
    authorList.add(new Author("Josh", "Juneau", juneauBio));
    authorList.add(new Author("Carl", "Dea", deaBio));
    authorList.add(new Author("Mark", "Beaty", beatyBio));
    authorList.add(new Author("John", "O'Conner", oConnerBio));
    authorList.add(new Author("Freddy", "Guime", guimeBio));
    return "example04_01a";
}

public String populateJavaEERecipesAuthorList() {
    System.out.println("initializng authors list");
    authorList = new ArrayList<>();
    authorList.add(new Author("Josh", "Juneau", juneauBio));
    return "example04_01b";

}

public String displayAuthor(String last) {
    for (Author author : authorList) {
        if (author.getLast().equals(last)) {
            current = author;
        }
    }
```

```java
        return "example04_01c";
    }

    /**
     * @return the authorList
     */
    public List getAuthorList() {
        return authorList;
    }

    /**
     * @return the current
     */
    public Author getCurrent() {
        return current;
    }

    /**
     * @param current the current to set
     */
    public void setCurrent(Author current) {
        this.current = current;
    }

    /**
     * @return the authorLast
     */
    public String getAuthorLast() {
        return authorLast;
    }

    /**
     * @param authorLast the authorLast to set
     */
    public void setAuthorLast(String authorLast) {
        this.authorLast = authorLast;
    }

    /**
     * @return the storeName
     */
    public String getStoreName() {
        return storeName;
    }

    /**
     * @param storeName the storeName to set
     */
    public void setStoreName(String storeName) {
        this.storeName = storeName;
    }
}
```

In the end, the overall application will look like Figure 4-4. To run the application from the sources, deploy the WAR file distribution to your application server, and then load the following URL into your browser: `http://your-server:port_number/JSFByExample/faces/chapter04/example04_01a.xhtml`.

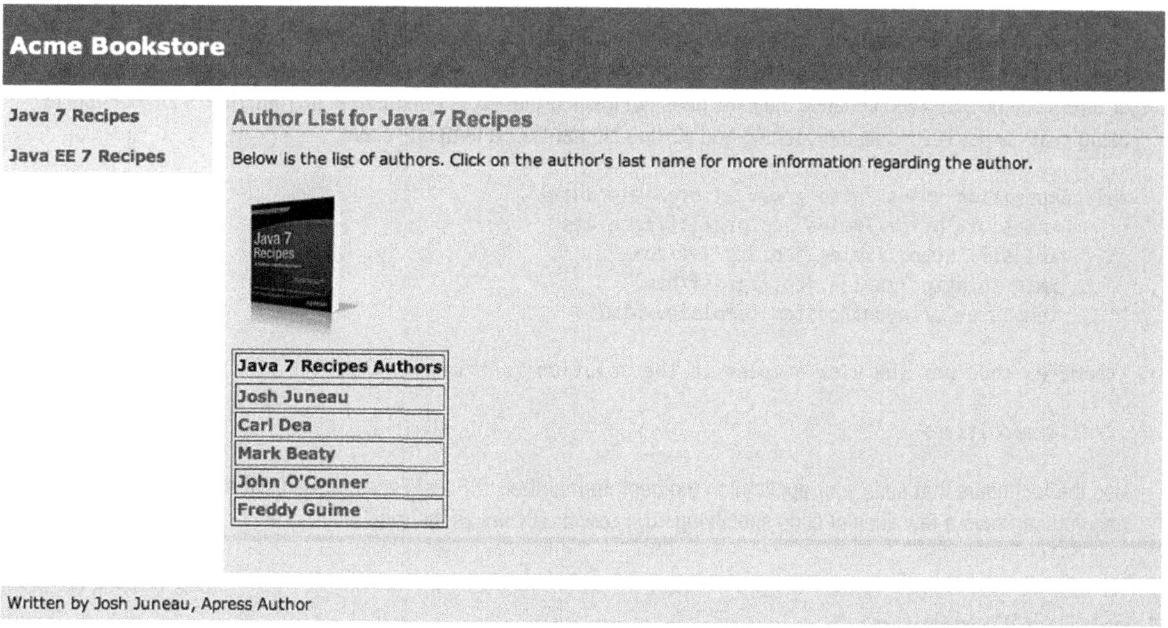

Acme Bookstore

Java 7 Recipes
Java EE 7 Recipes

Author List for Java 7 Recipes

Below is the list of authors. Click on the author's last name for more information regarding the author.

Java 7 Recipes Authors
Josh Juneau
Carl Dea
Mark Beaty
John O'Conner
Freddy Guime

Written by Josh Juneau, Apress Author

Figure 4-4. *Application using Facelets template*

Explanation

Applying a Facelets template to individual views within a JSF application is quite easy. Views that make use of a template are known as *template client*s. As mentioned in the first example in this chapter, a view template can specify individual ui:insert tags, along with the name attribute, in any location on the template where view content could be inserted. The name attribute within the ui:insert tag will pair up with the name attribute within the ui:define tag in the template client in order to determine what content is inserted.

■ **Note**   As noted in previously, each view that uses a Facelets template can be referred to as a *composition*. It can also be referred to as a *template client*. It is important to note that a template client, or composition, contains an opening and closing <ui:composition> tag. Everything outside of those tags is actually ignored at rendering time because the template body is used instead. You can also omit the <html> tags within a template client and just open and close the view using the <ui:composition> tags instead. Please see the "Opening/Closing Template Clients with <ui:composition>" sidebar for an example.

OPENING/CLOSING TEMPLATE CLIENTS WITH <UI:COMPOSITION>

It is common to see template client views using opening and closing `<html>` tags, as demonstrated with the example views in the solution to this example. However, since everything outside of the `<ui:composition>` tags is ignored at rendering time, you can omit those tags completely. It is sometimes useful to open and close a template client with the `<ui:composition>` tag. However, some page editors will be unable to work with the code or errors will be displayed because the view does not include the `<html>` element at its root. Here's an example of using `<ui:composition>` as the opening and closing elements of a template client:

```
<ui:composition xmlns="http://www.w3.org/1999/xhtml"
        xmlns:ui="http://xmlns.jcp.org/jsf/facelets"
        xmlns:f="http://xmlns.jcp.org/jsf/core"
        xmlns:h=http://xmlns.jcp.org/jsf/html
        template="./layout/custom_template.xhtml">

<<same as code per the view samples in the solution to this example>>

 </ui:composition>
```

Use the technique that suits your application the best! Remember, JSF and Facelets will treat each view the same, and you can save a few lines of code specifying `<ui:composition>` as the root.

Applying Templates

A template can be applied to a view by specifying it within the template attribute within the view's `ui:composition` tag. For instance, all the views within this example specify the same template, as you can see in the following excerpt:

```
<ui:composition template="./layout/custom_template.xhtml">
```

The name of the template in the example is `custom_template.xhtml`, and the path to the template is `./layout/`. The `ui:composition` tag should encapsulate all other markup within a Facelets view. All views that are to use the template must specify the `ui:composition` tag. A number of other useful Facelets template tags come along with Facelets, as described in Table 4-1.

The `ui:define` tag encloses content that will be inserted into the template at the location of the template's `ui:insert` tags. The `ui:define` tag is matched to a template's `ui:insert` tag based on the value of the name attribute that is common to each tag. As you can see from the first view listing in this example, the first `ui:define` tag specifies top for the name attribute, and this will correspond to the template `ui:insert` tag with a name attribute equal to top. But the template does not specify such a tag! That is OK; there does not have to be a one-to-one match between the `ui:define` and `ui:insert` tags. A view can specify any number of `ui:define` tags, and if they do not correspond to any of the `ui:insert` tags within the template, then they are ignored. Likewise, a template can specify any number of `ui:insert` tags, and if they do not correspond to a `ui:define` tag within the template client view, then the content that is defined within the template in that location will be displayed.

Looking at the same view, another `ui:define` tag contains a name attribute value equal to content, and this tag does correspond with a `ui:insert` tag within the template that also has a name attribute value of content. The following excerpt is taken from the template, and it shows the `ui:insert` tag that corresponds to the view's `ui:define` tag with the same name attribute. You can see the full listing for the template in the first example in this chapter.

```
<div id="content" class="left_content">
        <ui:insert name="content">Content</ui:insert>
</div>
```

The following excerpt, taken from example04_01a.xhtml, is the corresponding ui:define tag that will be inserted into the template at this location:

```
<ui:define name="content">
                <h:form id="componentForm">
                    <h1>Author List for Java 7 Recipes</h1>
                    <p>
                        Below is the list of authors.  Click on the author's last name
                        for more information regarding the author.
                    </p>

                    <h:graphicImage id="javarecipes" style="width: 10%; height: 20%" library="image"
                    name="java7recipes.png"/>
                    <br/>
                    <h:dataTable id="authorTable" border="1" value="#{faceletsAuthorController.
                    authorList}" var="author">
                        <f:facet name="header">
                            Java 7 Recipes Authors
                        </f:facet>
                        <h:column>
                            <h:commandLink id="authorName" action="#{faceletsAuthorController.
                            displayAuthor(author.last)}"
                                            value="#{author.first} #{author.last}"/>
                        </h:column>
                    </h:dataTable>
                    <br/>
                    <br/>

                </h:form>
            </ui:define
```

As you can see, it can be very powerful to define a view template that can be applied to several views within an application. Facelets templating provides a very powerful solution for defining such a template, allowing for consistent page layout and reusable page code.

Ensuring Resource Availability from All Views

It can become cumbersome managing references to resources within application web pages. JSF provides the ability to include resources, such as CSS, images, and JavaScript code to views, such that they become accessible for use from every view within your application. For instance, rather than hard-coding a URL to an image, you want to reference the image location and have the application dynamically create the URL to the image location at runtime.

Example

Create a resource directory and, optionally, subfolders within the resources directory to contain the resources that your application will utilize. Any CSS files, images, and so on, that are placed within subdirectories in the resources folder can be referenced within a JSF view via a JSF component's library attribute, rather than specifying the full path to the resource. In the following example, a cascading style sheet is used to style the table of authors within the application. For this example, you will use the styles.css sheet that was applied to the h:dataTable in in the previous chapter. The style sheet declaration will reside within the custom_template.xhtml template, and you will use an h:outputStylesheet component rather than a <link> tag. As a matter of fact, all of the <link> tags will be removed and replaced with h:outputStylesheet components to take advantage of the resources folder. The directory structure should look like Figure 4-5 when set up correctly.

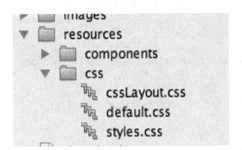

Figure 4-5. *Utilizing the resources directory*

The following listing is the updated custom_template.xhtml, because it now utilizes the h:outputStylesheet component rather than the <link> tag. Note that the library attribute is specified as css.

```
<?xml version='1.0' encoding='UTF-8' ?>
<!--
Author: J. Juneau
-->
<!DOCTYPE html PUBLIC "-//W3C//DTD XHTML 1.0 Transitional//EN" "http://www.w3.org/TR/xhtml1/DTD/
xhtml1-transitional.dtd">
<html xmlns="http://www.w3.org/1999/xhtml"
      xmlns:ui="http://xmlns.jcp.org/jsf/facelets"
      xmlns:h="http://xmlns.jcp.org/jsf/html">

    <h:head>
        <meta http-equiv="Content-Type" content="text/html; charset=UTF-8" />
        <h:outputStylesheet library="css" name="default.css"/>
        <h:outputStylesheet library="css" name="cssLayout.css"/>
        <h:outputStylesheet library="css" name="styles.css"/>
        <title>#{faceletsAuthorController.storeName}</title>
    </h:head>

    <h:body>

        <div id="top">
            <h2>#{faceletsAuthorController.storeName}</h2>
        </div>
```

```
        <div>
            <div id="left">
                <h:form id="navForm">
                    <h:commandLink action="#{faceletsAuthorController.
                    populateJavaRecipesAuthorList}" >Java 7 Recipes</h:commandLink>
                    <br/>
                    <br/>
                    <h:commandLink action="#{faceletsAuthorController.populateJavaEERecipesAuthorLis
                    t}">Java EE 7 Recipes </h:commandLink>
                </h:form>
            </div>
            <div id="content" class="left_content">
                <ui:insert name="content">Content</ui:insert>
            </div>
        </div>
        <div id="bottom">
            Written by Josh Juneau, Apress Author
        </div>

    </h:body>

</html>
```

The h:dataTable component that is used to list the authors within the views of the Acme Bookstore application can now make use of the styles that are listed within styles.css. The following excerpt from the XHTML document named example04_03.xhtml demonstrates the h:dataTable component with the styles applied:

```
<h:dataTable id="authorTable" border="1" value="#{faceletsAuthorController.authorList}"
                                    styleClass="authorTable"
                                    rowClasses="authorTableOdd, authorTableEven"
                                    var="author">
        <f:facet name="header">
            Java 7 Recipes Authors
        </f:facet>
        <h:column>
                <h:commandLink id="authorName"
                    action="#{faceletsAuthorController.displayAuthor(author.last)}"
                     value="#{author.first} #{author.last}"/>
        </h:column>
</h:dataTable>
```

The table should now look like Figure 4-6 when rendered on a page.

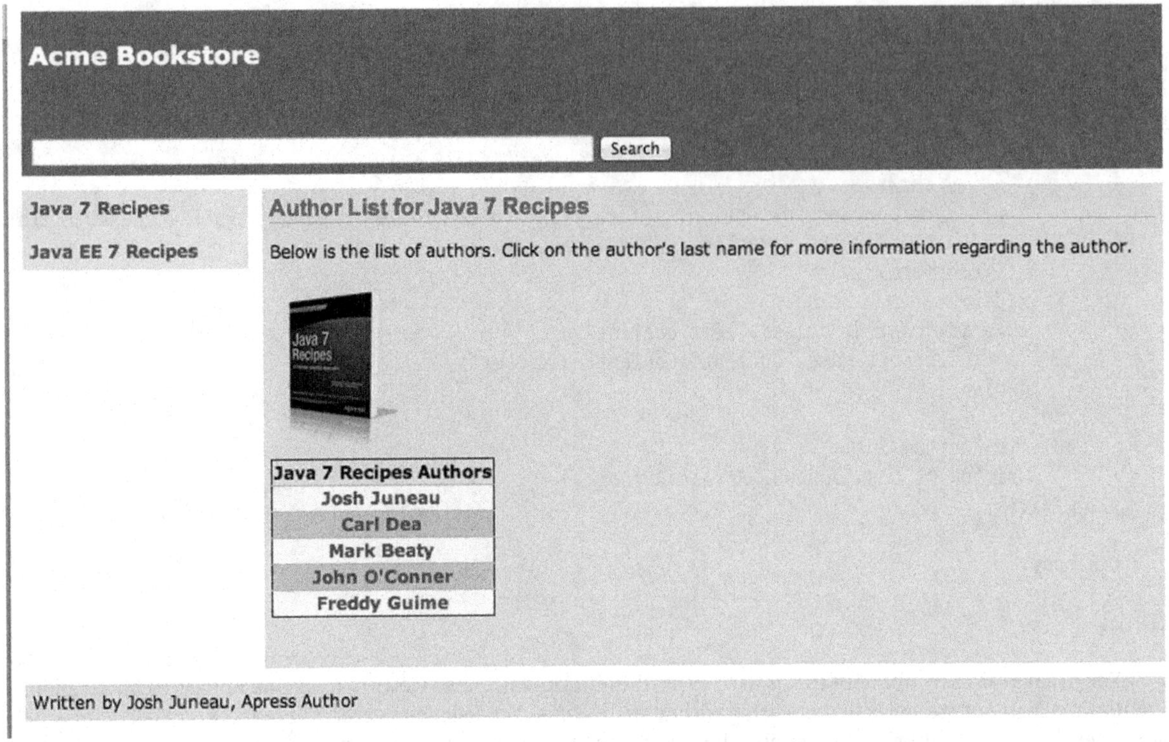

Figure 4-6. *Author table with styles applied*

Explanation

It is easy to add a resource to a JSF application because there is no need to worry about referring to a static path when declaring the resources. Since the release of JSF 2.0, the resources folder can be used to list subfolders, also known as *libraries*, into which the resources can be placed. The JSF components that can use resources now have the library attribute baked into them. This allows a specific library to be specified for such components so that the component will know where to find the resources that it requires.

To use the new resources folder, create a folder at the root of an application's web directory and name it resources. That resources folder can then contain subfolders, which will become the libraries that can be utilized within the JSF components. For instance, subfolders can be named css and images, and then those names can be specified for the library attribute of JSF components that utilize such resources. In the example, cascading style sheets are placed into the resources/css folder, and then they are referenced utilizing the h:outputStylesheet component and specifying the css library as follows:

```
<h:outputStylesheet library="css" name="default.css"/>
```

Other resources can be placed within such libraries. The h:graphicImage component also contains the library attribute, so the images for the books can be moved into a folder named resources/image, and then the h:graphicImage tag can reference the image as such:

```
<h:graphicImage id="javarecipes" library="image" style="width: 100px; height: 120px" name="java7recipes.png"/>
```

It has always been a challenge referencing resource files from the pages of a web application. To do so, a developer needs to know the exact path to the resource, and sometimes the path can be broken if folder names are changed or if the application is deployed in a different server environment. The use of the `resources` folder in JSF 2.0 along with the new `library` attribute has greatly reduced the complexity of managing such resources.

Creating Reusable Templates That Act As Components

One of the big benefits to using JSF is componentization, which allows one to encapsulate a component along with all of its resources so that it can be reused in any JSF view within your application.

Example

Create a new XHTML document that includes namespace declarations as required for use of the Facelets and JSF components, along with the Facelets tags required to create a composite component. The document can contain any valid JSF components or HTML markup needed to develop the component you desire. The Facelets tags that can be used to help develop composite components are `<composite:interface>` and `<composite:implementation>`. Any attributes that a component will accept will be declared within the `<composite:interface>` element, and the actual component implementation will be declared within the `<composite:implementation>` element. The component can then be used within another JSF view by declaring the namespace to the component XHTML document and then adding the component tag to the view. Let's take a look at an example.

The example contains a handful of source listings, each of which is required to construct and utilize the composite component. In this example, you'll create a component that will act as a search mechanism for authors who have books within the Acme Bookstore. A user will be able to type the name of an author in order to search for their bio. The search component will include an `h:inputText` component for accepting the search text, an `h:commandButton` for submitting the search text to the managed bean, and an `h:outputText` component for displaying a message if the search is unsuccessful. The component will utilize its own JSF managed bean for providing the business logic that is required to perform the search activity. Once the component construction is completed, a simple JSF tag can be added to any page in order to include said search component.

Creating the Composite Component: search.xhtml

You'll start by taking a look at the source for the composite component itself. The following code is for an XHTML document entitled `search.xhtml`, and it declares the composite component layout. The file should be saved into the `resources` folder within a JSF application, and for this example it is saved in the folder `resources/components/util`.

```
<?xml version='1.0' encoding='UTF-8' ?>
<!DOCTYPE html PUBLIC "-//W3C//DTD XHTML 1.0 Transitional//EN" "http://www.w3.org/TR/xhtml1/DTD/
xhtml1-transitional.dtd">
<html xmlns="http://www.w3.org/1999/xhtml"
      xmlns:h="http://xmlns.jcp.org/jsf/html"
      xmlns:composite="http://xmlns.jcp.org/jsf/composite">

    <!—OPTIONAL INTERFACE -->
    < composite:interface>
        < composite:attribute name="searchAction" default="#{searchController.searchAuthors(complete
AuthorController.completeAuthorList)}"
                     method-signature="java.lang.String action(java.util.List)"/>
    </ composite:interface>
```

```
    <!-- IMPLEMENTATION -->
    < composite:implementation>
        <h:form id="searchForm">
            <h:outputText id="error" value="#{searchController.errorText}"/>
            <br/>
            <h:inputText id="searchText" styleClass="searchBox" size="75" value="#{searchController.
searchText}"/>

            <h:commandButton id="searchButton" value="Search" action="#{cc.attrs.searchAction}"/>

        </h:form>
    </ composite:implementation>
</html>
```

Managed Bean Controller for Composite Component: SearchController.java

Next, let's look at the code for the JSF managed bean that is used for containing the business logic used for the component. The bean class is named SearchController.

```
package org.javaserverfaces.chapter04;
import javax.inject.Named;
import javax.enterprise.context.RequestScoped;
import javax.faces.bean.ManagedProperty;
import org.javaserverfaces.chapter04.Author;

/**
 * @author juneau
 */
@Named(name = "searchController")
@RequestScoped
public class SearchController implements java.io.Serializable {

    private String searchText;
    private String errorText;

    @ManagedProperty(value="authorController")
    private AuthorController authorController;

    /**
     * Creates a new instance of SearchController
     */
    public SearchController() {

    }

    public String searchAuthors(List<Author> authorList){
        String fullName = null;
        String returnString = null;
```

```
        for (Author author: authorList){
            fullName = author.getFirst() + " " + author.getLast();
            if (author.getFirst().equalsIgnoreCase(searchText)){
                returnString = getAuthorController().displayAuthor(author.getLast());
            } else if (author.getLast().equalsIgnoreCase(searchText)){
                returnString = getAuthorController().displayAuthor(author.getLast());
            } else if (fullName.equalsIgnoreCase(searchText)){
                returnString = getAuthorController().displayAuthor(author.getLast());
            }
        }
        if(returnString == null){
            setErrorText("No Author Found");
            returnString = "example04_04a";
        }
        return returnString;
    }

    /**
     * @return the searchText
     */
    public String getSearchText() {
        return searchText;
    }

    /**
     * @param searchText the searchText to set
     */
    public void setSearchText(String searchText) {
        this.searchText = searchText;
    }

    /**
     * @return the authorController
     */
    public AuthorController getAuthorController() {
        return authorController;
    }

    /**
     * @param authorController the authorController to set
     */
    public void setAuthorController(AuthorController authorController) {
        this.authorController = authorController;
    }

    /**
     * @return the errorText
     */
    public String getErrorText() {
        return errorText;
    }
```

```
    /**
     * @param errorText the errorText to set
     */
    public void setErrorText(String errorText) {
        this.errorText = errorText;
    }
}
```

Managed Bean Controller: AuthorController.java

Note that the managed bean contains an annotation, @ManagedProperty, which has not yet been covered up to this point in the book. I'll discuss that annotation a bit in the following section. Also note that in the composite component document, search.xhtml, another managed bean is referenced by the name of completeAuthorController. This managed bean is essentially the same as the JSF managed bean that was constructed in the first example in this chapter, with an added List declaration named completeAuthorList. This List is used to contain all of the Author objects for those who have books listed in the Acme Bookstore. The source listing for the updated AuthorContoller managed bean is as follows:

```
package org.javaserverfaces.chapter04.example04_04;

import org.javaserverfaces.chapter04.*;
import java.io.Serializable;
import java.util.ArrayList;
import java.util.List;
import javax.enterprise.context.SessionScoped;
import javax.inject.Named;

/**
 *
 * @author juneau
 */
@Named(value = "completeAuthorController")
@SessionScoped
public class AuthorController implements Serializable {

    private List<Author> authorList;
    private List<Author> completeAuthorList
    private String storeName = "Acme Bookstore";

    private String juneauBio =
            "Josh Juneau has been developing software"
            + " since the mid-1990s. PL/SQL development and database programming"
            + " was the focus of his career in the beginning, but as his skills developed,"
            + " he began to use Java and later shifted to it as a primary base for his"
            + " application development. Josh has worked with Java in the form of graphical"
            + " user interface, web, and command-line programming for several years. "
            + "During his tenure as a Java developer, he has worked with many frameworks"
            + " such as JSF, EJB, and JBoss Seam. At the same time, Josh has extended his"
            + " knowledge of the Java Virtual Machine (JVM) by learning and developing applications"
            + " with other JVM languages such as Jython and Groovy. His interest in learning"
            + " new languages that run on the JVM led to his interest in Jython. Since 2006,"
```

```
                    + " Josh has been the editor and publisher for the Jython Monthly newsletter. "
                    + "In late 2008, he began a podcast dedicated to the Jython programming language.";
private String deaBio = "This is Carl Dea's Bio";
private String beatyBio = "This is Mark Beaty's Bio";
private String oConnerBio = "This is John O'Connor's Bio";
private String guimeBio = "This is Freddy Guime's Bio";
private Author current;
private String authorLast;

/**
 * Creates a new instance of RecipeController
 */
public AuthorController() {
    populateJavaRecipesAuthorList();
    populateCompleteAuthorList();

}

public String populateJavaRecipesAuthorList() {

    authorList = new ArrayList<Author>();
    authorList.add(new Author("Josh", "Juneau", juneauBio));
    authorList.add(new Author("Carl", "Dea", deaBio));
    authorList.add(new Author("Mark", "Beaty", beatyBio));
    authorList.add(new Author("John", "O'Conner", oConnerBio));
    authorList.add(new Author("Freddy", "Guime", guimeBio));
    return "example04_04a";
}

public String populateJavaEERecipesAuthorList() {
    System.out.println("initializng authors list");
    authorList = new ArrayList<Author>();
    authorList.add(new Author("Josh", "Juneau", juneauBio));
    return "example04_04b";

}

private String populateCompleteAuthorList() {

    setCompleteAuthorList(null);

    setCompleteAuthorList(new ArrayList<Author>());
    getCompleteAuthorList().add(new Author("Josh", "Juneau", juneauBio));
    getCompleteAuthorList().add(new Author("Carl", "Dea", deaBio));
    getCompleteAuthorList().add(new Author("Mark", "Beaty", beatyBio));
    getCompleteAuthorList().add(new Author("John", "O'Conner", oConnerBio));
    getCompleteAuthorList().add(new Author("Freddy", "Guime", guimeBio));
    return "example04_04a";
}
```

```java
    public String displayAuthor(String last) {
        for (Author author : authorList) {
            if (author.getLast().equals(last)) {
                current = author;
            }
        }
        return "example04_04c";
    }

    /**
     * @return the authorList
     */
    public List<Author> getauthorList() {
        return authorList;
    }

    /**
     * @return the current
     */
    public Author getCurrent() {
        return current;
    }

    /**
     * @param current the current to set
     */
    public void setCurrent(Author current) {
        this.current = current;
    }

    /**
     * @return the authorLast
     */
    public String getAuthorLast() {
        return authorLast;
    }

    /**
     * @param authorLast the authorLast to set
     */
    public void setAuthorLast(String authorLast) {
        displayAuthor(authorLast);
    }

    /**
     * @return the storeName
     */
    public String getStoreName() {
        return storeName;
    }
```

```
    /**
     * @param storeName the storeName to set
     */
    public void setStoreName(String storeName) {
        this.storeName = storeName;
    }

    /**
     * @return the completeAuthorList
     */
    public List<Author> getCompleteAuthorList() {
        return completeAuthorList;
    }

    /**
     * @param completeAuthorList the completeAuthorList to set
     */
    public void setCompleteAuthorList(List<Author> completeAuthorList) {
        this.completeAuthorList = completeAuthorList;
    }
}
```

Utilizing the Composite Component: custom_template_search.xhtml

Now that all of the necessary sources have been written for the component, it can be utilized within a page. The Acme Bookstore would like to have the search component displayed at the top of each page, so you'll add it to the site template that was created in the first example in the chapter. The following code shows the updated markup for the template, and it has been saved into an XHTML document named custom_template_search.xhtml in the same folder as the original template:

```
<?xml version='1.0' encoding='UTF-8' ?>
<!--
Author: J. Juneau
-->
<!DOCTYPE html PUBLIC "-//W3C//DTD XHTML 1.0 Transitional//EN" "http://www.w3.org/TR/xhtml1/DTD/
xhtml1-transitional.dtd">
<html xmlns="http://www.w3.org/1999/xhtml"
      xmlns:ui="http://xmlns.jcp.org/jsf/facelets"
      xmlns:h="http://xmlns.jcp.org/jsf/html"
      xmlns:util="http://xmlns.jcp.org/jsf/composite/components/util">

    <h:head>
        <meta http-equiv="Content-Type" content="text/html; charset=UTF-8" />
        <h:outputStylesheet library="css" name="default.css"/>
        <h:outputStylesheet library="css" name="cssLayout.css"/>
        <h:outputStylesheet library="css" name="styles.css"/>
        <title>#{faceletsAuthorController.storeName}</title>
    </h:head>

    <h:body>
```

```
        <div id="top">
            <h2>#{faceletsAuthorController.storeName}</h2>
            <br/>
            <util:search id="searchAuthor"/>
        </div>
        <div>
            <div id="left">
                <h:form id="navForm">
                    <h:commandLink action="#{completeAuthorController.
populateJavaRecipesAuthorList}" >Java 7 Recipes</h:commandLink>
                    <br/>
                    <br/>
                    <h:commandLink action="#{completeAuthorController.populateJavaEERecipesAuthorLis
t}">Java EE 7 Recipes </h:commandLink>
                </h:form>
            </div>
            <div id="content" class="left_content">
                <ui:insert name="content">Content</ui:insert>
            </div>
        </div>
        <div id="bottom">
            Written by Josh Juneau, Apress Author
        </div>

    </h:body>

</html>
```

The search component is added to the template using the tag `<s:search id="searchAuthor"/>`, and it will now appear at the top of each page within the Acme Bookstore application. Figure 4-7 shows what the updated store application looks like.

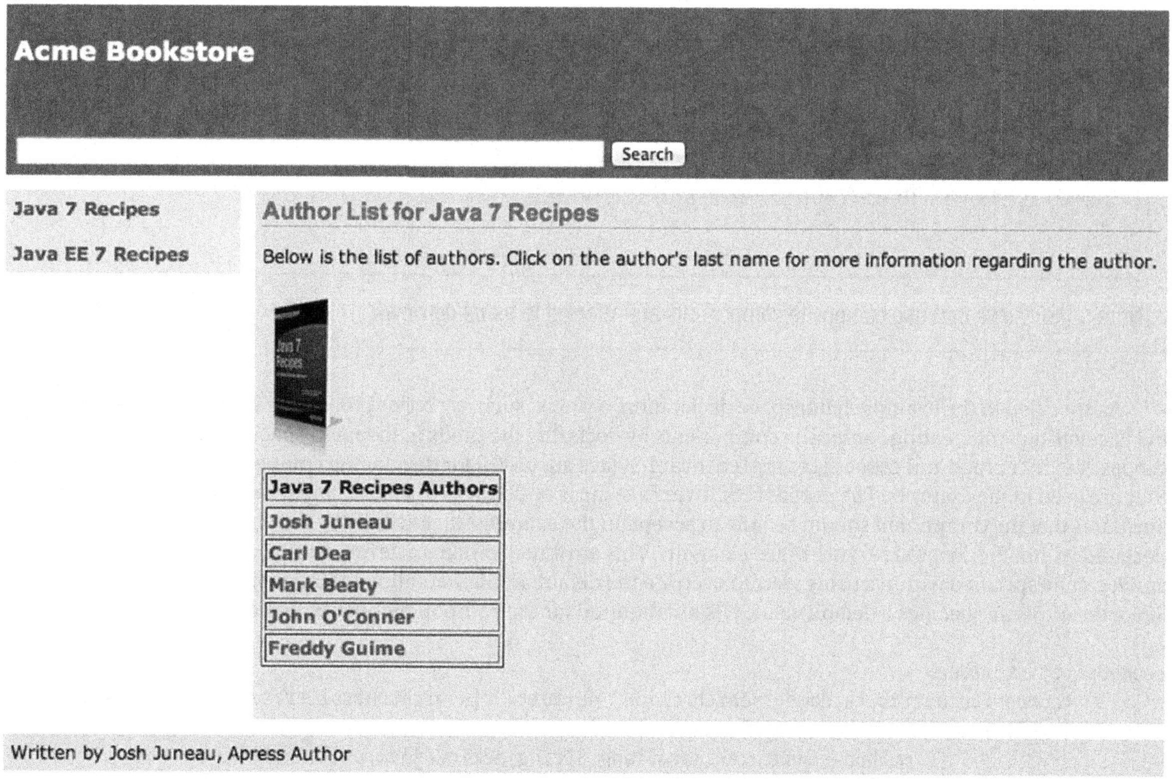

Figure 4-7. *Acme bookstore layout with search component*

▨ **Note** As of the release of JSF 2.2 with Java EE 7, it is possible to create composite components using Java code only with no markup. To learn more about doing so, please see the related example in Chapter 6.

Explanation

Creating JSF components has been a boon for the JSF technology because it allows portions of web views to be saved and reused in many places. The problem is that creating JSF components has always been a bit of a daunting task because there is quite a bit of work required to develop custom JSF components. However, when JSF 2.0 came about, the Facelets view definition language was baked in, and it included the ability to save portions of JSF views into their own components by utilizing the Facelets ui:component tag. Such components are referred to as *composite components*. Composite components are easy to develop and include most of the functionality that is required for standard application use.

The development of composite components consists of the creation of a separate XHTML document to contain the composite component layout, as well as an optional managed bean controller for containing any business logic that the composite component requires. In the example, an XHTML document entitled search.xhtml contains the layout for the composite component. The Facelets view definition language contains a handful of tags that can be useful for developing composite components. To use them, the required namespace must be declared within the composite component XHTML document. The following code excerpt from the search.xhtml document shows the declaration:

```
<html xmlns="http://www.w3.org/1999/xhtml"
      xmlns:h="http://xmlns.jcp.org/jsf/html"
      xmlns:composite"http://xmlns.jcp.org/jsf/composite">
```

■ **Note**   JSF views that use composite components are referred to as *using* views.

As specified in the example namespace declaration, a prefix, such as composite, can be used to reference the Facelets tags for creating composite components by declaring the prefix in the namespace. As such, the composite:interface and composite:implementation tags are useful for developing composite components, and they are used in the example. The composite:interface tag is optional as of JSF 2.2, and it can be used to specify any attributes that the component should be able to accept. In the example, an attribute by the name of searchAction is declared within the composite:interface elements. This attribute contains a default value and a method-signature, and it can be specified within a using view to override the default implementation method for the search component. Since the attribute specifies a default value, it is not required for the component's use within a view.

```
<composite:interface>
        <composite:attribute name="searchAction" default="#{searchController.searchAuthors(completeA
uthorController.completeAuthorList)}"
                        method-signature="java.lang.String action(java.util.List)"/>
</cc:interface>
```

Any number of attributes can be declared for a component, and if the attribute is used to specify a value rather than a method, then the method-signature attribute for the composite:interface tag does not have to be present. For instance, to declare an attribute that accepts a particular value for the name of a label, you may include an attribute such as the following:

```
<composite:attribute name="searchLabel" default="searchComponent"/>
```

The implementation for a composite component should be defined between opening and closing composite:implementation tags. The composite component in the example includes an h:form that will be used to submit search text to the SearchController managed bean. The composite component implementation also includes three JSF components: h:inputText to accept the search text, h:commandButton to invoke the searchAuthors method, and h:outputText to display a message if the search fails.

```
<composite:implementation>
        <h:form id="searchForm">
                <h:outputText id="error" value="#{searchController.errorText}"/>
                <br/>
                <h:inputText id="searchText" styleClass="searchBox" size="75" value="#{searchController.
searchText}"/>

                <h:commandButton id="searchButton" value="Search" action="#{cc.attrs.searchAction}"/>

        </h:form>
</composite:implementation>
```

The action that is specified for the h:commandButton is #{cc.attrs.searchAction}, and this corresponds to the searchAction attribute that was defined within the composite:interface element within the composite component view. Any attribute that is defined within the view can be referenced using the cc.attrs prefix. The word cc in JavaServer Faces is a reserved identifier for use with composite components. The cc.attrs identifier can be used to access composite component attributes. The default method that will be specified for the searchAction attribute in the example is #{searchController.searchAuthors}, but a using view can specify another method if needed. The value for both the h:inputText and h:outputText components within the composite component implementation are properties that are exposed from the SearchController managed bean class.

The SearchController managed bean class encapsulates the business logic for the search component. Within the class, an @ManagedProperty annotation is specified. The @ManagedProperty annotation is used to inject a value into the annotated property. If using CDI beans, one can also use the @Inject annotation to inject resources. In the example, the AuthorController managed bean is injected, so now any of the public fields or methods contained within AuthorController can be utilized from within the SearchController managed bean. The properties searchText and errorText are declared within the bean, and they are used within the component for setting the search text and displaying an error message, respectively. When the composite component's h:commandButton is clicked, the searchAuthors method is invoked, passing the complete list of authors, completeAuthorList, from the AuthorController managed bean. Taking a look at the method, it goes through each Author object within the complete author list and evaluates whether the searchText matches either the first, last, or full name of any author. If so, the AuthorController's displayAuthor method is invoked, passing the last field for the matching Author object, returning a String for the view name that should be rendered next. If the searchText does not match any of the Author objects, then the errorText property is populated with an error message, and the view named example04_04a.xhtml is displayed.

To use the composite component within a view, the XML namespace for the composite component must be declared and assigned a prefix. After doing so, the name of the composite component XHTML document should be specified as the tag name, followed by any attributes that are required. In the example, the namespace is declared as follows:

```
<html xmlns="http://www.w3.org/1999/xhtml"
    xmlns:ui="http://xmlns.jcp.org/jsf/facelets"
    xmlns:h="http://xmlns.jcp.org/jsf/html"
    xmlns:util"http://xmlns.jcp.org/jsf/composite/components/util">
```

The composite component can then be utilized within the page as follows:

```
<util:search id="searchAuthor"/>
```

Developing components for use within JSF applications has never been easier. The Facelets ui:component tag has certainly made component creation much easier on developers and allows for the reuse of view fragments throughout JSF applications.

Handling Variable-Length Data on a Page

The DataTable component can be handy for iterating over a list or collection of data. It is possible to style a DataTable component to make a look that applies to almost every situation. However, sometimes it can be easier to use standard HTML table markup for each row and column of the table in order to apply finer grained styling. The ui:repeat tag can be helpful in this situations.

Example

Use the Facelets ui:repeat tag for iterating over a collection of data rather than the h:dataTable component. Doing so allows for the same style of collection iteration, but it does not force the use of the h:dataTable component elements. For this example, the Acme Bookstore application has been rewritten so that it now contains the ability to list each author's books separately on their bio page. When an author name is chosen from the book listing or when an author is searched, then the bio page will appear, and the author's bio is displayed along with each of the books that the author has written.

■ **Note**   The example has been rewritten to make the application more robust. A new Book class has been created so that each book is now its own object. The Author class has been rewritten so that one or more Book objects can now be added to each Author object. The AuthorController has been rewritten so that the new Book and Author objects can be used to populate the author listing tables, and a new method has been added that allows for the initialization of each Book and Author object. To use the new classes, the application template (custom_template_neworg.xhtml), search component (search_neworg.xhtml), and each of the application views (example04_05a.xhtml, example04_05b.xhtml, example04_05c.xhtml) have been rewritten. Please refer to the sources in the org.javaserverfaces.chapter04. example04_05 package and the corresponding XHTML documents for complete listings.

The ui:repeat tag is used to iterate over a collection of the selected author's books within the author bio view, named example04_05c.xhtml. The author bio page can be reached by selecting an author from a listing of authors or searching for an author using the search component. The following code shows the view, example04_05c.xhtml, which is the bio view:

```
<?xml version="1.0" encoding="UTF-8"?>
<!--
Author: J. Juneau
-->
<!DOCTYPE html PUBLIC "-//W3C//DTD XHTML 1.0 Strict//EN" "http://www.w3.org/TR/xhtml1/DTD/xhtml1-
strict.dtd">
<html xmlns="http://www.w3.org/1999/xhtml"
    xmlns:f="http://xmlns.jcp.org/jsf/core"
    xmlns:ui="http://xmlns.jcp.org/jsf/facelets"
    xmlns:h="http://xmlns.jcp.org/jsf/html">
    <h:head>
        <meta http-equiv="Content-Type" content="text/html; charset=UTF-8"/>
        <title>Facelets Page Template</title>
    </h:head>
    <h:body>
        <ui:composition template="./layout/custom_template_search_neworg.xhtml">
            <ui:define name="content">
                <h:form id="componentForm">
                    <h1>#{uiRepeatAuthorController.current.first} #{uiRepeatAuthorController.
current.last}</h1>
                    <p>
                        #{uiRepeatAuthorController.current.bio}
                    </p>
```

```
                    <br/>
                    <h1>Author's Books</h1>
                    <table>
                    <ui:repeat id="bookList" var="book" value="#{uiRepeatAuthorController.current.
books}">
                        <tr>
                            <td>
                                <h:graphicImage id="bookImage"
                                                library="image"
                                                style="width: 100px; height: 120px" name="#{book.
image}"/>
                            </td>
                        </tr>
                        <tr>
                            <td>
                                <strong>#{book.title}</strong>
                            </td>
                        </tr>
                    </ui:repeat>
                    </table>
                </h:form>
            </ui:define>

        </ui:composition>
    </h:body>
</html>
```

Each Author object contains a list of books that an author has written, and when the bio page is rendered, it looks like Figure 4-8, displaying the list of books that the author has written using the ui:repeat tag.

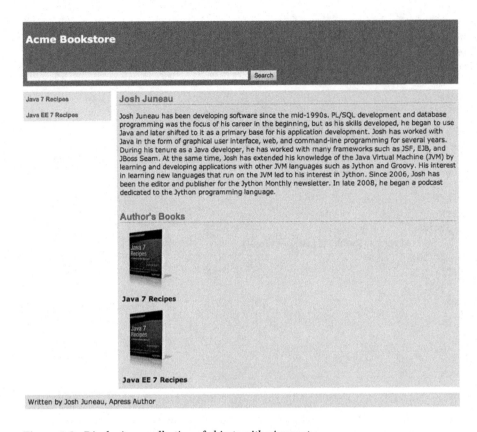

Figure 4-8. *Displaying a collection of objects with ui:repeat*

Explanation

The Facelets `ui:repeat` tag is a nice alternative to the `h:dataTable` component if you need to have more control over the HTML table that is rendered. The `h:dataTable` component is powerful in that it makes it easy to iterate over a collection of objects and display them within a page. However, sometimes it is useful to control the layout a bit more, and `ui:repeat` provides that level of control.

The `ui:repeat` tag has a handful of attributes that need to be specified in order to bind the tag to a collection of data within a managed bean. Specifically, the `value` and `var` attributes, much like those of the `h:dataTable` component, are used to specify the collection to iterate over and the variable that will be used to refer to a single object within the collection, respectively. In the example, the `value` attribute is set to `#{uiRepeatAuthorController.current.books}`, which is a collection of `Book` objects that is attached to the currently selected `Author`, and the `var` attribute is set to the value `book`.

The markup and JSF tags placed between the opening and closing `ui:repeat` tags will be processed for each iteration over the collection of objects. In the example, two table rows are placed inside `ui:repeat`; one row contains the book cover image, and the other contains the name of the book. The `Book` object fields are referenced within `ui:repeat` using the value of the `var` attribute, `book`.

In the example, the views that display the complete author list for each of the books use a List named authorList. The authorList is declared within the AuthorController managed bean and populated with Author objects. When an author is selected from the list, the displayAuthor method within AuthorController is invoked, which populates the current Author object. Let's take a look at the AuthorController for this example, which has been rewritten since its use within previous examples.

```java
package org.javaserverfaces.chapter04.example04_05;

import org.javaeerecipes.chapter04.*;
import java.io.Serializable;
import java.util.ArrayList;
import java.util.List;
import javax.enterprise.context.SessionScoped;
import javax.inject.Named;

/**
 *
 * @author juneau
 */
@Named(value = "uiRepeatAuthorController")
@SessionScoped
public class AuthorController implements Serializable {

    private List<Author> authorBookList;
    private List<Author> authorList;
    private List<Author> completeAuthorList;
    private String storeName = "Acme Bookstore";

    private String juneauBio =
            "Josh Juneau has been developing software"
            + " since the mid-1990s. PL/SQL development and database programming"
            + " was the focus of his career in the beginning, but as his skills developed,"
            + " he began to use Java and later shifted to it as a primary base for his"
            + " application development. Josh has worked with Java in the form of graphical"
            + " user interface, web, and command-line programming for several years. "
            + "During his tenure as a Java developer, he has worked with many frameworks"
            + " such as JSF, EJB, and JBoss Seam. At the same time, Josh has extended his"
            + " knowledge of the Java Virtual Machine (JVM) by learning and developing applications"
            + " with other JVM languages such as Jython and Groovy. His interest in learning"
            + " new languages that run on the JVM led to his interest in Jython. Since 2006,"
            + " Josh has been the editor and publisher for the Jython Monthly newsletter. "
            + "In late 2008, he began a podcast dedicated to the Jython programming language.";
    private String deaBio = "This is Carl Dea's Bio";
    private String beatyBio = "This is Mark Beaty's Bio";
    private String oConnerBio = "This is John O'Connor's Bio";
    private String guimeBio = "This is Freddy Guime's Bio";
    private Author current;
    private String authorLast;
```

```java
/**
 * Creates a new instance of RecipeController
 */
public AuthorController() {
    populateAuthors();
    populateJavaRecipesAuthorList();
    populateCompleteAuthorList();
}

private void populateAuthors(){

    Book book1 = new Book("Java 7 Recipes", "java7recipes.png");
    Book book2 = new Book("Java EE 7 Recipes", "javaEE 7recipes.png");
    Book book3 = new Book("Java FX 2.0: Introduction By Example", "javafx.png");
    authorBookList = new ArrayList<Author>();

    Author author1 = new Author("Josh", "Juneau", juneauBio);
    author1.addBook(book1);
    author1.addBook(book2);
    authorBookList.add(author1);

    Author author2 = new Author("Carl", "Dea", deaBio);
    author2.addBook(book1);
    author2.addBook(book3);
    authorBookList.add(author2);

    Author author3 = new Author("Mark", "Beaty", beatyBio);
    author3.addBook(book1);
    authorBookList.add(author3);

    Author author4 = new Author("John", "O'Conner", oConnerBio);
    author4.addBook(book1);
    authorBookList.add(author4);

    Author author5 = new Author("Freddy", "Guime", guimeBio);
    author5.addBook(book1);
    authorBookList.add(author5);
}

/**
 * Searches through all Author objects and populates the authorList
 * with only those authors who were involved with the Java 7 Recipes book
 * @return
 */
public String populateJavaRecipesAuthorList() {
    authorList = new ArrayList<>();
    for(Author author:authorBookList){
        List<Book>books = author.getBooks();
```

```java
            for(Book book:books){
                if(book.getTitle().equals("Java 7 Recipes")){
                    authorList.add(author);
                }
            }
        }

        return "example04_05a";
    }

    /**
     * Searches through all Author objects and populates the authorList
     * with only those authors who were involved with the Java EE 7 Recipes book
     * @return
     */
    public String populateJavaEERecipesAuthorList() {
        authorList = new ArrayList<>();
        for(Author author:authorBookList){
            List<Book>books = author.getBooks();
            for(Book book:books){
                if(book.getTitle().equals("Java EE 7 Recipes")){
                    authorList.add(author);
                }
            }
        }
        return "example04_05b";

    }

    /**
     * Populates completeAuthorList with each existing Author object
     * @return
     */
    private void populateCompleteAuthorList() {
        completeAuthorList = new ArrayList();
        for(Author author:authorBookList){
            completeAuthorList.add(author);
        }

    }

    public String displayAuthor(String last) {
        for (Author author : authorList) {
            if (author.getLast().equals(last)) {
                current = author;
            }
        }
        return "example04_05c";
    }
```

```java
/**
 * @return the authorList
 */
public List getauthorList() {
    return authorList;
}

/**
 * @return the current
 */
public Author getCurrent() {
    return current;
}

/**
 * @param current the current to set
 */
public void setCurrent(Author current) {
    this.current = current;
}

/**
 * @return the authorLast
 */
public String getAuthorLast() {
    return authorLast;
}

/**
 * @param authorLast the authorLast to set
 */
public void setAuthorLast(String authorLast) {
    displayAuthor(authorLast);
}

/**
 * @return the storeName
 */
public String getStoreName() {
    return storeName;
}

/**
 * @param storeName the storeName to set
 */
public void setStoreName(String storeName) {
    this.storeName = storeName;
}

/**
 * @return the completeAuthorList
```

```
    */
    public List<Author> getCompleteAuthorList() {
        return completeAuthorList;
    }

    /**
     * @param completeAuthorList the completeAuthorList to set
     */
    public void setCompleteAuthorList(List<Author> completeAuthorList) {
        this.completeAuthorList = completeAuthorList;
    }
}
```

When `displayAuthor` is invoked, the current `Author` object is populated with the currently selected author, and the bio page is rendered. The bio page source is listed in the solution to this example. Each `Author` object contains a `List` of `Book` objects that correspond to the books that particular author has written. The `ui:repeat` tag is used to iterate over this list of books.

The `ui:repeat` tag can be effective in various use cases. When deciding to use `h:dataTable` or `ui:repeat`, it is best to determine whether customization is going to be imperative. For those situations where more control is desired, `ui:repeat` is certainly the best choice.

Debugging View Content

JSF provides a facility for debugging on a view layout. This can make it easier to find unwanted bugs before placing a view into a production environment.

Example

Insert the `ui:debug` tag into the JSF view that you want to debug. One of the JSF views for the Acme Bookstore has been rewritten to include the `ui:debug` tag. The source for the view is as follows:

```xml
<?xml version='1.0' encoding='UTF-8' ?>
<!--
Author: J. Juneau
-->
<!DOCTYPE html PUBLIC "-//W3C//DTD XHTML 1.0 Transitional//EN" "http://www.w3.org/TR/xhtml1/DTD/
xhtml1-transitional.dtd">
<html xmlns="http://www.w3.org/1999/xhtml"
      xmlns:ui="http://xmlns.jcp.org/jsf/facelets"
      xmlns:f="http://xmlns.jcp.org/jsf/core"
      xmlns:h="http://xmlns.jcp.org/jsf/html">

    <body>

        <ui:composition template="./layout/custom_template_search_neworg.xhtml">
            <ui:define name="content">
                <ui:debug/>
                <h:form id="componentForm">
                    <h1>Author List for Java 7 Recipes</h1>
```

```
                <p>
                    Below is the list of authors.  Click on the author's last name
                    for more information regarding the author.
                </p>

                <h:graphicImage id="javarecipes" style="width: 100px; height: 120px" url="../
images/java7recipes.png"/>
                <br/>
                <h:dataTable id="authorTable" border="1" value="#{uiRepeatAuthorController.
authorList}"
                            var="author">
                    <f:facet name="header">
                        Java 7 Recipes Authors
                    </f:facet>
                    <h:column>
                        <h:commandLink id="authorName" action="#{uiRepeatAuthorController.
displayAuthor(author.last)}" value="#{author.first} #{author.last}"/>
                    </h:column>
                </h:dataTable>
                <br/>
                <br/>
            </h:form>
        </ui:define>
    </ui:composition>

    </body>
</html>
```

Once the view has been rendered in a browser, pressing the Ctrl+Shift+D keys will bring up a debug window for the page that looks like Figure 4-9.

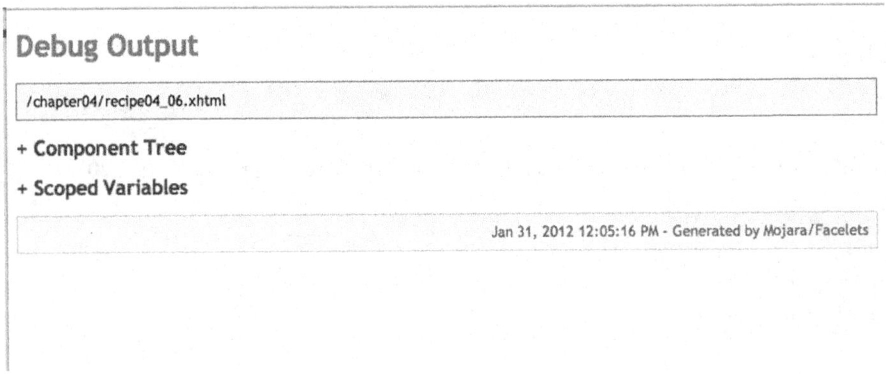

Figure 4-9. *The ui:debug output window*

Explanation

Debugging JSF views can sometimes prove to be frustrating, especially if there is an issue within some JSF EL within the view. Facelets provides a convenient tool known as ui:debug that helps satisfy the requirement of debugging troubled JSF views. To use the tool, add the ui:debug tag to the JSF view that you want to debug. In most environments, it can be most useful to add the tag to the application template so that each template client view inherits the tag. When the view is rendered in a browser, press the Ctrl+Shift+D keys to open the debug window for the view. The debug window contains a lot of information regarding the current state of the component tree, as well as the scoped variables within the application.

The ui:debug tag contains a rendered attribute that can be used to determine when the tag should be included in the view. For instance, an EL expression can be used for the rendered attribute to signify whether the environment is in development or production, returning a Boolean value that either renders the tag or not. The ui:debug tag also includes a hotkey attribute, which can be used to change the key that is pressed along with Ctrl+Shift in order to open the debug window. By default, the hot key is D, which stands for "debug."

Writing a Custom Resolver for Locating Facelets Templates and Resources

Facelets provide the ability to store resource files in an external JAR. A custom ResourceResolver can be used to locate Facelets resource files from an external JAR. This would allow one to package all resources within a single JAR that could be used by a suite of applications.

Example

FacesServlet will then use the custom resolver class to find the Facelets files you request. The following source listing, for a class named FaceletsResourceResolver, can be used to resolve the URL to the resource you require rather than using the native Facelets ResourceResolver.

```
package org.javaserverfaces.chapter04.example04_07;


import java.net.URL;
import javax.faces.view.facelets.ResourceResolver;
/**
 * @author juneau
 */
@FaceletsResourceResolver
public class FaceletsResourceResolver extends ResourceResolver {

    private ResourceResolver parent;

    public FaceletsResourceResolver(ResourceResolver parent) {
        this.parent = parent;
    }

    @Override
    public URL resolveUrl(String path) {
        System.out.println("Resolving URL " + path);
        URL url = parent.resolveUrl(path);
```

```
        if (url == null) {

            if (path.startsWith("/")) {
                path = path.substring(1);
            }
            url = Thread.currentThread().getContextClassLoader().
                    getResource(path);
        }
        return url;
    }

}
```

When the application is redeployed, the new FaceletsResourceResolver class will be used to resolve the URL for accessing resources, rather than the default resolver.

Explanation

Sometimes it makes sense to package resources into a JAR or WAR file so that they can be shared across multiple applications or with a number of different developers. The problem is that simply adding the JAR or WAR file to the application CLASSPATH will not allow for such resources to become accessible to the application. You must write a custom resource resolver in order to find the path to the custom resource, rather than relying upon the default resolver.

To write a resolver class, extend the ResourceResolver abstract class, and override the resolveUrl(String) method with the custom resolver implementation. The custom implementation should search the CLASSPATH for the resource and return a URL that corresponds to the resource's location. To register the resolver with Facelets, you can annotate the class using the @FaceletsResourceResolver annotation or modify the web.xml deployment descriptor (as described in the following note).

■ **Note**   Prior to JSF 2.2, a Facelets ResourceResolver had to be manually configured within the web.xml deployment descriptor. The ability to annotate the class with the @FaceletsResourceResolver was a new feature of Java EE 7 and JSF 2.2. It is good to note that if you have a resource resolver defined via an annotation and also via web.xml, the resolver defined within the web.xml file will take precedence.

If you are using JSF 2.1 or earlier, then to manually configure the ResourceResolver for the example, place the following lines of XML into the web.xml deployment descriptor:

<context-param>

　　<param-name>facelets.RESOURCE_RESOLVER</param-name>

　　<param-value>org.javaserverfaces.chapter04.FaceletsResourceResolver</param-value>

</context-param>

Utilizing Multiple Templates per Application

JSF 2.2 introduced a feature known as Resource Library Contracts, which allows one the ability to change the styling of an application very easily. One can supply multiple templates for an application, assigning each to various portions of an application to provide a different look and feel in those portions.

Example

To use Resource Library Contracts, create a directory at the root of your application named `contracts`, and then place subfolders containing necessary files for different application templates within the template directory. The file structure for each template folder should contain folders named `css` and `images`, each containing a style sheet for the template and images files, respectively. Figure 4-10 shows how the directory structure should look.

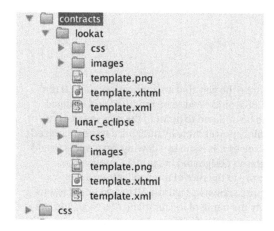

Figure 4-10. *Multitemplating directory structure*

Next, add the name of the template file to the `ui:composition` element on each view that you want to have the site template applied to. For example, the following excerpt from `chapter04/example04_08.xhtml` demonstrates how this is done:

```
<html xmlns="http://www.w3.org/1999/xhtml"
      xmlns:ui="http://xmlns.jcp.org/jsf/facelets"
      xmlns:f="http://xmlns.jcp.org/jsf/core"
      xmlns:h="http://xmlns.jcp.org/jsf/html">

    <body>

        <ui:composition template="template.xhtml">
            <ui:define name="content">
                ...
            </ui:define>
        </ui:composition>
    </body>
</html>
```

Lastly, to enable the new template system, add the `resource-library-contracts` section to the `faces-config.xml`, specifying the name of the template that you want to apply to the site.

```
<resource-library-contracts>
      <contract-mapping>
          <url-pattern>/admin/*</url-pattern>
          <contracts>lookat</contracts>
      </contract-mapping>
      <contract-mapping>
          <url-pattern>*</url-pattern>
          <contracts>lunar_eclipse</contracts>
      </contract-mapping>
</resource-library-contracts>
```

The `resource-library-contracts` element allows one to specify a different template to the views that reside within specified folders in an application.

Explanation

In the past, developers had to perform lots of tweaking in order to change the way that an application looks. If the background color or images needed to be changed on the site, then CSS would need to be modified and updated images copied into place. Moreover, configuration files would need to be updated to point to the new images and/or make use of the updated CSS. This is not a horrible task, but it is certainly preventable by utilizing a more organized templating system. In JSF 2.2, the Resource Library Contracts system solves this issue by allowing developers to add more than one template to an application and apply different templates to designated areas in an application.

To register templates with an application, add a `contracts` directory to the root of the application, as mentioned in the solution to this example. Follow the directory structure shown in Figure 4-10 to add templates to the application, as needed. To apply a given template to a page, specify the name of the template file. Next, add the `resource-library-contracts` section to `faces-config.xml` in order to map the different contracts to portions of the application via the url path.. At runtime, the specified template will be applied.

CHAPTER 5

JavaServer Faces Standard Components

The JSF framework allows developers to build applications utilizing a series of views, and each view consists of a series of components. The framework is kind of like a puzzle in that each piece must fit into its particular place in order to make things work smoothly. Components are just another piece of the puzzle. Components are the building blocks that make up JSF views. One of the strengths of using the JSF framework is the abundance of components that are available for use within views. To developers, components can be tags that are placed within the XHTML views. Components resemble standard HTML tags; they contain a number of attributes, an opening tag and a closing tag, and sometimes components that are to be embedded inside of others. Components can also be written in Java code, and their tags can be bound to Java code that resides within a JSF managed bean.

A number of components come standard with the JSF framework. The examples in this chapter will cover the standard components in detail, and it will provide examples that will allow you to begin using components in your applications right away.

This chapter focuses on the JSF standard component library, and toward the end it features some examples showing how to use external component libraries. The example in this chapter will grow from the first example final one. In the end, a newsletter page for the Acme Bookstore will be complete and full-featured.

Before tackling the examples, though, the following section provides a brief overview of the standard JSF components and associated common component tags. This will help you get the most out of the examples..

Component and Tag Primer

Table 5-1 lists the components that are available with a clean install of the JSF framework.

Table 5-1. *JSF HTML Components*

Component	Tag	Description
UIColumn	h:column	Represents a column of data in the dataTable component
UICommand	h:commandButton	Submits a form
	h:commandLink	Links pages or actions
UIData	h:dataTable	Represents a table used for iterating over collections of data
UIForm	h:form	Represents an input form
UIGraphic	h:graphicImage	Displays an image
UIInput	h:inputHidden	Includes a hidden variable in a form
	h:inputSecret	Allows text entry without displaying the actual text
	h:inputText	Allows text entry
	h:inputTextarea	Allows multiline text entry
UIOutcomeTarget	h:link	Links to another page or location
UIMessage	h:message	Displays a localized message
UIMessages	h:messages	Displays localized messages
UIOutput	h:outputFormat	Displays a formatted localized message
	h:outputLabel	Displays a label for a specified field
	h:outputLink	Links to another page or location
UIPanel	h:panelGrid	Displays a table
	h:panelGroup	Groups components
UISelectBoolean	h:selectBooleanCheckbox	Displays a Boolean choice
UISelectItem	h:selectItem	Represents one item in a list of items for selection
UISelectItems	h:selectItems	Represents a list of items for selection
UISelectMany	h:selectManyCheckbox	Displays a group of check boxes that allow multiple user choices
	h:selectManyListbox	Allows a user to select multiple items from a list
	h:selectManyMenu	Allows a user to select multiple items from a drop-down menu
UISelectOne	h:selectOneListbox	Allows a user to select a single item from a list
	h:selectOneMenu	Allows a user to select a single item from a drop-down menu
	h:selectOneRadio	Allows a user to select one item from a set

JSF provides a number of core tags that can be used to provide more functionality for the components. For example, these tags can be embedded inside JSF component tags and specify rules that can be used to convert the values that are displayed or used as input for the component. Other uses of the core tags are to provide a list of options for a select component, validate input, and provide action and event listeners. Table 5-2 describes the JSF core tags.

Table 5-2. *JSF Core Tags*

Tag	Function
f:actionListener	Registers an action listener method with a component
f:phaseListener	Registers a PhaseListener to a page
f:setPropertyActionListener	Registers a special form submittal action listener
f:valueChangeListener	Registers a value change listener with a component
f:converter	Registers an arbitrary converter with a component
f:convertDateTime	Registers a DateTimeConverter instance with a component
f:convertNumber	Registers a NumberConverter with a component
f:facet	Adds a nested component to particular enclosing parents
f:metadata	Registers a particular facet with a parent component
f:selectItem	Encapsulates one item in a list
f:selectItems	Encapsulates all items of a list
f:validateDoubleRange	Registers a DoubleRangeValidator with a component
f:validateLength	Registers a LengthValidator with a component
f:validateLongRange	Registers a LongRangeValidator with a component
f:validator	Registers a custom validator with a component
f:validateRegex	Registers a RegExValidator with a component (JSF 2.0)
f:validateBean	Delegates validation of a local value to a BeanValidator (JSF 2.0)
f:validateRequired	Ensures that a value is present in a parent component
f:viewAction	Allows for the execution of an application-specific command or action during one of the JSF lifecycle phases.

■ **Note** The common sources and the completed classes to run the application for Chapter 5 are contained within the org.javaserverfaces.chapter05 package, and one or more examples throughout this chapter will utilize classes contained within that package.

Common Component Tag Attributes

Each standard JSF component tag contains a set of attributes that must be specified in order to uniquely identify it from the others, register the component to a managed bean, and so on. There is a set of attributes that are common across each component tag, and this section lists those attributes, along with a description of each. *All attributes besides id can be specified as JSF EL.*

- binding: A managed bean property can be specified for this attribute, and it can be used to bind the tag to a component instance within a managed bean. Doing so allows you to programmatically control the component from within the managed bean.

- id: This attribute can be set to uniquely identify the component. If you do not specify a value for the id attribute, then JSF will automatically generate one. Each component within a view must have a unique id attribute, or an error will be generated when the page is rendered. *I recommend you specify a value for the id attribute on each component tag, because then it will be easy to statically reference the tag from a scripting language or a managed bean if needed. If you let JSF automatically populate this attribute, it may be different each time, and you will never be able to statically reference the tag from a scripting language.*

- immediate: This attribute can be set to true for input and command components in order to have them invoked during the Apply Request Values phase, rather than the Invoke Application phase.

- rendered: The rendered attribute can be used to specify whether the component should be rendered. This attribute is typically specified as a JSF EL expression that is bound to a managed bean property yielding a Boolean result. The EL expression must be an rvalue expression, meaning that it is read-only and cannot set a value.

- style: This attribute allows a CSS style to be applied to the component. The specified style will be applied when the component is rendered as output.

- styleClass: This attribute allows a CSS style class to be applied to the component. The specified style will be applied when the component is rendered as output.

- value: This attribute identifies the value of a given component. For some components, the value attribute is used to bind the tag to a managed bean property. In this case, the value specified for the component will be read from, or set within, the managed bean property. Other components, such as the commandButton component, use the value attribute to specify a label for the given component.

Common JavaScript Component Tags

Table 5-3 lists a number of attributes that are shared by many of the components, which enable JavaScript functionality to interact with the component.

Table 5-3. *Common Component Atrributes*

Attribute	Description
onblur	JavaScript code that should be executed when the component loses focus.
onchange	JavaScript code that should be executed when the component loses focus and the value changes.
ondblclick	JavaScript code that should be executed when the component has been clicked twice.
onfocus	JavaScript code that should be executed when the component gains focus.
onkeydown	JavaScript code that should be executed when user presses a key down and the component is in focus.
onkeypress	JavaScript code that should be executed when user presses a key and the component is in focus.
onkeyup	JavaScript code that should be executed when key press is completed and the component is in focus.
onmousedown	JavaScript code that should be executed when user clicks the mouse button and the component is in focus.
onmouseout	JavaScript code that should be executed when user moves mouse away from the component.
onmouseover	JavaScript code that should be executed when user moves mouse onto the component.
onmousemove	JavaScript code that should be executed when user moves mouse within the component.
onmouseup	JavaScript code that should be executed when mouse button click is completed and the component is in focus.
onselect	JavaScript code that should be executed when the component is selected by user.

Binding Components to Properties

All JSF components can be bound to managed bean properties. Do so by declaring a property for the type of component you want to bind within the managed bean and then by referencing that property using the component's binding attribute. For instance, the following dataTable component is bound to a managed bean property and then manipulated from within the bean.

In the view:

```
<h:dataTable id="myTable" binding="#{myBean.myTable}" value="#{myBean.myTableCollection}"/>
```

In the bean:

```
// Provide getter and setter methods for this property
private javax.faces.component.UIData myTable;
...
myTable.setRendered(true);
...
```

Binding can prove to be very useful in some cases, especially when you need to manipulate the state of a component programmatically before re-rendering the view.

Creating an Input Form

The JSF component library provides a number of useful components for input of data. Using the library, you can, for example, create an input form.

Example

Create an input form by enclosing child input components within a parent form component. There are four JSF components that will allow for text entry as input. Those components are inputText, inputSecret, inputHidden, and inputTextarea. Any or all of these components can be placed within a form component in order to create an input form that accepts text entry.

In the example, you will create an input form that will be used to sign up for the Acme Bookstore newsletter. The user will be able to enter their first and last names, an e-mail address, a password, and a short description of their interests.

The View: example05_01.xhtml

The following code is for the view example05_01.xhtml, which constructs the layout for the input form:

```
<?xml version='1.0' encoding='UTF-8' ?>
<!--
Author: J. Juneau
-->
<!DOCTYPE html PUBLIC "-//W3C//DTD XHTML 1.0 Transitional//EN" "
http://www.w3.org/TR/xhtml1/DTD/xhtml1-transitional.dtd">
<html xmlns="http://www.w3.org/1999/xhtml"
      xmlns:ui="http://xmlns.jcp.org/jsf/facelets"
      xmlns:f="http://xmlns.jcp.org/jsf/core"
      xmlns:h="http://xmlns.jcp.org/jsf/html">

    <body>

        <ui:composition template="layout/custom_template_search.xhtml">
            <ui:define name="content">
                <h:messages globalOnly="true"  errorStyle="color: red" infoStyle="color: green"/>
                <h:form id="contactForm">
                    <h1>Subscribe to Newsletter</h1>
                    <p>
                        Enter your information below in order to be added to the Acme Bookstore
                        newsletter.
                    </p>

                    <br/>
                    <label for="first">First: </label>
                    <h:inputText id="first" size="40" value="#{contactController1.current.first}"/>
                    <br/>
                    <label for="last">Last: </label>
                    <h:inputText id="last" size="40" value="#{contactController1.current.last}"/>
                    <br/>
                    <label for="email">Email: </label>
```

```
            <h:inputText id="email" size="40" value="#{contactController1.current.email}"/>
            <br/>
            <label for="password">Enter a password for site access:</label>
            <h:inputSecret id="password" size="40" value="#{contactController1.current.
            password}"/>
            <br/><br/>
            <label for="description">Enter your book interests</label>
            <br/>
            <h:inputTextarea id="description" rows="5" cols="100"
            value="#{contactController1.current.description}"/>
            <br/>
            <h:commandButton id="contactSubmit" action="#{contactController1.subscribe}"
            value="Save"/>
        </h:form>
      </ui:define>
    </ui:composition>

  </body>
</html>
```

■ **Note**   As you can see from the example, HTML can be mixed together with JSF component tags. An HTML label tag is used to specify a label for each input component in this example.

To learn more about how the commandButton component works, please see the next example.

Managed Bean: ContactController.java

Each view that contains an input form needs to have an associated managed bean, right? The managed bean in this case is RequestScoped, and the name of the bean class is ContactController. The listing for the ContactController class is as follows:

```
package org.javaserverfaces.chapter05.example05_01;

import java.util.ArrayList;
import java.util.LinkedHashMap;
import java.util.List;
import java.util.Map;
import javax.faces.application.FacesMessage;
import javax.inject.Named ;
import javax.enterprise.context.RequestScoped;
import javax.faces.component.UIComponent;
import javax.faces.context.FacesContext;
import javax.faces.event.ValueChangeEvent;
import javax.faces.model.SelectItem;
import javax.faces.validator.ValidatorException;
import javax.inject.Inject;
```

```java
/**
 * Chapter 5
 *
 * @author juneau
 */
@RequestScoped
@Named(value = "contactController")
public class ContactController implements java.io.Serializable {

    private Contact current;

    /**
     * Creates a new instance of ContactController
     */
    public ContactController() {

    }

    /**
     * Obtain the current instance of the Contact object
     * @return Contact
     */
    public Contact getCurrent(){
        if (current == null){
            current = new Contact();
        }
        return current;
    }

    /**
     * Adds a subscriber to the newsletter
     * @return String
     */
    public String subscribe(){
        // No implementation yet, will add to a database table in Chapter 7
        FacesMessage facesMsg = new FacesMessage(FacesMessage.SEVERITY_INFO,
                "Successfully Subscribed to Newsletter for " + getCurrent().getEmail(), null);
        FacesContext.getCurrentInstance().addMessage(null, facesMsg);
        return "SUBSCRIBE";
    }

    /**
     * Navigational method
     * @return String
     */
    public String add(){
        return "ADD_SUBSCRIBER";
    }
}
```

■ **Note**   At this time, nothing happens when the submit button is clicked other than a nice "Success" message being displayed on the screen. Later in the book, you will revisit the subscribe method and add the code for creating a record within an underlying database. The input screen should look like Figure 5-1 when rendered.

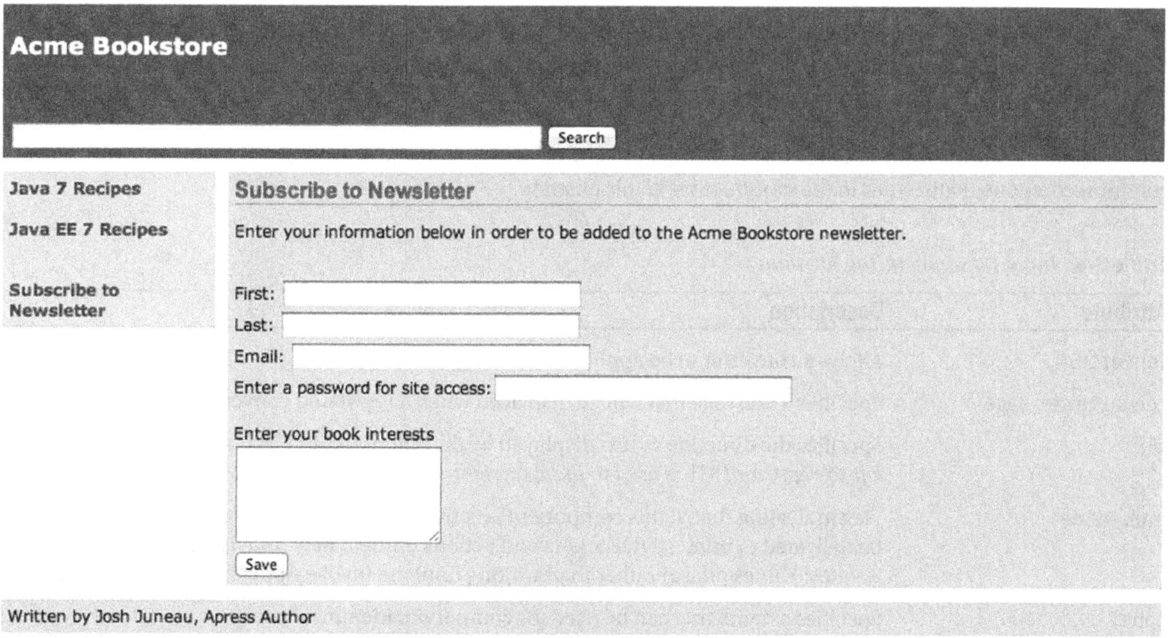

Acme Bookstore

Search

Java 7 Recipes

Java EE 7 Recipes

Subscribe to
Newsletter

Subscribe to Newsletter

Enter your information below in order to be added to the Acme Bookstore newsletter.

First:

Last:

Email:

Enter a password for site access:

Enter your book interests

Save

Written by Josh Juneau, Apress Author

Figure 5-1. *JSF input form for subscribing to the Acme Bookstore newsletter*

Explanation

The JavaServer Faces framework ships with a slew of standard components that can be utilized within JSF views. There are four standard components that can be used for capturing text input: inputText, inputSecret, inputHidden, and inputTextarea. These component tags, as well as all of the other standard JSF component tags, share a common set of attributes and some attributes that are unique to each specific tag. To learn more about the common attributes, please see the related section in the introduction to this chapter. In this example, I will go over the specifics for each of these input components. The form component, specified via the h:form tag, is used to create an input form within a JSF view. Each component that is to be processed within the form should be enclosed between the opening and closing h:form tags. Each form typically contains at least one command component, such as a commandButton. A view can contain more than one form component, and only those components that are contained within the form will be processed when the form is submitted.

■ **Note**   I recommend you always specify the id attribute for each component. Most importantly, specify the id attribute for the form component. If you do not specify the id attribute for a given JSF component, then one will be automatically generated for you. The automatic generation of JSF component ids prohibits the ability to statically reference a component from within a scripting language, such as JavaScript, or a managed bean. For instance, in the example, the form id attribute is set to contactForm, and the first inputText component id is set to first. This allows you to reference the component statically by appending the form id to the component id from a scripting language or managed bean. In the case of the example, you'd reference the first component as contactForm:first.

Each of the input tags support the list of attributes that is shown in Table 5-4, in addition to those already listed as common component attributes in the introduction to this chapter.

Table 5-4. *Input Component Tag Attributes*

Attribute	Description
converter	Allows a converter to be applied to the component's data.
converterMessage	Specifies a message that will be displayed when a registered converter fails.
dir	Specifies the direction of text displayed by the component. *(LTR is used to indicate left-to-right, and RTL is used to indicate right-to-left).*
immediate	Flag indicating that, if this component is activated by the user, notifications should be delivered to interested listeners and actions immediately (that is, during the Apply Request Values phase) rather than waiting until the Invoke Application phase.
label	Specifies a name that can be used for component identification.
lang	Allows a language code to be specified for the rendered markup.
required	Accepts a Boolean to indicate whether the user must enter a value for the given component.
requiredMessage	Specifies an error message to be displayed if the user does not enter a value for a *required* component.
validator	Allows a validator to be applied to the component.
valueChangeListener	Allows a managed bean method to be bound for event-handling purposes. The method will be called when there is a change made to the component.

The inputText component is used to generate a single-line text box within a rendered page. The inputText component value attribute is most commonly bound to a managed bean property so that the values of the property can be retrieved or set when a form is processed. In the example, the first inputText component is bound to the managed bean property named first. The EL expression #{contactController1.current.first} is specified for the component value, so if the managed bean's first property contains a value, then it will be displayed within the inputText component. Likewise, when the form is submitted, then any value that has been entered within the component will be saved within the first property in the managed bean.

The inputSecret component is used to generate a single-line text box within a rendered page, and when text is entered into the component, then it is not displayed; rather, asterisks are displayed in place of each character typed. This component makes it possible for a user to enter private text, such as a password, without it being displayed on the screen for others to read. The inputSecret component works identically to the inputText component, other than hiding the text with asterisks. In the example, the value of the inputSecret component is bound to a managed bean property named password via the #{contactController1.current.password} EL expression.

The inputTextarea component is used to generate a multiline text box within a rendered page. As such, this component has a couple of additional attributes that can be used to indicate how large the text area should be. The inputTextarea has the rows and cols attributes, which allow a developer to specify how many rows (height) and how many columns (wide) of space the component should take up on the page, respectively. Other than those two attributes, the inputTextarea component works in much the same manner as the inputText component. In the example, the value attribute of the inputTextarea component is specified as #{contactController1.current. description}, so the description property will be populated with the contents of the component when the form is submitted.

The input component I have not yet discussed is the inputHidden component. This component is used to place a hidden input field into the form. It works in the same manner as the inputText component, except that it is not rendered on the page for the user to see. The value for an inputHidden component can be bound to a managed bean property in the same way as the other components. You can use such a component for passing a hidden token to and from a form.

As you can see, the days of passing and receiving request parameters within JSP pages are over. Utilizing the JSF standard input components, it is possible to bind values to managed bean properties using JSF EL expressions. This makes it much easier for developers to submit values from an input form for processing. Rather than retrieving parameters from a page, assigning them to variables, and then processing, the JSF framework takes care of that overhead for you. Although I have not covered the usage of all input component attributes within this example, I will cover more in the examples that follow, as we will build upon the Acme Bookstore newsletter subscription page.

Invoking Actions from Within a Page

The JSF framework allows one to invoke server-side methods from a button or link within an application view.

Example

To invoke action methods within a managed bean, utilize the commandButton or commandLink components within your view. The command components allow for the user invocation of actions within managed beans. Command components bind buttons and links on a page directly to action methods, allowing developers to spend more time thinking about the development of the application and less time thinking about the Java servlet–processing life cycle.

In the example, a button and a link are added to the newsletter page for the Acme Bookstore. The button that will be added to the page will be used to submit the input form for processing, and the link will allow a user to log into the application and manage their subscription and bookstore account.

The View: example05_02.xhtml

The following code is for the newsletter subscription view including the command components. The sources are for the file named example05_02.xhtml.

```xml
<?xml version='1.0' encoding='UTF-8' ?>
<!--
Author: J. Juneau
-->
<!DOCTYPE html PUBLIC "-//W3C//DTD XHTML 1.0 Transitional//EN" "http://www.w3.org/TR/xhtml1/DTD/
xhtml1-transitional.dtd">
<html xmlns="http://www.w3.org/1999/xhtml"
      xmlns:ui="http://xmlns.jcp.org/jsf/facelets"
      xmlns:f="http://xmlns.jcp.org/jsf/core"
      xmlns:h="http://xmlns.jcp.org/jsf/html">

  <body>

        <ui:composition template="layout/custom_template_search.xhtml">
            <ui:define name="content">
                <h:messages globalOnly="true"  errorStyle="color: red" infoStyle="color: green"/>
                <h:form id="contactForm">
                    <h1>Subscribe to Newsletter</h1>
                    <p>
                        Enter your information below in order to be added to the Acme Bookstore
                        newsletter.
                    </p>

                    <br/>
                    <label for="first">First: </label>
                    <h:inputText id="first" size="40" value="#{contactController2.current.first}"/>
                    <br/>
                    <label for="last">Last: </label>
                    <h:inputText id="last" size="40" value="#{contactController2.current.last}"/>
                    <br/>
                    <label for="email">Email: </label>
                    <h:inputText id="email" size="40" value="#{contactController2.current.email}"/>
                    <br/>
                    <label for="password">Enter a password for site access:</label>
                    <h:inputSecret id="password" size="40" value="#{contactController2.current.
                    password}"/>
                    <br/><br/>
                    <label for="description">Enter your book interests</label>
                    <br/>
                    <h:inputTextarea id="description" rows="5" cols="100"
                    value="#{contactController2.current.description}"/>
                    <br/>
```

```
                    <h:commandButton id="contactSubmit" action="#{contactController2.subscribe}"
                        value="Save"/>
                    <br/><br/>
                    <h:commandLink id="manageAccount" action="#{contactController2.manage}"
                        value="Manage Subscription"/>
                </h:form>
            </ui:define>
        </ui:composition>

    </body>
</html>
```

Managed Bean: ContactController.java

The managed bean that contains the action methods is named `ContactController`, which was created in he first example. The following code excerpt is taken from the `ContactController` class, and it shows the updates that have been made to the methods for this example.

■ **Note**   The complete implementation of `ContactController` resides within the package `org.javaserverfaces.chapter05`.

```
...
    /**
     * Adds a subscriber to the newsletter
     * @return String
     */
    public String subscribe(){
        // Using a list implementation for now,
        // but will add to a database table in Chapter 7

        // Add the current contact to the subscription list
        subscriptionController.getSubscriptionList().add(current);
        FacesMessage facesMsg = new FacesMessage(FacesMessage.SEVERITY_INFO,
                "Successfully Subscribed to Newsletter for " + getCurrent().getEmail(), null);
        FacesContext.getCurrentInstance().addMessage(null, facesMsg);
        return "SUBSCRIBE";
    }

    /**
     * Navigational method
     * @return String
     */
    public String add(){
        return "ADD_SUBSCRIBER";
    }
```

```
/**
 * This method will allow a user to navigate to the manageAccount view.
 * This method will be moved into another managed bean that focuses on
 * authentication later on.
 * @return
 */
public String manage(){
    return "/chapter05/manageAccount";
}
```
...

When the view is rendered, the resulting page looks like Figure 5-2.

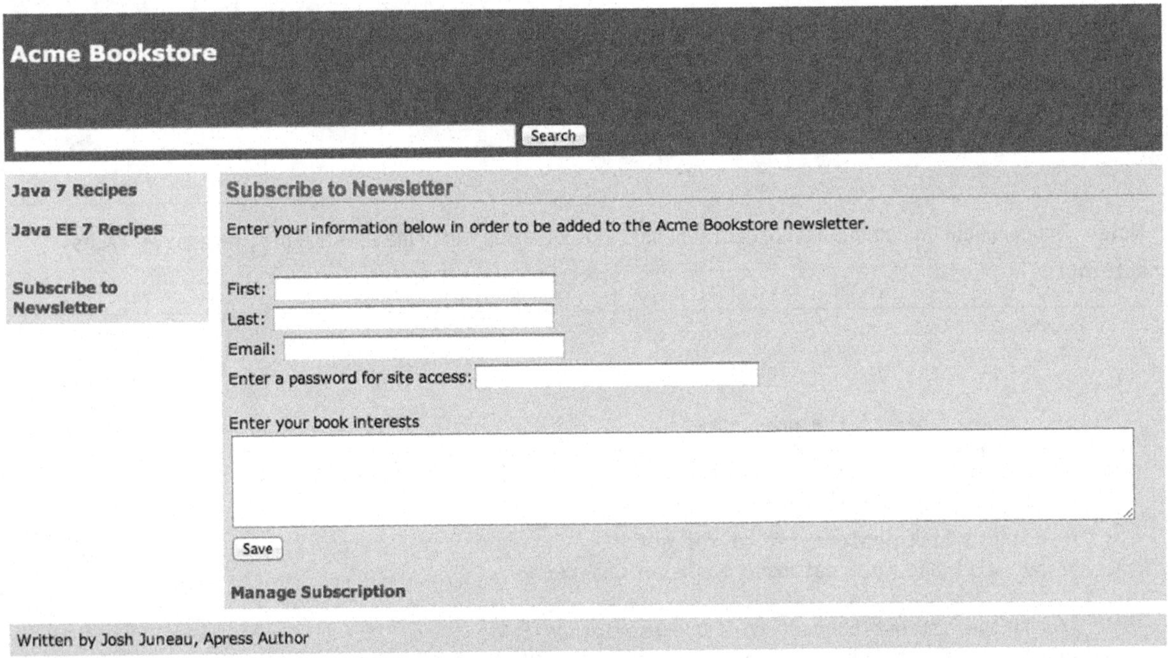

Figure 5-2. Utilizing command components within a view

Explanation

The command components make JSF vastly different from using JSP technology. In the older technologies, form actions were used to handle request parameters and perform any required business logic with them. With the JSF command components, Java methods can be bound directly to a button or a link and invoked when the components are activated (button or link clicked). In the example, both the commandButton and commandLink components are utilized. The commandButton component is used to submit the form request parameters for processing, and the commandLink component is bound to an action method that performs a redirect to another application page.

The command components have a handful of attributes that are of note. Those attributes, along with a description of each, are listed in Table 5-5 and Table 5-6.

Table 5-5. *commandButton Component Additional Attributes*

Attribute	Description
action	EL that specifies a managed bean action method that will be invoked when the user activates the component.
actionListener	EL that specifies a managed bean action method that will be notified when this component is activated. The action method should be public and accept an ActionEvent parameter, with a return type of void.
class	CSS style class that can be applied to the component.
dir	Direction indication for text (LTR: left-to-right; RTL: right-to-left).
disabled	A Boolean to indicate whether the component is disabled.
image	Absolute or relative URL to an image that will be displayed on the button.
immediate	Flag indicating that, if this component is activated by the user, notifications should be delivered to interested listeners and actions immediately (that is, during the Apply Request Values phase) rather than waiting until the Invoke Application phase.
label	Name for the component.
lang	Code for the language used for generating the component markup.
readonly	Boolean indicating whether the component is read only.
rendererType	Identifier of renderer instance.
tabindex	Index value indicating number of tab button presses it takes to bring the component into focus.
title	Tooltip that will be displayed when the mouse hovers over component.
transient	Boolean indicating whether component should be included in the state of the component tree.
type	Indicates type of button to create. Values are submit (default), reset, and button.

Table 5-6. *commandLink Component Additional Attributes*

Attribute	Description
action	EL that specifies a managed bean action method that will be invoked when the user activates the component.
accessKey	Access key value that will transfer the focus to the component.
cords	Position and shape of the hotspot on the screen.
dir	Direction indication for text (LTR: left-to-right; RTL: right-to-left).
disabled	Specifies a Boolean to indicate whether the component is disabled.
hreflang	Language code of the resource designated by the hyperlink.
immediate	Flag indicating that, if this component is activated by the user, notifications should be delivered to interested listeners and actions immediately (that is, during the Apply Request Values phase) rather than waiting until the Invoke Application phase.
lang	Code for the language used for generating the component markup.
rel	Relationship from the current document to the anchor specified by the hyperlink.
rev	Reverse anchor specified by this hyperlink to the current document.
shape	Shape of the hotspot on the screen.
tabindex	Index value indicating number of tab button presses it takes to bring the component into focus.
target	Name of a frame where the resource retrieved via the hyperlink will be displayed.
title	Tooltip that will be displayed when the mouse hovers over component.
type	Indicates type of button to create. Values are submit (default), reset, and button.
charset	Character encoding of the resource designated by the hyperlink.

The commandButton and commandLink components in the example to specify only a minimum number of attributes. That is, they both specify id, action, and value attributes. The id attribute is used to uniquely identify each of the components. The action attribute is set to the JSF EL, which binds the components to their managed bean action methods. The commandButton component has an action attribute of #{contactController2.subscribe}, which means that the ContactController class's subscribe method will be invoked when the button on the page is clicked. The commandLink has an action attribute of #{contactController2.manage}, which means that the ContactController class's manage method will be invoked when the link is clicked. Each of the components also specifies a value attribute, which is set to the text that is displayed on the button or link when rendered.

As you can see, only a handful of the available attributes are used within the example. However, the components can be customized using the additional attributes that are available. For instance, an actionListener method can be specified, which will bind a managed bean method to the component, and that method will be invoked when the component is activated. JavaScript functions can be specified for each of the attributes beginning with the word on, activating client-side functionality.

Command components vastly change the landscape of Java web application development. They allow the incorporation of direct Java method access from within user pages and provide an easy means for processing request parameters.

Displaying Output

It is useful to provide feedback to application users upon form submission. JSF allows one to display output via a number of different components.

Example

Output components are used to display static or dynamic text onto a page, as well as the results of expression language arithmetic. The standard JSF component library contains four components that render output: `outputLabel`, `outputText`, `outputFormat`, `outputLink`, and `link`. The Acme Bookstore utilizes each of these components within the bookstore newsletter application façade.

The View: example05_03.xhtml

In the following example, the newsletter subscription view has been rewritten to utilize some of the output components:

```
<?xml version='1.0' encoding='UTF-8' ?>
<!--
Author: J. Juneau
-->
<!DOCTYPE html PUBLIC "-//W3C//DTD XHTML 1.0 Transitional//EN" "http://www.w3.org/TR/xhtml1/DTD/
xhtml1-transitional.dtd">
<html xmlns="http://www.w3.org/1999/xhtml"
      xmlns:ui="http://xmlns.jcp.org/jsf/facelets"
      xmlns:f="http://xmlns.jcp.org/jsf/core"
      xmlns:h="http://xmlns.jcp.org/jsf/html">

    <body>

        <ui:composition template="layout/custom_template_search.xhtml">
            <ui:define name="content">
                <h:messages globalOnly="true"  errorStyle="color: red" infoStyle="color: green"/>
                <h:form id="contactForm">
                    <h1>Subscribe to Newsletter</h1>
                    <p>
                        <h:outputText id="newsletterSubscriptionDesc"
                                    value="#{contactController.newsletterDescription}"/>
                    </p>

                    <br/>
                    <h:outputLabel for="first" value="First: "/>
                    <h:inputText id="first" size="40" value="#{contactController.current.first}"/>
                    <br/>
                    <h:outputLabel for="last" value="Last: "/>
                    <h:inputText id="last" size="40" value="#{contactController.current.last}"/>
                    <br/>
```

```
                        <h:outputLabel for="email" value="Email: "/>
                        <h:inputText id="email" size="40" value="#{contactController.current.email}"/>
                        <br/>
                        <h:outputLabel for="password" value="Enter a password for site access: "/>
                        <h:inputSecret id="password" size="40" value="#{contactController.
                        current.password}"/>
                        <br/><br/>
                        <h:outputLabel for="description" value="Enter your book interests"/>
                        <br/>
                        <h:inputTextarea id="description" rows="5" cols="100"
                                            value="#{contactController.current.description}"/>
                        <br/>
                        <h:commandButton id="contactSubmit" action="#{contactController.subscribe}"
                                            value="Save"/>
                        <br/><br/>
                        <h:commandLink id="manageAccount" action="#{contactController.manage}"
                                            value="Manage Subscription"/>
                        <br/><br/>
                        <h:outputLink id="homeLink" value="home.xhtml">Home</h:outputLink>
                </h:form>
            </ui:define>
        </ui:composition>

    </body>
</html>
```

Managed Bean: ContactController.java

The ContactController managed bean has been modified throughout the examples within this chapter to incorporate new functionality as the examples move forward. In this example, a new property has been added to the ContactController that contains the description of the newsletter.

■ **Note** The hard-coded newsletter description is not a good idea for use in a production application. It is used in this example for demonstration purposes only. For a production application, utilization of resource bundles or database storage would be a more viable approach for storing Strings of text.

The following source excerpt from the ContactController class shows the changes:

```
...
private String newsletterDescription;

    /**
     * Creates a new instance of ContactController
     */
    public ContactController() {
        current = null;
        newsletterDescription = "Enter your information below in order to be " +
                "added to the Acme Bookstore newsletter.";
    }
```

```
...
/**
     * @return the newsletterDescription
     */
    public String getNewsletterDescription() {
        return newsletterDescription;
    }

    /**
     * @param newsletterDescription the newsletterDescription to set
     */
    public void setNewsletterDescription(String newsletterDescription) {
        this.newsletterDescription = newsletterDescription;
    }
...
```

The resulting page looks like Figure 5-3. Note that the text is the same, because it is merely reading the same text from a managed bean property. Also note that there is now an additional link added to the bottom of the page, which reads Home.

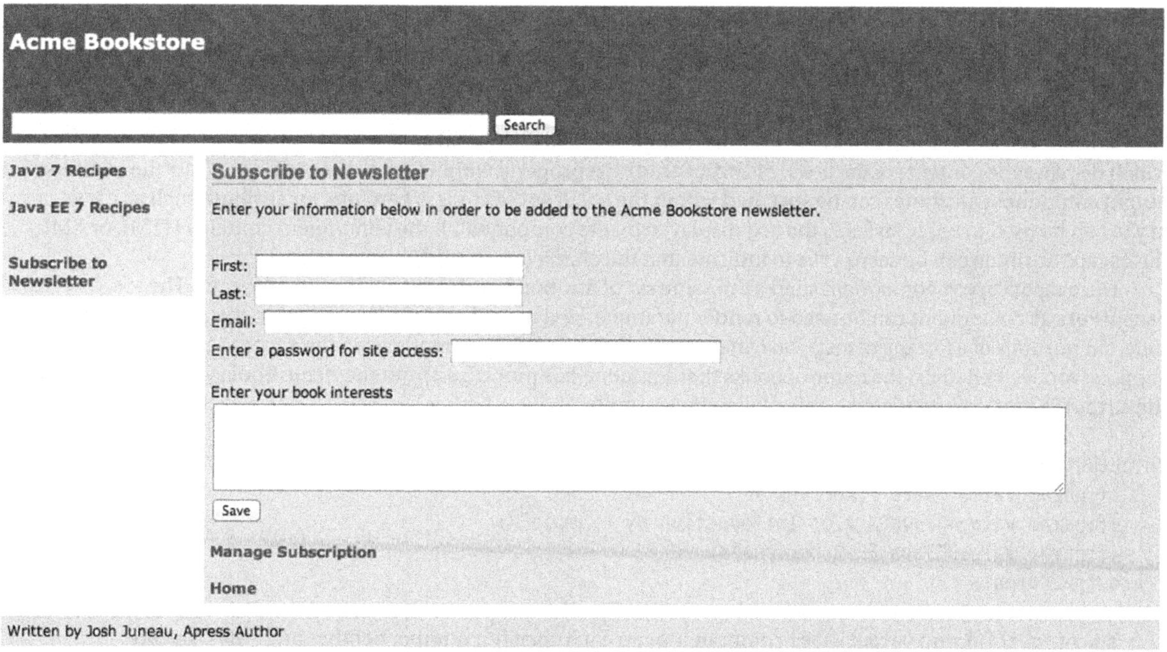

Figure 5-3. *Utilizing output components within a view*

Explanation

Output components can be used to display output that is generated within a managed bean or to render a link to another resource. They can be useful in many cases for displaying dynamic output to a web view. The example demonstrates three out of the five different output component types: outputText, outputLink, and outputLabel. Each of the components shares a common set of attributes, which are listed in Table 5-7.

■ **Note** The outputText component has become a bit less important since the release of JSF 2.0 because the Facelets view definition language implicitly wraps inline content with a similar output component. Therefore, the use of the outputText tag within JSF 2.0 is necessary only if you want to utilize some of the tag attributes for rendering, JavaScript invocation, or the like.

Table 5-7. *Common Output Component Attributes (Not Listed in Introduction)*

Attribute	Description
class	CSS class for styling
converter	Converter that is registered with the component
dir	Direction of text (LTR: left-to-right; RTL: right-to-left)
escape	Boolean value to indicate whether XML- and HTML-sensitive characters are escaped
lang	Code for language used when generating markup for the component
parent	Parent component
title	Tooltip text for the component
transient	Boolean indicating whether component should be included in the state of the component tree

The outputText component in the example contains a value of #{contactController.newsletterDescription}, which displays the contents of the newsletterDescription property within ContactController. Only the common output component attributes can be specified within the h:outputText tag. Therefore, an attribute such as class or style can be used to apply styles to the text displayed by the component. If the component contains HTML or XML, the escape attribute can be set to true to indicate that the characters should be escaped.

The outputFormat component shares the same set of attributes as the outputText component. The outputFormat component can be used to render parameterized text. Therefore, if you require the ability to alter different portions of a String of text, you can do so via the use of JSF parameters (via the f:param tag). For example, suppose you wanted to list the name of books that someone has purchased from the Acme Bookstore; you could use the outputFormat component like in the following example:

```
<h:outputFormat value="Cart contains the books {0}, {1}, {2}"/>
    <f:param value="Java 7 Recipes"/>
    <f:param value="JavaFX 2.0: Introduction by Example"/>
    <f:param value="Java EE 7 Recipes"/>
</h:outputFormat>
```

The outputLink and outputLabel components can each specify a number of other attributes that are not available to the previously discussed output components. The additional attributes are listed in Table 5-8 (outputLink) and Table 5-9 (outputLabel). The outputLink component can be used to create an anchor or link that will redirect an application user to another page when the link is clicked. In the example, the outputLink component is used to redirect a user to a view named home.xhtml. The value for the outputLink component can be set to a static page name, as per the example, or it can contain a JSF EL expression corresponding to a managed bean property. It is also possible to pass parameters to another page using the outputLink component by nesting f:param tags between opening and closing h:outputLink tags as follows:

```
<h:outputLink id="homeLink" value="home.xhtml">
    <h:outputText value="User Home Page"/>
    <f:param name="username" value="#{contactController.current.email}"/>
 </h:outputLink>
```

The previous example would produce a link with the text *User Home Page* when rendered on the page. It would produce the following HTML link, where emailAddress corresponds to the EL expression of #{contactController. current.email}:

```
<a href="home.xhtml?username=emailAddress">Home Page</a>
```

Similarly, rather than displaying a link as text on the page, an image can be used by embedding a graphicImage component.

The outputLabel component renders an HTML <label> tag, and it can be used in much the same way as the outputText component. In the example, the outputLabel component values are all using static text, but they could also utilize JSF EL expressions to make use of managed bean property values if that is more suitable for the application.

Table 5-8. *outputLink Additional Attributes*

Attribute	Description
acccessKey	Access key value that will transfer the focus to the component.
binding	ValueExpresssion linking this component to a property in a backing bean.
charset	The character encoding of the resource designated by this hyperlink.
cords	Position and shape of the hotspot on the screen.
dir	Direction indication for text (LTR: left-to-right; RTL: right-to-left).
disabled	Specifies a Boolean to indicate whether the component is disabled.
fragment	Identifier for the page fragment that should be brought into focus when the target page is rendered.
hreflang	Language code of the resource designated by the hyperlink.
lang	Code for the language used for generating the component markup.
rel	Relationship from the current document to the anchor specified by the hyperlink.
rev	Reverse anchor specified by this hyperlink to the current document.
shape	Shape of the hotspot on the screen.
tabindex	Index value indicating number of Tab button presses it takes to bring the component into focus.
target	Name of a frame where the resource retrieved via the hyperlink will be displayed.
title	Tooltip that will be displayed when the mouse hovers over component.
type	Type of button to create. Values are submit (default), reset, and button.

Table 5-9. *outputLabel Additional Attributes*

Attribute	Description
acccessKey	Access key value that will transfer the focus to the component.
binding	ValueExpresssion linking this component to a property in a backing bean.
dir	Direction indication for text (LTR: left-to-right; RTL: right-to-left).
escape	Flag indicating that characters that are sensitive in HTML and XML markup must be escaped.
for	Client identifier of the component for which this element is a label
lang	Code for the language used for generating the component markup.
tabindex	Index value indicating number of Tab button presses it takes to bring the component into focus.
title	Tooltip that will be displayed when the mouse hovers over component.
type	Type of button to create. Values are submit (default), reset, and button.

The last output component that I'll cover in this example is the link component. It was introduced to JSF in release 2.0, and it makes the task of adding links to a page just a bit easier. Both the outputLink and link components produce similar results, but link has just a couple of different attributes that make it react a bit differently. The value attribute of the h:link tag specifies the label or text that should be used when the link is rendered on the page, and the outcome attribute specifies the page that should be linked to. The following example of the link component produces the same output as the outputLink component in the example:

```
<h:link id="homeLink" value="Home" outcome="home"/>
```

Parameters and images can also embedded within the h:link tag, in the same manner as with outputLink. The link component also contains some custom attributes, as listed in Table 5-10.

Table 5-10. *link Component Additional Attributes*

Attribute	Description
charset	Character encoding of the resource that is designated by the hyperlink.
cords	Position and shape of the hotspot on the screen, usually used when generating maps or images containing multiple links.
disabled	Flag to indicate that the component should never receive focus.
fragment	Identifier for the page fragment that should be brought into focus when the link is clicked. The identifier is appended to the # character.
hreflang	Language of the resource designated by this link.
includeviewparams	Boolean indicating whether to include page parameters when redirecting.
outcome	Logical outcome used to resolve a navigational case.
rel	Relationship from the current document to the resource specified by link.
rev	Reverse link from the anchor specified from this link to the current document.
shape	Shape of the hotspot on the screen.
target	Name of the frame in which the resource linked to is to be displayed.
type	Content type of resource that is linked to.

This example provided a high-level overview of the JSF standard output components. In JSF 2.0+, it is important to note that you can simply include a JSF EL expression without using an output component to display text within a page. However, these components can still be quite useful under certain circumstances, making them an important set of components to have within your arsenal.

Adding Form Validation

It is important to ensure that valid data is being submitted via your form. One way of doing so is to provide validation on your input components, checking for the appropriate values or format. JSF provides the concept of component validators, which can be useful for performing validation to be certain that only the correct data is being entered. Bean validation is another technique that can be used to apply validation to managed or entity bean fields.

Example #1

Utilize prebuilt JSF validator tags on the view's input components where possible. JSF ships with a handful of prebuilt validators that can be applied to components within a view by embedding the validator tag within the component you want to validate. The following code excerpt is taken from a JSF view that defines the layout for the newsletter subscription page of the Acme Bookstore application. The sources can be found in the view named example05_04. xhtml, and the excerpt demonstrates applying prebuilt validators to some inputText components.

```
...
<h:outputLabel for="first" value="First: "/>
<h:inputText id="first" size="40" value="#{contactController.current.first}">
    <f:validateLength minimum="1" maximum="40"/>
 </h:inputText>
<br/>
<h:message id="firstError"
                    for="first"
                    errorStyle="color:red"/>
<br/>
<h:outputLabel for="last" value="Last: "/>
<h:inputText id="last" size="40" value="#{contactController.current.last}">
    <f:validateLength minimum="1" maximum="40"/>
</h:inputText>
<br/>
<h:message id="lastError"
                    for="last"
                    errorStyle="color:red"/>
<br/>
...
```

In the preceding code excerpt, you can see that the f:validateLength validator tags have been embedded in different inputText components. When the form is submitted, these validators will be applied to the values within the inputText component fields and will return an error message if the constraints have not been met.

Example #2

Utilize JSF bean validation by annotating managed bean fields with validation annotations. It is possible to perform validation from within the managed bean (or entity class) by annotating the property field declaration with the validation annotations that are needed. When the form is submitted, then the bean validation will be performed.

■ **Note** An f:validateBean tag can be embedded within the component in the view if making use of validationGroups in order to delegate the validation of the local value to the Bean Validation API. If using f:validateBean, the validationGroups attribute will serve as a filter that instructs which constraints should be enforced.

The following code excerpt is taken from the JSF view that defines the layout for the newsletter subscription page of the Acme Bookstore application. The sources can be found in the view named example05_04.xhtml.

```
...
<h:outputLabel for="email" value="Email: "/>
<h:inputText id="email" size="40" value="#{contactController.current.email}"/>
<br/>
<h:message id="emailError"
                for="email"
                errorStyle="color:red"/>
...
```

Next is an excerpt from the ContactController managed bean that demonstrates applying a validator annotation to the email property field declaration:

```
...
@Pattern(regexp = "[a-zA-Z0-9]+@[a-zA-Z0-9]+\\.[a-zA-Z0-9]+", message = "Email format is invalid.")
    private String email;
...
```

When the form is submitted, the validation on the email field will occur. If the value entered into the inputText component does not validate against the regular expression noted in the annotation, then the message will be displayed within the corresponding messages component.

Example #3

Create a custom validator method within a managed bean, and register that method with an input component by specifying the appropriate EL for the component's validator attribute. The following code excerpt is taken from the JSF view that defines the layout for the newsletter subscription page of the Acme Bookstore application. The sources can be found in the view named example05_04.xhtml, and the excerpt demonstrates a custom validator method to a component by specifying it for the validator attribute.

```
...
<h:outputLabel for="password" value="Enter a password for site access: "/>
<h:inputSecret id="password" size="40" redisplay="true" value="#{contactController.current.
password}"/>
<br/>
<h:outputLabel for="passwordConfirm" value="Confirm Password: "/>
<h:inputSecret id="passwordConfirm" size="40" redisplay="true"
                        validator="#{contactController.validatePassword}"/>
<br/>
<h:message id="passwordConfirmError"
                    for="passwordConfirm"
                    style="color:red"/>
...
```

> **Note** If you are thinking outside of the box, you'll see that the previous code fragment would be an excellent choice for creating into a composite component! If a composite component is created, then it would be as simple as adding a tag such as `<custom:passwordValidate>` to your form.

The validator attribute specifies the `validatePassword` method within the `ContactController` managed bean. The following excerpt is taken from `ContactController`, and it shows the validator method's implementation:

```
...
/**
    * Custom validator to ensure that password field contents match
    * @param context
    * @param component
    * @param value
    */
    public void validatePassword(FacesContext context,
                                    UIComponent component,
                                    Object value){
        Map map = context.getExternalContext().getRequestParameterMap();
        String passwordText = (String) map.get(("contactForm:password"));
        String confirmPassword = value.toString();

        if (!passwordText.equals(confirmPassword)) {
            throw new ValidatorException(new FacesMessage("Passwords do not match"));
        }
    }
...
```

When the form is submitted, the `validatePassword` method will be invoked during the Process Validations phase. The method will read the values of both the `password` and `passwordConfirm` fields, and an exception will be thrown if they do not match. For example, if the input form for the newsletter subscription page is submitted without any values, then the page should be re-rendered and look like Figure 5-4.

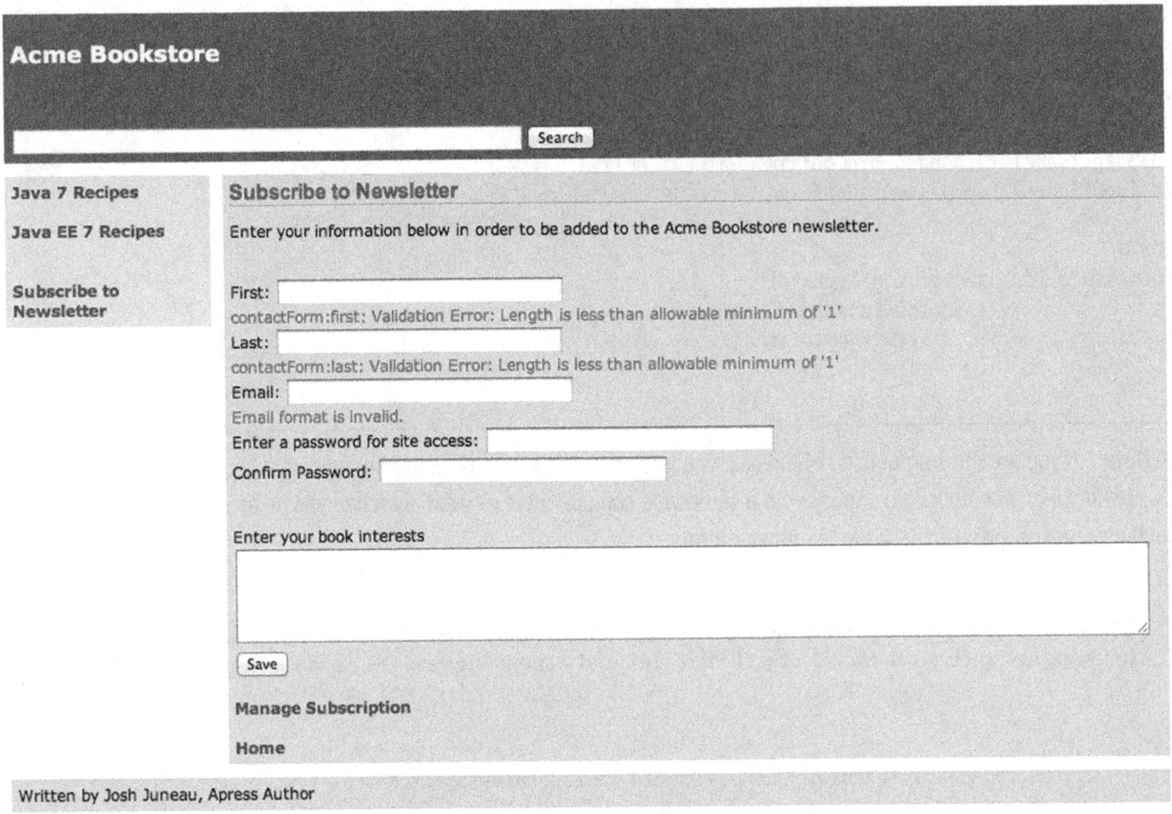

Figure 5-4. *Validation errors on input fields*

Explanation

There are a few different ways in which to apply validation to form input fields. The easiest way to apply validation to an input component is to utilize the prebuilt validator tags that ship with JSF. There are prebuilt tags for validating data for a specified length, range, and so on. Please see Table 5-2 in the introduction to this chapter for the complete list of validator tags. You can also choose to apply validation to input components using bean validation. Bean validation requires validation annotations to be placed on the property declaration within the managed bean. Yet another possible way to perform validation is to create a custom validation method and specify the method within the input component's `validator` attribute. This section will provide a brief overview of each prebuilt validation tag, cover the basics of bean validation, and demonstrate how to build a custom validation method.

■ **Note**   It is possible to create a class that implements the `Validator` interface to perform validation.

No matter which validation solution you choose to implement, the validation occurs during the Process Validations phase of the JSF life cycle. When a form is submitted, via a command component or an Ajax request, all validators that are registered on the components within the tree are processed. The rules that are specified within the attributes of the component are compared against the local value for the component. At this point, if any of the validations fails, the messages are returned to the corresponding `message` components and displayed to the user.

To utilize the prebuilt validation tags, they must be embedded between opening and closing input component tag and specify attributes according to the validation parameters you want to set. In Example #1, you learned how to use the f:validateLength validator tag, which allows validation of component data for a specified length. The minimum and maximum attributes are set to the minimum string length and maximum string length, respectively.

The f:validateLongRange validator can be used to check the range of a numeric value that has been entered. The minimum and maximum attributes of f:validateLongRange are used to determine whether the value entered falls within the lower and upper bounds, respectively.

Similar to f:validateLongRange is the f:validateDoubleRange validator, which is used to validate the range of a floating-point value. Again, the minimum and maximum attributes of f:validateDoubleRange are used to determine whether the value entered falls within the lower and upper bounds, respectively.

New with the release of JSF 2.0 was the f:validateRequired validator, which is used to ensure that an input field is not empty. No attributes are needed with this validator; simply embed it within a component tag to ensure that the component will not contain an empty value.

Another new validator that shipped with the JSF 2.0 release was the f:validateRegex validator. This validator uses a regular expression pattern to determine whether the value entered matches the specified pattern. The validator's pattern attribute is used to specify the regular expression pattern, as shown in the example for Example #1.

In Example #2, JSF bean validation is demonstrated, which was also a new feature of the JSF 2.0 release. Bean validation allows you to annotate a managed bean field with constraint annotations that indicate the type of validation that should be performed. The validation automatically occurs on the annotated fields when a form is submitted that contains input components referencing them. A handful of standard constraint annotations can be applied to bean fields, as listed in Table 5-11. Each annotation accepts different attributes; please see the online documentation at http://docs.oracle.com/javaee/7/api/ for more details.

Table 5-11. *Constraint Annotations Used for Bean Validation*

Annotation	Description
@AssertFalse	The annotated element must be false.
@AssertTrue	The annotated element must be true.
@DecimalMax	The annotated element must be a decimal that has a value less than or equal to the specified maximum.
@DecimalMin	The annotated element must be a decimal that has a value greater than or equal to the specified minimum.
@Digits	The annotated element must be a number within the accepted range.
@Future	The annotated element must be a date in the future.
@Max	The annotated element must be a number that has a value less than or equal to the specified maximum.
@Min	The annotated element must be a number that has a value greater than or equal to the specified minimum.
@NotNull	The annotated element must not be null.
@Null	The annotated element must be null.
@Past	The annotated element must be a date in the past.
@Pattern	The annotated element must match the pattern specified in the regular annotation's regular expression.
@Size	The annotated element must be between the specified boundaries.

When using bean validation, the input component that references an annotated bean field can contain an
f:validateBean tag to customize behavior. The f:validateBean tag's validationGroups annotation can be used to
specify validation groups that can be used for validating the component. For instance, such a solution may resemble
something like the following:

```
<h:inputText id="email" value="#{contactController.email}">
    <f:validateBean validationGroups="org.javaserverfaces.validation.groups.EmailGroup"/>
</h:inputText>
```

■ **Note**   Validation groups define a subset of constraints that can be applied for validation. A validation group is
represented by an empty Java interface. The interface name can then be applied to annotation constraints within a bean
class in order to assign such constraints to a particular group. For instance, the following field that is annotated with @
Size specifies a group of EmailGroup.class:

```
@Size(min=2, max=30, groups=Email.class)
private String email;
```

When utilizing the f:validateBean tag, any constraint annotations that are contained within the specified group will be
applied to the field for validation.

When using bean validation, a custom error message can be displayed if the validation for a field fails. To add a
custom message, include the message attribute within the annotation, along with the error message that you want to
have displayed. As a best practice, error messages should be pulled from a message bundle.

The example for Example #3 demonstrates the use of a custom validator method in order to perform validation
on an input component. The input component's validator attribute can reference a managed bean method that has
no return type and accepts a FacesContext, a UIComponent, and an Object, as a validation method. The method can
utilize the parameters to gain access to the current FacesContext, the UIComponent that is being validated, and the
current value that is contained in the object, respectively. The validation logic can throw a javax.faces.validator.
ValidatorException if the value does not pass validation and then return a message to the user via the exception.
In the example, the method named validatePassword is used to compare the two password field contents to ensure
that they match. The first two lines of code within the method are used to obtain the value of the component with the
id of password and save it into a local variable. The actual validation logic compares that value against the incoming
parameter's Object value, which is the current value of the component being validated, to determine whether there
is a match. If not, then a ValidationException is thrown with a corresponding message. That message will then be
displayed within the messages component that corresponds to the component being validated.

As mentioned at the beginning of this example, there are a few ways to validate input. None of them is any better
than the other; their usage depends upon the needs of your application. If you are going to be changing validation
patterns often, then you may want to stick with the prebuilt validator tags so that you do not need to recompile code
in order to change the validation. On the other hand, if you know that your validation will not change, then it may be
easier for you to work with the bean validation technique. Whatever the case, validation can be made even easier with
Ajax, and that topic will be covered in Chapter 6.

Adding Select Lists to Pages

A popular way to provide a selection option for users within web pages is to utilize a *select list* component. JSF provides a number of selection components, each allowing you to select one or more options from a list of items.

Example

To add a select list to your JSF view, use the JSF selectOneMenu, selectManyMenu, selectOneListbox, or selectManyListbox component, depending upon the type of list your application requires. Each of these selection components allows for either one or many selections to be made from a particular set of values. The example adds to the newsletter subscription page of the Acme Bookstore. The bookstore application will allow the customer to select their occupation from a drop-down list and to select one or more newsletters to which they would like to subscribe from a multiple-select list. Since they'll be selecting only a single option for their occupation, a selectOneMenu is used. However, since multiple newsletter selections can be made, a selectManyListbox is the best choice.

The View: example05_05.xhtml

The following excerpt is taken from the JSF view named example05_05.xhtml, and it demonstrates the usage of these components:

```
...
<h:outputLabel for="occupation" value="Occupation: "/>
<h:selectOneMenu id="occupation" value="#{contactController.current.occupation}">
    <f:selectItem itemLabel="" itemValue=""/>
    <f:selectItems value="#{contactController.occupationList}"/>
</h:selectOneMenu>
<br/><br/>
<h:outputLabel for="newsletterList" value="Newsletters:"/>
<h:selectManyListbox id="newsletterList" value="#{contactController.current.newsletterList}">
    <f:selectItems value="#{contactController.allNewsletters}"/>
</h:selectManyListbox>
...
```

Managed Bean: ContactController.java

The components are bound to properties within the ContactController managed bean. The following excerpt, taken from ContactController, shows the declaration of the properties, along with their corresponding accessor methods:

```
...
// Declaration of the managed bean properties
private List<String> occupationList;
private Map<String, Object> allNewsletters;
...
// Example of populating the object
private void populateOccupationList(){
        occupationList = new ArrayList();
        occupationList.add("Author");
        occupationList.add("IT Professional");
}
```

```java
// Example of populating the object
private void populateNewsletterList(){
    newsletterList = new LinkedHashMap<String,Object>();
    newsletterList.put("Java 7 Recipes Weekly", "Java");
    newsletterList.put("JavaFX Weekly", "FX");
    newsletterList.put("Oracle PL/SQL Weekly", "Oracle");
    newsletterList.put("New Books Weekly", "New Books");
}

...
/**
    * @return the occupationList
    */
public List<String> getOccupationList() {
    return occupationList;
}

/**
    * @param occupationList the occupationList to set
    */
public void setOccupationList(List<String> occupationList) {
    this.occupationList = occupationList;
}

/**
    * @return the newsletterList
    */
public Map<String,Object> getNewsletterList() {
    return newsletterList;
}

/**
    * @param newsletterList the newsletterList to set
    */
public void setNewsletterList(Map<String,Object> newsletterList) {
    this.newsletterList = newsletterList;
}
...
```

The newly updated newsletter subscription page should look like Figure 5-5.

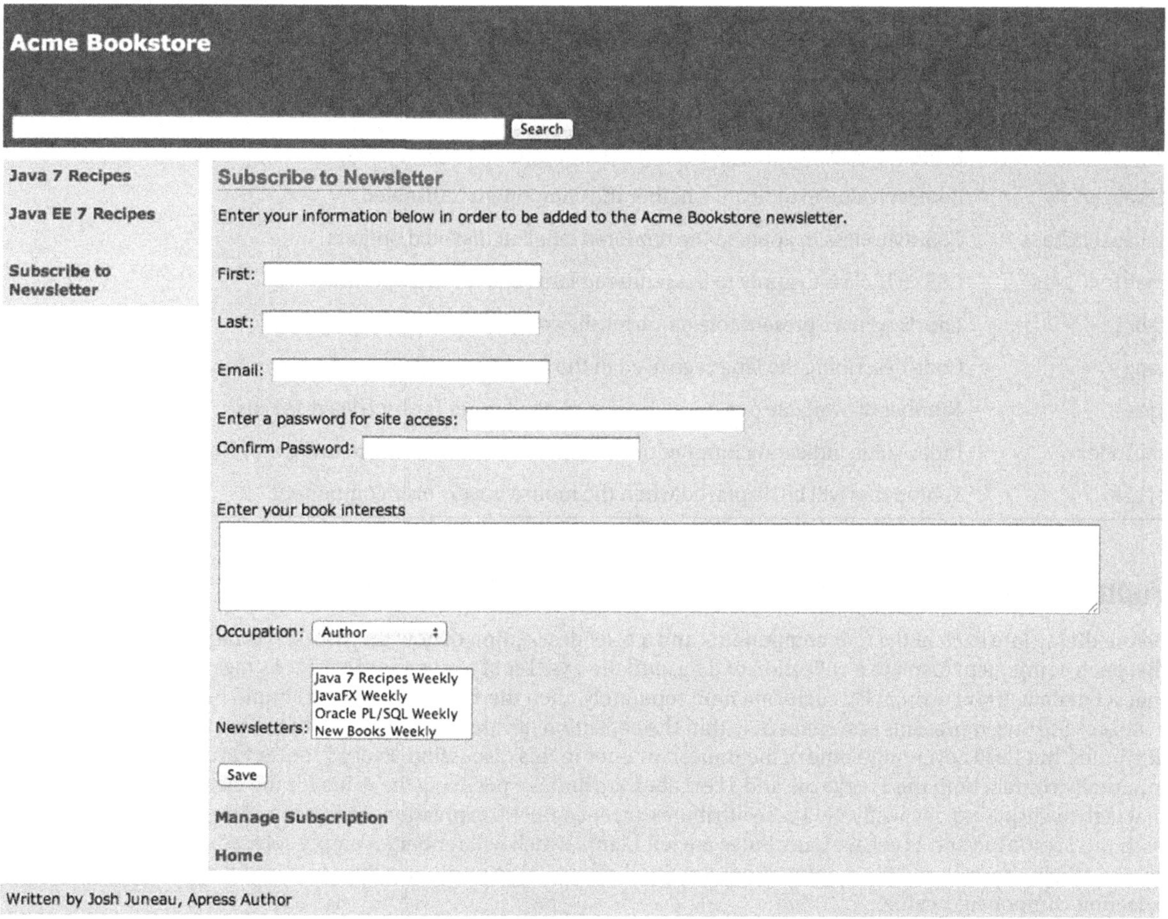

Figure 5-5. *Selection components including lists of values*

Explanation

To ensure data integrity, it is always a good idea to include input components that are prepopulated with data if possible. Doing so ensures that users are not entering free-text values of varying varieties into text boxes, and it also gives the user a convenient choice of options. Utilizing selection components provides the user with a list of values to choose from, allowing one or more selections to be made. The standard JSF component library ships with four input components that accept lists of data from which a user can choose one or more selections. The selection components are selectOneListbox, selectManyListbox, selectOneMenu, and selectManyMenu. Each of these components shares a common set of attributes. Those common attributes that were not already displayed within Table 5-2 are listed within Table 5-12.

Table 5-12. *Select Component Attributes*

Attribute	Description
accesskey	Access key that, when pressed, transfers focus to the component
dir	Direction indication for text (LTR: left-to-right; RTL: right-to-left)
disabled	Boolean value to indicate whether the component is disabled
disabledClass	CSS style class to apply to the rendered label on disabled options
enabledClass	CSS style class to apply to the rendered label on enabled options
label	Localized user-presentable name for the component
lang	Code describing the language used in the generate markup for the component
size	Number of available options to be shown at all times (selectManyListbox)
tabindex	Index value indicating number of Tab button presses it takes to bring the component into focus
title	Tooltip that will be displayed when the mouse hovers over component

Populating the Select Lists

Before diving into each of the four components and a brief description of how they work, it is important to note that each component displays a collection of data, and the f:selectItem or f:selectItems tags are used to specify that set of data. If you want to list each data item separately, then the f:selectItem tag should be used. One f:selectItem tag represents one element within the collection of values. The f:selectItem tag contains several attributes, but I will cover only some of the important ones in this discussion. Every f:selectItem tag should minimally contain both the itemValue and itemLabel attributes, specifying the value for the element and the label that is to be displayed, respectively. These attributes accept a JSF EL expression, or a string of text. In the example, both the itemValue and itemLabel attributes are left blank, which will render an empty selection for the first menu choice. When the user selects an option from the list, the itemValue attribute value is set into the corresponding selection component's value.

The f:selectItems tag can be used to specify a collection of data that should be used for the component. A List of SelectItem objects can be built within a managed bean and specified for the f:selectItems tag. Much like the f:selectItem tag, several attributes can be used with this tag, and I'll cover the essential ones here. Both the itemValue and itemLabel attributes can also be specified for the f:selectItems tag, corresponding to a List or Map of values, and a string label, respectively. However, most often, the value attribute is specified, referencing a managed bean property that contains a Collection or array of objects. The Collection or array can contain any valid Java object, and in the example a LinkedHashMap is used to populate the newsletterList property. Oftentimes it is easier to populate individual SelectItem objects and then load them into a List for use with the f:selectItems tag. The following lines of code show how to utilize SelectItem objects to populate the newsletters:

```
private void populateNewsletterList() {
        allNewsletters = new LinkedHashMap<String, Object>();
        allNewsletters.put("Java 7 Recipes Weekly", "Java");
        allNewsletters.put("JavaFX Weekly", "FX");
        allNewsletters.put("Oracle PL/SQL Weekly", "Oracle");
        allNewsletters.put("New Books Weekly", "New Books");
    }
```

Regarding Each Component Type

The selectOneMenu is probably the most commonly used selection component, and it renders a collection of data into a drop-down list. The user can select one entry from the menu, and the selected entry will be set into the managed bean property that is specified for the value attribute of the component. In the example, the value is set to #{contactController.current.occupation}, so when an entry from the list is selected, then it will be set into the currently selected Contact object's occupation field.

The selectOneListbox allows a user to select one value from a list of data. The user can see at least a few of the entries within the list within a box on the screen and can select one of the options from the list box. The selectOneListbox contains an additional attribute named collectionType, which allows the type of collection to be specified using a literal value.

Both the selectManyMenu and selectManyListbox components allow the user to choose more than one option in the selection list. The example demonstrates how to use a selectManyListbox component, allowing the user to choose more than one newsletter from the list. The main difference when using one of these components is that the managed bean property value for the component must be able to accept more than one value. In the example, the selectManyListbox component value references the Contact class's newsletterList field. The newsletterList field is declared as a List of String objects, so when the user selects more than one value from the newsletterList, all of the choices can be stored in the current Contact object.

In the example, two components are used to display lists of options for selection. One of the components allows a user to select one value from the collection and displays the options in a drop-down list, and the other allows a user to select more than one value and displays the options within a list box.

Adding Graphics to Your Pages

To incorporate a graphic into a site template or other select application pages, utilize a graphicImage component.

Example

To display images within a JSF view, place the images that you want to display into a library within your application's resources folder, and then use the graphicImage component to display them. The book.xhtml view for the Acme Bookstore application contains an image of each book in the store. To render the image, the book image name is populated from the image field of the Book managed bean. The following code excerpt taken from book.xhtml demonstrates how to use the h:graphicImage tag:

```
<h:graphicImage id="bookImage"
                         library="image"
            style="width: 100px; height: 120px" name="#{book.image}"/>
```

Explanation

Since the inception of JSF, the graphicImage component has been used to display images. Using the library attribute of the graphicImage component, a JSF view can reference an image resource without needing to specify a fully qualified path to the image file. In the example, the value specified for the library attribute is image, meaning that the image can be found within the resource\image folder. It also provides the convenience of accepting JSF EL in attributes as needed so that images can be dynamically loaded based upon the current values within the corresponding managed bean properties. The graphicImage component makes it easy to display images, both dynamically and statically.

The h:graphicImage tag supports a number of attributes, above and beyond the standard JSF component attributes, as listed in Table 5-13.

Table 5-13. *graphicImage Component-Specific Attributes*

Attribute	Description
alt	Alternate textual description of the element rendered by the component
dir	Direction indication for text (LTR: left-to-right; RTL: right-to-left)
height	Overrides the height of the image
ismap	Boolean indicating whether the image is to be used as a server-side image map
lang	Code describing the language used in the generated markup for the component
longdesc	URI to a long description of the image represented by the element
title	Advisory title information about the markup elements generated by the component
usemap	Name of a client-side image map for which this element provides the image
width	Overrides the width of the image

When the page is rendered in the example, the image that resides within the application's resources/image directory that corresponds to the name attribute on the tag will be displayed. If the user selects a different book from the menu, then that book's image will be displayed using the same graphicImage component, because the name specified for the image can be changed depending upon the currently selected book object in the managed bean.

By utilizing a graphicImage within your views, you enable your images to take on the dynamic characteristics of standard JSF components.

Adding Check Boxes to a View

Another convenient technique for allowing users to select options on an application page is to provide a series of checkboxes. The JSF framework provides a number of components for rendering checkboxes.

Example

The selectOneCheckbox and selectManyCheckbox components can be added within a view to render checkboxes for selection. These components allow you to specify a Boolean value as input by simply checking a box for a true value and deselecting the check box for a false value.

The View: example05_07.xhtml

The following code excerpt is taken from the view named example05_07.xhtml, and it demonstrates the usage of these components:

```
...
<h:outputLabel for="notifyme" value="Would you like to receive other promotional email?"/>
<h:selectBooleanCheckbox id="notifyme"
value="#{contactController.current.receiveNotifications}"/>
<br/><br/>
<h:outputLabel for="notificationTypes"
                        value="What type of notifications are you interested in recieving?"/>
<h:selectManyCheckbox id="notifyTypes" value="#{contactController.current.notificationType}">
    <f:selectItems value="#{contactController.notificationTypes}"/>
</h:selectManyCheckbox>
...
```

Managed Bean Controllers

Each of the components is bound to a Contact object, so when the form is submitted, the current Contact object will receive the data if valid. The following listing contains excerpts from the updated Contact class, an object that is used to hold the contact's information. For the complete listing, please see the Contact.java sources within the org.javaserverfaces.chapter05 packages in the sources.

```
...
private boolean receiveNotifications;
private Map<String, Object> notificationType;
...

/**
    * @return the receiveNotifications
    */
public boolean isReceiveNotifications() {
    return receiveNotifications;
}

/**
    * @param receiveNotifications the receiveNotifications to set
    */
public void setReceiveNotifications(boolean receiveNotifications) {
    this.receiveNotifications = receiveNotifications;
}

/**
    * @return the notificationTypes
    */
    public Map<String, Object> getNotificationTypes() {
        return notificationTypes;
    }
```

```java
    /**
     * @param notificationTypes the notificationTypes to set
     */
    public void setNotificationTypes(Map<String, Object> notificationTypes) {
        this.notificationTypes = notificationTypes;
    }
```

The last piece of the puzzle is the list of notification types that are bound to the f:selectItems tag that is embedded within the h:selectManyCheckbox component. These are bound to a property named notificationTypes in the ContactController managed bean. The following listing contains the relevant excerpts from that class.

```java
...
// Declaration
private Map<String, Object> notificationTypes;
...
// Population occurs within the constructor, calling the populateNotificationTypes method
/**
     * Creates a new instance of ContactController
     */
public ContactController() {
    current = null;
    passwordConfirm = null;
    newsletterDescription = "Enter your information below in order to be " +
            "added to the Acme Bookstore newsletter.";
    populateOccupationList();
    populateNewsletterList();
    populateNotificationTypes();

}

private void populateNotificationTypes() {
        notificationTypes = new HashMap<>();
        notificationTypes.put("Product Updates", "1");
        notificationTypes.put("Best Seller Alerts","2");
        notificationTypes.put("Spam", "3");

    }
...
```

The resulting newsletter subscription input screen for the Acme Bookstore application including the new check box components will look like Figure 5-6.

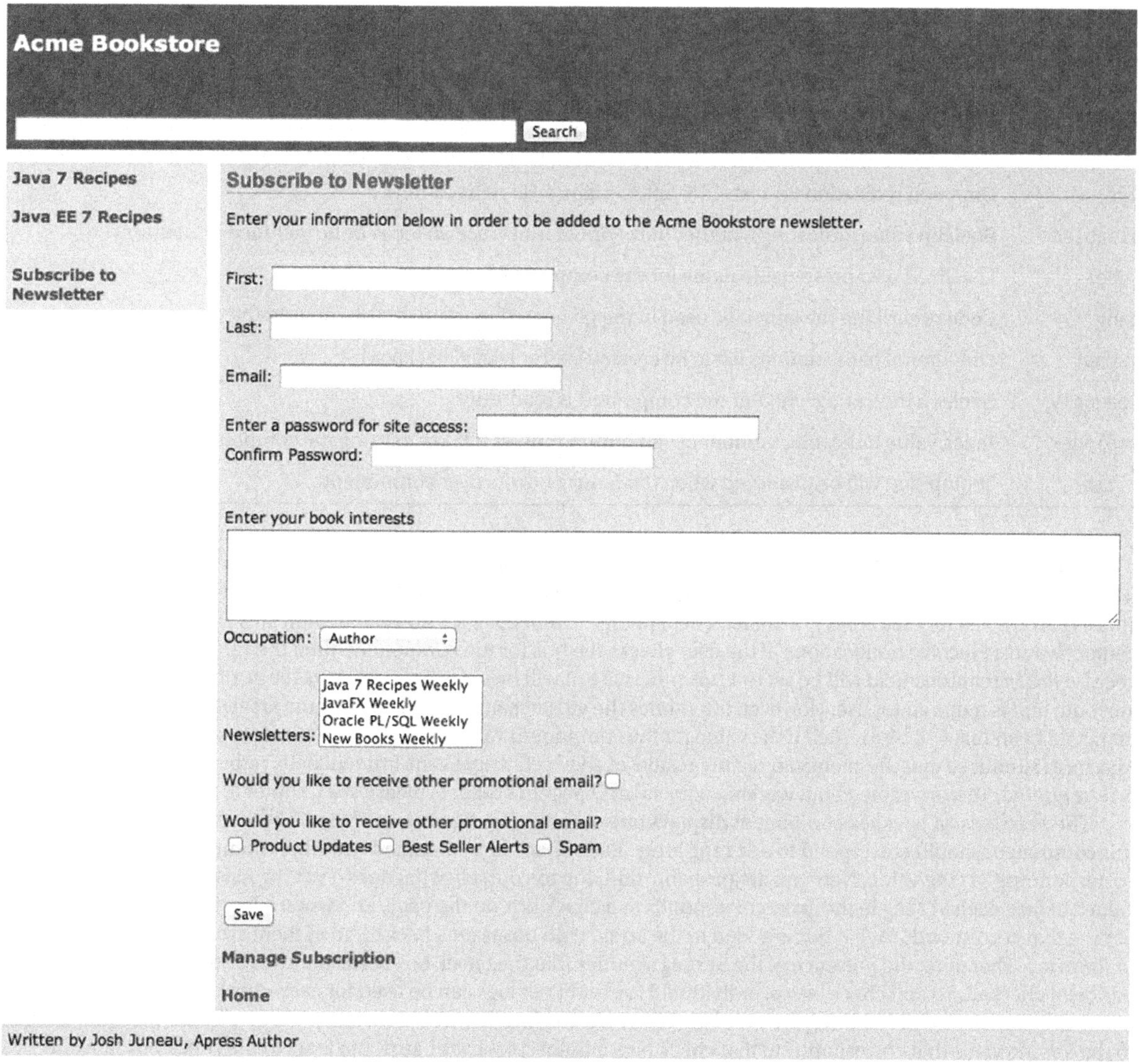

Acme Bookstore

Search

Java 7 Recipes

Java EE 7 Recipes

Subscribe to
Newsletter

Subscribe to Newsletter

Enter your information below in order to be added to the Acme Bookstore newsletter.

First:

Last:

Email:

Enter a password for site access:

Confirm Password:

Enter your book interests

Occupation: Author

Newsletters: Java 7 Recipes Weekly / JavaFX Weekly / Oracle PL/SQL Weekly / New Books Weekly

Would you like to receive other promotional email? ☐

Would you like to receive other promotional email?
☐ Product Updates ☐ Best Seller Alerts ☐ Spam

Save

Manage Subscription

Home

Written by Josh Juneau, Apress Author

Figure 5-6. *Incorporating check boxes into your pages*

Explanation

Check boxes are very common in applications because they provide an easy means for a user to enter a Boolean value. The box is either checked or not, and a checked box relates to a `true` value, leaving an unchecked box relating to a `false` value. The JSF standard component library ships with a couple of different check box selection components, namely, the `selectBooleanCheckbox` and the `selectManyCheckbox`. The `selectBooleanCheckbox` renders a single HTML input element with `type="checkbox"` on the page, whereas the `selectManyCheckbox` component renders multiple HTML input elements with `type="checkbox"`. As with all JSF components, the check box selection components share a standard set of attributes above and beyond the common JSF component attributes, which are listed in Table 5-14.

Table 5-14. *Check Box Selection Component Attributes*

Attribute	Description
accessKey	Access key that, when pressed, transfers focus to the element
border	Width of the border to be drawn around the table containing the options list (selectManyCheckbox)
dir	Direction indication for text (LTR: left-to-right; RTL: right-to-left)
disabled	Boolean value indicating whether the element must receive focus or be included in a submit
label	Localized user presentable name for the component
lang	Code describing the language used in the generated markup for the component
layout	Orientation of the options list to be created (selectManyCheckbox)
readonly	Boolean indicating whether the component is read-only
tabindex	Index value indicating number of Tab button presses it takes to bring the component into focus
title	Tooltip that will be displayed when the mouse hovers over component

A selectBooleanCheckbox component value attribute EL expression should correspond to a Boolean property within the managed bean. In the example, the selectBooleanCheckbox value is set to #{contactController. current.receiveNotifications}, a Boolean field in the current Contact object that indicates whether the contact wants to receive notifications. If the user checks the box for the component, then the value for the receiveNotifications field will be set to true; otherwise, it will be set to false. The value attribute is the only attribute that is required for use. However, oftentimes the valueChangeListener attribute is set to a method within a managed bean that will be invoked if the value for the component value changes. This is most useful when using an Ajax form submit so that the client can see the results of a ValueChangeEvent immediately, rather than after the form is re-rendered. To learn more about working with valueChangeListeners, please see Chapter 6.

The selectManyCheckbox component displays one or more check boxes on a page. The value attribute for this component should correspond to a String array. Each check box contained within the component has a corresponding String value. Now you are probably thinking to yourself, what does a String have to do with a Boolean value? In fact, each String in the array corresponds to a check box on the page, and when a box is checked, the String that corresponds to that box is added to the array. If no boxes are checked, then there are no Strings added to the array. Therefore, the presence of the String signifies that the check box corresponding to that String value has been checked. To add check boxes, individual f:selectItem tags can be used for each check box, or a collection of check boxes can be added using the f:selectItems tag. If using f:selectItem, then the itemValue attribute is set to the String value that corresponds to that check box, and the itemLabel attribute is set to the check box label. In the example, the f:selectItems tag is used to populate check boxes for the component. The f:selectItems tag in the example contains a value attribute that is set to #{contactController.notificationTypes}, which corresponds to the notificationTypes field in the ContactController class. If you take a look at the notificationTypes field, you will see that it is declared as a Map<String, Object>, and each element in the array will correspond to a check box. When the ContactController class is instantiated, the populateNotificationTypes method is called, which populates the Map with the values for each check box. The following listing is that of the populateNotificationTypes method. Each element in the Map corresponds to a check box.

```
private void populateNotificationTypes() {
        notificationTypes = new HashMap<>();
        notificationTypes.put("Product Updates", "1");
        notificationTypes.put("Best Seller Alerts","2");
        notificationTypes.put("Spam", "3");

    }
```

Check boxes make it easy for a user to indicate a `true` or `false` (checked or unchecked) value for a given option. The JSF check box selection components help organize content on a page, and they provide a good means of ensuring data integrity since the user does not have to enter free text.

Adding Radio Buttons to a View

The JSF component library provides the `SelectOneRadio` component to render radio buttons within a view.

Example

Use radio buttons on your page to provide the user the option of selecting one item from a set. Radio buttons are often a nice solution when you want to display all options on the screen at once but allow only one selection. For this example, the Acme Bookstore wants to add a radio button on the newsletter subscription page to determine whether the subscriber is male or female.

The View: example05_08.xhtml

The following excerpt is taken from the JSF view named `example05_08.xhtml`, and it demonstrates the `selectOneRadio` component:

```
...
<h:outputLabel for="gender" value="Gender: "/>
<h:selectOneRadio id="gender" value="#{contactController.current.gender}">
    <f:selectItem itemValue="M" itemLabel="Male"/>
    <f:selectItem itemValue="F" itemLabel="Female"/>
</h:selectOneRadio>
<br/><br/>
<h:message id="genderError"
           for="gender"
           errorStyle="color:red"/>
<br/>
...
```

Managed Bean

The component is bound to a managed bean property named gender that has been added to the `Contact` class. The following listing contains excerpts from the `Contact` class, which show the updates for incorporating the new field:

```
...
private String gender;
...
/**
    * @return the gender
    */
public String getGender() {
    return gender;
}
```

```
/**
    * @param gender the gender to set
    */
public void setGender(String gender) {
    this.gender = gender;
}
...
```

When the selectOneRadio component is rendered on the screen, it adds a radio button for each of the available options. The updated Acme Bookstore newsletter page looks like that in Figure 5-7.

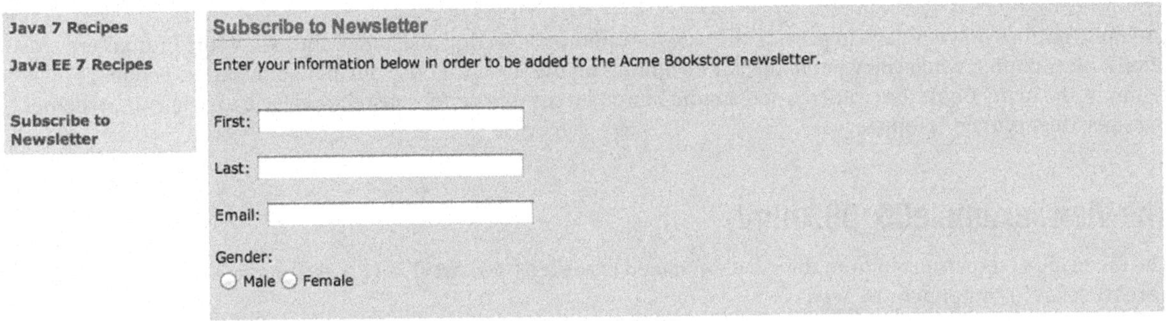

Figure 5-7. *Using a selectOneRadio component*

Explanation

Radio buttons are very similar to check boxes in that they provide the user with an on or off value for a designated page value. The value added to using radio buttons is that they make it easy to display several options on the screen at once and allow the user to select only one of them. If a user tries to select a different option, then the currently selected item becomes unselected, forcing the user to select only one option. The JSF selectOneRadio component is used to render radio buttons on a page, and the component works in much the same manner as the selectManyCheckbox.

The selectOneRadio shares all of the same attributes as the selectBooleanCheckbox component. Please see Table 5-14 for a listing of those attributes. The selectOneRadio component also contains a number of additional attributes, as listed in Table 5-15.

Table 5-15. *selectOneRadio Attributes (in Addition to Those Listed in Table 5-14)*

Attribute	Description
disabledClass	CSS style class to apply to the rendered label on disabled options
enabledClass	CSS style class to apply to the rendered label on enabled options

To use the selectOneRadio component, the value attribute should be set to a String. In the example, the value for the selectOneRadio component is set to the gender field in the current Contact object. When one of the radio buttons is selected, the String value corresponding to that button will be set into the field value. The radio buttons are populated using either the f:selectItem tag or the f:selectItems tag, much like the selectManyCheckbox component. In the example, two f:selectItem tags are used to add two radio buttons to the component; the itemValue attribute is the String that will be submitted for the selected button, and the itemLabel attribute is the String that is displayed next to the corresponding button.

If you want to use an f:selectItems tag to populate a collection of radio buttons, the f:selectItems value attribute should be set to a managed bean property that is declared as a String array, a Map, or a List of SelectItem objects. To see an example, please review the example for the selectManyCheckbox component in the previous example.

Radio buttons are an easy way to display multiple options to a user and allow them to select one. If you understand how a selectManyCheckbox component works, then the selectOneRadio is very similar.

Structuring View Layout

One of the most important ingredients to building a successful application is to provide a clean, user-friendly interface. Two of the traditional options for providing a structured layout are to use HTML tables or CSS. JSF provides components that allow one to design a view using an HTML table structure.

Example

To design an HTML table layout, construct the page using a number of panelGrid and panelGroup components. The panelGrid component renders into an HTML table, so it allows JSF components to be organized using a table structure. For this example, the newsletter subscription page of the Acme Bookstore has been reorganized using a series of panelGrid and panelGroup components in an attempt to better organize the components into page sections. The components within each section of the page now correspond to each other so that the form is more intuitive for a user to populate.

The following listing is that of the view named example05_09.xhtml, which is the reorganized JSF view for the newsletter subscription page:

```
<?xml version='1.0' encoding='UTF-8' ?>
<!--
Author: J. Juneau
-->
<!DOCTYPE html PUBLIC "-//W3C//DTD XHTML 1.0 Transitional//EN" "http://www.w3.org/TR/xhtml1/DTD/
xhtml1-transitional.dtd">
<html xmlns="http://www.w3.org/1999/xhtml"
      xmlns:ui="http://xmlns.jcp.org/jsf/facelets"
      xmlns:f="http://xmlns.jcp.org/jsf/core"
      xmlns:h="http://xmlns.jcp.org/jsf/html">
```

```
<body>

    <ui:composition template="layout/custom_template_search.xhtml">
        <ui:define name="content">
            <h:messages globalOnly="true"  errorStyle="color: red" infoStyle="color: green"/>
            <h:form id="contactForm">
                <h1>Subscribe to Newsletter</h1>
                <p>
                    <h:outputText id="newsletterSubscriptionDesc"
                                  value="#{contactController.newsletterDescription}"/>
                </p>

                <br/>
                <h:panelGrid columns="2" bgcolor="" border="0">
                    <h:panelGroup>
                        <h:outputLabel for="first" value="First: "/>
                        <h:inputText id="first" size="40" value="#{contactController.current.
                        first}">
                            <f:validateLength minimum="1" maximum="40"/>
                        </h:inputText>
                    </h:panelGroup>
                    <h:panelGroup>

                        <h:outputLabel for="last" value="Last: "/>
                        <h:inputText id="last" size="40" value="#{contactController.current.
                        last}">
                            <f:validateLength minimum="1" maximum="40"/>
                        </h:inputText>
                    </h:panelGroup>

                    <h:message id="firstError"
                               for="first"
                               errorStyle="color:red"/>

                    <h:message id="lastError"
                               for="last"
                               errorStyle="color:red"/>
                    <h:panelGroup>
                        <h:outputLabel for="email" value="Email: "/>
                        <h:inputText id="email" size="40" value="#{contactController.current.
                        email}"/>
                    </h:panelGroup>
                    <h:panelGroup/>
                    <h:message id="emailError"
                               for="email"
                               errorStyle="color:red"/>
                    <h:panelGroup/>
```

```
        <h:selectOneRadio title="Gender" id="gender"
            value="#{contactController.current.gender}">
            <f:selectItem  itemValue="M" itemLabel="Male"/>
            <f:selectItem itemValue="F" itemLabel="Female"/>
        </h:selectOneRadio>
        <h:panelGroup>
            <h:outputLabel for="occupation" value="Occupation: "/>
            <h:selectOneMenu id="occupation" value="#{contactController.current.
            occupation}">
                <f:selectItems  itemvalue="#{contactController.occupationList}"/>
            </h:selectOneMenu>
        </h:panelGroup>
        <h:message id="genderError"
                   for="gender"
                   errorStyle="color:red"/>

</h:panelGrid>
<br/>
<h:outputLabel for="description" value="Enter your book interests"/>
<br/>
<h:inputTextarea id="description" rows="5" cols="75"
    value="#{contactController.current.description}"/>

<br/>
<h:panelGrid columns="2">
    <h:outputLabel for="password" value="Enter a password for site access: "/>
    <h:inputSecret id="password" size="40"
        value="#{contactController.current.password}"/>

    <h:outputLabel for="passwordConfirm" value="Confirm Password: "/>
    <h:inputSecret id="passwordConfirm" size="40"
        value="#{contactController.passwordConfirm}"
                validator="#{contactController.validatePassword}"/>
</h:panelGrid>
<h:message id="passwordConfirmError"
           for="passwordConfirm"
           style="color:red"/>
<br/>
<hr/>
<br/>

<h:panelGrid columns="3">
    <h:panelGroup>
        <h:outputLabel for="newsletterList" value="Newsletters:" style=" "/>
        <h:selectManyListbox id="newsletterList"
            value="#{contactController.current.newsletterList}">
            <f:selectItems value="#{contactController.newsletterList}"/>
        </h:selectManyListbox>
    </h:panelGroup>
    <h:panelGroup/>
    <h:panelGroup>
```

```
                            <h:panelGrid columns="1">
                                <h:panelGroup>
                                    <h:outputLabel for="notifyme"
                                       value="Would you like to receive other promotional email?"/>
                                    <h:selectBooleanCheckbox id="notifyme"
                                           value="#{contactController.current.receiveNotifications}"/>
                                </h:panelGroup>
                                <h:panelGroup/>
                                <hr/>
                                <h:panelGroup/>
                                <h:panelGroup>
                                    <h:outputLabel for="notificationTypes"
                                    value="What type of notifications are you interested in
recieving?"/>

                                    <br/>
                                    <h:selectManyCheckbox id="notifyTypes"
                                    value="#{contactController.current.notificationType}">
                                        <f:selectItems value="#{contactController.
notificationTypes}"/>

                                    </h:selectManyCheckbox>
                                </h:panelGroup>
                            </h:panelGrid>
                        </h:panelGroup>
                    </h:panelGrid>
                    <hr/>
                    <br/>

                    <h:commandButton id="contactSubmit" action="#{contactController.subscribe}"
                                            value="Save"/>
                    <h:panelGrid columns="2" width="400px;">
                        <h:commandLink id="manageAccount" action="#{contactController.manage}"
                                            value="Manage Subscription"/>

                        <h:outputLink id="homeLink" value="home.xhtml">Home</h:outputLink>
                    </h:panelGrid>
                </h:form>
            </ui:define>
        </ui:composition>

    </body>
</html>
```

When the reorganized page is rendered, it will look similar to what is shown in Figure 5-8.

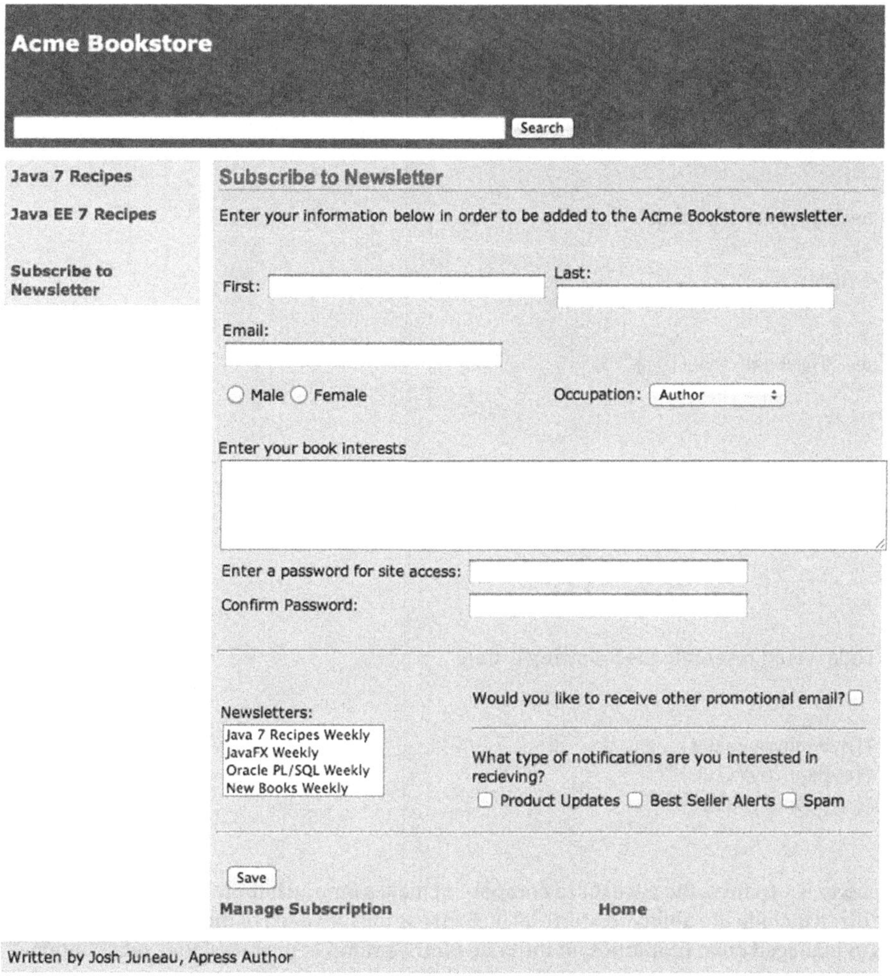

Figure 5-8. *Organizing page content with panelGrid and panelGroup*

Explanation

Sometimes it makes sense to organize the layout of a web page using Cascading Style Sheets. This is often the case when there are a series of page sections, images that must be placed in precise locations, and fonts of varying styles and sizes. Other times it makes sense to organize the layout of a web page using HTML tables. Such is true when there are various fields that share similar fonts and organization needs to be uniform, whereas the fields are laid out with respect to the fields around them. Table-based layout is usually easy to apply to input forms that include a multitude of input components with corresponding labels. Uniform layout for input forms can help the overall user experience, making page flow that creates an easy experience. The JSF standard component known as the panelGrid is rendered into an HTML table, and it can be used to create uniform layout with ease.

You may ask, why would I use a panelGrid when a standard HTML table will do? There are a few good reasons to use a panelGrid as opposed to an HTML table. The best reason is for readability. To create a three-column table using HTML markup, you would have to write something similar to the following code:

```
<table>
    <tr>
        <td>
        <h:outputText value="#{myBean.myValue}"/>
        </td>
    </tr>
    <tr>
        <td>
        <h:outputText value="#{myBean.myValue}"/>
        </td>
    </tr>
    <tr>
        <td>
         <h:outputText value="#{myBean.myValue}"/>
        </td>
    </tr>
</table>
```

If using a panelGrid, the code would resemble the following listing:

```
<h:panelGrid columns="3">
    <h:outputText value="#{myBean.myValue}"/>
    <h:outputText value="#{myBean.myValue}"/>
    <h:outputText value="#{myBean.myValue}"/>
</h:panelGrid>
```

As you can see from the previous variance, the panelGrid component makes for much more readable markup. The other reasons to use panelGrid include the ability to utilize ValueExpressions for each of the attributes and the ability to bind panelGrids to managed bean properties. In the code for the example, the newsletter subscription page has been reworked to include a section on the top pertaining to the personal information about the contact individual, as well as a section at the bottom pertaining to the subscription. Fields have been organized using panelGrid components, along with some panelGroup components nested throughout. The panelGrid component contains a set of attributes that allow you to style the header, rows, footer, and so forth. Table 5-16 contains a listing of the attributes, with the exception of JavaScript code attributes that are shared with the other JSF standard components.

Table 5-16. *panelGrid Attributes*

Attribute	Description
bgcolor	Name or code of the background color for the table.
bodyrows	Comma-separated list of row indices for which a new `<tbody>` element should be started.
border	Width (pixels) of the border to be drawn around the table.
captionClass	Space-separated list of CSS style classes that will be applied to any caption generated for the table.
captionStyle	CSS style(s) to be applied when the caption is rendered.
cellpadding	Definition of how much space the user agent should leave between the border of each cell and its contents.
cellspacing	Definition of how much space the user agent should leave between the left side of the table and the leftmost column, the top of the table and the top of the top side of the topmost row, and so on, for the right and bottom of the table. This also specifies how much space to leave between cells.
columnClasses	Comma-delimited list of CSS styles that will be applied to the columns of the table. A space-separated list of classes may also be specified for any individual column.
columns	Number of columns to render before starting a new row.
dir	Direction indication for text (LTR: left-to-right; RTL: right-to-left).
footerClass	Space-separated list of CSS style classes that will be applied to any footer generated for the table.
frame	Code specifying which sides of the frame surrounding the table will be visible.
headerClass	Space-separated list of CSS style classes that will be applied to any header generated for the table.
lang	Code describing the language used in the generated markup for the component.
rowClasses	Comma-delimited list of CSS style classes that will be applied to the rows of the table. A space-separated list of classes can also be specified for each individual row.
rules	Code specifying which rules will appear between the cells of the table. Valid values include none, groups, rows, cols, and all.
summary	Summary of the table's purpose and structure, for user agents rendering to nonvisual media.
title	Advisory title information about markup elements generated for the component.
width	Width of the entire table.

When using a panelGrid, the columns and rows attributes determine how many columns and rows the rendered table will include. For instance, a panelGrid that specifies columns="3" and rows="4" will have four rows of three columns of cells, for a total of 12 cells. The panelGroup component can be utilized for grouping one or more JSF components together so they occupy a single cell within the panelGrid. Any number of components can be embedded inside opening and closing h:panelGroup tags in order to have them treated as a single component within the table and, therefore, have them grouped into the same table cell. The panelGroup component contains a number of attributes, but they are rarely needed. In the example, the panelGroup component is used to group the input fields together with their labels in most cases. The following excerpt from the example demonstrates the use of the panelGroup component:

```
<h:panelGroup>
    <h:outputLabel for="newsletterList" value="Newsletters:" style=" "/>
    <h:selectManyListbox id="newsletterList"
        value="#{contactController.current.newsletterList}">
            <f:selectItems value="#{contactController.newsletterList}"/>
    </h:selectManyListbox>
</h:panelGroup>
```

Just like HTML tables, panelGrid components can be nested inside each other. If there comes a need to create a table within a table, then doing so is very easy. The newly formatted newsletter subscription page contains a nested panelGrid component for laying out the subscription details section.

Page layout can be very important for the usability of an application. If a page is difficult to navigate, then users will become frustrated, and the application will be difficult to use at best. For years, HTML tables have been used as a means of structuring forms in an organized fashion. The panelGrid component adds value to this technique, making it the preferred way to organize JSF views in situations where CSS is not going to be a major benefit.

Displaying a Collection of Data

Traditionally, HTML tables have been used in web pages to provide a convenient display for a collection of data. JSF provides the DataTable, which is a component providing the ease of use of an HTML table, while adding the ability to bind the table to a collection of data.

Example

A dataTable component can be used to iterate over a collection of data, providing a handle for each row object so that column data can be interrogated if need be or simply displayed. For this example, the book page is being updated to display the table of contents for a chosen book. The table of contents will be displayed within a dataTable component that has been customized for readability.

The View: example05_10.xhtml

The following listing is that of the view named example05_10.xhtml, which is an incomplete snapshot of the book.xhtml view:

```
<?xml version='1.0' encoding='UTF-8' ?>
<!--
Author: J. Juneau
-->
<!DOCTYPE html PUBLIC "-//W3C//DTD XHTML 1.0 Transitional//EN" "http://www.w3.org/TR/xhtml1/DTD/
xhtml1-transitional.dtd">
<html xmlns="http://www.w3.org/1999/xhtml"
      xmlns:ui="http://xmlns.jcp.org/jsf/facelets"
      xmlns:f="http://xmlns.jcp.org/jsf/core"
      xmlns:h="http://xmlns.jcp.org/jsf/html">
<h:head>
        <meta http-equiv="Content-Type" content="text/html; charset=UTF-8"/>
        <title>Acme Bookstore</title>
```

```
    </h:head>
    <h:body>
        <ui:composition template="./layout/custom_template_search.xhtml">

            <ui:define name="content">
                <h:form id="componentForm">
                    <h1>Author List for #{ch5AuthorController.currentBook.title}</h1>
                    <p>
                        Below is the list of authors.  Click on the author's last name
                        for more information regarding the author.
                    </p>

                    <h:graphicImage    id="javarecipes" library="image"
                                    style="width: 100px; height: 120px"
                                    name="#{ch5AuthorController.currentBook.image}"/>
                    <br/>
                    <h:dataTable id="authorTable" border="1" value="#{ch5AuthorController.
                    authorList}"
                                    var="author">
                        <f:facet name="header">
                            #{ch5AuthorController.currentBook.title} Authors
                        </f:facet>
                        <h:column>
                            <h:commandLink id="authorName" action="#{ch5AuthorController.
displayAuthor(author.last)}"
                                            value="#{author.first} #{author.last}"/>
                        </h:column>
                    </h:dataTable>
                    <br/><br/>
                    <h:dataTable id="bookDetail" border="1"
                                    value="#{ch5AuthorController.currentBook.chapters}"
                                    var="book" style="width:100%"
                                    rowClasses="tocTableOdd, tocTableEven" columnClasses="col1">
                        <f:facet name="header">
                            #{ch5AuthorController.currentBook.title} Details
                        </f:facet>

                        <h:column>
                            <f:facet name="header">
                                Chapter
                            </f:facet>
                            <h:outputText value="#{book.chapterNumber}"/>
                        </h:column>
                        <h:column>
                            <f:facet name="header">
                                Title
                            </f:facet>
                            <h:outputText value="#{book.title}"/>
                        </h:column>
```

```
                    </h:dataTable>
                    <br/>
                    <br/>
                </h:form>
            </ui:define>
        </ui:composition>
    </h:body>
</html>
```

CSS

The dataTable utilizes some CSS style classes in order to make it easier to read. The following excerpt is taken from the Acme Bookstore application style sheet named styles.css, and it contains the styles utilized by the table. The styles.css sheet is linked to the view because it is declared as a resource within the template.

```css
.tocTableOdd{
    background: #c0c0c0;
}

.tocTableEven{
    background: #e0e0e0;
}

.col1{
    text-indent: 15px;
    font-weight: bold;
}
```

Managed Bean

To accommodate the new table, a class named Chapter has been added to the application. The Chapter class is an object that will contain the chapter number, the title, and a description of each chapter. There is to be one Chapter object instantiated for each chapter in every book. To view the listing, please see the org.javaserverfaces. chapter05.Chapter class in the sources. To populate the Chapter objects for each book, the AuthorController managed bean has been updated. The following excerpt is taken from the AuthorController managed bean, and it shows how the chapters are populated into the Book objects.

■ **Note**   The example demonstrates hard-coding of Strings within Java classes. This is generally a bad idea, and the use of a database or resource bundle for obtaining Strings is a better fit for enterprise applications.

```
...
public void populateAuthors(){
...
    Book book1 = new Book("Java 7 Recipes", "java7recipes.png");
    book1 = addChapters1(book1);
...
}
...
private Book addChapters1(Book book){
    Chapter chapter1 = new Chapter(1, "Getting Started with Java 7", null);
    Chapter chapter2 = new Chapter(2, "Strings", null);
    Chapter chapter3 = new Chapter(3, "Numbers and Dates", null);
    Chapter chapter4 = new Chapter(4, "Data Structures, Conditionals, and Iteration", null);
    Chapter chapter5 = new Chapter(5, "Input and Output", null);
    Chapter chapter6 = new Chapter(6, "Exceptions, Logging, and Debugging", null);
    Chapter chapter7 = new Chapter(7, "Object Oriented Java", null);
    Chapter chapter8 = new Chapter(8, "Concurrency", null);
    Chapter chapter9 = new Chapter(9, "Debugging and Unit Testing", null);
    Chapter chapter10 = new Chapter(10, "Unicode, Internationalization, and Currency Codes", null);
    Chapter chapter11 = new Chapter(11, "Working with Databases (JDBC)", null);
    Chapter chapter12 = new Chapter(12, "Java 2D Graphics and Media", null);
    Chapter chapter13 = new Chapter(13, "Java 3D", null);
    Chapter chapter14 = new Chapter(14, "Swing API", null);
    Chapter chapter15 = new Chapter(15, "JavaFX Fundamentals", null);
    Chapter chapter16 = new Chapter(16, "Graphics with JavaFX", null);
    Chapter chapter17 = new Chapter(17, "Media with JavaFX", null);
    Chapter chapter18 = new Chapter(18, "Working with Servlets", null);
    Chapter chapter19 = new Chapter(19, "Applets", null);
    Chapter chapter20 = new Chapter(20, "JavaFX on the Web", null);
    Chapter chapter21 = new Chapter(21, "Email", null);
    Chapter chapter22 = new Chapter(22, "XML and Web Services", null);
    Chapter chapter23 = new Chapter(23, "Networking", null);
    List <Chapter> chapterList = new ArrayList();
    chapterList.add(chapter1);
    chapterList.add(chapter2);
    chapterList.add(chapter3);
    chapterList.add(chapter4);
    chapterList.add(chapter5);
    chapterList.add(chapter6);
    chapterList.add(chapter7);
    chapterList.add(chapter8);
    chapterList.add(chapter9);
    chapterList.add(chapter10);
    chapterList.add(chapter11);
    chapterList.add(chapter12);
    chapterList.add(chapter13);
    chapterList.add(chapter14);
    chapterList.add(chapter15);
    chapterList.add(chapter16);
    chapterList.add(chapter17);
    chapterList.add(chapter18);
```

```
chapterList.add(chapter19);
chapterList.add(chapter20);
chapterList.add(chapter21);
chapterList.add(chapter22);
chapterList.add(chapter23);
book.setChapters(chapterList);
return book;

}
...
```

The resulting table of contents within the book page will look like Figure 5-9.

Java 7 Recipes Details	
Chapter	**Title**
1	Getting Started with Java 7
2	Strings
3	Numbers and Dates
4	Data Structures, Conditionals, and Iteration
5	Input and Output
6	Exceptions, Logging, and Debugging
7	Object Oriented Java
8	Concurrency
9	Debugging and Unit Testing
10	Unicode, Internationalization, and Currency Codes
11	Working with Databases (JDBC)
12	Java 2D Graphics and Media
13	Java 3D
14	Swing API
15	JavaFX Fundamentals
16	Graphics with JavaFX
17	Media with JavaFX
18	Working with Servlets
19	Applets
20	JavaFX on the Web
21	Email
22	XML and Web Services
23	Networking

Figure 5-9. *Using a dataTable component*

Explanation

The JSF dataTable component can be used to display collections of data in a uniform fashion. The dataTable component is easy to work with, and it allows the flexibility to work with each field within a data collection. There are other means of displaying collections of data, such as the ui-repeat Facelets tag or the use of a panelGrid component, but a dataTable makes a developer's life easy if the table does not need to be customized to the nth degree.

The dataTable component contains various attributes that can be used to customize the look and feel of the table, as well as some behavioral characteristics. Each of those attributes is listed in Table 5-17. Each dataTable also contains column components, which are declared within a dataTable component using the h:column tag. As with any other JSF tag, there are many attributes that correspond to the h:column tag, as listed in Table 5-18.

Table 5-17. *dataTable Attributes*

Attribute	Description
bgcolor	Name or code of the background color for the table.
bodyrows	Comma-separated list of row indices for which a new <tbody> element should be started.
border	Width (pixels) of the border to be drawn around the table.
captionClass	Space-separated list of CSS style classes that will be applied to any caption generated for the table.
captionStyle	CSS style to be applied when the caption is rendered.
cellpadding	Definition of how much space the user agent should leave between the border of each cell and its contents.
cellspacing	Definition of how much space the user agent should leave between the left side of the table and the leftmost column, the top of the table and the top of the top side of the topmost row, and so on, for the right and bottom of the table. This also specifies how much space to leave between cells.
columnClasses	Comma-delimited list of CSS styles that will be applied to the columns of the table. A space-separated list of classes can also be specified for any individual column.
columns	Number of columns to render before starting a new row.
dir	Direction indication for text (LTR: left-to-right; RTL: right-to-left).
footerClass	Space-separated list of CSS style classes that will be applied to any footer generated for the table.
frame	Code specifying which sides of the frame surrounding the table will be visible.
headerClass	Space-separated list of CSS style classes that will be applied to any header generated for the table.
lang	Code describing the language used in the generated markup for the component.
rowClasses	Comma-delimited list of CSS style classes that will be applied to the rows of the table. A space-separated list of classes may also be specified for each individual row.
rules	Code specifying which rules will appear between the cells of the table. Valid values include none, groups, rows, cols, and all.
summary	Summary of the table's purpose and structure for user agents rendering to nonvisual media.
title	Advisory title information about markup elements generated for the component.
width	Width of the entire table.

Table 5-18. h:column Attributes

Attribute	Description
footerClass	CSS class that will be applied to the column footer
headerClass	CSS class that will be applied to the column header

The easiest way to describe the dataTable is to walk through an example. The example contains a JSF view, in which there are two dataTable components utilized. The first dataTable has an id attribute of authorTable, and the second has an id attribute of bookTable. You are most interested in the second dataTable, whose id attribute equals bookTable, although the first dataTable functions in much the same way. The bookTable component is used to iterate over a collection of Chapter objects and display the corresponding chapter number and title for the currently selected book. The value attribute of the dataTable is set to #{ch5AuthorController.currentBook.chapters}, which corresponds to a List<String> property within the AuthorController managed bean. A dataTable can iterate over many different collection types, including a List, DataModel, and array. Beginning with the release of JSF 2.2, the common Collection interface also became supported. The var attribute of the dataTable component is used to specify a handle that allows access to the collection data at the row level. This means you can hone in on a specific field of the data collection if needed. The dataTable tag does not display anything on its own; it must have column components embedded within it in order to display the content. Each h:column tag within a dataTable correlates to a single column of the resulting table when it is rendered. For instance, if you look at the first h:column tag within the dataTable that has an id of bookDetail, it has an embedded outputText component, which specifies a value of #{book.chapterNumber}. This specific column is used to display the chapter number, which is a field within the Chapter object that correlates to the currentBook object's chapters List.

A column component can contain any valid JSF component, or it can contain plain JSF EL correlating to a data field within the collection. If you look at the dataTable that has an id attribute of authorTable, you will see that a commandLink component is used within one of the columns. Oftentimes such is the case, because you may want to link to the currently selected row's data from within a table cell. The dataTable with an id of authorTable contains a good example of doing just that. The commandLink in the table contains an action attribute that specifies a method within the AuthorController class, and the currently selected row's value, lastName, is passed to the method as a parameter. The underlying method uses that parameter to retrieve all the data for the selected row and display it in a different view.

```
<h:commandLink id="authorName" action="#{ch5AuthorController.displayAuthor(author.last)}"
                    value="#{author.first} #{author.last}"/>
```

To place a header or footer on the table, you must embed a facet into the table using an f:facet tag. The f:facet tag contains a number of typical JSF component attributes, but one that stands out for this component is the name attribute. The name attribute is used to specify what type of facet the tag is, and in the case of the dataTable those names are header and footer. To create the table header or footer, simply embed the f:facet tag, specifying the name of the facet (type of facet to create) inside the dataTable component.

■ **Note** A unique data type that can be used for a dataTable collection is the DataModel. To have the ability to display row numbers, use a DataModel.

The dataTable component can be extremely useful in situations when you need to display a collection of data. One of the pitfalls to using the dataTable is that it does not provide an overabundance of customizability. However, it is very possible to extend the functionality of the dataTable to suit one's need. There are plenty of third-party component libraries that do just that; they provide extended dataTables that feature sorting, row expansion, inline editing, and so forth. To learn more about using these custom dataTable components, please see Chapter 6.

Utilizing Custom JSF Component Libraries

One of the boons to using JSF is the ability to incorporate multiple third party component libraries for creating sophisticated views. There are a number of highly praised component libraries available for use, and it is easy to incorporate them into an application.

Example

Obtain the latest stable version of the JSF component library that you'd like to utilize, and configure it for use within your application. This example will cover the configuration of the RichFaces and PrimeFaces component libraries, both of which contain a number of customized components that can add a great deal of functionality to your applications. To download RichFaces, please visit the site `www.richfaces.org`, and to download the PrimeFaces library, please visit the site `www.primefaces.org`. Each of these component sites can be used together within a single JSF application.

Once you have downloaded the libraries, add them to your JSF application by adding the component library JAR file to the `WEB-INF/lib` directory within your application's web source directory. Note that you may also need to include additional JAR files with your application in order to utilize external libraries. Please see each library's documentation for complete details on each external JAR that needs to be included within your application in order to gain full functionality.

After the libraries have been placed within the `WEB-INF/lib` directory, you can begin to utilize the library's components within your application by declaring their corresponding tag libraries within the application views in which you want to use them. The following tag declarations are used to allow usage of RichFaces and PrimeFaces components within a JSF view:

```
xmlns:rich="http://richfaces.org/rich"
xmlns:a4j="http://richfaces.org/a4j"
xmlns:p="http://primefaces.org/ui"
```

Explanation

The JSF standard component library contains a vast number of components for use within applications. However, many individuals and organizations require the use of more customized components and components that build upon the functionality of the standard components. Utilizing a third-party JSF component library is very easy and usually involves nothing more than downloading the distribution, including the recommended JAR files within your application, and referencing the tag libraries from within the views. However, it is best to take care when utilizing more than one third-party JSF component library within the same application, because there may be some compatibility issues/conflicts that arise between them.

Once you have followed the procedures outlined in the example, you will be able to begin adding components from the RichFaces and PrimeFaces libraries into your views. These libraries include exciting components such as the `autoComplete` component, which renders an input text box that will automatically complete a string of text when the user begins to type. While I will not delve into any details of the components in this chapter, you will begin using them within Chapter 6.

Implementing File Uploading

A common requirement in a web application is the need to upload documents or images to the server. JSF provides a component for filling this requirement.

Example

Make use of the JSF file upload component to create an Ajax or non-Ajax-based file upload system for your application. To utilize the inputFile component, it must be placed within a JSF form that has an enctype set to multipart/form-data and does not specify an id attribute. The h:form element contains the attributes enctype and prependId, which can be used to specify these requirements, respectively. A JSF command component or the f:ajax tag should be set to an action method within the managed bean that will save the file to disk.

The following JSF view demonstrates the use of the inputFile component in a non-Ajax solution:

```
<h:form prependId="false" enctype="multipart/form-data">
    Choose a file to upload to the server:     <br/>
     <h:inputFile id="uploadFile" value="#{ajaxBean.file}"/>
    <br/>     <h:commandButton action="#{ajaxBean.uploadFile()}" value="Upload File"/></h:form>
```

The sources for the uploadFile method that is invoked via the commandButton are as follows:

```
public void uploadFile() {

        try(InputStream is = file.getInputStream();) {
            byte[] b = new byte[1024];
            is.read(b);
            String fileName = file.getName();
            FileOutputStream os = new FileOutputStream("/Java_Dev/" + fileName);

        } catch (IOException ex) {
            Logger.getLogger(AjaxBean.class.getName()).log(Level.SEVERE, null, ex);
        }

}
```

Explanation

JSF 2.2 includes a new file upload component that relies upon new Servlet 3.1 file upload support. The file upload support can be Ajax-enabled or non-Ajax-enabled. A new JSF component named inputFile has been added to the list of standard JSF components. This component can be used with or without the f:ajax tag, so files can be uploaded with a page refresh (non-Ajax) or without (Ajax).

The following line of code demonstrates how to set the attributes for a form containing an inputFile component:

```
<h:form prependId="false" enctype="multipart/form-data">
```

The value attribute of the inputFile component is set to a variable of type javax.servlet.http.Part within the AjaxBean managed bean, and the commandButton has an action set to the managed bean's uploadFile method. To make the solution utilize Ajax, simply embed an f:ajax tag into the commandButton, which invokes the underlying managed bean method.

The addition of a native file upload component to JSF is much welcomed. For years now, JSF developers have had to rely on third-party libraries to handle file-uploading procedures. The scope of components that requires third-party integration is becoming more narrow, and the default JSF component tool set is becoming complete enough to be the only requirement for standard enterprise applications.

CHAPTER 6

Advanced JavaServer Faces and Ajax

A task that can be run in the background, independent of other running tasks, is known as an *asynchronous* task. JavaScript is the most popular modern browser language that is used to implement asynchronous tasking in web applications. Ajax is a set of technologies that allows you to perform asynchronous tasks using JavaScript in the background, sending responses from the client browser to the server, and then sending a response back to the client. That response is used to update the page's Document Object Model (DOM). Enhancing an application to make use of such asynchronous requests and responses can greatly improve the overall user experience. The typical web applications from years past included a series of web pages, including buttons that were used to navigate from one page to the next. The browser had to repaint each new page, and when a user was finished with the next page, they'd click another button to go to a subsequent page, and so on. The days of page reloads are long gone, and client-side asynchronous processing is now the norm. Ajax technology has overtaken the industry of web application development, and users now expect to experience a richer and more desktop-like experience when using a web application.

The JSF framework allows developers to create rich user experiences via the use of technologies such as Ajax and HTML5. Much of the implementation detail behind these technologies can be abstracted away from the JSF developer using JSF components so that the developer needs to worry only about how to use a JSF component tag and relate it to a server-side property.

This chapter delves into using Ajax with the JSF web framework. Along the way, you will learn how to spruce up applications and make the user interface richer and more user friendly so that it behaves more like that of a desktop application. You'll also learn how to listen to different component phases and system events, allowing further customization of application functionality.

■ **Note** This chapter contains examples using the third-party component library PrimeFaces. To use PrimeFaces with Java EE 7 or greater, you must utilize PrimeFaces 4.x+, as earlier releases are not compatible with JSF 2.2.

Validating Input with Ajax

When performing Ajax validation, values should be validated immediately after the user has entered text or moved to a different field, rather than at form submission time. JSF facilitates this functionality via the use of the f:ajax tag.

Example

Perform validation on the field(s) by embedding the f:ajax tag within each component whose values you want to validate. Specify appropriate values for the event and render attributes so that the Ajax validation will occur when the field(s) loses focus, and any validation errors will be identified immediately. The following listing is the JSF view for the newsletter subscription page of the Acme Bookstore application. It has been updated to utilize Ajax validation so that the validation occurs immediately, without the need to submit the form before corresponding errors are displayed.

■ **Note**   To utilize the f:ajax tag, you must be sure to declare the document head section within the
<h:head> </h:head> tags. The component looks for the h:head tags when searching for various <script> tags.

```
<?xml version='1.0' encoding='UTF-8' ?>
<!--
Author: J. Juneau
-->
<!DOCTYPE html PUBLIC "-//W3C//DTD XHTML 1.0 Transitional//EN" "http://www.w3.org/TR/xhtml1/DTD/
xhtml1-transitional.dtd">
<html xmlns="http://www.w3.org/1999/xhtml"
      xmlns:ui="http://xmlns.jcp.org/jsf/facelets"
      xmlns:f="http://xmlns.jcp.org/jsf/core"
      xmlns:h="http://xmlns.jcp.org/jsf/html">

    <body>

        <ui:composition template="layout/custom_template_search.xhtml">
            <ui:define name="content">
                <h:messages globalOnly="true"  errorStyle="color: red" infoStyle="color: green"/>
                <h:form id="contactForm">
                    <h1>Subscribe to Newsletter</h1>
                    <p>
                        <h:outputText id="newsletterSubscriptionDesc"
                         value="#{ch6ContactController.newsletterDescription}"/>
                    </p>

                    <br/>
                    <h:panelGrid columns="2" bgcolor="" border="0">
                        <h:panelGroup>
                            <h:outputLabel for="first" value="First: "/>
                            <h:inputText id="first" size="40"
                             value="#{ch6ContactController.current.first}">
                                <f:validateLength minimum="1" maximum="40"/>
                                <f:ajax event="blur" render="firstError"/>
                            </h:inputText>
                        </h:panelGroup>
```

```
    <h:panelGroup>

        <h:outputLabel for="last" value="Last: "/>
        <h:inputText id="last" size="40"
         value="#{ch6ContactController.current.last}">
            <f:validateLength minimum="1" maximum="40"/>
            <f:ajax event="blur" render="lastError"/>
        </h:inputText>
    </h:panelGroup>

    <h:message id="firstError"
             for="first"
             errorStyle="color:red"/>

    <h:message id="lastError"
             for="last"
             errorStyle="color:red"/>
    <h:panelGroup>
        <h:outputLabel for="email" value="Email: "/>
        <h:inputText id="email" size="40"
         value="#{ch6ContactController.current.email}">
            <f:ajax event="blur" render="emailError"/>
        </h:inputText>
    </h:panelGroup>
    <h:panelGroup/>
    <h:message id="emailError"
             for="email"
             errorStyle="color:red"/>
    <h:panelGroup/>

    <h:selectOneRadio title="Gender" id="gender"
             value="#{ch6ContactController.current.gender}">
        <f:selectItem  itemValue="M" itemLabel="Male"/>
        <f:selectItem itemValue="F" itemLabel="Female"/>
    </h:selectOneRadio>
    <h:panelGroup>
        <h:outputLabel for="occupation" value="Occupation: "/>
        <h:selectOneMenu id="occupation"
         value="#{ch6ContactController.current.occupation}">
            <f:selectItems value="#{ch6ContactController.occupationList}"/>
        </h:selectOneMenu>
    </h:panelGroup>
    <h:message id="genderError"
             for="gender"
             errorStyle="color:red"/>

</h:panelGrid>
<br/>
<h:outputLabel for="description" value="Enter your book interests"/>
<br/>
<h:inputTextarea id="description" rows="5" cols="75"
             value="#{ch6ContactController.current.description}"/>

<br/>
```

```
<h:panelGrid columns="2">
    <h:outputLabel for="password" value="Enter a password for site access: "/>
    <h:inputSecret id="password" size="40"
        value="#{ch6ContactController.current.password}">
        <f:validateRequired/>
        <f:ajax event="blur" render="passwordError"/>
    </h:inputSecret>

    <h:outputLabel for="passwordConfirm" value="Confirm Password: "/>
    <h:inputSecret id="passwordConfirm" size="40"
        value="#{ch6ContactController.passwordConfirm}"
                validator="#{ch6ContactController.validatePassword}">
        <f:ajax event="blur" render="passwordConfirmError"/>
    </h:inputSecret>
</h:panelGrid>
<h:message id="passwordError"
        for="password"
        style="color:red"/>
<br/>
<h:message id="passwordConfirmError"
        for="passwordConfirm"
        style="color:red"/>
<br/>
<hr/>
<br/>

<h:panelGrid columns="3">
    <h:panelGroup>
        <h:outputLabel for="newsletterList" value="Newsletters:" style=" "/>
        <h:selectManyListbox id="newsletterList"
         value="#{ch6ContactController.current.newsletterList}">
            <f:selectItems value="#{ch6ContactController.newsletterList}"/>
        </h:selectManyListbox>
    </h:panelGroup>
    <h:panelGroup/>
    <h:panelGroup>
        <h:panelGrid columns="1">
            <h:panelGroup>
                <h:outputLabel for="notifyme"
    value="Would you like to receive other promotional email?"/>
                <h:selectBooleanCheckbox id="notifyme"
                        value="#{ch6ContactController.current.
                        receiveNotifications}"/>
            </h:panelGroup>
            <h:panelGroup/>
            <hr/>
            <h:panelGroup/>
```

```
                  <h:panelGroup>
                      <h:outputLabel for="notificationTypes"value="What type of
                       notifications are you interested in recieving?"/>
                      <br/>
                      <h:selectManyCheckbox id="notifyTypes"
                          value="#{ch6ContactController.current.notificationType}">
                      <f:selectItems value="#{ch6ContactController.
                          notificationTypes}"/>
                      </h:selectManyCheckbox>
                  </h:panelGroup>
              </h:panelGrid>
          </h:panelGroup>
      </h:panelGrid>
      <hr/>
      <br/>

      <h:commandButton id="contactSubmit"
          action="#{ch6ContactController.subscribe}" value="Save"/>
      <h:panelGrid  columns="2" width="400px;">
          <h:commandLink id="manageAccount"
          action="#{ch6ContactController.manage}" value="Manage Subscription"/>

          <h:outputLink id="homeLink" value="home.xhtml">Home</h:outputLink>
      </h:panelGrid>
    </h:form>
  </ui:define>
 </ui:composition>

 </body>
</html>
```

Once the input components have been "Ajaxified" by embedding the f:ajax tag within them, then tabbing through the fields (causing the onBlur event to occur for each field) will result in a form that resembles Figure 6-1.

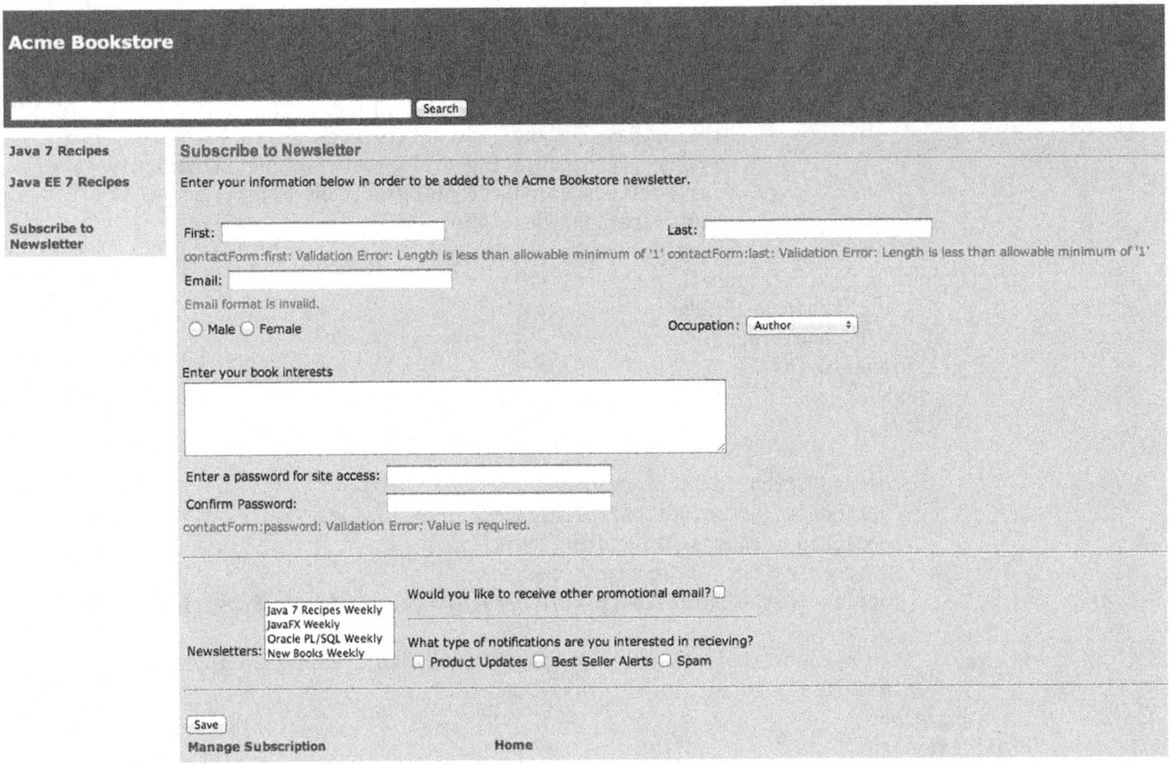

Figure 6-1. *Ajax validation using the f:ajax tag*

Explanation

In releases of JSF prior to 2.0, performing immediate validation required the manual coding of JavaScript or a third-party component library. The f:ajax tag was added to the JSF arsenal with the release of 2.0, bringing with it the power to easily add immediate validation (and other asynchronous processes) to JSF views using standard or third-party components. The f:ajax tag can be embedded within any JSF input component in order to immediately enhance the component, adding Ajax capabilities to it. This provides many benefits to the developer in that there is no longer a need to manually code JavaScript to perform client-side validation. It also allows validation to occur on the server (in Java code within a JSF managed bean) asynchronously, providing seamless interaction between the client and server and generating an immediate response to the client. The result is a rich Internet application that behaves in much the same manner as a native desktop application. Validation can now occur instantaneously in front of an end user's eyes without the need to perform several page submits in order to repair all of the possible issues.

To use the f:ajax tag, simply embed it within any JSF component. There are a number of attributes that can be specified with f:ajax, as described in Table 6-1. If an attribute is not specified, then the default values are substituted. It is quite possible to include no attributes in an f:ajax tag, and if this is done, then the default attribute values for the component in which the f:ajax tag is embedded will take effect.

Table 6-1. f:ajax Tag Attributes

Attribute	Description
delay	A value that is specified in milliseconds, corresponding to the amount of delay between sending Ajax requests from the client-side queue to the server. The value none can be specified to disable this feature.
disabled	Boolean value indicating the tag status. A value of true indicates that the Ajax behavior should not be rendered, and a value of false indicates that the Ajax behavior should be rendered. The default value is false.
event	A String that identifies the type of event to which the Ajax action shall apply. If specified, it must be one of the supported component events. The default value is the event that triggers the Ajax request for the parent component of the Ajax behavior. The default event is action for ActionSource components and is valueChange for EditableValueHolder components.
execute	A collection that identifies a list of components to be executed on the server. A space-delimited String of component identifiers can be specified as the value for this attribute, or a ValueExpression (JSF EL) can be specified. The default value is @this, meaning the parent component of the Ajax behavior.
immediate	Boolean value indicating whether the input values are processed early in the life cycle. If true, then the values are processed, and their corresponding events will be broadcast during the Apply Request Values phase; otherwise, the events will be broadcast during the Invoke Applications phase.
listener	Name of the listener method that is called when an AjaxBehaviorEvent has been broadcast for the listener.
onevent	Name of the JavaScript function used to handle UI events.
onerror	Name of the JavaScript function used to handle errors.
render	Collection that identifies the components to be rendered on the client when the Ajax behavior is complete. A space-delimited String of component identifiers can be specified as the value for this attribute, or a ValueExpression (JSF EL) can be specified. The default value is @none, meaning that no components will be rendered when the Ajax behavior is complete.

The execute and render attributes of the f:ajax tag can specify a number of keywords to indicate which components are executed on the server for the Ajax behavior or which are rendered again after the Ajax behavior is complete, respectively. Table 6-2 lists the values that can be specified for both of these two attributes.

Table 6-2. f:ajax Tag execute and render Attribute Values

Attribute Value	Description
@all	All component identifiers
@form	The form that encloses the component
@none	No component identifiers (default for render attribute)
@this	The Ajax behavior parent component
Component IDs	Space-separated list of individual component identifiers
JSF EL	Expression that resolves to a collection of string identifiers

In the example, an f:ajax tag has been embedded inside many of the input components within the form. Each of those components has been Ajaxified, in that the data entered as the value for the components will now have the ability to be processed using the JavaScript resource library associated with JSF. Behind the scenes, the jsf.ajax.request() method of the JavaScript resource library will collect the data for each component that has been Ajaxified and post the request to the JavaServer Faces life cycle. In effect, the data is sent to the managed bean property without submitting the page in a traditional fashion. Notice that the event attribute specifies a JavaScript event that will be used to trigger the Ajax behavior. The JavaScript events that can be specified for the event attribute are those same JavaScript event attributes that are available on the parent component's tag, but the on prefix has been removed. For instance, if you want to perform an Ajax behavior on an inputText component when it loses focus, you would specify blur for the f:ajax event attribute rather than onBlur. Applying this concept to the example, when a user leaves the first or last name field, they will be validated using their associated f:validate tags immediately because the f:ajax tag has been embedded in them and the event on the f:ajax tag is specified as blur. When the Ajax behavior (the validation in this case) is complete, then the components whose identifiers are specified in the f:ajax render attribute will be re-rendered. In the case of the first and last inputText fields, their associated message components will be re-rendered, displaying any errors that may have occurred during validation.

UTILIZING AN ACTION LISTENER

It is possible to bind an action listener to an f:ajax tag so that when the invoking action occurs, the listener method is invoked. Why would you want to bind an action listener? There are any reasons to do so. For instance, suppose you wanted to capture the text that a user is typing into a text field. You could do so by binding an action method within a managed bean to the listener attribute of an inputText field's corresponding f:ajax tag and then obtaining the current component's value from the AjaxBehaviorEvent object within the action method. For instance, suppose that you wanted to test a password for complexity and display a corresponding message indicating whether a password was strong enough. The inputSecret component for the password could be modified to include an f:ajax tag with an event specification of keyup and a listener specified as #{ch6ContactController.passwordStrength}, such as the following listing demonstrates.

Within the view:

```
<h:outputLabel for="password" value="Enter a password for site access: "/>
<h:inputSecret id="password" size="40" value="#{ch6ContactController.current.password}">
    <f:validateRequired/>
    <f:ajax event="keyup" listener="#{ch6ContactController.passwordStrength}"
        render="passwordStrengthMessage"/>
</h:inputSecret>
...
```

Within the managed bean:

```
public void passwordStrength(AjaxBehaviorEvent event){
        UIInput password = (UIInput) event.getComponent();
        boolean isStrong = false;
        String input = password.getValue().toString();

        if(input.matches("((?=.*\\d)(?=.*[a-z])(?=.*[A-Z]).{6,})")) {
            isStrong = true;
        }
```

```
        if(isStrong == true){
            setPasswordStrengthMessage("Password is strong");
        } else {
            setPasswordStrengthMessage("Password is weak");
        }
    }
```

The code in this example would create a listener event that, when a user types a value, would check the present entry to determine whether it met the given criteria for a secure password. A message would then be displayed to the user to let them know whether the password was secure.

Using the f:ajax tag makes it easy to add Ajax behavior to a JSF component. Before the f:ajax tag, special third-party JavaScript libraries were often used to incorporate similar behaviors within JSF views. f:ajax adds the benefit of allowing the developer to choose between using Ajax behaviors, without the need for coding a single line of JavaScript.

Submitting Pages Without Page Reloads

Submitting an input form using Ajax provides the ability process input fields without reloading the page. In essence, Ajax causes an input form to react more like that of a desktop application.

Example

To submit input fields in a JSF form without causing a page reload, embed an <f:ajax/> tag within the command component in the view so that the managed bean action is. Enable f:ajax to update the messages component in the view so that any errors or success messages that result from the processing can be displayed. In this example, the newsletter subscription page for the Acme Bookstore will be changed so that the form is submitted using Ajax, and the commandLink component is processed without submitting the form in a traditional manner. The following excerpt from the newsletter subscription form sources from example06_02.xhtml, which demonstrates how to add Ajax functionality to the action components within the form:

```
<h:commandButton id="contactSubmit" action="#{ch6ContactController.subscribe}"
            value="Save">
    <f:ajax event="action" execute="@form" render="@all"/>
</h:commandButton>
<h:panelGrid  columns="2" width="400px;">
```

When the button or link is clicked, JavaScript will be used in the background to process the request so that the results will be displayed immediately without needing to refresh the page.

Explanation

The user experience for web applications has traditionally involved a point, click, and page refresh mantra. While this type of experience is not particularly a bad one, it is not as nice as the immediate response that is oftentimes presented within a native desktop application. The use of Ajax within web applications has helped create a more unified user experience, allowing a web application the ability to produce an "immediate" response much like that of a native desktop application. Field validation (covered in the previous example) is a great candidate for immediate feedback, but another area where immediate responses work well is when forms are being submitted.

The f:ajax tag can be embedded in an action component in order to invoke the corresponding action method using JavaScript behind the scenes. The f:ajax tag contains a number of attributes, covered in Table 6-1, that can be used to invoke Ajax behavior given a specified event and re-render view components when that Ajax behavior is complete. Please refer to Table 6-2 to see the values that can be specified for the execute and render attributes of the f:ajax tag.

In the example, the commandButton component with an identifier of contactSubmit contains an f:ajax tag that specifies the event attribute as action, the execute attribute as @form, and the render attribute as @all. This means that when the button is invoked, the ch6ContactController.subscribe method will be called asynchronously using JavaScript, and it will send all the input component values from the form to the server (managed bean) for processing. When the Ajax behavior (subscribe method) is complete, all of the components within the view will be re-rendered. By re-rendering all the components in the view, this allows those message components to display any messages that have been queued up as a result of failed validation or a successful form submission. It is possible to process or render only specified components during an Ajax behavior.

■ **Note**   Note that the event attribute has a default value of action when the f:ajax tag is embedded within a UICommand component. However, it is specified in the code for this example for consistency.

Adding Ajax actions to a page has been simplified since the addition of the f:ajax tag with the 2.0 release of JSF. Validation and page actions are easy to process asynchronously by utilizing a single tag, f:ajax, to incorporate Ajax functionality into any JSF component.

Making Partial-Page Updates

It can be beneficial at times to execute only a section of a page using an Ajax event and then render the corresponding section's components when the Ajax behavior is complete.

Example

Use the f:ajax tag to add Ajax functionality to the components that you want to execute and render when the Ajax behavior is completed. Specify only the component identifiers corresponding to those components, or @form, @this, or one of the other execute keywords, for the f:ajax tag execute attribute. Likewise, specify only the component identifiers for the corresponding message components within the render attribute.

Suppose that the Acme Bookstore wants to execute the submission of the newsletter subscription form values and update the form's global message only when the submission is complete. The following commandButton component would execute only the form in which it is placed and the component corresponding to the identifier newsletterSubscriptionMsgs:

```
<h:commandButton id="contactSubmit" action="#{ch6ContactController.subscribe}" value="Save">
    <f:ajax event="action" execute="@form" render="newsletterSubscriptionMsgs"/>
</h:commandButton>
```

When the button is clicked, the current form component values will be processed with the request, and the ContactController managed bean's subscribe method will be invoked. Once the subscribe method is complete, the component within the form that contains an identifier of newsletterSubscriptionMsgs (in this case, a messages component) will be re-rendered.

> **Note** In the case of the newsletter subscription form for the Acme Bookstore, a partial-page render upon completion is a bad idea. This is because the form will never be submitted if the values within the form do not validate correctly. In this case, if some of the form values do not validate correctly, then nothing will be displayed on the page when the Save button is clicked because the `subscribe` method will never be invoked. If the `f:ajax` tag's `render` attribute is set to `@all`, then all of the components that failed validation will have a corresponding error message that is displayed. This example should demonstrate how important it is to process the appropriate portions of the page for the result you are trying to achieve.

Explanation

The `f:ajax` tag makes it simple to perform partial-page updates. To do so, specify the identifiers for those components that you want to execute for the `f:ajax` execute attribute. As mentioned in the example, suppose you want to execute only a portion of a page, rather than all of the components on the given page. You could do so by identifying the components that you want to execute within the view, specifying them within the `f:ajax` execute attribute, and then rendering the corresponding message components when the Ajax behavior was completed. If nothing is specified for an `f:ajax` execute attribute, then the `f:ajax` tag must be embedded inside a component, in which case the parent component would be executed. Such is the default behavior for the `f:ajax` execute attribute. In the example, the execute attribute of the `f:ajax` tag specifies the `@form` keyword, rather than a specific component id. A number of keywords can be specified for both the execute and render attributes of the `f:ajax` tag. Those keywords are listed in Table 6-2, which describes that the `@form` keyword indicates that all components within the same form as the given `f:ajax` tag will be executed when the Ajax behavior occurs. Therefore, all fields within the newsletter subscription form in this example will be sent to the managed bean for processing when the button is clicked.

The same holds true for the render attribute, and once the Ajax behavior has completed, any component specified for the render attribute of the `f:ajax` tag will be re-rendered. Thus, if a validation occurs when a component is being processed because of the result of an `f:ajax` method call, a corresponding validation failure message can be displayed on the page after the validation fails. Any component can be rendered again, and the same keywords that can be specified for the execute attribute can also be used for the render attribute. In the example, the `newsletterSubscriptonMsgs` component is rendered once the Ajax behavior is completed.

Partial-page updates, a common use of the `f:ajax` tag, are easy to implement and can enhance the functionality and usability of an application. Later in this chapter you will learn how to utilize some third-party component libraries to perform partial-page updates, creating highly usable interfaces for editing data and the like.

Applying Ajax Functionality to a Group of Components

It can become cumbersome to apply Ajax functionality to components on a one-by-one basis. The `f:ajax` tag can also enclose multiple components to provide Ajax functionality to each of the components in the group.

Example

Enclose any components to which you want to apply Ajax functionality within an `f:ajax` tag. The `f:ajax` tag can be the parent to one or more JSF components, in which case each of the child components inherits the given Ajax behavior. Applying Ajax functionality to multiple components is demonstrated in the following code listing. In the example, the newsletter subscription view of the Acme Bookstore application is adjusted so that each of the `inputText` components that contains a validator is enclosed by a single `f:ajax` tag. Given that each of the `inputText` components is embodied within the same f:ajax tag, the f:ajax render attribute has been set to specify the message component for each of the corresponding inputText fields in the group.

```xml
<?xml version='1.0' encoding='UTF-8' ?>
<!--
Author: J. Juneau
-->
<!DOCTYPE html PUBLIC "-//W3C//DTD XHTML 1.0 Transitional//EN"
"http://www.w3.org/TR/xhtml1/DTD/xhtml1-transitional.dtd">
<html xmlns="http://www.w3.org/1999/xhtml"
      xmlns:ui="http://xmlns.jcp.org/jsf/facelets"
      xmlns:f="http://xmlns.jcp.org/jsf/core"
      xmlns:h="http://xmlns.jcp.org/jsf/html">

    <body>

        <ui:composition template="layout/custom_template_search.xhtml">
            <ui:define name="content">
                <h:form id="contactForm">
                    <h1>Subscribe to Newsletter</h1>
                    <p>
                        <h:outputText id="newsletterSubscriptionDesc"
                            value="#{ch6ContactController.newsletterDescription}"/>
                    </p>

                    <br/>
                    <h:messages id="newsletterSubscriptionMsgs" globalOnly="true"
                    errorStyle="color: red" infoStyle="color: green"/>
                    <br/>
                    <f:ajax event="blur" render="firstError lastError emailError genderError
                        passwordError passwordConfirmError">
                    <h:panelGrid columns="2" bgcolor="" border="0">
                        <h:panelGroup>
                            <h:outputLabel for="first" value="First: "/>
                            <h:inputText id="first" size="40"
                                value="#{ch6ContactController.current.first}">
                                <f:validateLength minimum="1" maximum="40"/>

                            </h:inputText>
                        </h:panelGroup>
                        <h:panelGroup>

                            <h:outputLabel for="last" value="Last: "/>
                            <h:inputText id="last" size="40"
                                value="#{ch6ContactController.current.last}">
                                <f:validateLength minimum="1" maximum="40"/>

                            </h:inputText>
                        </h:panelGroup>
```

```
        <h:message id="firstError"
                   for="first"
                   errorStyle="color:red"/>

        <h:message id="lastError"
                   for="last"
                   errorStyle="color:red"/>
        <h:panelGroup>
            <h:outputLabel for="email" value="Email: "/>
            <h:inputText id="email" size="40"
               value="#{ch6ContactController.current.email}">

            </h:inputText>
        </h:panelGroup>
        <h:panelGroup/>
        <h:message id="emailError"
                   for="email"
                   errorStyle="color:red"/>
        <h:panelGroup/>

        <h:selectOneRadio title="Gender" id="gender"
           value="#{ch6ContactController.current.gender}">
            <f:selectItem  itemValue="M" itemLabel="Male"/>
            <f:selectItem itemValue="F" itemLabel="Female"/>
        </h:selectOneRadio>
        <h:panelGroup>
            <h:outputLabel for="occupation" value="Occupation: "/>
            <h:selectOneMenu id="occupation"
               value="#{ch6ContactController.current.occupation}">
                <f:selectItems value="#{ch6ContactController.occupationList}"/>
            </h:selectOneMenu>
        </h:panelGroup>
        <h:message id="genderError"
                   for="gender"
                   errorStyle="color:red"/>

</h:panelGrid>
<br/>
<h:outputLabel for="description" value="Enter your book interests"/>
<br/>
<h:inputTextarea id="description" rows="5" cols="75"
   value="#{ch6ContactController.current.description}"/>

<br/>
<h:panelGrid columns="2">
    <h:outputLabel for="password" value="Enter a password for site access: "/>
    <h:inputSecret id="password" size="40"
       value="#{ch6ContactController.current.password}">
        <f:validateRequired/>
        <f:ajax event="keyup" listener="#{ch6ContactController.passwordStrength}" r
           ender="passwordStrengthMessage"/>
    </h:inputSecret>
```

```
            <h:outputLabel for="passwordConfirm" value="Confirm Password: "/>
            <h:inputSecret id="passwordConfirm" size="40"
               value="#{ch6ContactController.passwordConfirm}"
               validator="#{ch6ContactController.validatePassword}">

            </h:inputSecret>
      </h:panelGrid>
      <h:panelGroup>
            <h:outputText id="passwordStrengthMessage"
               value="#{ch6ContactController.passwordStrengthMessage}"/>
            <h:message id="passwordError"
                    for="password"
                    style="color:red"/>
      </h:panelGroup>
      <br/>
      <h:message id="passwordConfirmError"
                    for="passwordConfirm"
                    style="color:red"/>
      <br/>
      <hr/>
      <br/>

      <h:panelGrid columns="3">
          <h:panelGroup>
              <h:outputLabel for="newsletterList" value="Newsletters:" style=" "/>
              <h:selectManyListbox id="newsletterList"
                 value="#{ch6ContactController.current.newsletterList}">
                 <f:selectItems value="#{ch6ContactController.newsletterList}"/>
              </h:selectManyListbox>
          </h:panelGroup>
          <h:panelGroup/>
          <h:panelGroup>
              <h:panelGrid columns="1">
                  <h:panelGroup>
                      <h:outputLabel for="notifyme"
                         value="Would you like to receive other promotional email?"/>
                      <h:selectBooleanCheckbox id="notifyme"
                         value="#{ch6ContactController.current.receiveNotifications}"/>
                  </h:panelGroup>
                  <h:panelGroup/>
                  <hr/>
                  <h:panelGroup/>
                  <h:panelGroup>
                      <h:outputLabel for="notificationTypes" value="What type of
                         notifications are you interested in recieving?"/>
                      <br/>
```

```
                    <h:selectManyCheckbox id="notifyTypes"
                        value="#{ch6ContactController.current.notificationType}">
                            <f:selectItems value="#{ch6ContactController.notificationTypes}"/>
                    </h:selectManyCheckbox>
                </h:panelGroup>
            </h:panelGrid>
        </h:panelGroup>
    </h:panelGrid>
    <hr/>
    <br/>
    </f:ajax>
    <h:commandButton id="contactSubmit" action="#{ch6ContactController.subscribe}"
    value="Save">
        <f:ajax event="action" execute="@form" render="@all"/>
    </h:commandButton>
    <h:panelGrid  columns="2" width="400px;">
        <h:commandLink id="manageAccount" action="#{ch6ContactController.manage}"
        value="Manage Subscription">
            <f:ajax event="action" execute="@this" render="@all"/>
        </h:commandLink>
        <h:outputLink id="homeLink" value="home.xhtml">Home</h:outputLink>
    </h:panelGrid>
        </h:form>
    </ui:define>
    </ui:composition>

    </body>
</html>
```

When the page is rendered, each component will react separately given their associated validations. That is, if validation fails for one component, only the message component that corresponds with the component failing validation will be displayed, although each component identified within the f:ajax render attribute will be re-rendered.

■ **Note**   As a result of specifying a global f:ajax tag, the password component can now execute two Ajax requests. One of the Ajax requests for the field is responsible for validating to ensure that the field is not blank, and the other is responsible for ensuring that the given password String is strong.

Explanation

Grouping multiple components with the same Ajax behavior has its benefits. For one, if the behavior needs to be adjusted for any reason, one change can now be made to the Ajax behavior, and each of the components in the group can benefit from the single adjustment. However, the f:ajax tag is smart enough to enable each component to still utilize separate functionality, such as validation or actions, so each can still have their own customized Ajax behavior. To group components under a single f:ajax tag, they must be added to the view as subelements of the f:ajax tag. That is, any child components must be enclosed between the opening and closing f:ajax tags. All of the enclosed components will then use Ajax to send requests to the server using JavaScript in an asynchronous fashion.

In the example, a handful of the `inputText` components within the newsletter subscription view have been embodied inside an `f:ajax` tag so that their values will be validated using server-side bean validation when they lose focus. The `f:ajax` tag that is used to group the components has an event attribute set to `blur`, and its render attribute contains the `String`-based identifier for each of the `message` components corresponding to the components that are included in the group. The space-separated list of component `id`s is used to re-render each of the message components when the Ajax behavior is complete, displaying any errors that occur as a result of the validation.

Custom Processing of Ajax Functionality

For those times when custom Ajax processing is required, the JSF framework provides the `jsf.ajax.request()` function, which can be used in place of an `f:ajax`.

Example

Write the JavaScript that will be used for processing your request, and utilize the `jsf.ajax.request()` function along with one of the standard JavaScript event-handling attributes for a JSF component. The following example is the JSF view for the newsletter subscription page for the Acme Bookstore application. All of the `f:ajax` tags that were previously used for validating `inputText` fields have been removed, and the `onblur` attribute of each `inputText` component has been set to use the `jsf.ajax.request()` method in order to Ajaxify the component. The following excerpt is taken from the view named example06_05.xhtml, representing the updated newsletter subscription JSF view:

...

```
<h:outputScript name="jsf.js" library="javax.faces" target="head"/>
<h1>Subscribe to Newsletter</h1>
<p>
    <h:outputText id="newsletterSubscriptionDesc"
                    value="#{ch6ContactController.newsletterDescription}"/>
</p>

<br/>
<h:messages id="newsletterSubscriptionMsgs" globalOnly="true"
    errorStyle="color: red" infoStyle="color: green"/>
<br/>

<h:panelGrid columns="2" bgcolor="" border="0">
    <h:panelGroup>
        <h:outputLabel for="first" value="First: "/>
        <h:inputText id="first" size="40" value="#{ch6ContactController.current.
        first}"
                        onblur="jsf.ajax.request(this, event, {execute: 'first',
                        render: 'firstError'});
                return false;">
            <f:validateLength minimum="1" maximum="40"/>
        </h:inputText>
    </h:panelGroup>
```

```
<h:panelGroup>
    <h:outputLabel for="last" value="Last: "/>
    <h:inputText id="last" size="40" value="#{ch6ContactController.current.last}"
        onblur="jsf.ajax.request(this, event,
        {execute: 'last', render: 'lastError'});
         return false;">
     <f:validateLength minimum="1" maximum="40"/>
    </h:inputText>
</h:panelGroup>

<h:message id="firstError"
           for="first"
           errorStyle="color:red"/>

<h:message id="lastError"
           for="last"
           errorStyle="color:red"/>
<h:panelGroup>
    <h:outputLabel for="email" value="Email: "/>
    <h:inputText id="email" size="40"
    value="#{ch6ContactController.current.email}"
                onblur="jsf.ajax.request(this, event,
                {execute: 'email', render: 'emailError'});
            return false;"/>
</h:panelGroup>
<h:panelGroup/>
<h:message id="emailError"
           for="email"
           errorStyle="color:red"/>
<h:panelGroup/>
```
...

Using this technique, the inputText components that specify Ajax behavior for the onblur event will asynchronously have their values validated when they lose focus. If any custom JavaScript code needs to be used, it can be added to the same inline JavaScript call to jsf.ajax.request().

▪ **Note**   Method calls cannot be made using the jsf.ajax.request() technique, so it is not possible to invoke a listener explicitly with the Ajax request.

Explanation

The JavaScript API method jsf.ajax.request(), a JSF 2.x feature, can be accessed directly by a Facelets application, enabling a developer to have slightly more control than using the f:ajax tag. Behind the scenes, the f:ajax tag is converted into a call to jsf.ajax.request(), sending the parameters as specified via the tag's attributes. To use this technique, you must include the jsf.js library within the view. A JSF outputScript tag should be included in the view, specifying jsf.js as the script name and javax.faces as the library. The jsf.js script within this example will be placed in the head of the view, which is done by specifying head for the target attribute of the outputScript tag. The following excerpt from the example demonstrates what the tag should look like:

```
<h:outputScript name="jsf.js" library="javax.faces" target="head"/>
```

> ■ **Note**   To avoid nested IDs, it is a good idea to specify the h:form attribute of prependId="false" when using jsf.ajax.request() manually. For instance, the form tag should look as follows:
>
> ```
> <h:form prependId="false">
> ```

The jsf.ajax.request() method can be called inline, as is the case with the example, and it can be invoked from within any of the JavaScript event attributes of a given component. The format for calling the JavaScript method is as follows:

```
jsf.ajax.request(component, event,{execute:'id or keyword', render:'id or keyword'});
```

Usually when the request is made using an inline call, the this keyword is specified for the first parameter, signifying that the current component should be passed. The event keyword is passed as the second parameter, and it passes with it the current event that is occurring against the component. Lastly, a map of name-value pairs is passed, specifying the execute and render attributes along with the component identifiers or keywords that should be executed and rendered after the execution completes, respectively. For a list of the valid keywords that can be used, please refer to Table 6-2.

> ■ **Note**   You can also utilize the jsf.ajax.request method from within a managed bean by specifying the @ResourceDependency annotation as follows:
>
> ```
> @ResourceDependency(name="jsf.js" library="javax.faces" target="head")
> ```

The majority of developers will never need to utilize a manual call to the JSF JavaScript API. However, if the need ever arises, calling the jsf.ajax.request() method is fairly straightforward.

Custom Conversion of Input Values

It is possible to create a custom converter for those occasions when custom logic is required to convert an input value.

Example

To apply custom conversion processing, create a custom converter class containing the logic that is required for converting the values, and then apply that converter to the inputText components as needed. For this example, the Acme Bookstore has decided that it would like all first and last names in the subscriber list to appear in uppercase. The store would also like all e-mail addresses in lowercase. Therefore, a custom converter will be developed to perform the String conversion automatically behind the scenes.

The following listing is for the conversion class, LowerConverter, which accepts values from registered components and returns a formatted String value in lowercase:

```java
import javax.faces.component.UIComponent;
import javax.faces.context.FacesContext;
import javax.faces.convert.Converter;
import javax.faces.convert.FacesConverter;

/**
 *
 * @author juneau
 */
@FacesConverter("org.javaserverfaces.converter.LowerConverter")
public class LowerConverter implements Converter {

    @Override
    public Object getAsObject(FacesContext context, UIComponent component,
            String value) {
        // Return String value in lower case
        return value.toString().toLowerCase();
    }

    @Override
    public String getAsString(FacesContext context, UIComponent component,
            Object value) {

        // Return String value
        return value.toString().toLowerCase();

    }

}
```

The code that is used to create the uppercase converter is very similar, except that the getAsObject and getAsString methods make use of different String functions to return the uppercase values. The sources reside within a class named org.javaserverfaces.chapter6.converter.UpperConverter, and they are nearly identical to the LowerConverter class with the exception of calling the toUpperCase() method, rather than toLowerCase().

Now that the conversion classes have been built, it is time to apply the converters to the JSF components where applicable. The following excerpt is taken from the newsletter subscription page of the Acme Bookstore application, and it demonstrates the use of the converters for the first, last, and e-mail input components.

```xml
...
<h:panelGroup>
    <h:outputLabel for="first" value="First: "/>
    <h:inputText id="first" size="40" value="#{ch6ContactController.current.first}">
        <f:validateLength minimum="1" maximum="40"/>
        <f:converter converterId="org.javaserverfaces.converter.UpperConverter"/>
    </h:inputText>
</h:panelGroup>
```

```
<h:panelGroup>

    <h:outputLabel for="last" value="Last: "/>
    <h:inputText id="last" size="40" value="#{ch6ContactController.current.last}">
        <f:validateLength minimum="1" maximum="40"/>
        <f:converter converterId="org.javaserverfaces.converter.UpperConverter"/>
    </h:inputText>
</h:panelGroup>

<h:message id="firstError"
           for="first"
           errorStyle="color:red"/>

<h:message id="lastError"
           for="last"
           errorStyle="color:red"/>
<h:panelGroup>
    <h:outputLabel for="email" value="Email: "/>
    <h:inputText id="email" size="40" value="#{ch6ContactController.current.email}">
        <f:converter converterId="org.javaserverfaces.converter.LowerConverter"/>
    </h:inputText>
</h:panelGroup>
<h:panelGroup/>
<h:message id="emailError"
           for="email"
           errorStyle="color:red"/>
<h:panelGroup/>
...
```

Now if a user types in lowercase for the first or last name or in uppercase for the e-mail field, the values will automatically be converted during the Apply Request Values phase.

Explanation

How many times have you seen an application's data become unmanageable because of inconsistencies? Maybe you have seen some records where a particular field contains a value in lowercase and other records contain the same value in uppercase...maybe even a mixture of cases! Applying conversion to data before it is persisted (usually in a database) is the best way to ensure data integrity. As you may have read about in Chapter 3, the JSF framework ships with a library of standard converters that can be applied to JSF components in order to convert data into a manageable format. While the standard converters will do the job for most applications, there may be situations when custom converters are needed in order to manipulate values into a manageable format for your application. In such cases, JSF custom converter classes can be used to develop the custom conversion logic; they are very easy to develop and apply to JSF components with minimal configuration.

■ **Note**   Beginning with JSF 2.2, converters and validators can be used as injection targets.

To develop a custom converter class, you must implement the javax.faces.convert.Converter interface, overriding two methods: getAsString and getAsObject. The getAsString method should accept three parameters: FacesContext, UIComponent, and a String. It should perform the desired conversion and return the converted value in String format. In the case of the LowerConverter example, simply applying toLowerCase() to the String and returning it is all the functionality you require. The getAsObject method should accept the same parameters as the getAsString method, and it should also apply the desired conversion and then return an object of any type. In the case of LowerConverter, you return a String in lowercase, just like the getAsString method. If you follow along and look through the same methods in UpperConverter, the opposite conversion is applied, returning an uppercase String.

To make a converter class available for use within a view, you must annotate the class by applying @FacesConverter to the class declaration. Pass a String into the annotation, being the String-based fully qualified name of the converter class. The UpperConverter @FacesConverter annotation reads as follows:

```
@FacesConverter("org.javaserverfaces.converter.UpperConverter")
```

Once the converter class has been written and annotated as required, the converter can be used just like a standard JSF converter tag. The logic contained within the converter can be much more complex than that which is demonstrated in this example, and given the wide variety of prebuilt converters, a custom converter usually does contain complex conversion logic.

Maintaining Managed Bean Scopes for a Session

JSF provides a number of different scopes into which a managed bean can be placed.

Example

Develop using the proper JSF managed bean scope that your situation requires. Managed beans utilize annotations to determine how long they are retained, so if your application needs to maintain state within a managed bean for a certain time frame, the scope can be set by annotating the managed bean class. In this example, you will be adding a shopping cart to the Acme Bookstore web site. The cart will be maintained for a browser session at this time, so if a book is added to the cart, then it will remain there until the current session ends. This example builds upon those concepts that were covered in earlier in the book because it demonstrates how to use SessionScoped managed beans.

Let's take a look at the JSF views that are being used for the shopping cart implementation. You are adding a couple of views to the application and modifying one view to accommodate the navigational buttons for the cart. The following excerpt is taken from the book view, which is displayed when a user clicks one of the book titles from the left menu. You are adding buttons to the bottom of the page to add the book to the cart and to view the current cart contents. To view the sources in entirety, please see the view located within the sources: web/chapter06/book.xhtml.

```
...
<h:panelGrid columns="2" width="45%">
    <h:commandButton id="addToCart" action="#{ch6CartController.addToCart}"
                        value="Add to Cart">
                            <f:ajax render="shoppingCartMsgs"/>
    </h:commandButton>
    <h:commandButton id="viewCart" action="#{ch6CartController.viewCart}"
                        value="View Cart">
    </h:commandButton>
</h:panelGrid>
...
```

The two buttons that have been added to the book view reference a new class, referred to as ch6CartController, although the name of the class is CartController. The CartController class is a JSF managed bean that contains the shopping cart implementation. The new buttons in the book view are used to add the current book title to the shopping cart and to view the cart. At this time, the shopping cart is a list of Item objects, and each Item object contains a Book object and a quantity. The sources for the Item class can be seen in the next listing:

```java
package org.javaserverfaces.chapter06;

/**
 * Object to hold a single cart item
 * @author juneau
 */
public class Item implements java.io.Serializable {
    private Book book = null;
    private int quantity = 0;

    public Item(Book book, int qty){
        this.book = book;
        this.quantity = qty;
    }

    /**
     * @return the book
     */
    public Book getBook() {
        return book;
    }

    /**
     * @param book the book to set
     */
    public void setBook(Book book) {
        this.book = book;
    }

    /**
     * @return the quantity
     */
    public int getQuantity() {
        return quantity;
    }

    /**
     * @param quantity the quantity to set
     */
    public void setQuantity(int quantity) {
        this.quantity = quantity;
    }

}
```

For the new shopping cart implementation, the Book class has been updated to include a description field; to see the sources for the Book class, please refer to src/org/javaserverfaces/chapter06/Book.java. The most important class in this example is the CartController managed bean. The sources for this class are listed here:

```java
package org.javaserverfaces.chapter06;

import java.io.Serializable;
import javax.inject.Named;
import javax.faces.application.FacesMessage;
import javax.enterprise.context.SessionScoped;
import javax.faces.context.FacesContext;
import javax.inject.Inject;

/**
 * Chapter 6
 *
 * @author juneau
 */
@SessionScoped
@Named(value = "ch6CartController")
public class CartController implements Serializable {

    private Cart cart = null;
    private Item currentBook = null;
    @Inject
    AuthorController authorController;

    /**
     * Creates a new instance of CartController
     */
    public CartController() {
    }

    public String addToCart() {
        if (getCart() == null) {
            cart = new Cart();
            getCart().addBook(authorController.getCurrentBook(), 1);
        } else {
            System.out.println("adding book to cart...");
            getCart().addBook(authorController.getCurrentBook(),
                    searchCart(authorController.getCurrentBook().getTitle())+1);
        }
        FacesMessage facesMsg = new FacesMessage(FacesMessage.SEVERITY_INFO,
                "Succesfully Updated Cart", null);
        FacesContext.getCurrentInstance().addMessage(null, facesMsg);
        return null;
    }
```

```java
/**
 * Determines if a book is already in the shopping cart
 * @param title
 * @return
 */
public int searchCart(String title) {
    int count = 0;

    for (Item item : getCart().getBooks()) {
        if (item.getBook().getTitle().equals(title)) {
            count++;
        }
    }
    return count;
}

public String viewCart() {
    if (cart == null) {
        FacesMessage facesMsg = new FacesMessage(FacesMessage.SEVERITY_INFO,
                "No books in cart...", null);
        FacesContext.getCurrentInstance().addMessage(null, facesMsg);
    }

    return "/chapter06/cart";
}

public String continueShopping(){
    return "/chapter06/book";
}

public String editItem(String title) {
    for (Item item : cart.getBooks()) {
        if (item.getBook().getTitle().equals(title)) {
            currentBook = item;
        }
    }
    return "/chapter06/reviewItem";

}

public String updateCart(String title) {
    Item foundItem = null;
    if (currentBook.getQuantity() == 0) {
        for (Item item : cart.getBooks()) {
            if (item.getBook().getTitle().equals(title)) {
                foundItem = item;
            }
        }
    }
```

```
        cart.getBooks().remove(foundItem);
        FacesMessage facesMsg = new FacesMessage(FacesMessage.SEVERITY_INFO,
                "Succesfully Updated Cart", null);
        FacesContext.getCurrentInstance().addMessage(null, facesMsg);
        return "/chapter06/cart";
    }

    /**
     * @return the cart
     */
    public Cart getCart() {
        return cart;
    }

    /**
     * @param cart the cart to set
     */
    public void setCart(Cart cart) {
        this.cart = cart;
    }

    /**
     * @return the currentBook
     */
    public Item getCurrentBook() {
        return currentBook;
    }

    /**
     * @param currentBook the currentBook to set
     */
    public void setCurrentBook(Item currentBook) {
        this.currentBook = currentBook;
    }
}
```

There is another class that has been added to the application in order to accommodate the shopping cart. The Cart class is an object that is used to hold the List of books in the shopping cart. The listing for the Cart class is as follows:

```
public class Cart implements java.io.Serializable {
    // List containing book objects
    private List<Item> books = null;

    public Cart(){
        books = null;
    }
```

```java
/**
 * @return the books
 */
public List <Item> getBooks() {
    return books;
}

/**
 * @param books the books to set
 */
public void setBooks(List books) {
    this.books = books;
}

/**
 * Utility method to add a book and quantity
 */
public void addBook(Book title, int qty){
    if (books == null){
        books = new ArrayList();
    }
    books.add(new Item(title, qty));
}
}
```

Lastly, let's take a look at the views that are used to display the contents of the shopping cart. The cart view is used to display the Cart object contents. The contents are displayed using a dataTable component, and each row in the table contains a commandLink that can be clicked to edit that item's quantity. The cart.xhtml listing is as follows:

```xml
<?xml version="1.0" encoding="UTF-8"?>

<!DOCTYPE html PUBLIC "-//W3C//DTD XHTML 1.0 Strict//EN"
"http://www.w3.org/TR/xhtml1/DTD/xhtml1-strict.dtd">
<html xmlns="http://www.w3.org/1999/xhtml"
    xmlns:f="http://xmlns.jcp.org/jsf/core"
    xmlns:ui="http://xmlns.jcp.org/jsf/facelets"
    xmlns:h="http://xmlns.jcp.org/jsf/html">
    <h:head>
        <meta http-equiv="Content-Type" content="text/html; charset=UTF-8"/>
        <title>Acme Bookstore</title>
    </h:head>
    <h:body>
        <ui:composition template="./layout/custom_template_search.xhtml">
            <ui:define name="content">
                <h:form id="shoppingCartForm">
                    <h1>Shopping Cart Contents</h1>
                    <p>
                        Below are the contents of your cart.
                    </p>
```

```
<h:messages id="cartMessage" globalOnly="true"
            errorStyle="color: red" infoStyle="color: green"/>
<br/>
<h:dataTable id="cartTable" value="#{ch6CartController.cart.books}" var="book"
            border="1" rendered="#{ch6CartController.cart.books ne null}">
    <h:column id="title">
        #{book.book.title}
    </h:column>
    <h:column id="quantity">
        <h:inputText readonly="true" size="10" value="#{book.quantity}"/>
    </h:column>
    <h:column id="edit">
        <h:commandLink id="editItem"
            action="#{ch6CartController.editItem(book.book.title)}" value="Edit"/>
    </h:column>

</h:dataTable>

<h:outputText id="emptyCart" value="No items currently in cart."
              rendered="#{ch6CartController.cart.books eq null}"/>
<br/>
<h:commandLink id="continueLink" action="#{ch6CartController.continueShopping}"
    value="Continue Shopping"/>
        </h:form>
    </ui:define>
</ui:composition>
</h:body>
</html>
```

The cart view will look like Figure 6-2 when it is rendered.

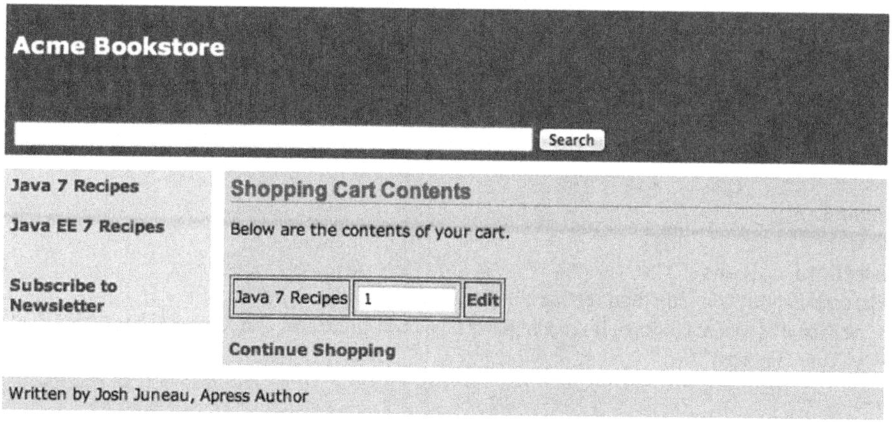

Figure 6-2. *Shopping cart view*

Finally, when the edit link is clicked, the current book selection quantity can be edited. The view for editing the shopping cart items is named reviewItem.xhtml, and the sources are as follows:

```xml
<?xml version='1.0' encoding='UTF-8' ?>
<!--
Author: J. Juneau
-->
<!DOCTYPE html PUBLIC "-//W3C//DTD XHTML 1.0 Transitional//EN"
"http://www.w3.org/TR/xhtml1/DTD/xhtml1-transitional.dtd">
<html xmlns="http://www.w3.org/1999/xhtml"
      xmlns:ui="http://xmlns.jcp.org/jsf/facelets"
      xmlns:f="http://xmlns.jcp.org/jsf/core"
      xmlns:h="http://xmlns.jcp.org/jsf/html">
    <h:head>
        <meta http-equiv="Content-Type" content="text/html; charset=UTF-8"/>
        <title>Acme Bookstore</title>
    </h:head>
    <h:body>
        <ui:composition template="./layout/custom_template_search.xhtml">

            <ui:define name="content">
                <h:form id="bookForm">
                    <h1>Review Item</h1>
                    <br/>
                    <h:messages id="reviewMsg" globalOnly="true"
                                errorStyle="color: red" infoStyle="color: green"/>
                    <br/>

                    #{ch6CartController.currentBook.book.title}
                    <br/>
                    <h:graphicImage    id="javarecipes" library="image"
                                       style="width: 100px; height: 120px"
                                       name="#{ch6CartController.currentBook.book.image}"/>
                    <br/>
                    <h:outputLabel for="quantity" value="Quantity: "/>
                    <h:inputText id="quantity"
                                 value="#{ch6CartController.currentBook.quantity}">

                    </h:inputText>
                    <br/>
                    <h:panelGrid columns="2">
                        <h:commandButton id="updateCart"
                          action="#{ch6CartController.updateCart(ch6CartController.currentBook.book.title)}"
                          value="Update"/>
```

```
                    <h:commandButton id="viewCart" action="#{ch6CartController.viewCart}"
                            value="Back To Cart">
                    </h:commandButton>
                </h:panelGrid>
                <br/>
                <br/>
            </h:form>
        </ui:define>
    </ui:composition>

    </h:body>
</html>
```

Figure 6-3 demonstrates what the item review form will look like once it is rendered.

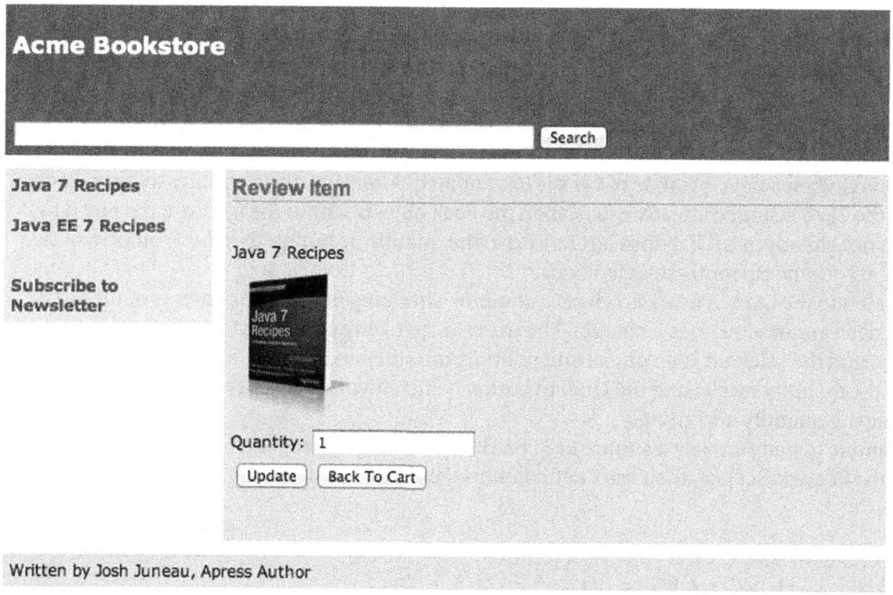

Figure 6-3. *Review cart item*

■ **Note**   The session scope is not the best implementation for a shopping cart because it ties the managed bean contents to a particular browser session. What happens when the user needs to leave for a few minutes and then comes back to the browser to see that the session has expired or the browser has been closed? A more functional scope for handling this situation is the Conversation scope.

Explanation

Annotating the managed bean class with the scope annotation corresponding to how long you need your managed bean to remain valid controls scope. Typically, one or more JSF views belong to a corresponding managed bean controller. *Scope* refers to how long a JSF view value needs to be retained in a browser session. Sometimes the value can be reset after a request is placed, and other times the value needs to be retained across several pages. Table 3-1 in Chapters 3 lists the annotations.

■ **Note**   Be aware that two different sets of annotations are available for use with Java EE 7. To apply a scope to a JSF managed bean, be sure you import the correct annotation class, or your results may vary. Typically, the classes you need to be importing for managing the JSF managed bean scopes reside within the package `javax.enterprise.context` to utilize CDI.

In this example, you will focus on the use of the `@SessionScoped` annotation. The shopping cart managed bean, `CartController`, has been annotated with `@SessionScoped`, so it becomes instantiated when a new session begins, and values that are stored within the bean are maintained throughout the client session. When someone visits the Acme Bookstore and decides to add a book to their shopping cart, they click the `commandButton` labeled *Add to Cart* on the book view. When this occurs, the addToCart method within the `CartController` is invoked, and if a Cart instance has not yet been created, then a new instance of Cart is instantiated. After that, the currently selected Book object is added to the cart. If the Cart instance already exists, then the Book objects within the Cart are traversed to make sure that the book does not already exist. If it does already exist, the quantity is bumped up by 1; otherwise, a quantity of 1 is added to the Cart for the currently selected book.

After a book has been added to the Cart, a user can elect to continue shopping or edit the contents of the Cart. This is where the `@SessionScoped` annotation does its magic. The user can go to any other page within the application and then re-visit the cart view, and the selected Book object and quantity are still persisted. If the user elects to edit the Cart object, they can update the quantity by clicking the Update button, which invokes the `CartController` class's updateCart method, adjusting the quantity accordingly.

This is an exhaustive example to demonstrate a simple task, marking a managed bean as `@SessionScoped`. If the bean had been annotated with `@RequestScoped`, then the Cart contents would be lost when the user navigates to a new page in the application.

Listening for System-Level Events

JSF provides the ability to wire action methods to lifecycle system events. The `SystemEventListener` interface can be utilized to provide this functionality.

Example

Create a system event listener class by implementing the `SystemEventListener` interface and overriding the `processEvent(SystemEvent event)` and `isListenerForSource(Object source)` methods. Implement these methods accordingly to perform the desired event processing. The following code listing is for a class named `BookstoreAppListener`, and it is invoked when the application is started up or when it is shutting down:

```
package org.javaserverfaces.chapter06.example06_08;

import javax.faces.application.Application;
import javax.faces.event.*;
```

```
/**
 * @author juneau
 */
public class BookstoreAppListener implements SystemEventListener {

    @Override
    public void processEvent(SystemEvent event) throws AbortProcessingException {
        if(event instanceof PostConstructApplicationEvent){
            System.out.println("The application has been constructed...");
        }

        if(event instanceof PreDestroyApplicationEvent){
            System.out.println("The application is being destroyed...");
        }
    }

    @Override
    public boolean isListenerForSource(Object source) {
        return(source instanceof Application);
    }

}
```

Next, the system event listener must be registered in the faces-config.xml file. The following excerpt is taken from the faces-config.xml file for the Acme Bookstore application:

```
...
<application>

                <system-event-listener>
                                <system-event-listener-class>
org.javaserverfaces.chapter06.example06_08.BookstoreAppListener
                                </system-event-listener-class>
                                <system-event-class>
                                                javax.faces.event.PostConstructApplicationEvent
                                </system-event-class>
                </system-event-listener>

                <system-event-listener>
                                <system-event-listener-class>
org.javaserverfaces.chapter06.example06_08.BookstoreAppListener
                                </system-event-listener-class>
                                <system-event-class>
                                                javax.faces.event.PreDestroyApplicationEvent
                                </system-event-class>
        </system-event-listener>

    </application>
...
```

When the application is started, the message "The application has been constructed..." will be displayed in the server log. When the application is shutting down, the message "The application is being destroyed..." will be displayed in the server log.

Explanation

The ability to perform tasks when an application starts up can sometimes be useful. For instance, let's say you'd like to have an e-mail sent to the application administrator each time the application starts. You can do this by performing the task of sending an e-mail within a class that implements the SystemEventListener interface. A class that implements SystemEventListener must then override two methods, processEvent(SystemEvent event) and isListenerForSource(Object source). The processEvent method is where the real action occurs, because it is the method into which your custom code should be placed. Whenever a system event occurs, the processEvent method is invoked. In this method, you will need to perform a check to determine what type of event has occurred so that you can process only those events that are pertinent. To determine the event that has occurred, perform an instanceof check on the SystemEvent object. In the example, there are two if statements used to determine the type of event that is occurring and to print a different message for each. If the event type is of PostConstructApplicationEvent, then that means the application is being constructed. Otherwise, if the event type is of PreDestroyApplicationEvent, the application is about to be destroyed. The PostConstructApplicationEvent event is called just after the application has been constructed, and PreDestroyApplicationEvent is called just prior to the application destruction.

The other method that must be overridden within the SystemEventListener class is named isListenerForSource. This method must return true if this listener instance is interested in receiving events from the instance referenced by the source parameter. Since the example class is built to listen for system events for the application, a true value is returned if the source parameter is an instance of Application.

After the system event listener class has been written, it needs to be registered with the application. In the example, you want to listen for both the PostConstructApplicationEvent and the PreDestroyApplicationEvent, so there needs to be a system-event-listener element added to the faces-config.xml file for each of these events. Within the system-event-listener element, specify the name of the event listener class within a system-event-listener-class element and the name of the event within a system-event-class element.

Listening for Component Events

Similar to invoking an action when a system level event occurs, it is possible to invoke actions when component level events occur.

Example

Embed an f:event tag within the component for which you want to listen for events. The f:event tag allows components to invoke managed bean listener methods based upon the current component state. For instance, if a component is being rendered or validated, a specified listener method could be invoked. In the example, an outputText component is added to the book view of the Acme Bookstore application to specify whether the current book is in the user's shopping cart. When the outputText component is being rendered, a component listener is invoked that checks the current state of the cart to see whether the book is contained within it. If it is in the cart, then the outputText component will render a message stating so; if not, then the outputText component will render a message stating that it is not in the cart.

The following excerpt is taken from a view named example06_09.xhtml, a derivative of the book view for the application. It demonstrates the use of the f:event tag within a component. Note that the outputText component contains no value attribute because the value will be set within the event listener.

```
...
<h:outputText id="isInCart" style="font-style: italic; color: ">
    <f:event type="preRenderComponent" listener="#{ch6CartController.isBookInCart}"/>
</h:outputText>
...
```

The CartController class contains a method named isBookInCart. The f:event tag in the view references this listener method via the CartController managed bean name, ch6CartController. The listener method is responsible for constructing the text that will be displayed in the outputText component.

```
public void isBookInCart(ComponentSystemEvent event) {
        UIOutput output = (UIOutput) event.getComponent();
        if (cart != null) {
            if (searchCart(authorController.getCurrentBook().getTitle()) > 0) {
                output.setValue("This book is currently in your cart.");
            } else {
                output.setValue("This book is not in your cart.");
            }
        } else {
            output.setValue("This book is not in your cart.");
        }
    }
```

Explanation

Everything that occurs within JSF applications is governed by the JSF application life cycle. As part of the life cycle, JSF components go through different phases within their lifetimes. Listeners can be added to JSF components to perform different tasks when a given phase is beginning or ending. There are two pieces to the puzzle for creating a component listener: the tag that is embedded within the component for which your listener will perform tasks and the listener method itself. To add a listener to a component, the f:event tag should be embedded within the opening and closing tags of the component that will be interrogated. The f:event tag contains a handful of attributes, but only two of them are mandatory for use: type and listener. The type attribute specifies the type of event that will be listened for, and the listener attribute specifies the managed bean listener method that will be invoked when that event occurs. The valid values that could be specified for the name attribute are preRenderComponent, postAddToView, preValidate, and postValidate. In addition to these event values, any Java class that extends javax.faces.event.ComponentSystemEvent can also be specified for the name attribute.

The listener method must accept a ComponentSystemEvent object. In the example, the listener checks to see whether the shopping cart is null, and if it is, then a message indicating an empty cart will be set for the outputText component's value. Otherwise, if the cart is not empty, then the method looks through the List of books in the cart to see whether the currently selected book is in the cart. A message indicating whether the book is in the cart is then added to the value of the outputText component. Via the listener, the actual value of the component was manipulated. Such a technique could be used in various ways to alter components to suit the needs of the situation.

Invoking a Managed Bean Action on Render

It can be useful to invoke action methods when a view is rendered. The ViewAction tag provides this functionality for JSF.

Example

To invoke an action when a view is rendered, add an f:metadata tag to the head of your view, and then embed a viewAction component within it, specifying the action method you want to invoke. This technique can be handy for executing back-end code prior to loading a page. As such, this technique can also be used to replace the f:event tag in order to create a bookmarkable URL. In this example, the Acme Bookstore author bio page has been updated so that it can be directly linked to, passing in an author's last name as a view parameter via the URL. The viewAction component is executed before the view is rendered, invoking the business logic to search for the requested author by last name and to populate the view components with the found author's information.

The following listing is for example06_10.xhtml, and it can be invoked by visiting a URL such as http://your-server:8080/JSFByExample/faces/chapter06/example06_10.xhtml?authorLast=juneau:

```xml
<?xml version="1.0" encoding="UTF-8"?>
<!--
Author: J. Juneau
-->
<ui:composition xmlns="http://www.w3.org/1999/xhtml"
                xmlns:f="http://xmlns.jcp.org/jsf/core"
                xmlns:ui="http://xmlns.jcp.org/jsf/facelets"
                xmlns:h="http://xmlns.jcp.org/jsf/html"
                template="./layout/custom_template_search.xhtml">
    <f:metadata>
        <f:viewParam name="authorLast" value="#{ch6AuthorController.authorLast}"/>
        <f:viewAction action="#{ch6AuthorController.findAuthor}" />
    </f:metadata>
            <ui:define name="content">
                <h:form id="componentForm">
                    <h1>#{ch6AuthorController.current.first} #{ch6AuthorController.current.last}</h1>
                    <p>
                        #{ch6AuthorController.current.bio}
                    </p>

                    <br/>
                    <h1>Author's Books</h1>
                    <ui:repeat id="bookList" var="book" value="#{ch6AuthorController.current.books}">
                        <tr>
                            <td>
                                <h:graphicImage id="bookImage"
                                                library="image"
                                                style="width: 100px; height: 120px"
                                                name="#{book.image}"/>
                            </td>
                        </tr>
```

```
                    <tr>
                        <td>
                            <strong>#{book.title}</strong>
                        </td>
                    </tr>
                </ui:repeat>
            </h:form>
        </ui:define>

    </ui:composition>
```

The next piece of code is an excerpt from the `AuthorController` managed bean class. This method is the implementation for the `action` method that is specified within the `viewAction` component. This method is responsible for finding the author by last name and loading the current Author object with the found object.

```
public void findAuthor(){
    if (this.authorLast != null){
        for(Author author:authorList){
            if(author.getLast().equalsIgnoreCase(authorLast)){
                this.current = author;
            }
        }
    } else {
        FacesContext facesContext = FacesContext.getCurrentInstance();
        facesContext.addMessage(null,
            new FacesMessage("No last name specified."));

    }
}
```

Explanation

The `viewAction` component was added to JSF in release 2.2, and with it comes the ability to perform evaluations before a page is rendered. The `viewAction` component is very similar to `f:event`, except for some notable differences.

- The view action timing is controllable.

- The same context as the GET request can be used for the action.

- Both the initial and postback requests are supported since the view action is incorporated into the JSF life cycle.

- `viewAction` supports both implicit and explicit navigation.

The `viewAction` component contains a number of attributes, as described in Table 6-3.

Table 6-3. *viewAction Component Attributes*

Attribute	Description
action	Method expression representing the application action to invoke when this component is activated by the user
onPostback	Boolean value to indicate whether the action should operate on postback (default: false)
if	Boolean value to indicate whether the component should be enabled (default: true)
immediate	Boolean value to indicate whether notifications should be delivered to interested listeners and actions immediately, during the Apply Requests Values phase
phase	String that specifies the phase in which the action invocation should occur using the name of the phase constraint in the PhaseId class (default: INVOKE_APPLICATION)

In the example, the viewAction component is used to invoke a managed bean method, which searches for the author whose last name equals that which is contained within the authorLast property. An action method must accept no parameters, and it must return a String, which is then passed to the NavigationHandler for the application.

Asynchronously Updating Components

Many web applications provide periodic updates to pages without the need to perform a manual refresh. The PrimeFaces library makes this possible vie the use of its Poll component.

Example

Utilize an Ajax polling component (available from a third-party JSF component library) to poll the data asynchronously and re-render display components with the updated data without any user interaction. In this example, the site template for the Acme Bookstore application has been updated to include the current time and date. The clock will be updated each second so that, from a user's point of view, it resembles a digital clock.

The following code is that of the view template entitled chapter06/layout/custom_template_search.xhtml, and it demonstrates how to use the PrimeFaces poll component:

```
<?xml version='1.0' encoding='UTF-8' ?>
<!--
Author: J. Juneau
-->
<!DOCTYPE html PUBLIC "-//W3C//DTD XHTML 1.0 Transitional//EN"
"http://www.w3.org/TR/xhtml1/DTD/xhtml1-transitional.dtd">
<html xmlns="http://www.w3.org/1999/xhtml"
      xmlns:ui="http://xmlns.jcp.org/jsf/facelets"
      xmlns:h="http://xmlns.jcp.org/jsf/html"
      xmlns:p="http://primefaces.org/ui"
      xmlns:s="http://xmlns.jcp.org/jsf/composite/components/util">
```

```
<h:head>
    <meta http-equiv="Content-Type" content="text/html; charset=UTF-8" />
    <h:outputStylesheet library="css" name="default.css"/>
    <h:outputStylesheet library="css" name="cssLayout.css"/>
    <h:outputStylesheet library="css" name="styles.css"/>

    <title>#{ch6AuthorController.storeName}</title>
</h:head>

<h:body>

    <div id="top">
        <h2>#{ch6AuthorController.storeName}</h2>
        <br/>
        <h:panelGrid width="100%" columns="2">
            <s:search id="searchAuthor"/>

            <h:form>
            <p:poll id="poll" interval="1" update="dayAndTime"/>

            <h:outputText id="dayAndTime" value="#{bookstoreController.dayAndTime}"/>
            </h:form>
        </h:panelGrid>
    </div>
    <div>
        <div id="left">
            <h:form id="navForm">
                <h:commandLink action="#{ch6AuthorController.populateJavaRecipesAuthorList}">
                    Java 7 Recipes</h:commandLink>
                <br/>
                <br/>
                <h:commandLink action="#{ch6AuthorController.populateJavaEERecipesAuthorList}">
                    Java EE 7 Recipes </h:commandLink>
                <br/>
                <br/>
                <br/>
                <h:commandLink action="#{ch6ContactController.add}">Subscribe to Newsletter
                </h:commandLink>
            </h:form>
        </div>
        <div id="content" class="left_content">
            <ui:insert name="content">Content</ui:insert>
        </div>
    </div>
    <div id="bottom">
        Written by Josh Juneau, Apress Author
    </div>

</h:body>

</html>
```

Here's the class:

```java
package org.javaserverfaces.chapter06;

import javax.inject.Named;
import javax.enterprise.context.SessionScoped;
import java.io.Serializable;
import java.util.Date;

/**
 *
 * @author juneau
 */
@Named(value = "bookstoreController")
@SessionScoped
public class BookstoreController implements Serializable {

    private Date dayAndTime = null;

    /**
     * Creates a new instance of BookstoreController
     */
    public BookstoreController() {
    }

    /**
     * @return the dayAndTime
     */
    public Date getDayAndTime() {
        dayAndTime = new Date();
        return dayAndTime;
    }

    /**
     * @param dayAndTime the dayAndTime to set
     */
    public void setDayAndTime(Date dayAndTime) {
        this.dayAndTime = dayAndTime;
    }
}
```

The date and time will appear on the right side of the header for the bookstore. The resulting solution should resemble that in Figure 6-4.

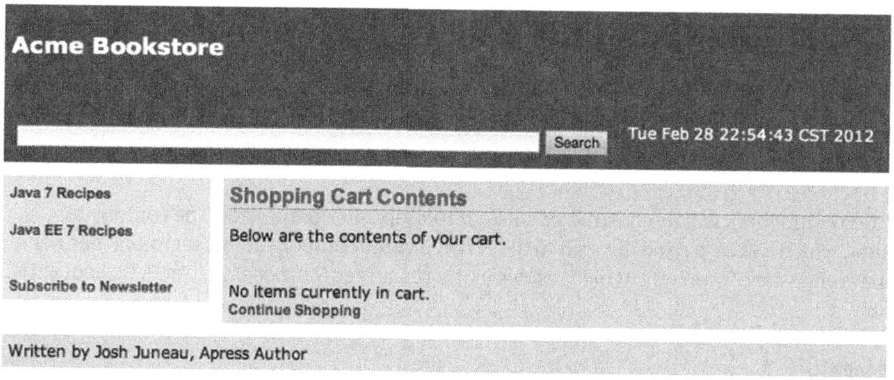

Acme Bookstore

Search   Tue Feb 28 22:54:43 CST 2012

Java 7 Recipes

Java EE 7 Recipes

Subscribe to Newsletter

Shopping Cart Contents

Below are the contents of your cart.

No items currently in cart.
Continue Shopping

Written by Josh Juneau, Apress Author

Figure 6-4. *Ajax poll component used to update date/time*

Explanation

The poll component of the PrimeFaces JSF component library can be used to update a specified portion of a view asynchronously on a timed interval. This can make web site content more dynamic because features can refresh in real time without any user interaction. For instance, the poll component would work well for a stock market graph to asynchronously update the graph every minute or so. In the example, the PrimeFaces poll component is used to display the current time and date within the Acme Bookstore application, updating the time every second.

For starters, you must ensure you have installed the PrimeFaces component library to utilize the poll component. To learn more about installing a third-party component library, please see Chapter 5. Both PrimeFaces and RichFaces have a poll component, so you can take your pick of which to use. You may choose one over the other based upon the library that you like to use best. After the library has been installed, you must add the namespace for the taglib reference to each page in which the components will be utilized. In the example, the xmlns:p="http://primefaces.org/ui" namespace is added within the <html> tag. After the namespace has been referenced in the view, the PrimeFaces components can be added to the view.

The poll component can be added to a view by including a tag that uses the p prefix, therefore, p:poll. To utilize the p:poll tag, you must set an update interval. This can be done by setting the interval attribute to a numerical value, which defines an interval in seconds between the previous response and the next request. In the example, the interval is set to 1 and, therefore, every second. The update attribute of the poll component is used to specify which component(s) to update each time the specified interval of time goes by. It is really as easy as that. In the example, the update attribute is set to the component identifier of dayAndTime. If you look down a few lines in the code, you can see that dayAndTime is actually an outputText component that is used to display the current contents of the dayAndTime property within the BookstoreController managed bean via the EL #{bookstoreController.dayAndTime}. Diving into the code for the managed bean, it is easy to see that each time the dayAndTime property is obtained, it is set equal to a new Date() object. A new Date() object contains the current time and date at the time of instantiation. Therefore, the date and time will always remain current.

The poll component is just one simplistic example of how third-party component libraries can assist in the development of more dynamic applications. Although the poll component is not very complex or difficult to use, it provides a large amount of functionality for an application view in just one line of code. I recommend you download the latest user guides for both the RichFaces and PrimeFaces component libraries and read about all the components that are available. If you have a basic understanding of what is available, it will help you formulate a plan for the development of your application when starting your next project.

Developing JSF Components Containing HTML5

JSF makes it possible to create composite components that include HTML5 markup.

Example

For this example, an HTML5 video component will be constructed into a JSF composite component. The composite component will declare attributes, which will be passed through to the HTML5 video component in a seamless manner.

The first listing is that of the composite component, which resides in the `resources/components/html5/video.xhtml` file of the sources for this book.

```
<?xml version='1.0' encoding='UTF-8' ?>
<!DOCTYPE html PUBLIC "-//W3C//DTD XHTML 1.0 Transitional//EN"
"http://www.w3.org/TR/xhtml1/DTD/xhtml1-transitional.dtd">
<html xmlns="http://www.w3.org/1999/xhtml"
      xmlns:h="http://xmlns.jcp.org/jsf/html"
      xmlns:cc="http://xmlns.jcp.org/jsf/composite">

    <!-- INTERFACE -->
    <cc:interface>
        <cc:attribute name="id"/>
        <cc:attribute name="width" default="450"/>
        <cc:attribute name="height" default="300"/>
        <cc:attribute name="controls" default="controls"/>
        <cc:attribute name="library" default="movie"/>
        <cc:attribute name="source"/>
        <cc:attribute name="type" default="video/mp4"/>
    </cc:interface>

    <!-- IMPLEMENTATION -->
    <cc:implementation>
        <video width="#{cc.attrs.width}" height="#{cc.attrs.height}" controls="#{cc.attrs.controls}">
            <source src="#{cc.attrs.source}" type="#{cc.attrs.type}" />

                Your browser does not support the video tag.
        </video>
    </cc:implementation>
</html>
```

To keep an aesthetically pleasing look to your pages, you will place a `video` component within the Acme Bookstore view named example06_12.xhtml. And the view that uses the component will look as follows:

```
<?xml version='1.0' encoding='UTF-8' ?>
<!--
Author: J. Juneau
-->
<!DOCTYPE html PUBLIC "-//W3C//DTD XHTML 1.0 Transitional//EN"
"http://www.w3.org/TR/xhtml1/DTD/xhtml1-transitional.dtd">
<html xmlns="http://www.w3.org/1999/xhtml"
      xmlns:ui="http://xmlns.jcp.org/jsf/facelets"
      xmlns:h5="http://xmlns.jcp.org/jsf/composite/components/html5">
    <head>
    </head>

    <body>

        <ui:composition template="layout/custom_template_search.xhtml">
            <ui:define name="content">

                <h1>Bear Movie</h1>
                <p>
                    <h5:video id="myvideo" width="300"
                                source="http://www.w3schools.com/html5/movie.mp4"/>
                </p>

            </ui:define>
        </ui:composition>

    </body>
</html>
```

When the view is rendered, the user will see a page that resembles Figure 6-5.

Figure 6-5. Using HTML5 components within JSF 2 composite components

Explanation

The use of HTML5 has become prevalent across the Web over the past few years. It is becoming the standard markup for producing web components that contain rich user interfaces. The JSF 2.2 release is being aligned with HTML5 so that the two technologies can coexist within the same views seamlessly. Prior to JSF 2.2, this was still a possible option, but some issues still may have been encountered when attempting to utilize some of the HTML5 components.

In the example, an HTML5 component is embedded within a JSF composite component, and the result is a JSF-based video component that has the ability to accept the same attributes as the HTML5 `video` component and configure default attributes where possible. If you have not yet reviewed how to create composite components, please go to Chapter 4 and review the content there. The following are the major differences between the example in Chapter 4 and this example:

- HTML5 is specifically used in this example, and it is not in Chapter 4.

- No server-side code is written for this composite component.

The composite component is placed within the `resources/components/html5` folder, so it will be made available for use within the application views automatically. All that is required for use within a client view is the definition of the `taglib` namespace within the `html` element. The name of the XHTML file that contains the composite component markup is `video.xhtml`, and it defines the namespace for the JSF composite component library inside the `<html>` element.

```
xmlns:cc="http://xmlns.jcp.org/jsf/composite".
```

The HTML5 video component accepts a number of attributes, and each of these is made available to the resulting JSF composite component by adding an interface to the component. This is done by supplying the opening and closing cc:interface tags, and each of the attributes that are to be made available for use with the composite component should be declared between the opening and closing tags. Each attribute is declared by adding a cc:attribute tag, along with the name of the attribute and a default value if needed. Here, you can see that the width attribute for the component will default to 450px if the user does not specify a width:

```
<cc:attribute name="width" default="450"/>
```

The actual component implementation takes place between the opening and closing cc:implementation tags, and the HTML5 video component is placed there. As you can see, each of the attributes is obtained from the composite component's interface, so any of the attributes specified for the composite component will accept values and pass them through to their corresponding attributes within the video component using the #{cc.attrs.X} syntax, where X is the name of the attribute that is being passed. That's it...the component is now ready to be used within a view.

To use the component, specify the namespace to the taglib within the client view's <html> element, and then the tag will be made available. As you can see in the example, the namespace given to the taglib for this JSF HTML5 video component is h5:

```
xmlns:h5="http://xmlns.jcp.org/jsf/composite/components/html5"
```

Once that has been completed, the composite component can be used in the same manner as any standard JSF component or one from a third-party library. HTML5 can add exciting features to your web applications, and I expect the number of JSF custom components utilizing HTML5 (a mix of JavaScript and markup) to increase.

Listening to JSF Phases

It is possible to listen for different phases in a JSF application lifecycle using a PhaseListener.

Example

To listen for different phases, create a class that implements the javax.faces.event.PhaseListener interface, and then implement the class's beforePhase, afterPhase, and getPhaseId methods to suit the needs of your application. The following class demonstrates the creation of a PhaseListener:

```
package org.javaserverfaces.chapter06;

import javax.faces.context.FacesContext;
import javax.faces.event.PhaseEvent;
import javax.faces.event.PhaseId;

public class BookstorePhaseListener implements javax.faces.event.PhaseListener {

    @Override
    public void beforePhase(PhaseEvent event) {
        FacesContext.getCurrentInstance().getExternalContext().log("Before the Phase - "
                + event.getPhaseId());
    }
```

```
    @Override
    public void afterPhase(PhaseEvent event) {
        FacesContext.getCurrentInstance().getExternalContext().log("After the Phase - "
                + event.getPhaseId());
    }

    @Override
    public PhaseId getPhaseId() {
        return PhaseId.ANY_PHASE;
    }
}
```

Any view that wants to use the PhaseListener should then be registered with the listener by adding an f:phaseListener tag to the view as follows:

```
<f:phaseListener type="org.javaserverfaces.chapter06.BookstorePhaseListener" />
```

In the end, when the application is launched and any view containing the f:phaseListener tag shown previously is rendered, a series of events will be published to the server log such as the following whenever a component is accessed:

```
INFO: PWC1412: WebModule[null] ServletContext.log():Before the Phase - APPLY_REQUEST_VALUES 2
INFO: PWC1412: WebModule[null] ServletContext.log():Before the Phase - APPLY_REQUEST_VALUES 2
INFO: PWC1412: WebModule[null] ServletContext.log():After the Phase - APPLY_REQUEST_VALUES 2
INFO: PWC1412: WebModule[null] ServletContext.log():After the Phase - APPLY_REQUEST_VALUES 2
INFO: PWC1412: WebModule[null] ServletContext.log():Before the Phase - PROCESS_VALIDATIONS 3
INFO: PWC1412: WebModule[null] ServletContext.log():Before the Phase - PROCESS_VALIDATIONS 3
INFO: PWC1412: WebModule[null] ServletContext.log():After the Phase - PROCESS_VALIDATIONS 3
INFO: PWC1412: WebModule[null] ServletContext.log():After the Phase - PROCESS_VALIDATIONS 3
INFO: PWC1412: WebModule[null] ServletContext.log():Before the Phase - RENDER_RESPONSE 6
INFO: PWC1412: WebModule[null] ServletContext.log():Before the Phase - RENDER_RESPONSE 6
INFO: PWC1412: WebModule[null] ServletContext.log():After the Phase - RENDER_RESPONSE 6
INFO: PWC1412: WebModule[null] ServletContext.log():After the Phase - RENDER_RESPONSE 6
```

■ **Note**   For more detail regarding the life-cycle phases of a JSF application, please visit the online documentation at http://docs.oracle.com/javaee/7/tutorial/doc/bnaqq.html, or refer to Recipe 3-1 for a brief explanation.

Explanation

It is possible to listen to individual phases for each of the components within a view. Sometimes developers want to do this so that they can customize the component activity during these phases. A custom class can implement the PhaseListener interface in order to perform this level of scrutiny against components in your views. The class can then override the beforePhase and afterPhase methods to implement custom tasks that will be performed prior to or after the phase of your choice.

To create a PhaseListener class, implement the javax.faces.event.PhaseListener interface. Doing so will force you to implement the abstract methods: beforePhase, afterPhase, and getPhaseId. The getPhaseId method returns the phase that the listener will fire its actions against. In the example, the getPhaseId returns PhaseId.ANY_PHASE, which will cause the listener to be invoked before and after each phase. There are static identifiers for each of the other phases too, so you can cause the PhaseListener to invoke its actions only when a specific phase is occurring. Specifically, the other options are APPLY_REQUEST_VALUES, INVOKE_APPLICATION, PROCESS_VALIDATIONS, RENDER_RESPONSE, RESTORE_VIEW, and UPDATE_MODEL_VALUES.

The beforePhase method takes a PhaseEvent object, and it is invoked before the phase that is returned by the getPhaseId method. Therefore, in the case of the example, the beforePhase method will be fired before any phase occurs. The example simply prints out to the server log which phase is currently beginning.

The afterPhase method also takes a PhaseEvent object, and it is invoked after the phase that is returned by the getPhaseId method occurs. Therefore, in the case of the example, the afterPhase method will be fire after any phase occurs. The example prints out to the server log which phase has just ended.

To register a view with the PhaseListener, you need to add an f:phaseListener tag to it and set the tag's type attribute to the PhaseListener class that you have created. Doing so will register the listener with the view such that when the view is rendered, the PhaseListener will kick in and begin listening for the phases that are specified by the getPhaseId method.

Adding Autocompletion to Text Fields

Sophisticated applications provide the ability to utilize input fields that in turn utilize auto-completion to help the user select the appropriate choice rather than having to type the entire text free-hand. JSF third party libraries contain auto-completion components, making it easy to develop user friendly interfaces.

Example

Utilize a third-party component library, and add an autocomplete text field to your application. For this example, the search box that is used for querying books and authors within the example Acme Bookstore application will be adjusted so that it auto-populates with text when a user starts typing. The following code is that of the custom search component view named search.xhtml, contained within the web/resources/components/util directory of the JSFByExample NetBeans project bundle. It has been updated to utilize a PrimeFaces autoComplete component as opposed to standard inputText.

■ **Note** This source comprises a JSF composite component. To learn more about JSF composite components, please refer to Recipe 4-4.

```
<?xml version='1.0' encoding='UTF-8' ?>
<!DOCTYPE html PUBLIC "-//W3C//DTD XHTML 1.0 Transitional//EN"
"http://www.w3.org/TR/xhtml1/DTD/xhtml1-transitional.dtd">
<html xmlns="http://www.w3.org/1999/xhtml"
      xmlns:h="http://xmlns.jcp.org/jsf/html"
      xmlns:cc="http://xmlns.jcp.org/jsf/composite"
      xmlns:p="http://primefaces.org/ui">

    <!-- INTERFACE -->
    <cc:interface>
        <cc:attribute name="searchAction" default="#{bookstoreSearchController.searchAuthors
            (ch6AuthorController.completeAuthorList)}"
                      method-signature="java.lang.String action(java.util.List)"/>
    </cc:interface>
```

```
<!-- IMPLEMENTATION -->
<cc:implementation>
    <h:form id="searchForm">
        <h:outputText id="error" value="#{bookstoreSearchController.errorText}"/>
        <br/>

        <p:autoComplete id="searchText" value="#{bookstoreSearchController.searchText}"
                completeMethod="#{ch6AuthorController.complete}"/>
        <h:commandButton id="searchButton" value="Search" action="#{cc.attrs.searchAction}"/>

    </h:form>
</cc:implementation>
</html>
```

Note that the autoComplete component contains a value attribute, which is set to the searchText property of the BookstoreSearchController managed bean, and a completeMethod attribute, which is used to specify the name of the method to use for autocompletion of the text. In this case, the method is named complete, and it resides within the AuthorController class. The following excerpt of code shows the complete method, which is excerpted from the AuthorController class (contained in the sources for Chapter 6):

```
/**
 * Auto-completes author names from the authorBookList
 *
 * @param text
 * @return
 */
public List<String> complete(String text){
    List<String> results = new ArrayList();
    // This should print each time you type a letter in the autocomplete box
    System.out.println("completing: " + text);
    for (Author author:authorBookList){
        if(author.getLast().toUpperCase().contains(text.toUpperCase())){
            results.add(author.getLast().toUpperCase() + " " + author.getFirst().toUpperCase());
        }
    }
    return results;
}
```

■ **Note** The searching logic in this application is suitable for smaller data sets. For larger data sets, a different approach would likely be used, such as a fully featured search engine solution.

When the component is rendered on the page and the user begins to type, then a drop-down list of matching author names will appear, allowing the user to choose one from the list. The drop-down will resemble that in Figure 6-6.

Explanation

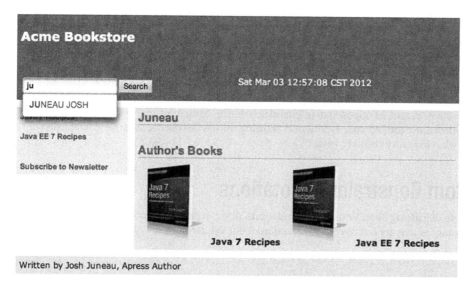

Figure 6-6. *The PrimeFaces autoComplete component*

The autocomplete text box is one of the most sought after components for anyone looking to build a web input form. They are an ingenious invention because they help the user to choose from a list of available options, while narrowing down that list as the user types characters. In the end, the user will be less likely to enter invalid data since a selection list is made available while typing, and this will decrease the likelihood for invalid data. Unfortunately, the standard JSF component library does not ship with an autocomplete component, but luckily there are several available for use from other third-party libraries. This example covers usage of the PrimeFaces autoComplete component. The PrimeFaces autoComplete component provides a myriad of choices to the developer, and a handful of them will be covered here. For complete documentation regarding the autoComplete component, please visit the PrimeFaces online documentation.

To use the PrimeFaces component, the namespace must be declared for the PrimeFaces tag library within the view where the autoComplete component will be used. In the example, the namespace is declared as p, so the autoComplete tag is written as p:autoComplete. The example makes use of only three attributes, and two of them are essential for the use of the component. The first attribute is id, which is the unique identifier for the component within the view. Next is the value attribute, which is set to a managed bean property where the ending value will be stored. The value attribute for the autoComplete component is analogous to the value attribute of an inputText component. The final attribute used in the example is completeMethod, which is set to the managed bean method used to perform the autocompletion of the text.

The completeMethod is where the real work occurs, because this is where the text that has been entered into the component is compared against a list of values to determine which of the list elements are possible choices for the autoComplete component value. A List of Strings is returned from the completeMethod, and the values of the List will be displayed within a drop-down menu below the component when the results are returned. The completeMethod is executed each time the user presses another key, and the text that has been entered into the component thus far is sent to the method each time for evaluation. In the example, the text is compared to the author's last name, and any author whose last name contains the text that has been entered will be added to the return List. Oftentimes the text from the component is compared against database table record values, as opposed to List elements, but the List demonstrates the technique fine too.

Those pieces of the puzzle that have been addressed already are the only essential pieces for making the autoComplete component function as expected. However, the PrimeFaces autoComplete component has a variety of attributes that can be used to customize the functionality of the autoComplete component. For instance, the component contains a minQueryLength attribute that can specify the minimum number of characters that need to be typed before the completeMethod will be invoked. The effect attribute can specify a range of different effects to apply to the autocomplete animation. The forceSelection attribute can be set to true to force a user to make a selection, and so forth. As mentioned previously, for a complete set of documentation covering the PrimeFaces autoComplete component, along with each of its attributes, please refer to the online documentation at www.primefaces.org.

The ability to autocomplete a user's text entry while they are typing the characters provides a wide variety of benefits to an application. First, the data integrity of the application can benefit from the use of standard entries that are displayed via the autocomplete feature, as opposed to freehand text entries from many different users. Second, autocomplete solutions provide a more unified user experience, allowing the user to choose from an available list of options rather than guessing what the entry should contain.

Developing Custom Constraint Annotations

Just as it is possible to make use of existing Bean Validation annotations, one can create custom constraint annotations to cover those instances that are not covered by standard Bean Validation.

Example

Create a custom annotation class, specifying the properties you want the annotation to accept, and create a validator class that will perform the actual validation on the property. In this example, you'll create a constraint annotation that can be used to validate the length of an inputSecret component value, that is, the length of a password. The following code is for a class named PasswordLength, which is used for creating the annotation that will be used for validating the password length:

```
package org.javaserverfaces.chapter06.annotation;

import static java.lang.annotation.ElementType.*;
import static java.lang.annotation.RetentionPolicy.*;

import java.lang.annotation.Documented;
import java.lang.annotation.Retention;
import java.lang.annotation.Target;

import javax.validation.Constraint;
import javax.validation.Payload;
import org.javaserverfaces.chapter06.validator.CheckPasswordValidator;

@Target( { METHOD, FIELD, ANNOTATION_TYPE })
@Retention(RUNTIME)
@Constraint(validatedBy = CheckPasswordValidator.class)
@Documented
```

```
public @interface PasswordLength {

    String message() default "{org.javaserverfaces.constraints.password}";

     * @return password length
     */
    int passwordLength();

}
```

Note that in the annotation class there is a reference to the CheckPasswordValidator class, which is where the actual validation takes place. The validator class for the annotation contains the logic for performing the actual validation, and the sources for the CheckPasswordValidator class are as follows:

```
package org.javaserverfaces.chapter06.validator;

import javax.validation.ConstraintValidator;
import javax.validation.ConstraintValidatorContext;
import org.javaserverfaces.chapter06.annotation.PasswordLength;

/**
 * Custom validation class to ensure password is long enough
 * @author juneau
 */
public class CheckPasswordValidator implements
        ConstraintValidator<PasswordLength, Object> {
    private int passwordLength;

    private String password;
    @Override
    public void initialize(PasswordLength constraintAnnotation) {
        // Initilize implementation here
        passwordLength = constraintAnnotation.passwordLength();
    }

    @Override
    public boolean isValid(Object value, ConstraintValidatorContext context) {
        boolean returnValue = false;
        if (value.toString().length() >= passwordLength){
            returnValue = true;
        } else {
            returnValue = false;
        }
        return returnValue;
    }
}
```

To make use of the annotation, place it before a field declaration just as with standard bean validation.

```
@PasswordLength(passwordLength=8)
    private String password;
```

Explanation

Annotations can be placed before a class, method, variable, package, or parameter declaration to indicate that it be treated in a different manner than a standard class or method. Annotations have been referred to as *syntactic metadata*, and they change the way that a piece of code functions at runtime. To create an annotation, you must create a piece of code that is very similar to a standard Java interface. At a glance, the main feature that separates a standard interface from an annotation is the @ character that is prefixed on the interface keyword. However, they have many differences, and special guidelines must be followed when creating them.

The name of the annotation when it is in use will be the same as the name of the @interface that is used to create the annotation. In the example, the annotation being created has a signature of @interface PasswordLength, and later the annotation will be used by specifying @PasswordLength, along with any parameters that go along with it. Annotations can contain method declarations, but the declaration must not contain any parameters. Method declarations should not contain any throws clauses, and the return types of method declarations should be one of the following:

- String

- Class

- Enum

- Primitive

- Array

Annotations can contain special annotations themselves that can be used only within the context of annotations. Those annotations are @Target, @Retention, @Constraint, @Documented, and @Inherited. I will briefly cover each of these annotation types, but it is important to note that custom constraint annotations require the @Constraint annotation to be placed before the @interface declaration, whereas other types of annotations do not.

The @Target annotation is used to signify which program elements can make use of the annotation. Table 6-4 describes the options that can be used within the @Target annotation.

Table 6-4. *@Target Annotation Values*

Value	Description
TYPE	The annotation can be placed on a class, interface, or enum.
FIELD	The annotation can be placed on a class member field.
METHOD	The annotation can be placed on a method.
PARAMETER	The annotation can be placed on a method parameter.
CONSTRUCTOR	The annotation can be placed on a constructor.
LOCAL_VARIABLE	The annotation can be placed on a local variable or a catch clause.
ANNOTATION_TYPE	The annotation can be placed on an annotation type.
PACKAGE	The annotation can be placed on a Java package.

For the purposes of creating a constraint annotation, the @Target annotation usually contains the following, as in the example:

```
@Target( { METHOD, FIELD, ANNOTATION_TYPE })
```

The @Retention annotation is used to indicate how long the annotation will be retained. The options are class, source, and runtime. Table 6-5 describes these three types of retention.

Table 6-5. *Annotation Retention Values*

Value	Description
class	The annotation is discarded during the class load.
source	The annotation is discarded after compilation.
runtime	The annotation is never discarded, available for reflection at runtime.

The @Documentation annotation can be added to ensure that the @interface is added to the JavaDoc for the specific project that it is contained within. The @Constraint annotation is used to declare which constraint class will be used for testing the validity of the value contained within the field being annotated. In the example, the @Constraint annotation contains a validatedBy parameter value of CheckPasswordValidator.class, and this signifies that the CheckPasswordValidator class will be used to validate the value. You will take a more in-depth look at the CheckPasswordValidator class in a moment.

The last annotation that can be specified within an @interface declaration is @Inherited. This is used to allow the annotation to inherit properties of another class. In other words, if the @Inherited annotation is placed on an @interface declaration, then the properties of an annotation that has been placed on a class can be inherited by another class, which extends it. Therefore, if ClassA contains your custom annotation and the @Inherited annotation has been specified in the declaration of the custom annotation, then if ClassB extends ClassA, it also inherits the properties of the custom annotation.

To briefly explain the annotation member elements and methods, both the message() and passwordLength() elements are exposed for use with the annotation, so a developer can specify @PasswordLength(message="some message" passwordLength=6), for instance. You can add any number of elements to the annotation, utilizing any data type that makes sense for your annotation requirements, although most of the time an int or String data type is specified. In the case of the validation annotation, you may want to expose one or more of the elements within the validator class. I'll show you how to do that after a brief explanation of how the validator class works.

■ **Note**   Any member element in an annotation @interface can contain a default value by specifying the keyword default and specifying the default value afterward. Doing so would enable a developer to use the annotation without specifying the element when using the annotation.

The last piece of the puzzle for developing a custom validator annotation is the validator class itself. The validator class must implement ConstraintValidator. In the validator class, override the initialize and isValid methods for the implementation. The initialize method accepts an object of the annotation type that you created. In the example, you can see that the intialize method accepts a PasswordLength object. The initialize method is where you set up all the local fields that will be needed to validate the contents of the field that the annotation has been placed on. In the example, a couple of member fields have been declared: passwordLength and password. The passwordLength field is set to the value specified by the annotation element that is exposed to the developer. To capture this value, in the initialize method, the annotation object is used to obtain the value. In the example, passswordLength is set equal to constraintAnnotation.passwordLength(). The isValid method is then invoked, and the actual value that is contained within the annotated managed bean property is passed into this method. This is where the actual validation occurs. The isValid method should return a Boolean value indicating whether the value is valid. In the example, if the value is greater than or equal to the passwordLength field value, then it is valid, and isValue returns a true value.

Although there are a few pieces, it isn't difficult to create a custom validation annotation once you've done it a time or two. There are some good use cases for developing custom annotations, so they make for a good tool to have in your arsenal.

Customizing Data Tables

Some of the JSF component libraries contain highly sophisticated DataTable components. Such components can be used to create interfacees by which users can create, edit, and delete data.

Example

To make use of a custom DataTable, use a third-party component library dataTable component to provide custom options for your application needs. In this example, you'll use the PrimeFaces dataTable component to create a editable dataTable for the Acme Bookstore shopping cart. Rather than clicking a link within a table row in order to edit the data for that row, this updated implementation will allow you to edit the table data inline, without the need to navigate to different page for editing the data. Everything will be done asynchronously via the use of Ajax, and the best part is that all of the dirty work is done for you. There is no need to code a single line of JavaScript. Let's take a look at this solution!

Let's look at an listing for the cart view that has been updated to use the p:dataTable (PrimeFaces dataTable component) and its inline row-editing capabilities. The following listing is the updated cart view, which resides in the file named example 06_16.xhtml:

```
<?xml version="1.0" encoding="UTF-8"?>

<ui:composition xmlns="http://www.w3.org/1999/xhtml"
                xmlns:f="http://xmlns.jcp.org/jsf/core"
                xmlns:ui="http://xmlns.jcp.org/jsf/facelets"
                xmlns:h="http://xmlns.jcp.org/jsf/html"
                xmlns:p="http://primefaces.org/ui"
                template="./layout/custom_template_search.xhtml">
    <ui:define name="content">
        <h:form id="shoppingCartForm">
            <h1>Shopping Cart Contents</h1>
            <p>
                Below are the contents of your cart.
            </p>
            <h:messages id="cartMessage" globalOnly="true"
                        errorStyle="color: red" infoStyle="color: green"/>
            <br/>
```

```
        <p:dialog id="updateDialog" widgetVar="updateDlg"
                modal="true"
                height="40" resizable="false"
                closable="false" showHeader="false" >

            <h:graphicImage id="loading" library="image" name="ajaxloading.gif"/>
        </p:dialog>
        <p:dataTable id="cartTable" value="#{ch6CartController.cart.books}" var="book"
                    rendered="#{ch6CartController.cart.books ne null}">
            <p:ajax id="rowEditAjax" event="rowEdit" execute="@this" update="@this"
                    listener="#{ch6CartController.updateRowData}"
                    onstart="updateDlg.show();"
                    oncomplete="updateDlg.hide();"
                    onerror="updateDlg.hide();"/>

            <p:column id="title" headerText="Title">
                #{book.book.title}
            </p:column>
            <p:column id="quantity" headerText="Quantity">
                <p:cellEditor>
                    <f:facet name="output">
                        <h:inputText readonly="true" size="10" value="#{book.quantity}"/>
                    </f:facet>
                    <f:facet name="input">
                        <h:inputText id="bookQty" size="10" value="#{book.quantity}"/>
                        </f:facet>
                </p:cellEditor>
            </p:column>
            <p:column id="edit" headerText="Edit">
                <p:rowEditor />
            </p:column>

        </p:dataTable>

        <h:outputText id="emptyCart" value="No items currently in cart."
                    rendered="#{ch6CartController.cart.books eq null}"/>
        <br/>
        <h:commandLink id="continueLink" action="#{ch6CartController.continueShopping}"
            value="Continue Shopping"/>
    </h:form>
  </ui:define>
</ui:composition>
```

Note that the view also contains another PrimeFaces component, the dialog. It is used to present a pop-up dialog, and in this case it shows an animation when the updating is occurring. Next, let's look at the code behind the logic of the inline editing and the shopping cart in general. The following listing is an excerpt from the CartController class (in the Chapter 6 sources), showing a method named updateRowData, which is responsible for updating the data in the table.org.primefaces.event.RowEditEvent class into the source in order to make use of the RowEditEvent:

...

```
public void updateRowData(RowEditEvent e) {
    System.out.println("Perform editing logic here...");
    currentBook = (Item)e.getObject();
    // Call the updateCart method, passing the title of the current book.
    updateCart(((Item)e.getObject()).getBook().getTitle());
}
```

...

When the final cart view is rendered, it will look like that in Figure 6-7 when the table is being edited inline.

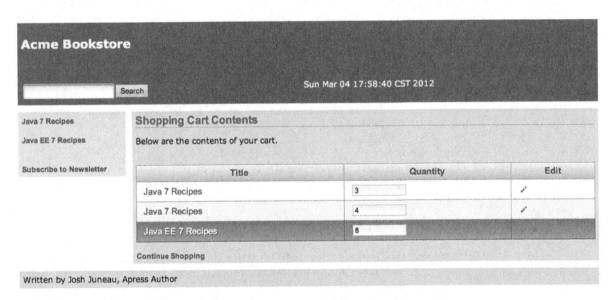

Figure 6-7. *PrimeFaces dataTable Component: inline table editing*

Explanation

The world of custom dataTable components is ever-changing, and there are a number of available implementations from which to choose. The RichFaces library offers its own flavor of the custom dataTable, providing sorting and editing options just like the PrimeFaces dataTable. To see a demo of each, please visit the RichFaces demo at http://livedemo.exadel.com/richfaces-demo/index.jsp and the PrimeFaces demo at www.primefaces.org/showcase/ui/home.jsf. This example demonstrates the editable dataTable available from the PrimeFaces component library. As always, the first step to using a component from a third-party library is to install the library for your application to use.

It should be noted that the PrimeFaces dataTable offers many options, and this example covers only one of them, that is, inline editing. There are options for sorting, adding headers and footers, filtering, selecting one or more rows, grouping, and so on. An entire chapter could be written about using the many options of the PrimeFaces dataTable.

I will not cover these features in this example; please see the PrimeFaces documentation for more information on using those features. I think you will find that PrimeFaces takes an "example" approach for demonstrating the use of its components. You can visit its showcase, see the components in action, and then look at the code on the same page. In this example, I will cover one of the more difficult features to customize: inline data editing.

Out of the box, the inline editing feature for PrimeFaces dataTables is very simple. A p:dataTable component works in the same manner as a standard JSF dataTable component, in that it accepts a List, DataModel, or Collection of data.

■ **Note** In a later chapter that makes use of database tables and entity classes, you will see a version of this example utilizing collections for the dataTable data type. The use of collections for dataTable components is new in JSF release 2.2.

In the example, you can see the p:dataTable component accepts a value of #{ch6CartController.cart.books}, which is a List of Item objects. The Item objects are those that are contained within the current session's cart. If you look directly below the p:dataTable component, you will notice a p:ajax tag, which will provide extra functionality to the p:dataTable. You can ignore the p:ajax tag for now; it is not necessary to implement the inline editable table. However, in this example, you use it to gain control over the underlying update of the row.

Moving down the code, the column declarations are also very similar to that of a standard h:dataTable component. Instead of denoting columns with h:column, use p:column tags, and reference the data for each column using the p:dataTable's var attribute keyword. In the example, var is set to book, so #{book.book.title} will return the title of the book, which is the first column's output. Note that the second column contains an embedded p:cellEditor component. A p:cellEditor component indicates that this column will be made editable, and each p:cellEditor component must contain two facets, one for the output and another for the input. The <f:facet name="ouput"> tag should be used to enclose what the column's output should display. In the example, an inputText component with a readonly attribute set to true is used to display the book quantity. The other facet within the p:cellEditor component is for the input, the facet tag should read <f:facet name="input">, and it should enclose the input component for this column's value. In the example, an inputText component is embedded within the input facet, and the value is set to #{book.quantity}. This time, the readonly attribute is not specified, and therefore the inputText component renders an editable text field. Following the input facet is a closing p:cellEditor tag, followed by the closing p:column tag for that column.

The last column of the table is also a p:column component, and embedded inside is a p:rowEditor component, which will display a pencil icon that the user can click to toggle the row of data and make it editable. Following along with the p:cellEditor logic that was covered in the previous paragraph, when the table is initially rendered, the content that is embedded within the cellEditor's output facet is displayed. When the edit icon is clicked, the cellEditor's output facet contents are hidden, and the input facet contents are displayed. At this point, the rowEditor component turns into a check mark and an X. If the user makes a change to the editable row contents, they can click the check mark to save the changes; otherwise, they can click the X to close the editable row and cancel the change.

The editable dataTable component works fine with just the constructs I've discussed, and all of the row editing takes place behind the scenes. That is, PrimeFaces does a good job of abstracting the implementation details from the developer, allowing the developer more time to work on other more important tasks. However, what if you want to perform some custom business logic when the row is edited? Perhaps you want to validate the data or track what data has been changed. Intercepting the edit is easy to do, and it has been done in this example. By adding the p:ajax tag to the p:dataTable component, you can intercept the rowEdit event. When the rowEdit event is executed, it is intercepted by the p:ajax listener, which in the example is set to the updateRowData method of the CartController class. To create a listener method for a rowEdit event, you must write a method that has no return value and accepts a RowEditEvent object. The RowEditEvent contains the actual row contents that are being edited. In the case of this example, the RowEditEvent is an Item object, and the listener method sets the currentBook object in the CartController class equal to the Item object and updates the cart accordingly.

■ **Note**   If you do not want to intercept the `rowEdit` event, simply leave out the embedded `p:ajax` tag. Doing so will cause the `p:dataTable` to take care of the update logic behind the scenes.

In this example, I touched upon one of the most widely used components in any data-related JSF application, the `dataTable`. There are many ways in which a `dataTable` can be customized, and plenty of third-party component libraries ship with customized `dataTable` components. This example demonstrates the use of the PrimeFaces `dataTable` component, which I highly recommend to anyone looking for a custom and easy-to-use `dataTable` component. Utilizing a PrimeFaces `dataTable` component and making it editable allows for the inline editing of table row data. This will provide users with the ability to edit data in a spreadsheet-like fashion, which is sometimes much easier than drilling into each record separately. To learn more about all of the custom options available with the PrimeFaces `dataTable`, please check out `http://primefaces.org`.

■ **Note**   As mentioned in the introduction to this chapter, in order to use PrimeFaces with Java EE 7, you must download and utilize the PrimeFaces 4.x release, as PrimeFaces 3.x or prior will not work correctly with JSF 2.2. Therefore, this example will only work with PrimeFaces 4.x.

Developing a Page Flow

JSF provides the ability to create a flow of views, such that a particular flow contains both entry and exit points.

Example

To create a flow, define it using the faces flow technology that was introduced in JSF 2.2. The faces flow solution allows a defined set of views to be interrelated with one another to share a common set of data, and views outside of the flow do not have access to the flow's data. Flows also have their own set of navigational logic, so they are almost like a subprogram within an application. To enable an application to utilize faces flow, a `<flow-definition>` section should be added to the `faces-config.xml` file. The section can be empty, because the navigational logic can instead reside in a separate configuration file for the flow. The following `faces-config.xml` file demonstrates how to enable faces flow for an application:

```
<faces-config version="2.2"
     xmlns="http://xmlns.jcp.org/xml/ns/javaee"
     xmlns:xsi="http://www.w3.org/2001/XMLSchema-instance"
     xsi:schemaLocation="http://xmlns.jcp.org/xml/ns/javaee
     http://xmlns.jcp.org/xml/ns/javaee/web-facesconfig_2_2.xsd">

  ...
    <flow-definition>
   </flow-definition>
  ...
</faces-config>
```

The views belonging to a flow should be separated from the rest of the application views and placed into a folder at the root of the application's web directory. The folder containing the flow views should be named the same as the flow identifier. Navigation and configuration code is contained within a separate XML configuration file that resides within the flow view directory, and the file is named flowname-flow.xml, where flowname is the flow identifier. The following configuration file demonstrates the configuration for a very basic flow identified by exampleFlow. You can find more information regarding the different elements that can be used within the flow configuration in the "Explanation" section.

```
<?xml version="1.0" encoding="UTF-8"?>
<!DOCTYPE html>

<html xmlns="http://www.w3.org/1999/xhtml"
      xmlns:f="http://xmlns.jcp.org/jsf/core"
      xmlns:j="http://xmlns.jcp.org/jsf/flow">

    <f:metadata>
        <j:faces-flow-definition id="exampleFlow">

            <!-- A faces-flow-definition in a facelet page without any other
            children declares a faces flow equivalent to this:

              <start-node>the name of this page without any extension</start-node>
              <view id="the name of this page without any extension">
                <vdl-document>the name of this page with the extension</vdl-document>
              </view>

            -->
        </j:faces-flow-definition>
    </f:metadata>
</html>
```

The views belonging to the flow should reside within the flow folder alongside the flow configuration file. Each of the views can access a managed bean that is dedicated to facilitating the flow. The flows share a context that begins when the flow is accessed and ends when the flow exits. The following view demonstrates the entry point to a flow named exampleFlow. This example view can be found in the book sources in the file example06_17.xhtml.

```
<ui:composition xmlns:ui="http://xmlns.jcp.org/jsf/facelets"
                xmlns:f="http://xmlns.jcp.org/jsf/core"
                xmlns:h="http://xmlns.jcp.org/jsf/html"
                template="layout/custom_template_search.xhtml">
    <ui:define name="content">
        <h:messages globalOnly="true"  errorStyle="color: red" infoStyle="color: green"/>
        <h:form id="flowForm">
            <p>
                Faces Flow Example
            </p>
            <h:commandButton value="Begin Flow" action="exampleFlow"/>
            <h:commandButton value="Stay Here" action="stay"/>

        </h:form>
    </ui:define>
</ui:composition>
```

Next, let's take a look at a view that is accessing the managed bean that is dedicated to the flow. In the following view, the managed bean named FlowBean is accessed to invoke a method, which will return an implicit navigational String directing the application to the next view in the flow. Notice that this view also accesses the facesContext.application.flowHandler, which I will discuss more in the "Explanation" section.

```
<h:body>
        <f:view>
            <h:form>
        <p>
            This is the first view of the flow.
            <br/><br/>
            Flow ID: #{facesContext.application.flowHandler.currentFlow.id}
            <br/>
            <h:commandLink value="Go to another view in the flow" action="#{flowBean.navMethod()}"/>
        </p>
            </h:form>
        </f:view>
    </h:body>
```

Each subsequent view within the flow can also access the resources of the flow's managed bean. Lastly, you'll look at the code that is contained within org.javaserverfaces.chapter06.FlowBean, which is the managed bean that is dedicated to the flow.

```
import javax.faces.flow.FlowScoped;
import javax.inject.Named;

@Named
@FlowScoped("exampleFlow")
public class FlowBean implements java.io.Serializable {

    private String flowValue;
    private String parameter1;
    /**
     * Creates a new instance of FlowBean
     */
    public FlowBean() {
    }

    /**
     * Initializes the flow
     */

    public void initializeIt(){
        System.out.println("Initialize the flow...");
    }
    /**
     * Finalizes the flow
     */

    public void finalizeIt(){
        System.out.println("Finalize the flow...");
    }
```

```java
    public String navMethod(){
        return "intermediateFlow";
    }

    public String testMethod(){
        return "intermediate";
    }

    public String endFlow(){
        return "endingFlow";
    }

    /**
     * @return the flowValue
     */
    public String getFlowValue() {
        return flowValue;
    }

    /**
     * @param flowValue the flowValue to set
     */
    public void setFlowValue(String flowValue) {
        this.flowValue = flowValue;
    }

    /**
     * @return the parameter1
     */
    public String getParameter1() {
        return parameter1;
    }

    /**
     * @param parameter1 the parameter1 to set
     */
    public void setParameter1(String parameter1) {
        this.parameter1 = parameter1;
    }
}
```

This solution provided a quick overview of the files that are required for creating a flow within a JSF application. In the next section, I'll cover the features in more detail.

Explanation

The concept of session management has been a difficult feat to tackle since the beginning of web applications. A *web flow* refers to a grouping of web views that are related and must have the ability to share information with each view within the flow. Many web frameworks have attempted to tackle this issue by creating different solutions that would facilitate the sharing of data across multiple views. Oftentimes, a mixture of session variables, request parameters, and cookies are used as a patchwork solution.

In JSF 2.2, a solution has been adopted for binding multiple JSF views to each other, allowing them to share information among each other. This solution is referenced as *faces flow*; and it allows a group of interrelated views to belong to a *flow instance*, and information can be shared across all the views belonging to a flow instance. Flows contain separate navigation that pertains to the flow itself and not the entire application. As such, flow navigation can be defined in an XML format or via code. A flow contains a single point of entry, and it can be called from any point within an application.

Defining a Flow

As mentioned in the solution to this example, the `faces-config.xml` file for a JSF application that will utilize the flow feature must contain a `<flow-definition>` section. This section of the `faces-config.xml` file can contain information specific to one or more flows residing within an application. However, for the purposes of this example, the solution utilizes a separate XML configuration file for use with the flow. Either way will work; the syntax does vary just a bit because the XML configuration file that is flow-specific uses a new JSF `taglib` for accessing the flow-specific configuration tags. To learn more about using the `faces-config.xml` file for flow configuration, please refer to the online documentation. Even if a flow is not using the `faces-config.xml` file for defining the flow configuration, the `<flow-definition>` section must exist to tell the JSF runtime that flows are utilized within the application.

The flow-specific configuration file and all flow-related views should reside within the same folder, at the root of the application's web directory. The name of the folder should be the same as the flow identifier. As mentioned in the solution, the flow configuration file should be named `flowname-flow.xml`, where `flowname` is the same as the flow identifier. The URI, `http://xmlns.jcp.org/jsf/flow`, should be added to the flow configuration file in order to make flow-specific tags available for configuration use. The `taglib` declarations for a simple JSF view that includes flows may look like the following:

```
<html xmlns="http://www.w3.org/1999/xhtml"
      xmlns:f="http://xmlns.jcp.org/jsf/core"
      xmlns:h="http://xmlns.jcp.org/jsf/html"
      xmlns:j="http://xmlns.jcp.org/jsf/flow">
```

The Flow Managed Bean

A flow contains its own managed bean annotated as `@FlowScoped`, which differs from `@SessionScoped` because the data can be accessed only by other views (`ViewNodes`) belonging to the flow. The `@FlowScoped` annotation relies upon Contexts and Dependency Injection (CDI), because `FlowScoped` is a CDI scope that causes the runtime to consider classes with the `@FlowScoped` annotation to be in the scope of the specified flow. A `@FlowScoped` bean maintains a life cycle that begins and ends with a flow instance. Multiple flow instances can exist for a single application, and if a user begins a flow within one browser tab and then opens another, a new flow instance will begin in the new tab. This solution resolves many lingering issues around sessions and new-age browsers that allow users to open multiple tabs. To maintain separate flow instances, the `ClientId` is used by JSF to differentiate among multiple instances.

Each flow can contain an `initializer` and a `finalizer` (that is, a method that will be invoked when a flow is entered and a method that will be invoked when a flow is exited, respectively). To declare an initializer, specify a child element named `<initializer>` within the flow configuration `<flow-definition>`. The initializer element can be an EL expression that declares the managed bean initializer method, as such:

```
...
<initializer>#{flowBean.initializeIt}</initializer>
...
```

Similarly, a `<finalizer>` element can be specified within the flow configuration to define the method that will be called when the flow is exited. The following demonstrates how to set the finalizer to an EL expression declaring the managed bean finalizer method:

```
...
<finalizer>#{flowBean.finalizeIt}></finalizer>
...
```

Flows can contain method calls and variable values that are accessible only via the flow nodes. These methods and variables should be placed within the `FlowScoped` bean and used the same as standard managed bean methods and variables. The main difference is that any method or variable that is defined within a `FlowScoped` bean is available only for a single flow instance.

Navigating Flow View Nodes

Flows contain their own navigational rules, which can be defined within the `faces-config.xml` file or the individual flow configuration files. These rules can be straightforward and produce a page-by-page navigation, or they can include conditional logic. There are a series of elements that can be specified within the navigation rules, which will facilitate conditional navigation. Table 6-6 lists the different elements, along with an explanation of what they do.

Table 6-6. *Flow Navigational Elements*

Element	Description
view	Navigates to a standard JSF view.
switch	Represents one or more EL expressions that conditionally evaluate to `true` or `false`. If `true`, then navigation occurs to the specified view node.
flow-return	Outcome determined by the caller of the flow.
flow-call	Represents a call to another flow; creates a nested flow.
method-call	Arbitrary method call that can invoke a method that returns a navigational outcome.

The following navigational sequence is an example of a flow navigation that contains conditional logic using the elements listed in Table 6-6:

```
<j:flow-definition>

    <start-node>exampleFlow</j:start-node>

    <switch id="startNode">
        <navigation-case>
            <if>#{flowBean.someCondition}</if>
                <from-outcome>newView</from-outcome>
        </navigation-case>
    </switch>
```

```
        <view id="oneFlow">
            <vdl-document>oneFlow.xhtml</vdl-document>
        </view>

        <flow-return id="exit">
            <navigation-case>
                <from-outcome>exitFlow</from-outcome>
            </navigation-case>
        </flow-return>

        <finalizer>#{flowBean.finalizeIt}</finalizer>

    </j:flow-definition>
```

Flow EL

Flows contain a new EL variable named facesFlowScope. This variable is associated with the current flow, and it is a map that can be used for storing arbitrary values for use within a flow. The key-value pairs can be stored and read via a JSF view or through Java code within a managed bean. For example, to display the content for a particular map key, you could use the following:

```
The content for the key is: #{facesFlowScope.myKey}
```

Constructing a JSF View in Pure HTML5

Using JSF and HTML5 friendly markup, it is possible to develop a JSF view in pure HTML5. This can be beneficial in cases where page designers are not familiar with JSF, or when there are JavaScript frameworks in use that do not work nicely with stateful frameworks such as JSF.

Example

Utilize the HTML-friendly markup for use within JSF views. By using HTML5 within JSF views directly, you can take advantage of the entire JSF stack while coding views in pure HTML5. To use this solution, HTML5 tags have the ability to access the JSF infrastructure via the use of a new taglib URI specification jsf="http://xmlns.jcp.org/jsf", which can be utilized within JSF views beginning with JSF 2.2 and beyond. In views that specify the new taglib URI, HTML tags can utilize attributes that expose the underlying JSF architecture.

In the following example view, HTML5 tags are used to compose an input form that is backed by a JSF managed bean. To visit the sources for this example, please visit the view example06_18.xhtml within the sources for the book.

```
<?xml version="1.0" encoding="UTF-8"?>
<!DOCTYPE html PUBLIC "-//W3C//DTD XHTML 1.0 Strict//EN" "http://www.w3.org/TR/xhtml1/DTD/xhtml1-
strict.dtd">
<html xmlns="http://www.w3.org/1999/xhtml"
    xmlns:f="http://xmlns.jcp.org/jsf/core"
    xmlns:jsf="http://xmlns.jcp.org/jsf">
    <head jsf:id="head">
        <meta http-equiv="Content-Type" content="text/html; charset=UTF-8"/>

    </head>
```

```
<body jsf:id="body">
    <form jsf:id="form" jsf:prependId="false">
        <input type="email" jsf:id="value1" value="#{ajaxBean.value1}">
        </input>
        <br/><br/>
        <input type="text" jsf:id="value2" value="#{ajaxBean.value2}">

        </input>
        <br/>
        <br/>
        <input type="submit" jsf:id="status" jsf:value="#{ajaxBean.status}"
                jsf:action="#{ajaxBean.process()}" value="Process"/>
        <label for="status">Message: </label>
        <output jsf:id="status">#{ajaxBean.status}</output>
    </form>
</body>
</html>
```

Note   This feature is only available to views written in Facelets. It is not available to views written in JSP.

Explanation

The JSF 2.2 release includes the ability to utilize HTML5 markup within JSF views. As a matter of fact, the markup is not limited to HTML5; it can also include HTML4, and so on. The addition of a new taglib URI makes this possible, because it allows existing HTML tags to be bound to the JSF life cycle via the use of new namespace attributes. It is now possible to develop entire JSF views without using any JSF tags at all.

To utilize the new namespace attributes, your JSF view must import the new taglib URI jsf="http://xmlns.jcp.org/jsf". The new taglib can then be referenced as attributes within existing HTML tags, setting the underlying JSF attributes that are referenced. For instance, to utilize an HTML input tag with JSF, you would add the jsf:id attribute and set it equal to the JSF ID that you want to assign to that component. You would then set an attribute of jsf:value equal to the managed bean value.

Note   There is no need to import the http://xmlns.jcp.org/jsf/html taglib because you are no longer utilizing JSF component tags in the view.

The new syntax provides several benefits for web developers. Although not all web developers are familiar with JSF component tags, HTML tags are well known. Utilizing the new syntax, both JSF and HTML developers alike can create web views that utilize the power of JSF along with the flexibility of HTML. The new syntax also makes it easier to bind HTML tags with JavaScript, if needed. You no longer need to worry about JSF view IDs getting in the way when working with HTML and JavaScript. With the addition of new JSF taglib namespace for use with HTML tags, both JSF and HTML alike have been improved.

Index

Get the eBook for only $10!

Now you can take the weightless companion with you anywhere, anytime. Your purchase of this book entitles you to 3 electronic versions for only $10.

This Apress title will prove so indispensible that you'll want to carry it with you everywhere, which is why we are offering the eBook in 3 formats for only $10 if you have already purchased the print book.

Convenient and fully searchable, the PDF version enables you to easily find and copy code—or perform examples by quickly toggling between instructions and applications. The MOBI format is ideal for your Kindle, while the ePUB can be utilized on a variety of mobile devices.

Go to www.apress.com/promo/tendollars to purchase your companion eBook.

Apress®
THE EXPERT'S VOICE™